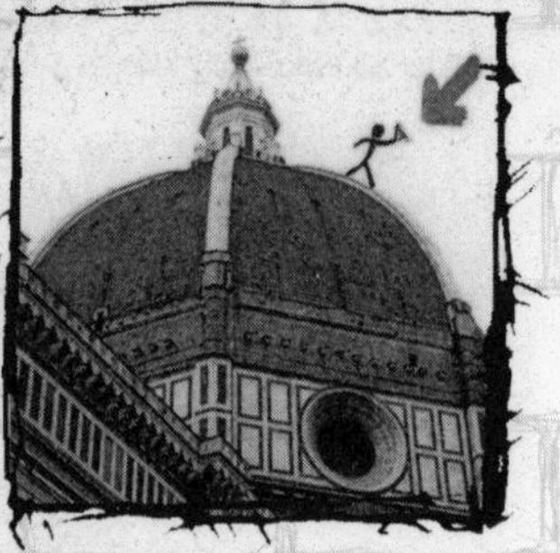

I turned 22 years old in February. Recently (actually for quite a while now), I'm more and more aware of my lack of life experience as I work. How does it look when an artist uses a foreign country as his stage, but he has never traveled abroad himself...? Consequently, I have a growing desire to travel...

—Kentaro Yabuki, 2001

Kentaro Yabuki made his manga debut with ***Yamato Gensoki***, a short series about a young empress destined to unite the warring states of ancient Japan and the boy sworn to protect her. His next series, ***Black Cat***, commenced serialization in the pages of ***Weekly Shonen Jump*** in 2000 and quickly developed a loyal fan following. ***Black Cat*** has also become an animated TV series, first hitting Japan's airwaves in the fall of 2005.

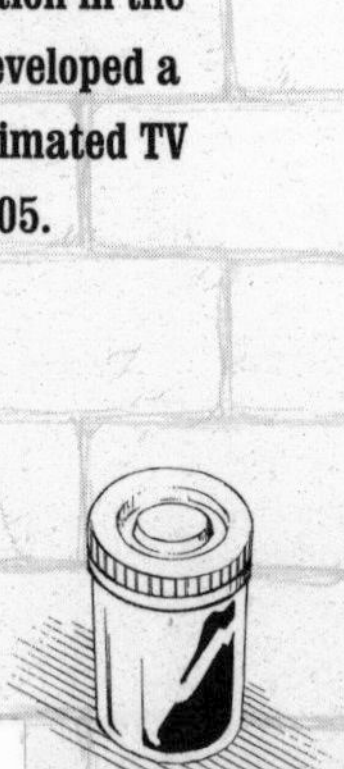

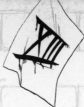

BLACK CAT VOL. 7
The SHONEN JUMP Manga Edition

STORY AND ART BY
KENTARO YABUKI

English Adaptation/Kelly Sue DeConnick
Translation/JN Productions
Touch-up Art & Lettering/Gia Cam Luc
Design/Courtney Utt
Editor/Jonathan Tarbox

Managing Editor/Frances E. Wall
Editorial Director/Elizabeth Kawasaki
VP & Editor in Chief/Yumi Hoashi
Sr. Director of Acquisitions/Rika Inouye
Sr. VP of Marketing/Liza Coppola
Exec. VP of Sales & Marketing/John Easum
Publisher/Hyoe Narita

BLACK CAT © 2000 by Kentaro Yabuki
All rights reserved. First published in Japan in 2000 by
SHUEISHA Inc., Tokyo. English translation rights in the United
States of America and Canada arranged by SHUEISHA Inc.
The stories, characters and incidents mentioned in this
publication are entirely fictional.

Printed in the U.S.A.

Published by VIZ Media, LLC
P.O. Box 77010
San Francisco, CA 94107

SHONEN JUMP Manga Edition
10 9 8 7 6 5 4 3 2 1
First printing, March 2007

THE WORLD'S
MOST POPULAR MANGA

viz
media

www.viz.com

www.shonenjump.com

PARENTAL ADVISORY
BLACK CAT is rated T+ for Older Teen and is recommended for ages 16
and up. This volume contains tobacco use and graphic, realistic violence.

RATED
T+
FOR OLDER
TEEN

List
PULLMAN ▷

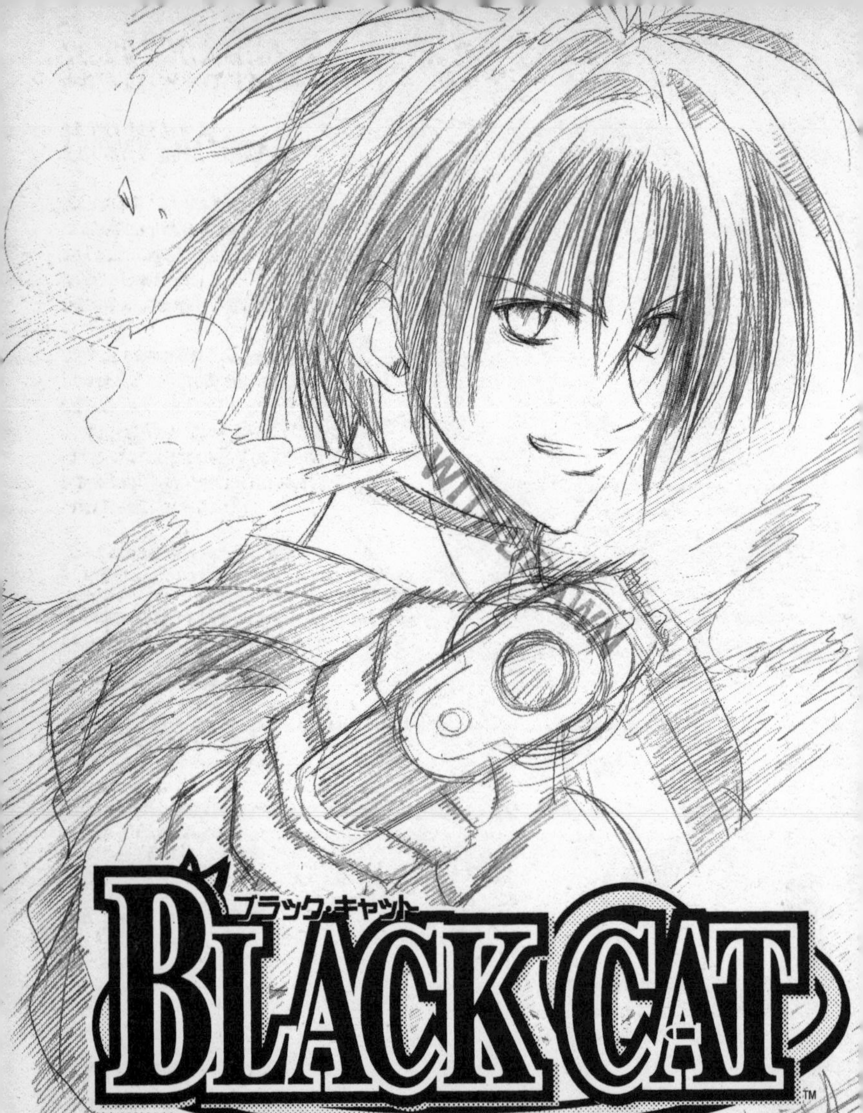
ブラック・キャット
BLACK CAT™

VOLUME 7

TIME FOR VENGEANCE

STORY & ART BY KENTARO YABUKI

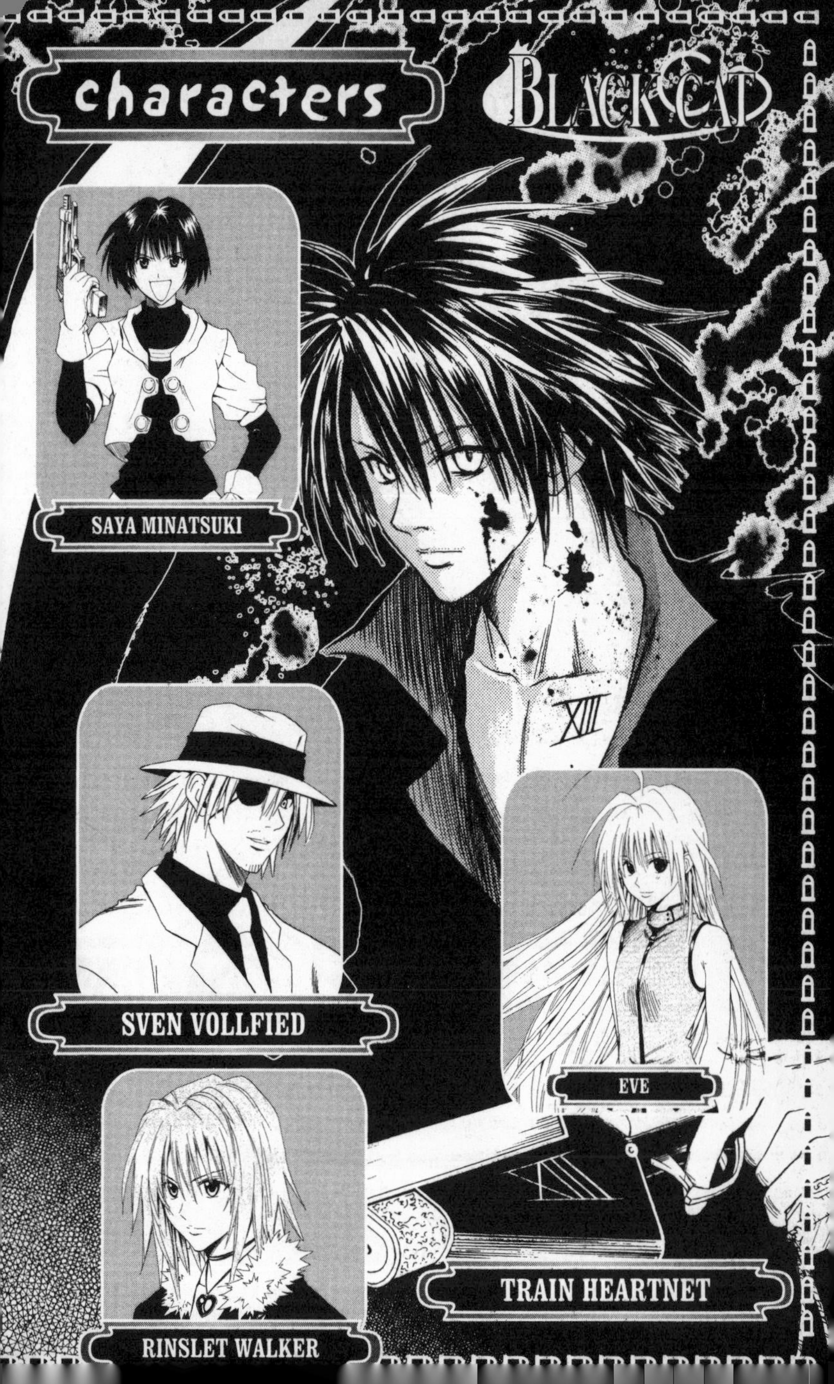
characters
BLACK CAT
SAYA MINATSUKI
SVEN VOLLFIED
EVE
TRAIN HEARTNET
RINSLET WALKER

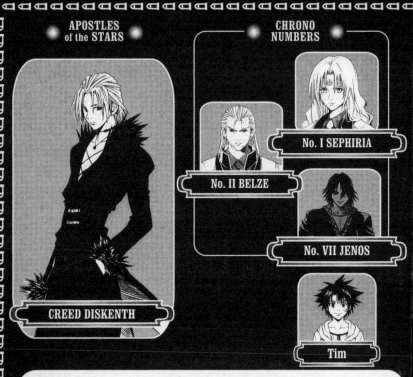

APOSTLES of the STARS

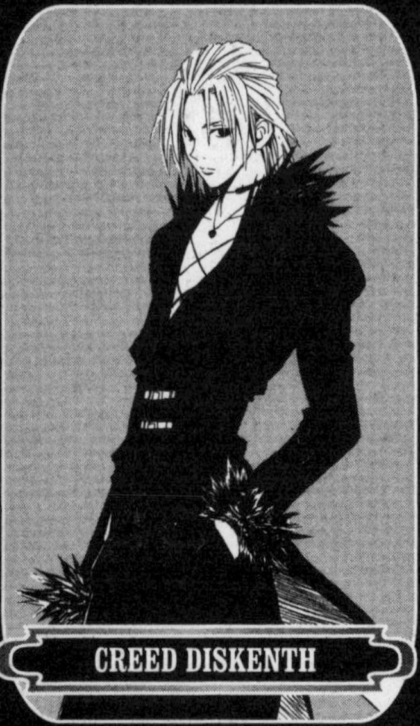

CREED DISKENTH

CHRONO NUMBERS

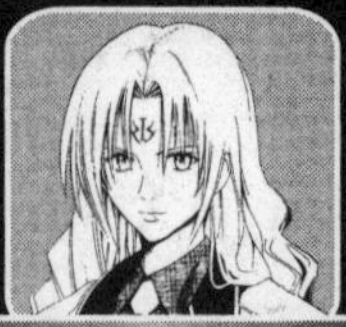

No. I SEPHIRIA

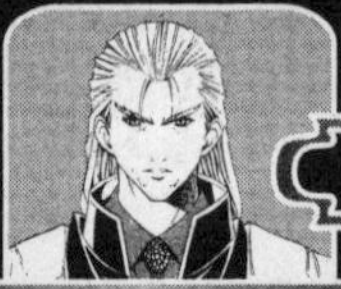

No. II BELZE

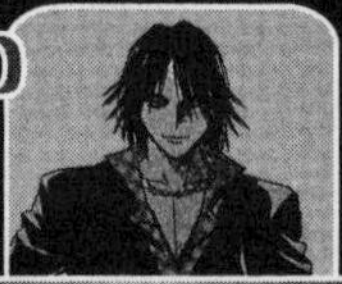

No. VII JENOS

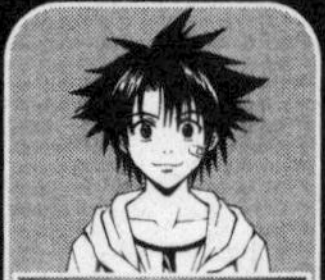

Tim

A fearless "eraser" responsible for the deaths of countless powerful men, Train "Black Cat" Heartnet carries an ornate pistol called "Hades." The gun is engraved with the Roman numeral XIII, Train's agent number as an assassin for the crime syndicate Chronos, a mysterious organization that quietly controls one-third of the world's economy. Two years after his departure from Chronos, Train lives a carefree wanderer's life, working with his partner Sven as a bounty hunter ("sweeper") and pursuing Creed Diskenth, the man who murdered Train's beloved friend Saya. The two sweepers are allied with sexy thief-for-hire Rinslet Walker and Eve, a young girl (and experimental living weapon) whom they rescued from a nanotech lab.

When Train and Creed finally cross paths, Train is shocked to learn that his enemy wants to join forces in a revolution against Chronos and the world. When Train declines, a fierce battle ensues…but ends in a stalemate. When Creed and his followers, the Apostles of the Stars, attempt an attack on a summit of world leaders, Chronos responds by sending their top agent Sephiria Arks to recruit Train to defend the leaders. After one of the Apostles attacks Eve, Sven decides it is time to part ways with her, as their association was proving too dangerous for the girl. But Eve is not so easily gotten rid of…

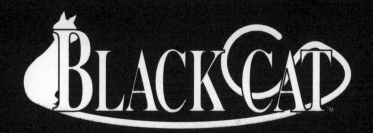

BLACK CAT

VOLUME 7 TIME FOR VENGEANCE

CONTENTS

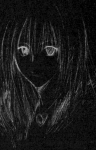

ブラック・キャット
BLACK CAT

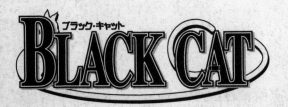

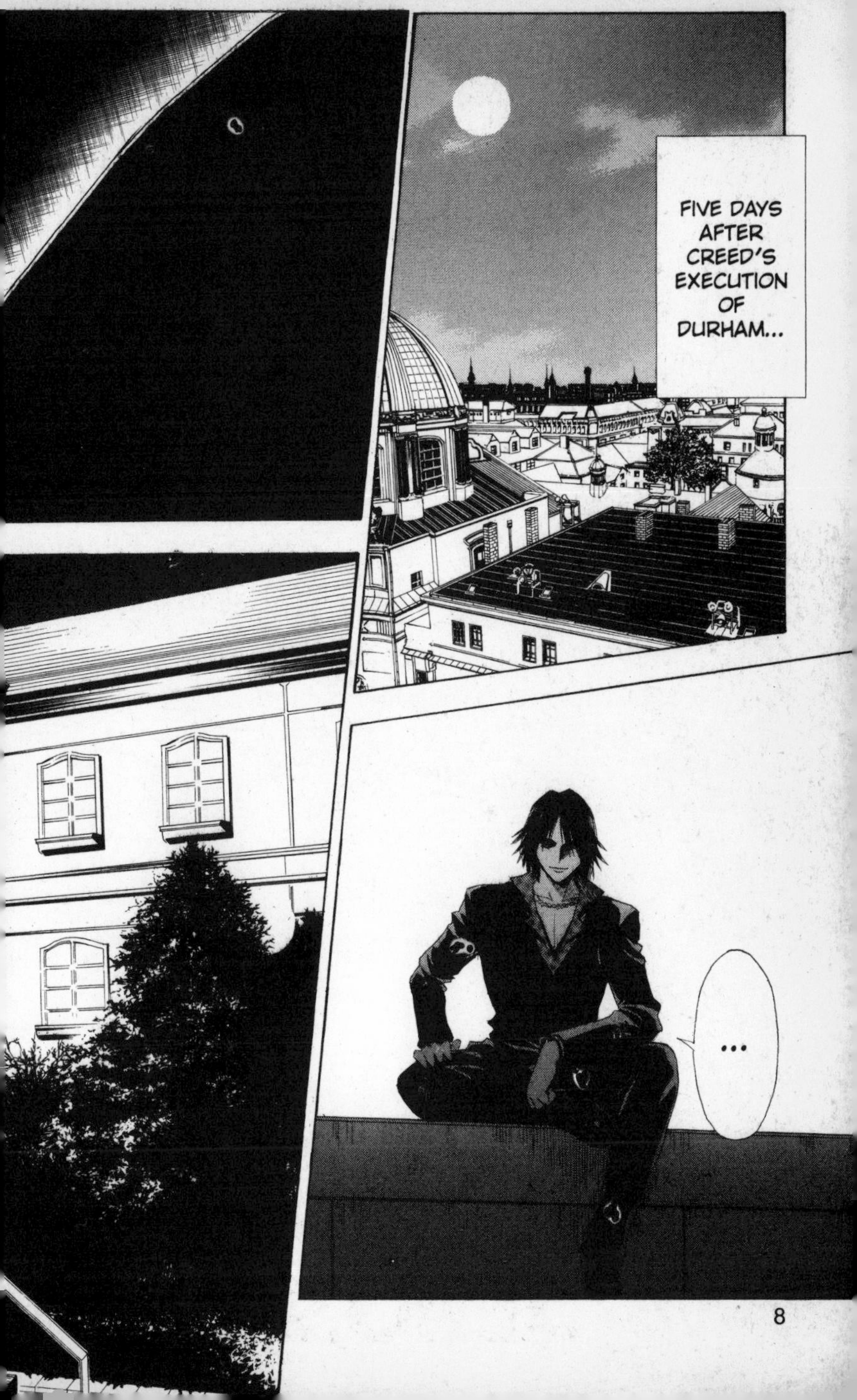
FIVE DAYS AFTER CREED'S EXECUTION OF DURHAM...
...

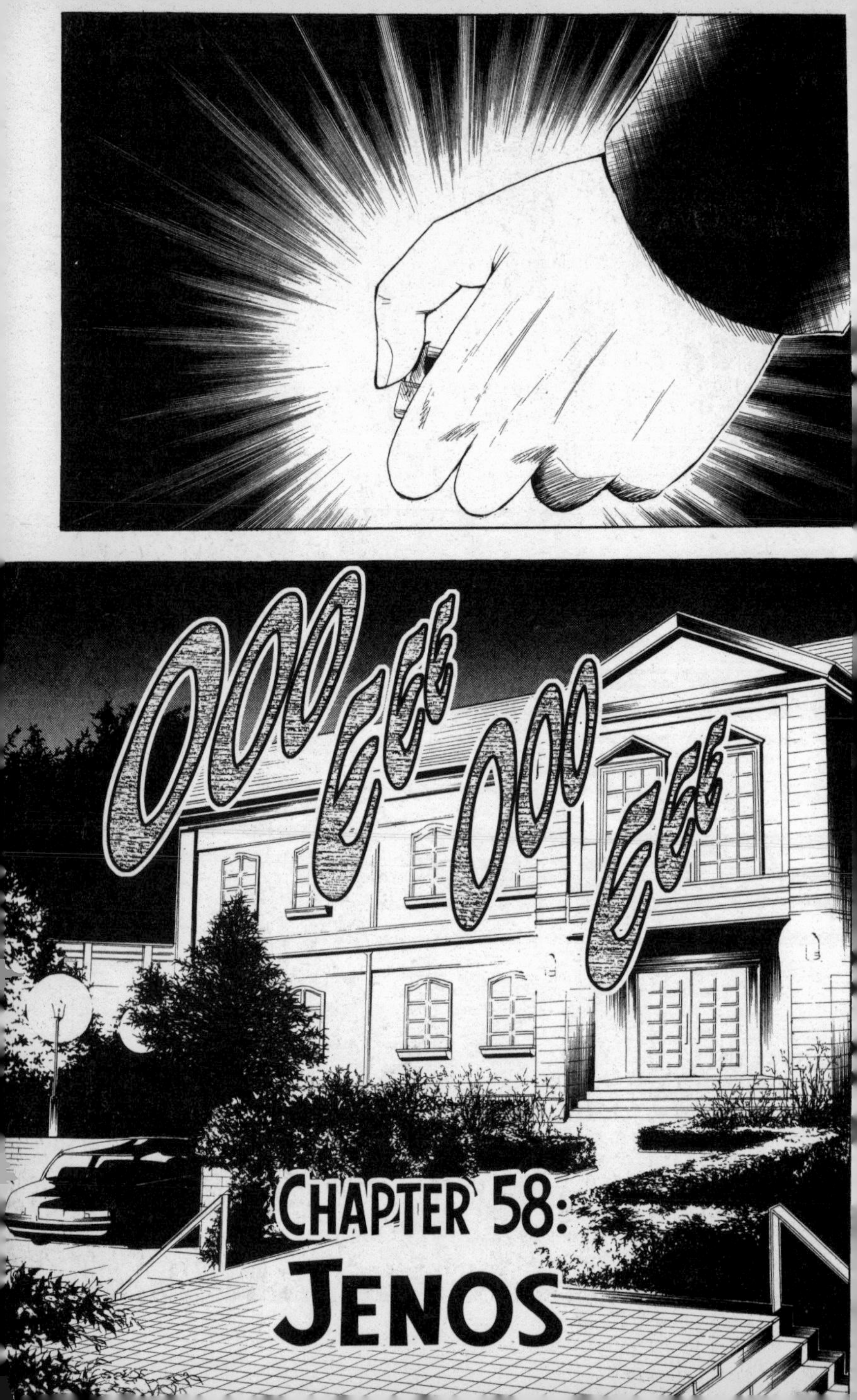
OOOZZZ OOOZZZ
CHAPTER 58:
JENOS

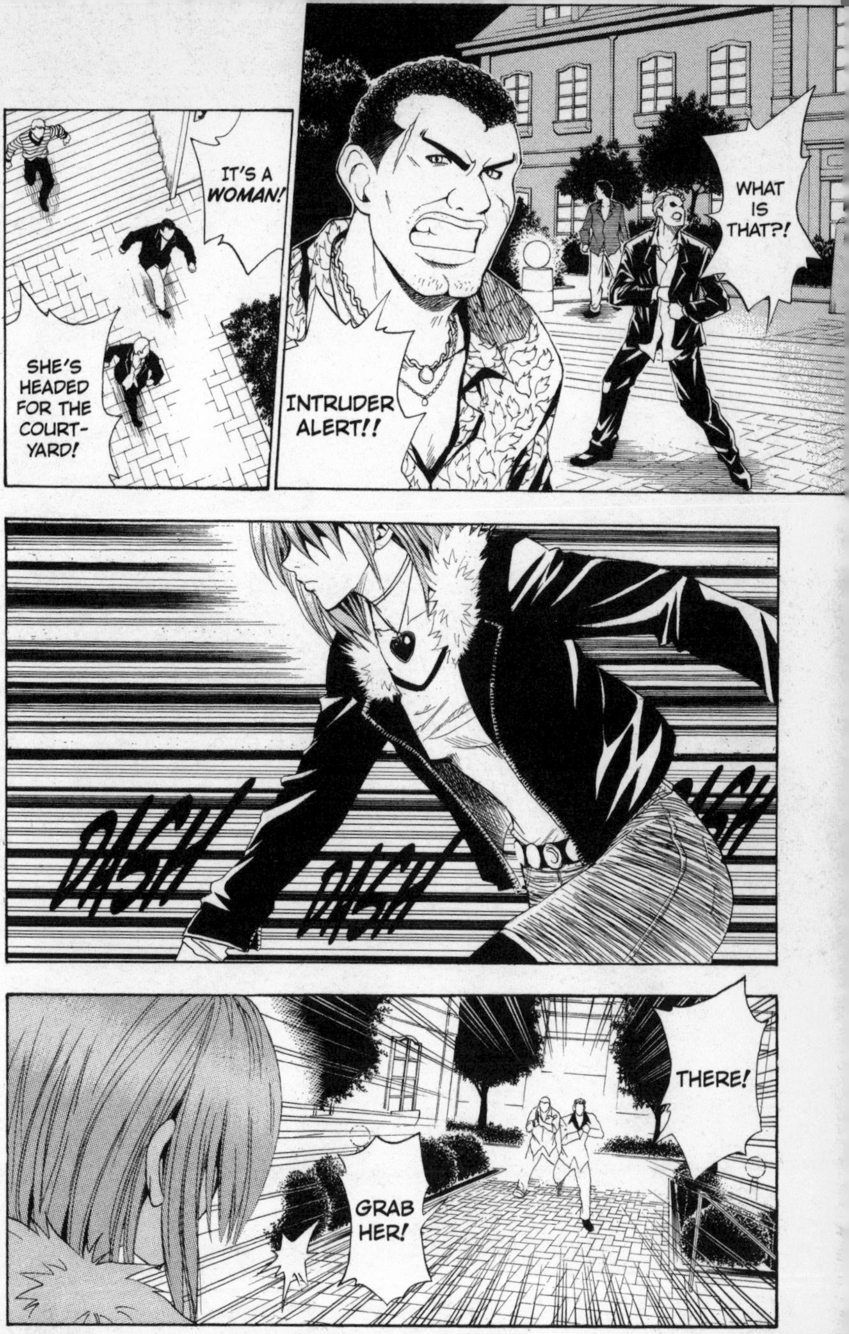
WHAT IS THAT?!
INTRUDER ALERT!!
IT'S A WOMAN!
SHE'S HEADED FOR THE COURT-YARD!
DASH
DASH
DASH
THERE!
GRAB HER!

READ THIS WAY

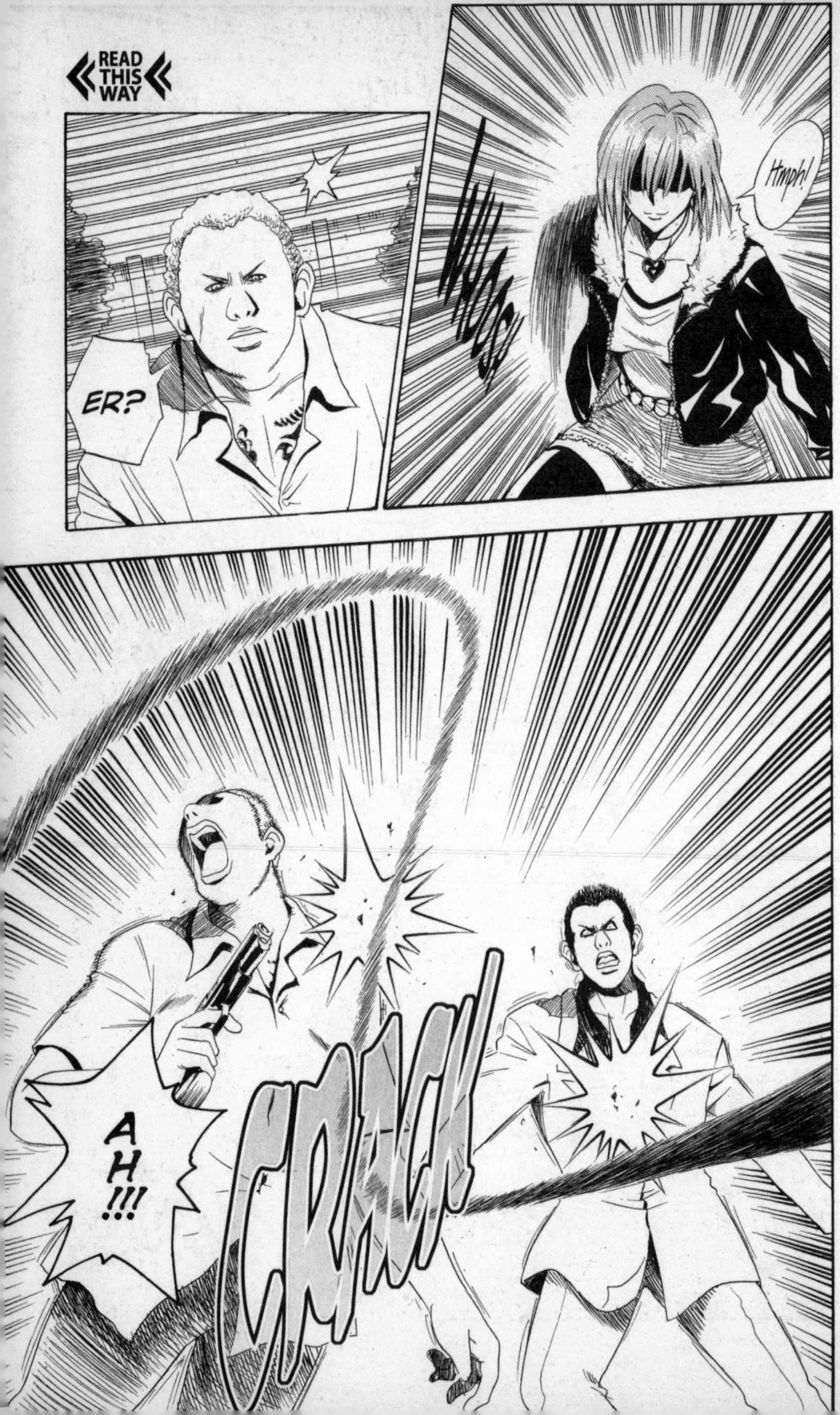
WHOOSH
Hmph!
ER?
CRACK
AH!!!

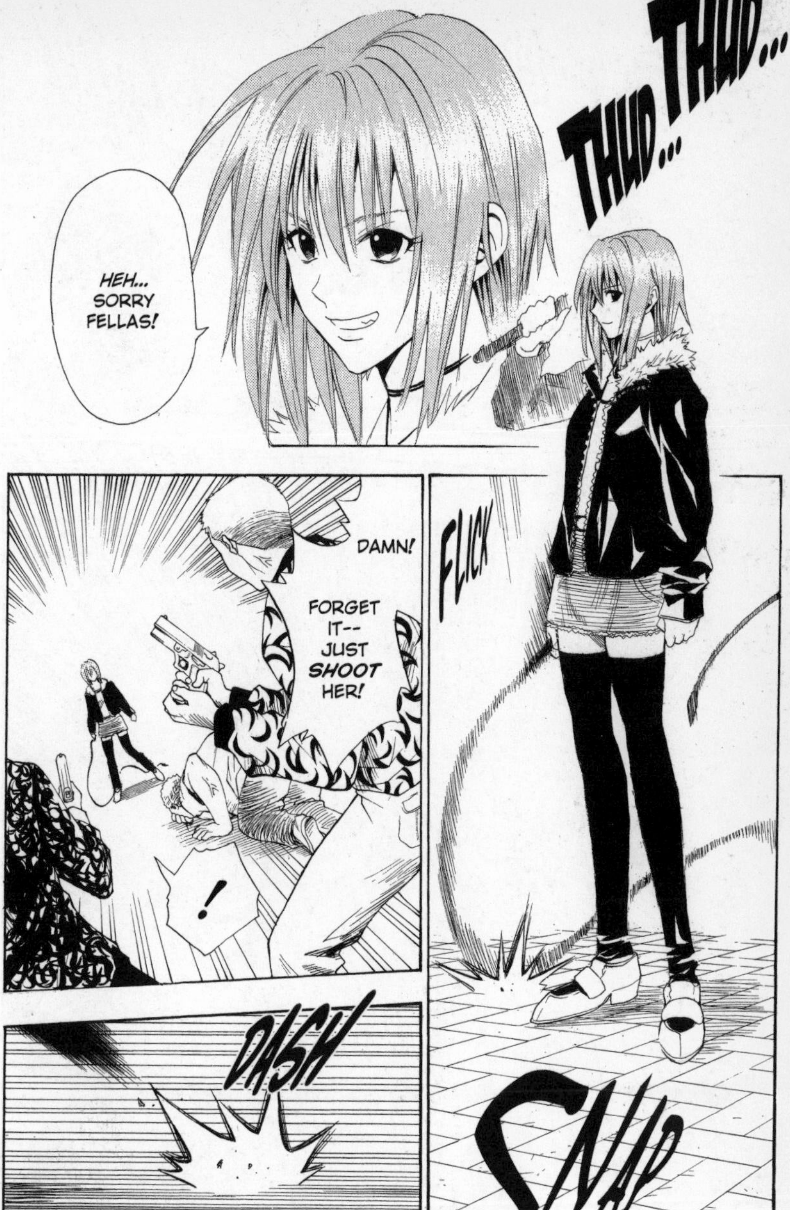
THUD...THUD...
HEH... SORRY FELLAS!
FLICK
SNAP
DAMN!
FORGET IT-- JUST SHOOT HER!
!
DASH

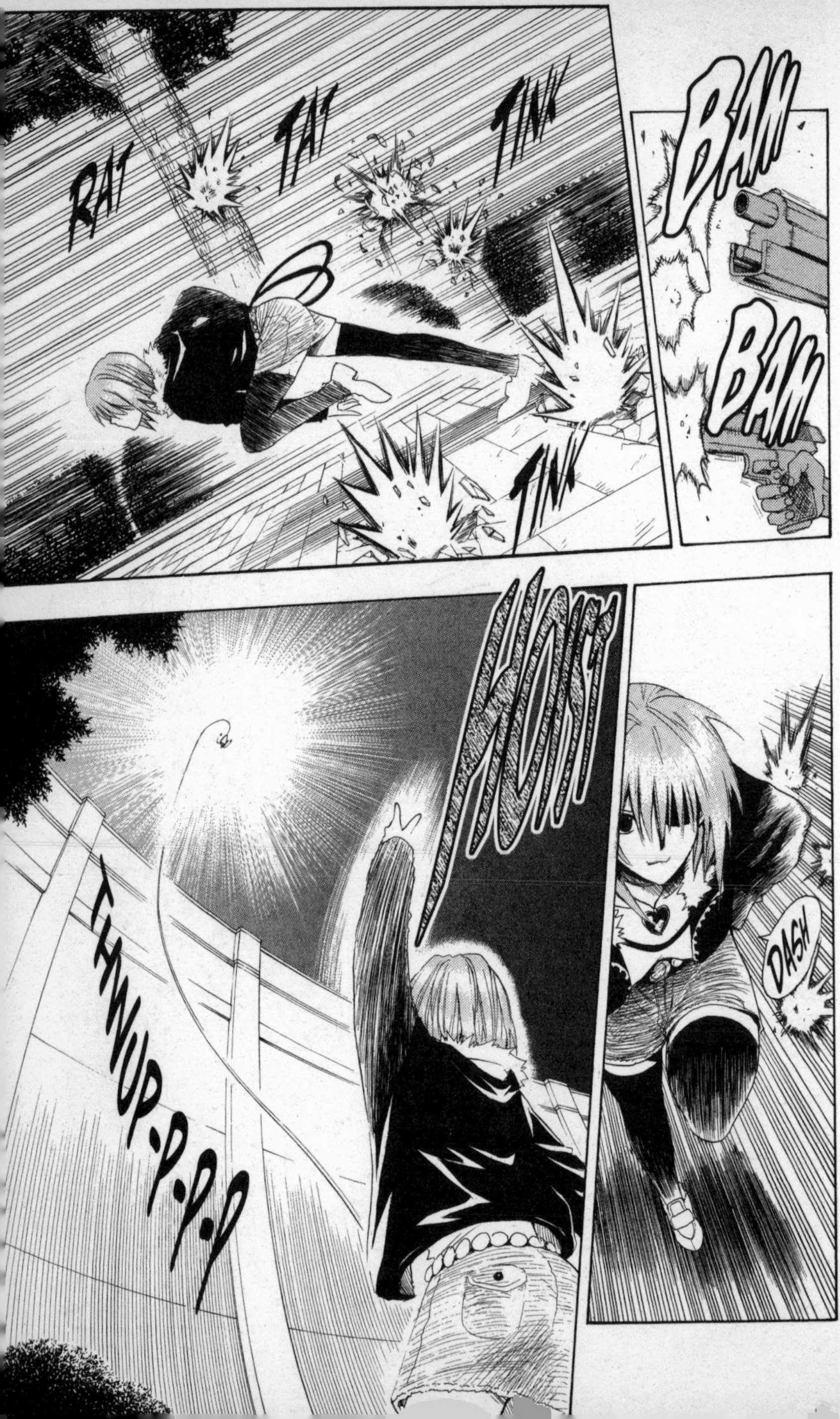
BAM
BAM
RAT
TAT
TINK
TINK
DASH
HOIST
THWUP-P-P-P

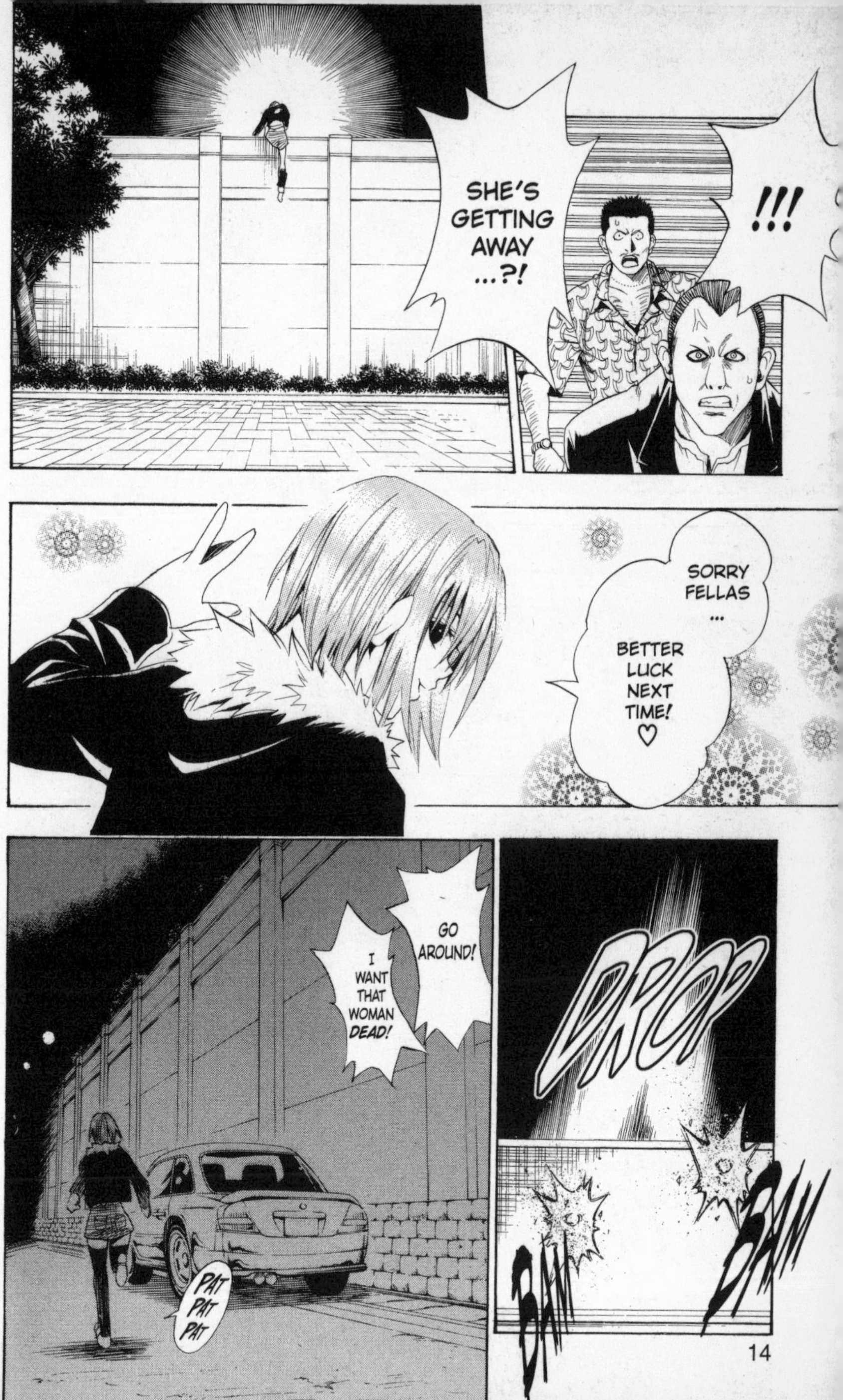
SHE'S GETTING AWAY ...?!
!!!
SORRY FELLAS ...
BETTER LUCK NEXT TIME! ♡
DROP
BAM
BAM
GO AROUND!
I WANT THAT WOMAN DEAD!
PAT PAT PAT

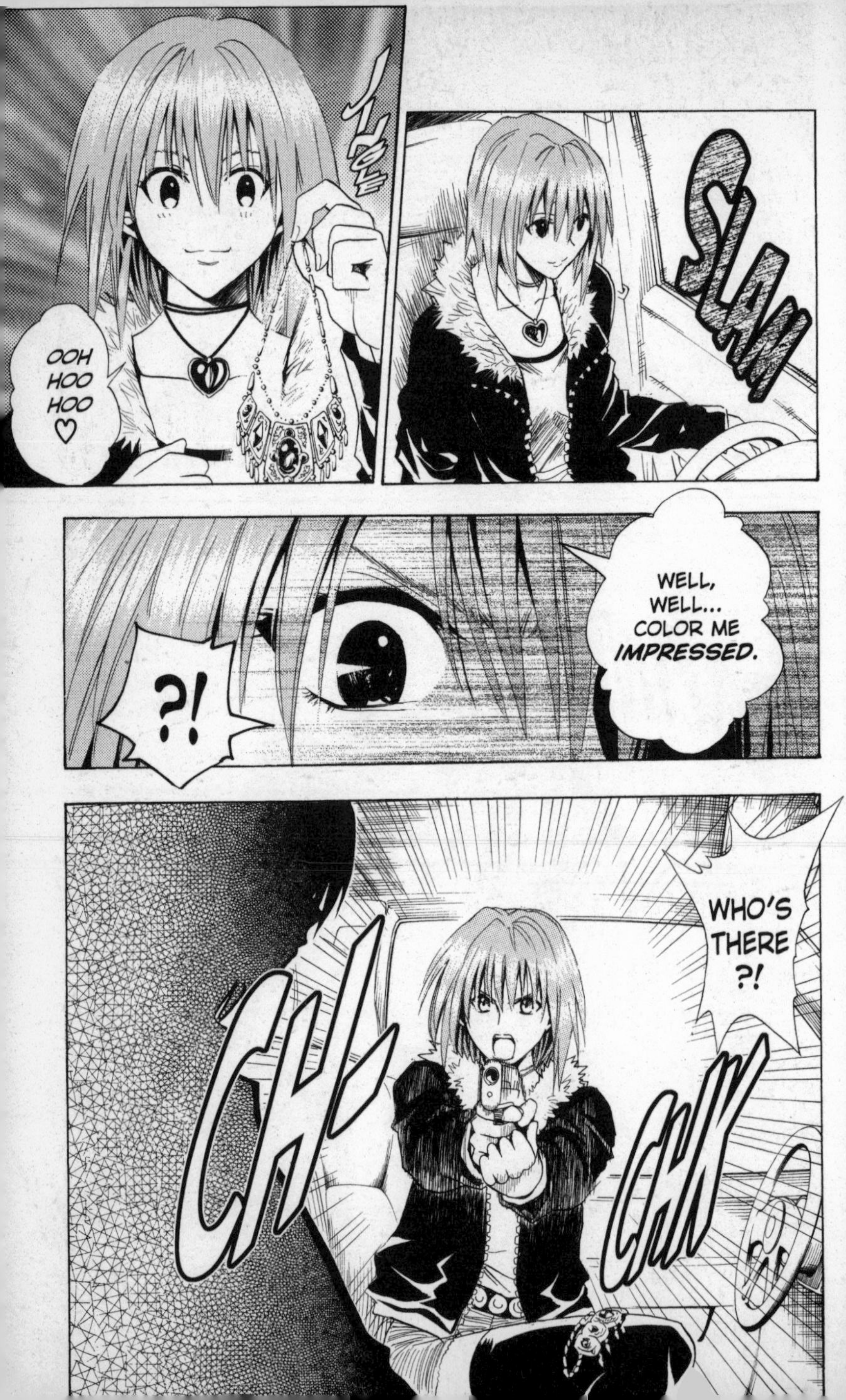
SLAM
JINGLE
OOH HOO HOO ♡
WELL, WELL... COLOR ME IMPRESSED.
?!
WHO'S THERE ?!
CHK CHK

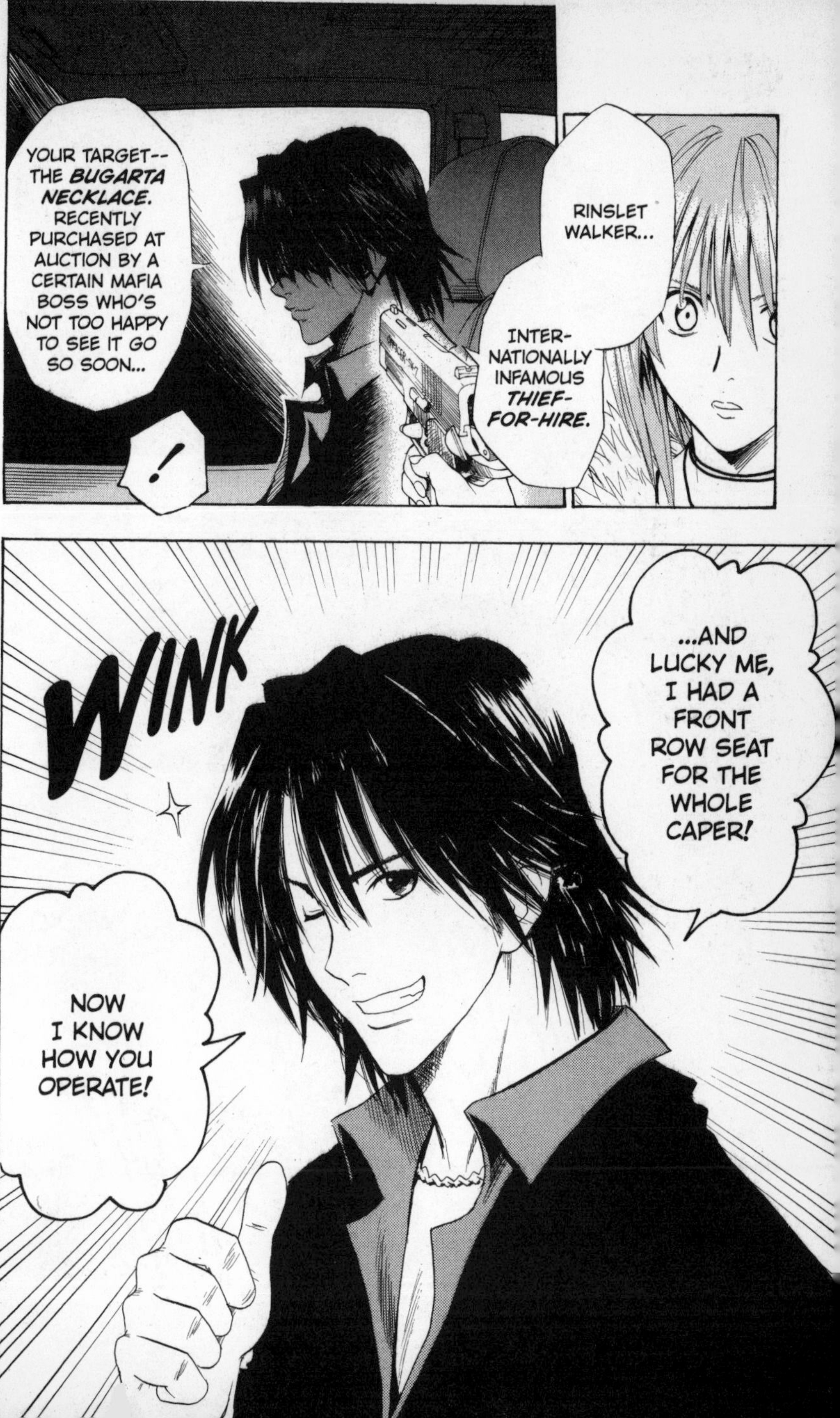
RINSLET WALKER...
INTER-NATIONALLY INFAMOUS *THIEF-FOR-HIRE.*
YOUR TARGET-- THE *BUGARTA NECKLACE.* RECENTLY PURCHASED AT AUCTION BY A CERTAIN MAFIA BOSS WHO'S NOT TOO HAPPY TO SEE IT GO SO SOON...
!
...AND LUCKY ME, I HAD A FRONT ROW SEAT FOR THE WHOLE CAPER!
WINK
NOW I KNOW HOW YOU OPERATE!

READ THIS WAY

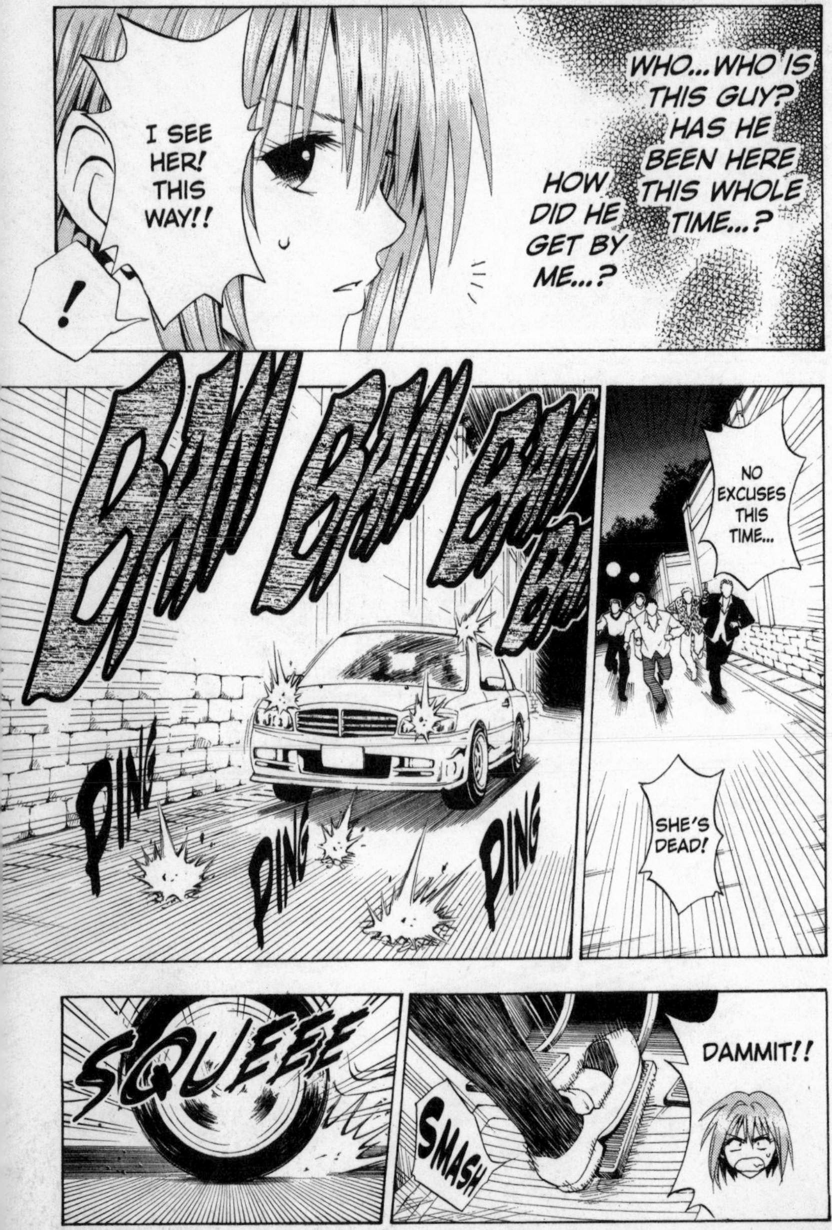

WHO...WHO IS THIS GUY? HAS HE BEEN HERE THIS WHOLE TIME...?
HOW DID HE GET BY ME...?
I SEE HER! THIS WAY!!
!
NO EXCUSES THIS TIME...
SHE'S DEAD!
BAM BAM BAM
PING
PING
PING
DAMMIT!!
SMASH
SQUEEE

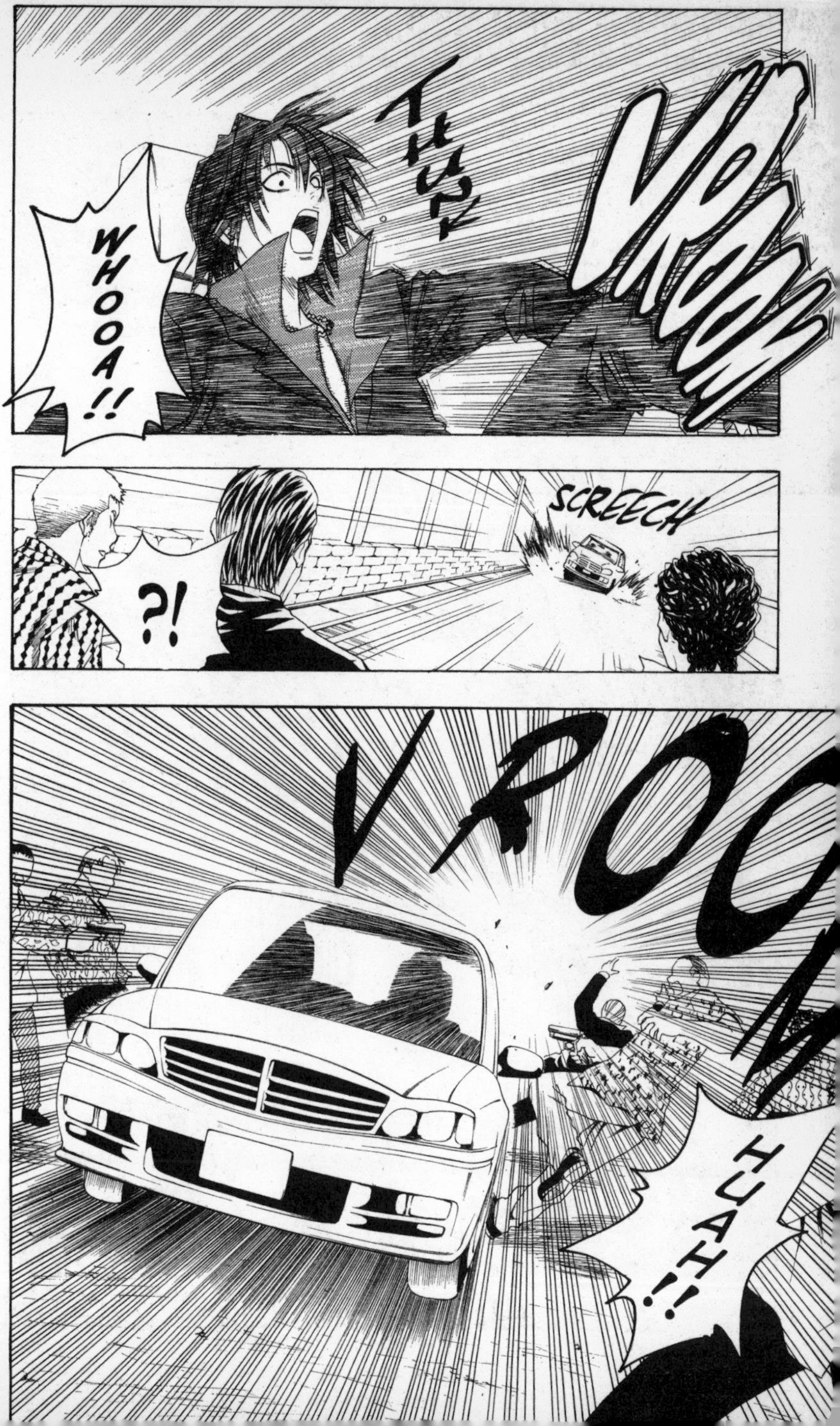
VROOM
THUNK
WHOOA!!
SCREECH
?!
VROOM
HUAH!!!

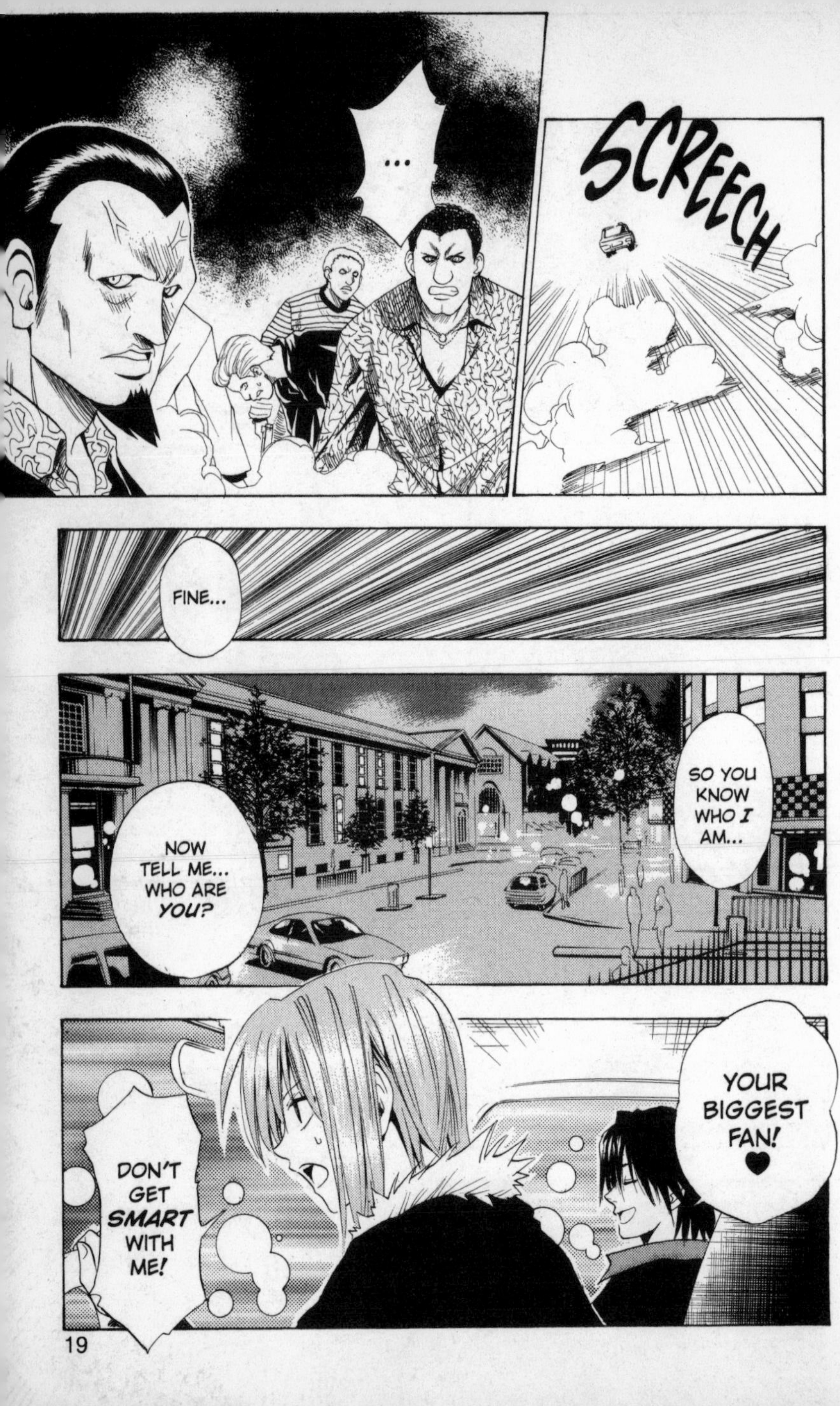
SCREECH
...
FINE...
SO YOU KNOW WHO I AM...
NOW TELL ME... WHO ARE YOU?
YOUR BIGGEST FAN! ♥
DON'T GET SMART WITH ME!

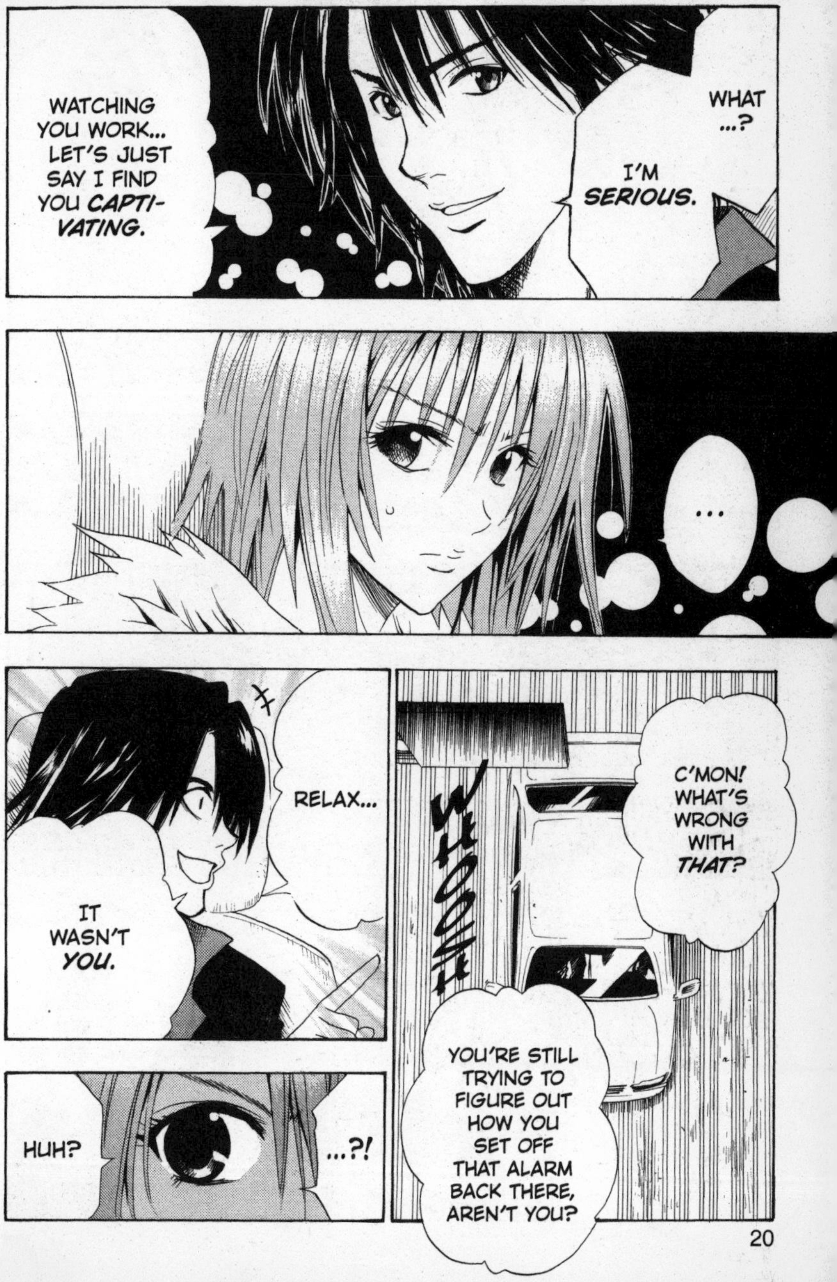
WHAT ...?
WATCHING YOU WORK... LET'S JUST SAY I FIND YOU *CAPTI-VATING.*
I'M *SERIOUS.*
...
C'MON! WHAT'S WRONG WITH *THAT?*
WHOOSH
YOU'RE STILL TRYING TO FIGURE OUT HOW YOU SET OFF THAT ALARM BACK THERE, AREN'T YOU?
RELAX...
IT WASN'T *YOU.*
...?!
HUH?

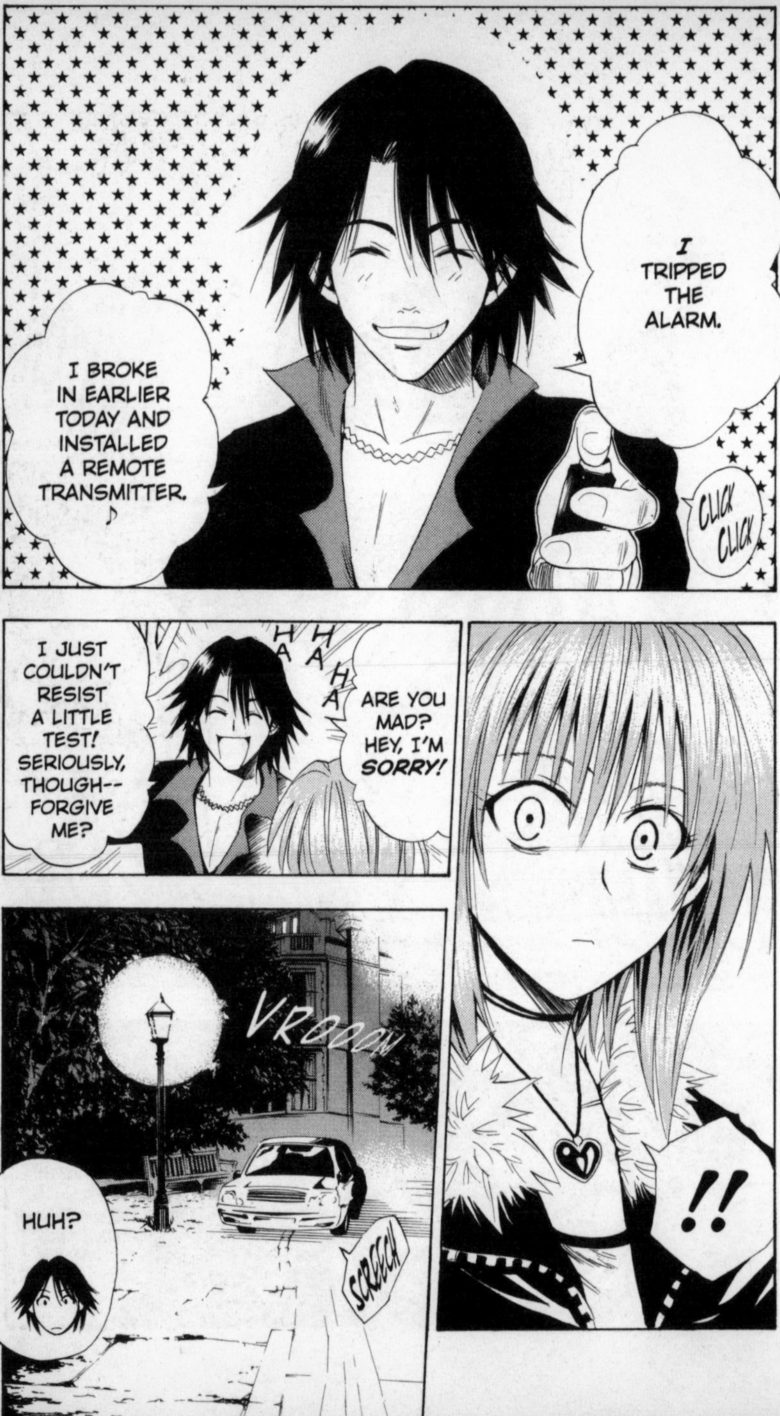
I TRIPPED THE ALARM.
CLICK CLICK
I BROKE IN EARLIER TODAY AND INSTALLED A REMOTE TRANSMITTER. ♪
!!
HAHAHA
ARE YOU MAD? HEY, I'M *SORRY!*
I JUST COULDN'T RESIST A LITTLE TEST! SERIOUSLY, THOUGH-- FORGIVE ME?
VROOOOM
SCREECH
HUH?

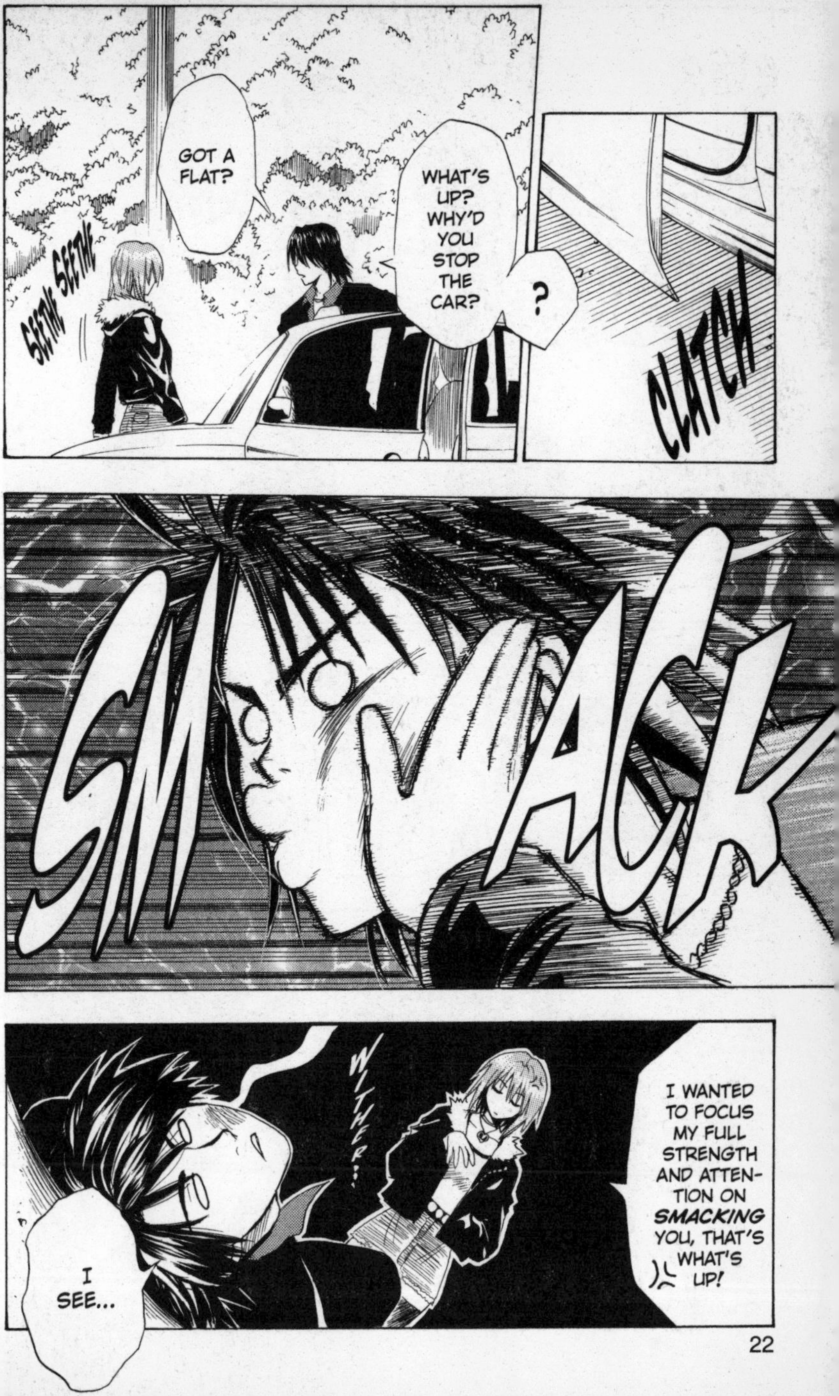
CLATCH
?
WHAT'S UP? WHY'D YOU STOP THE CAR?
GOT A FLAT?
SEETHE SEETHE
SMACK
I WANTED TO FOCUS MY FULL STRENGTH AND ATTEN-TION ON SMACKING YOU, THAT'S WHAT'S UP!
WITHER...
I SEE...

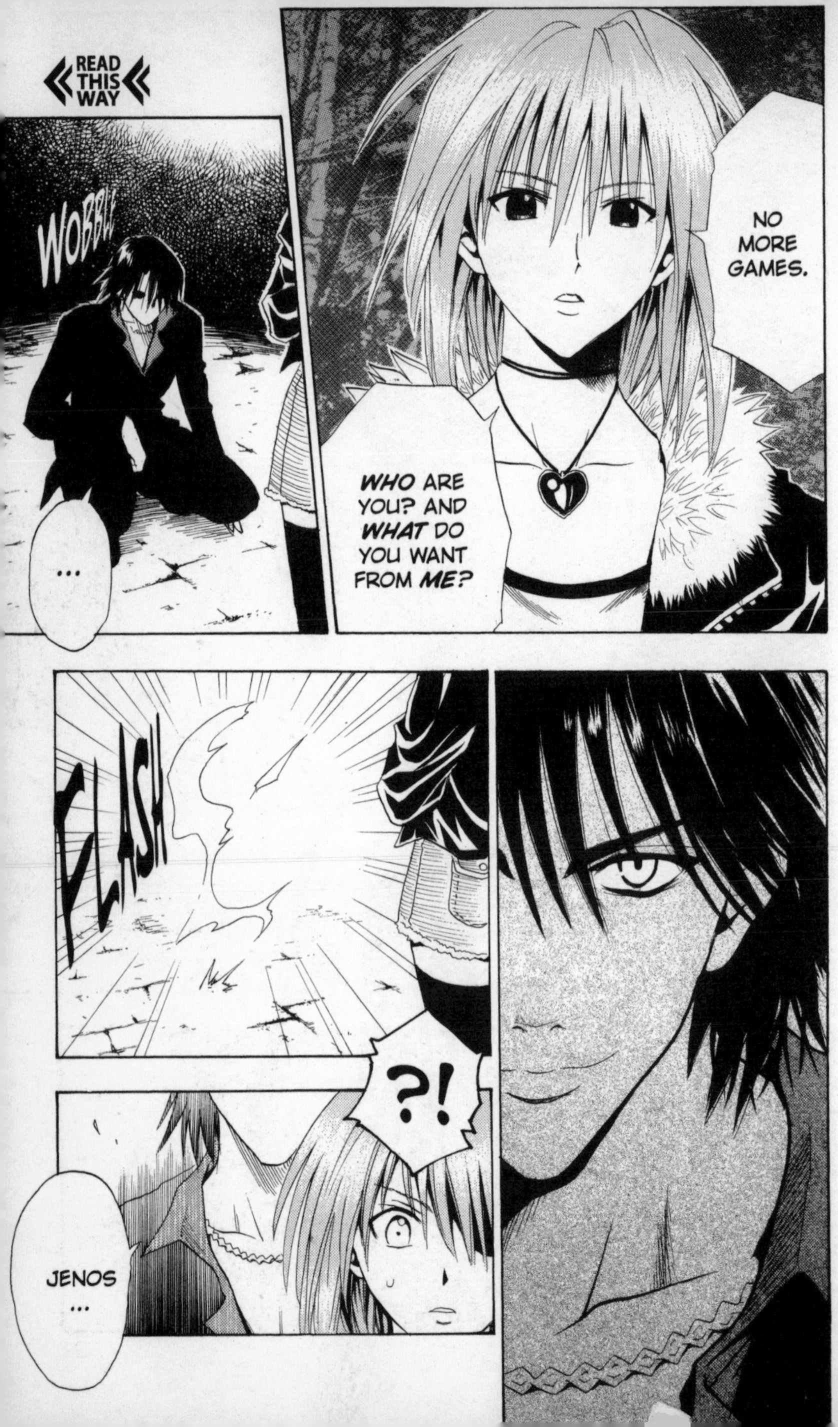
READ THIS WAY
NO MORE GAMES.
WHO ARE YOU? AND *WHAT* DO YOU WANT FROM *ME?*
WOBBLE
...
FLASH
?!
JENOS ...

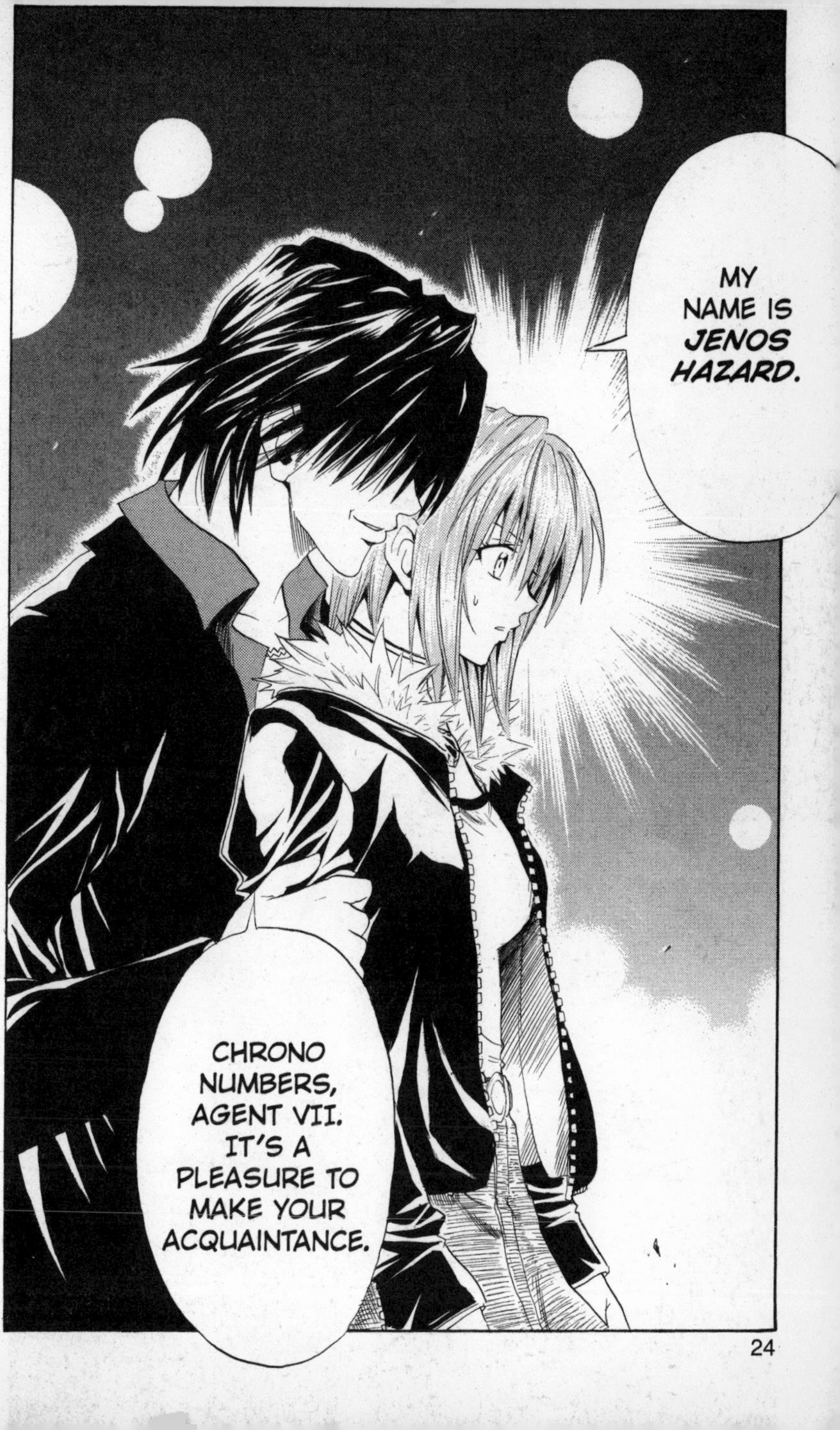
MY NAME IS *JENOS HAZARD.*
CHRONO NUMBERS, AGENT VII. IT'S A PLEASURE TO MAKE YOUR ACQUAINTANCE.

READ THIS WAY

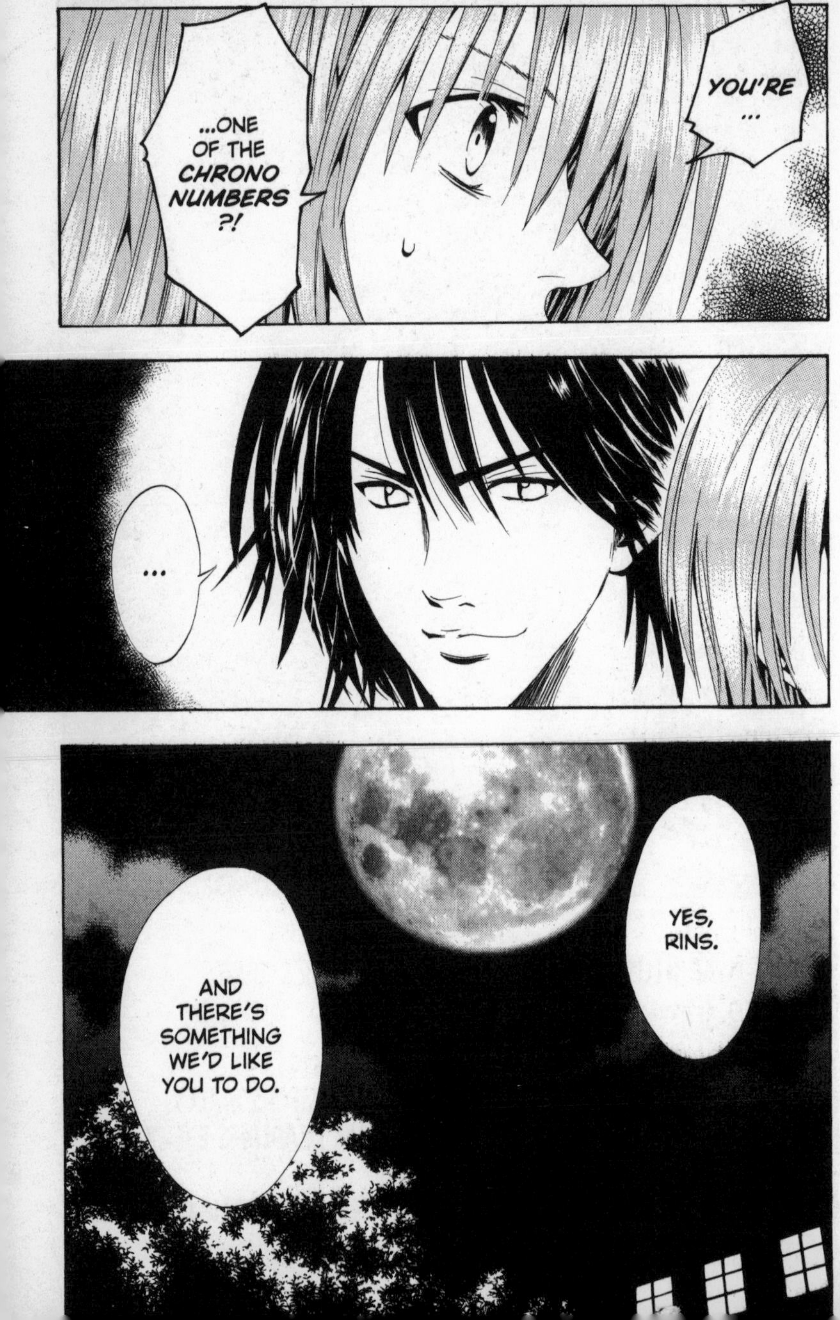
YOU'RE ...
...ONE OF THE CHRONO NUMBERS ?!
...
YES, RINS.
AND THERE'S SOMETHING WE'D LIKE YOU TO DO.

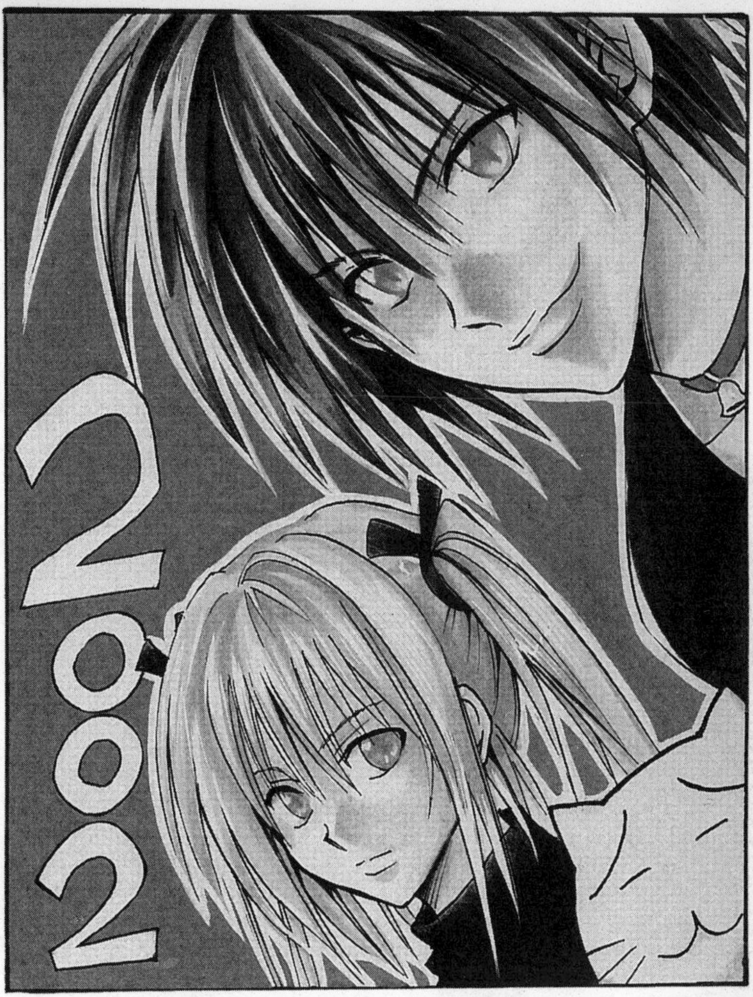
2002

☆ THIS IS AN ILLUSTRATION FROM THE NEW YEAR'S CARD THAT I SENT THIS YEAR.

I WISH I COULD REPLY TO ALL YOUR LETTERS PERSONALLY, BUT IT'S AN IMPOSSIBLE TASK WHEN I HAVE DEADLINES EVERY WEEK.

YOUR KIND WORDS AND WISHES ARE EXTREMELY GRATIFYING, THOUGH, SO I KEEP HOPING I CAN WORK SOMETHING OUT...

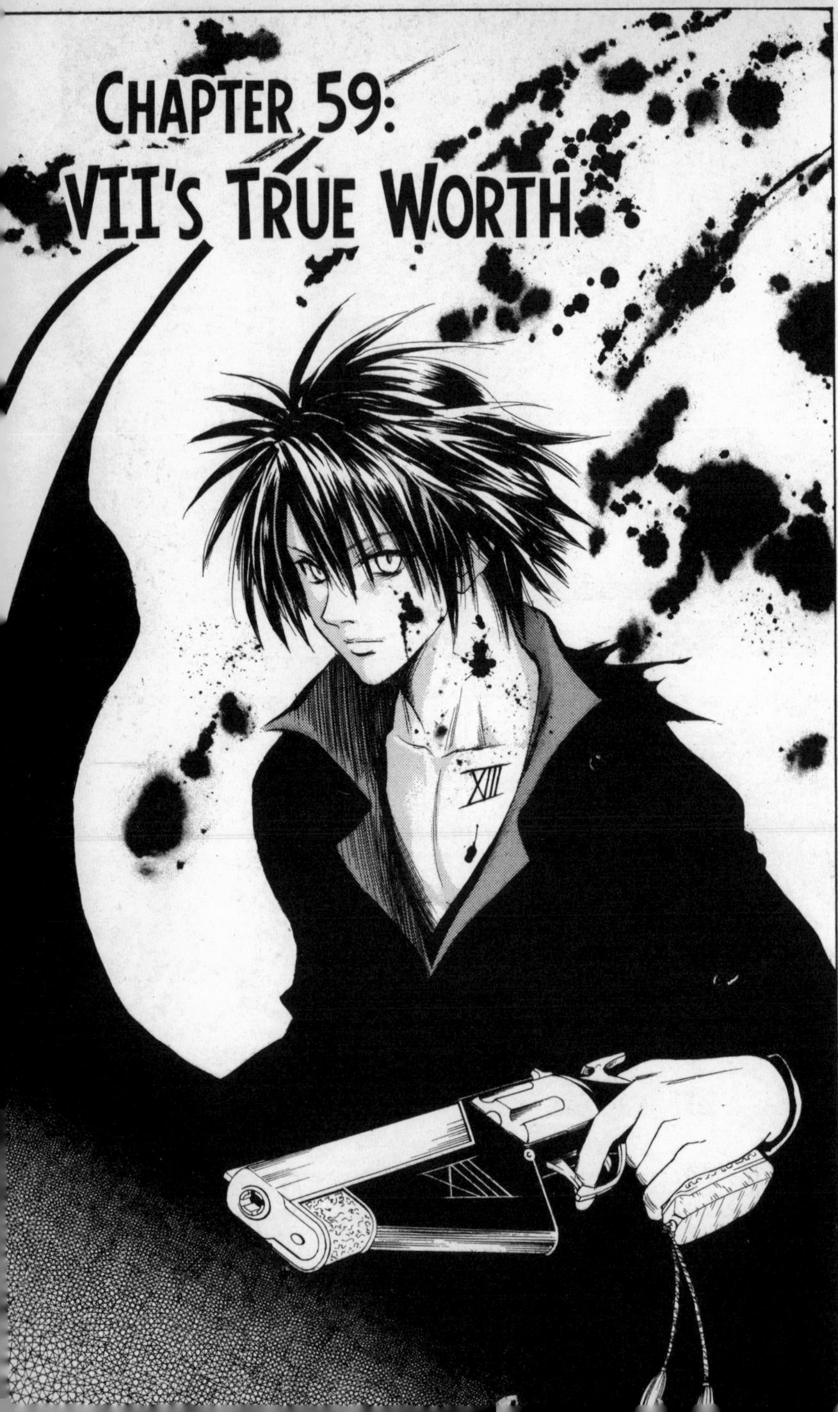
CHAPTER 59:
VII's TRUE WORTH

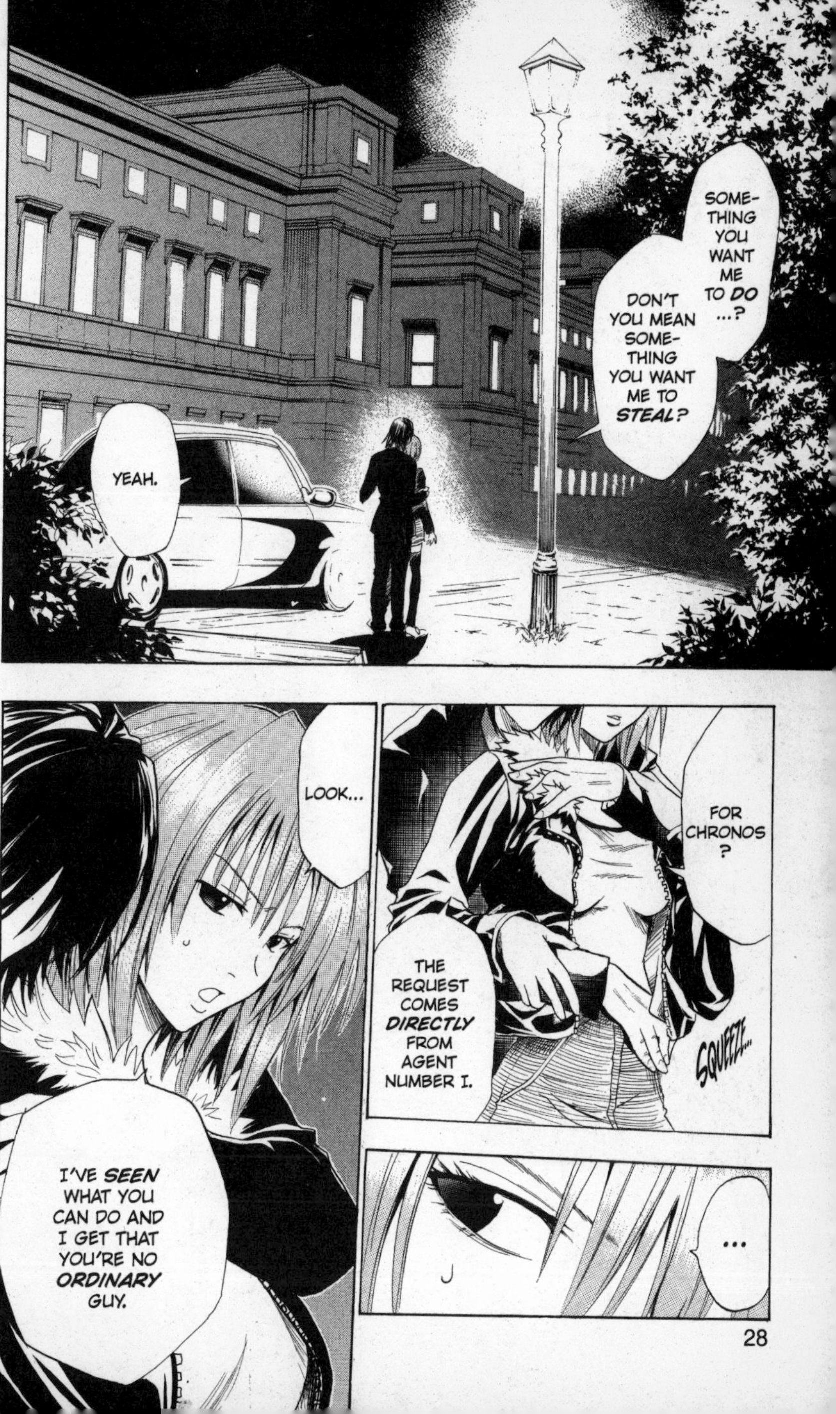
SOME-THING YOU WANT ME TO *DO* ...?
DON'T YOU MEAN SOME-THING YOU WANT ME TO *STEAL*?
YEAH.
FOR CHRONOS?
THE REQUEST COMES *DIRECTLY* FROM AGENT NUMBER I.
SQUEEZE...
...
LOOK...
I'VE *SEEN* WHAT YOU CAN DO AND I GET THAT YOU'RE NO *ORDINARY* GUY.

READ THIS WAY

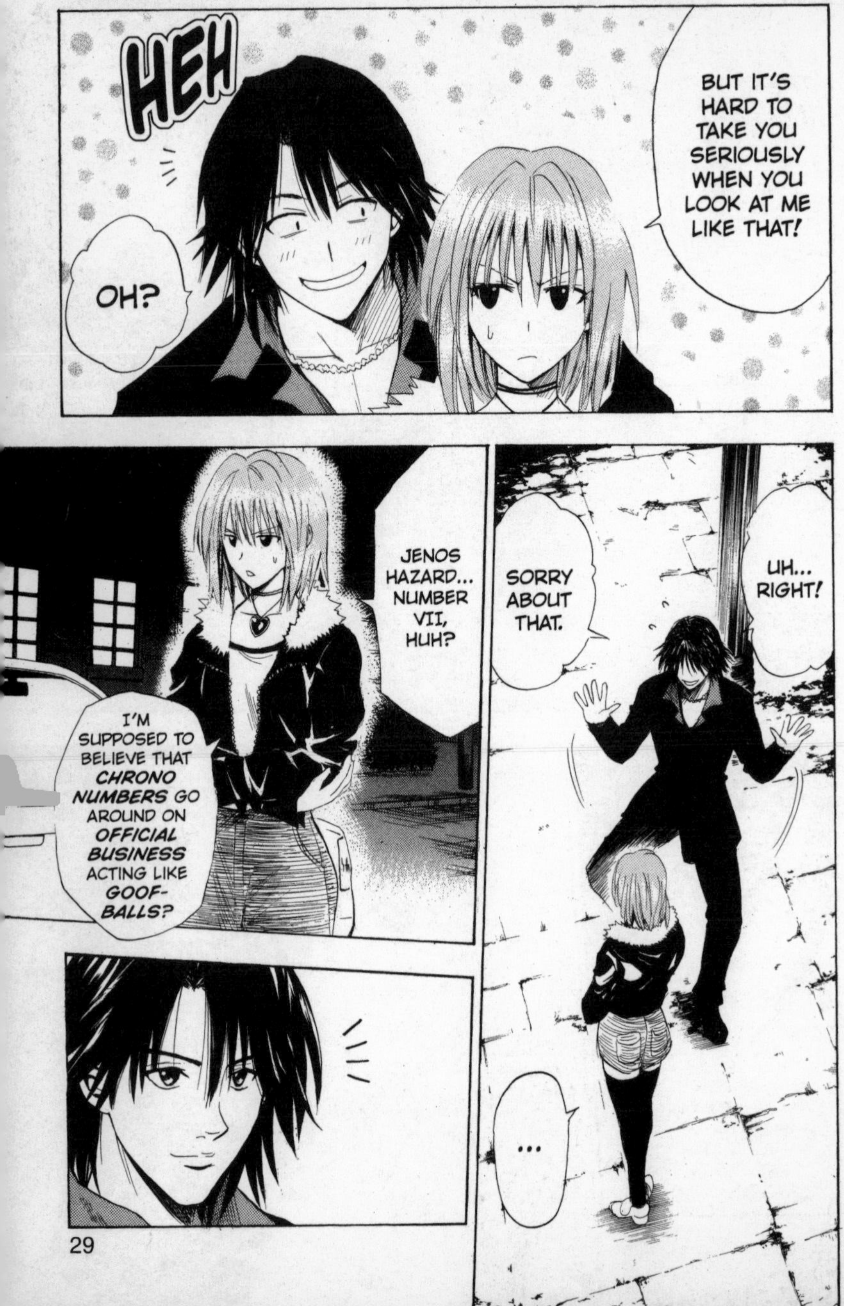

BUT IT'S HARD TO TAKE YOU SERIOUSLY WHEN YOU LOOK AT ME LIKE THAT!
HEH
OH?
UH... RIGHT!
SORRY ABOUT THAT.
...
JENOS HAZARD... NUMBER VII, HUH?
I'M SUPPOSED TO BELIEVE THAT CHRONO NUMBERS GO AROUND ON OFFICIAL BUSINESS ACTING LIKE GOOF-BALLS?

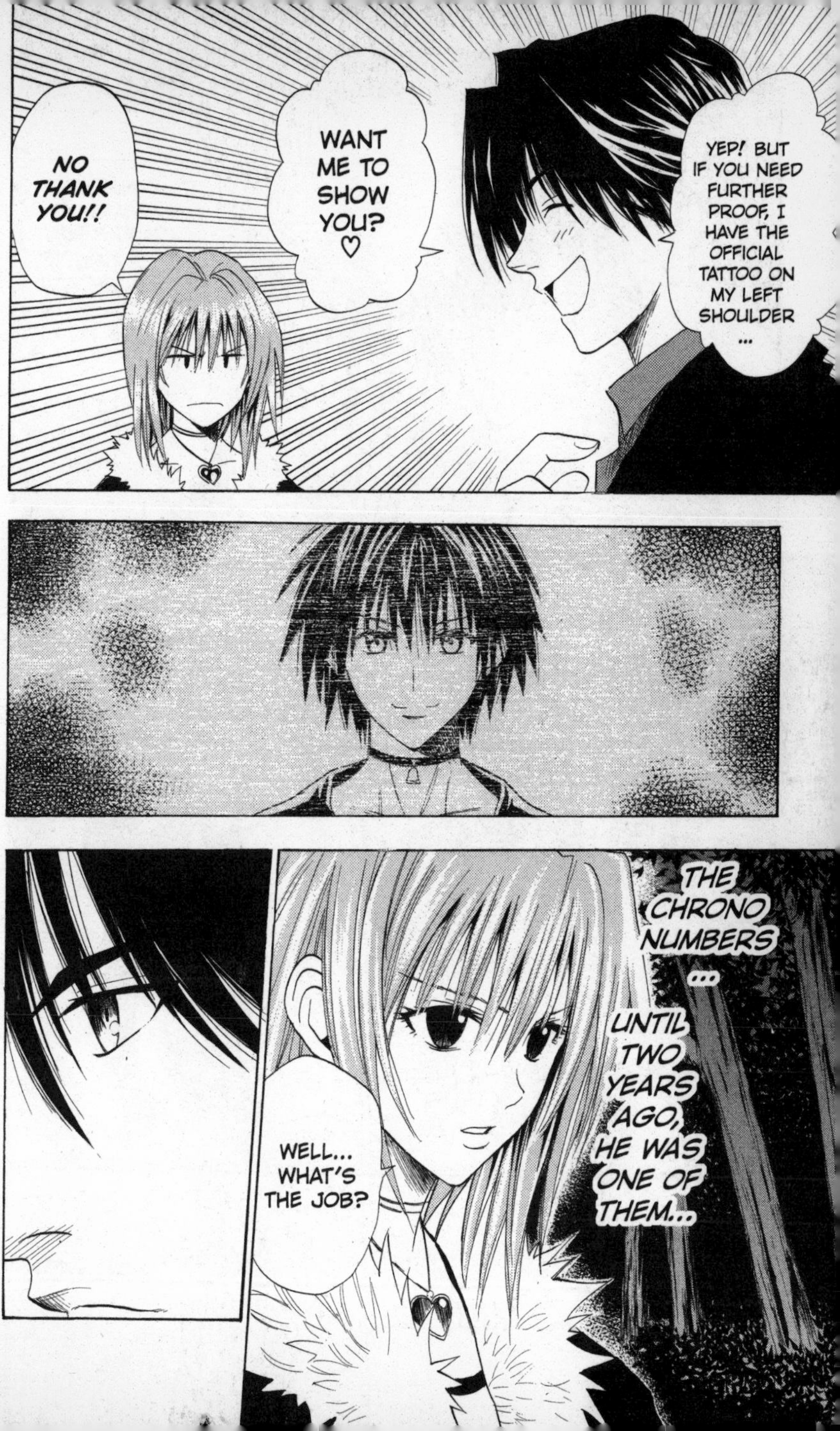
YEP! BUT IF YOU NEED FURTHER PROOF, I HAVE THE OFFICIAL TATTOO ON MY LEFT SHOULDER ...
WANT ME TO SHOW YOU? ♡
NO THANK YOU!!
THE CHRONO NUMBERS ...
UNTIL TWO YEARS AGO, HE WAS ONE OF THEM...
WELL... WHAT'S THE JOB?

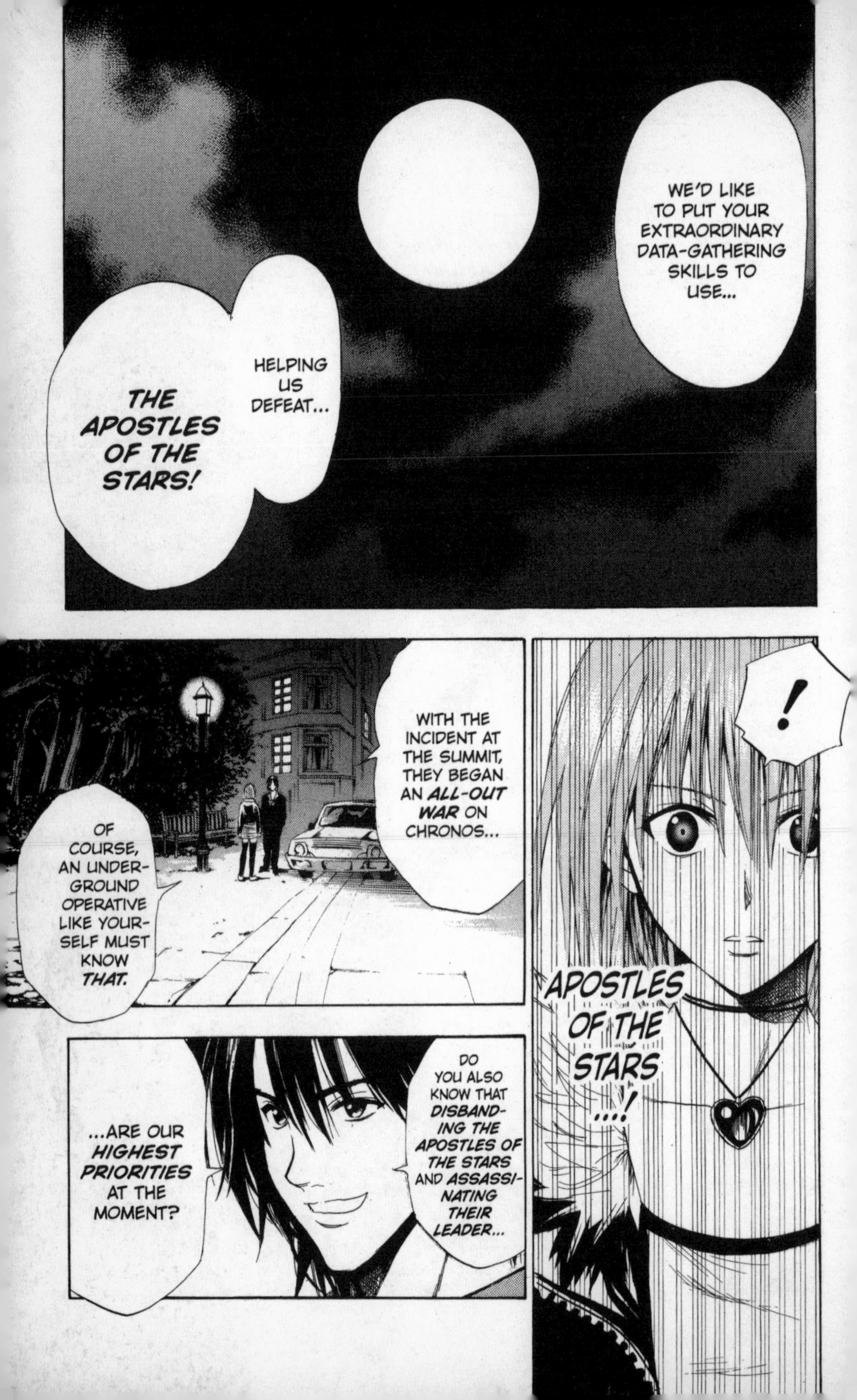
WE'D LIKE TO PUT YOUR EXTRAORDINARY DATA-GATHERING SKILLS TO USE...
HELPING US DEFEAT...
THE APOSTLES OF THE STARS!
!
APOSTLES OF THE STARS...!
WITH THE INCIDENT AT THE SUMMIT, THEY BEGAN AN ALL-OUT WAR ON CHRONOS...
OF COURSE, AN UNDER-GROUND OPERATIVE LIKE YOUR-SELF MUST KNOW THAT.
DO YOU ALSO KNOW THAT DISBAND-ING THE APOSTLES OF THE STARS AND ASSASSI-NATING THEIR LEADER...
...ARE OUR HIGHEST PRIORITIES AT THE MOMENT?

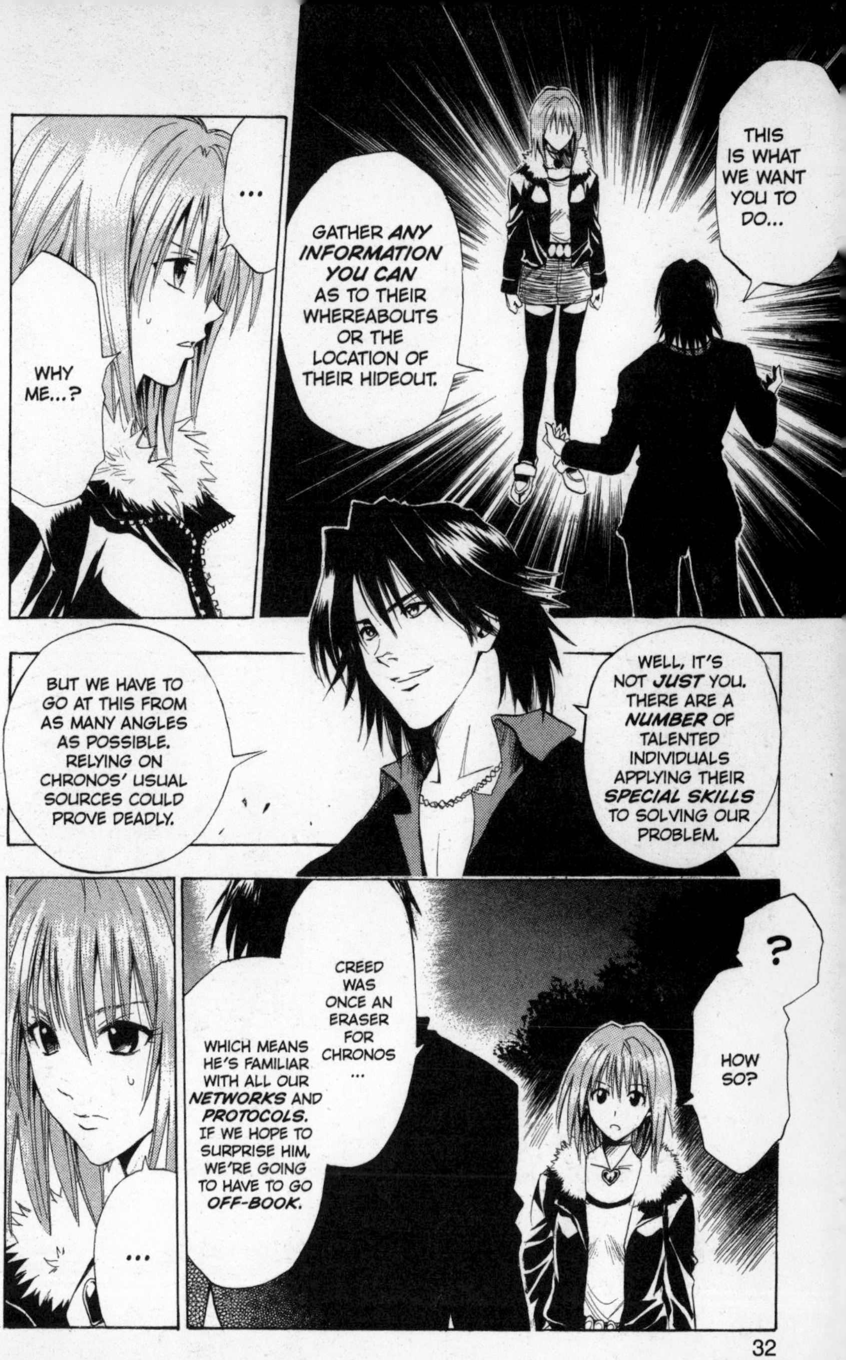

THIS IS WHAT WE WANT YOU TO DO...
GATHER ANY INFORMATION YOU CAN AS TO THEIR WHEREABOUTS OR THE LOCATION OF THEIR HIDEOUT.
...
WHY ME...?
WELL, IT'S NOT JUST YOU. THERE ARE A NUMBER OF TALENTED INDIVIDUALS APPLYING THEIR SPECIAL SKILLS TO SOLVING OUR PROBLEM.
BUT WE HAVE TO GO AT THIS FROM AS MANY ANGLES AS POSSIBLE. RELYING ON CHRONOS' USUAL SOURCES COULD PROVE DEADLY.
?
HOW SO?
CREED WAS ONCE AN ERASER FOR CHRONOS...
WHICH MEANS HE'S FAMILIAR WITH ALL OUR NETWORKS AND PROTOCOLS. IF WE HOPE TO SURPRISE HIM, WE'RE GOING TO HAVE TO GO OFF-BOOK.
...

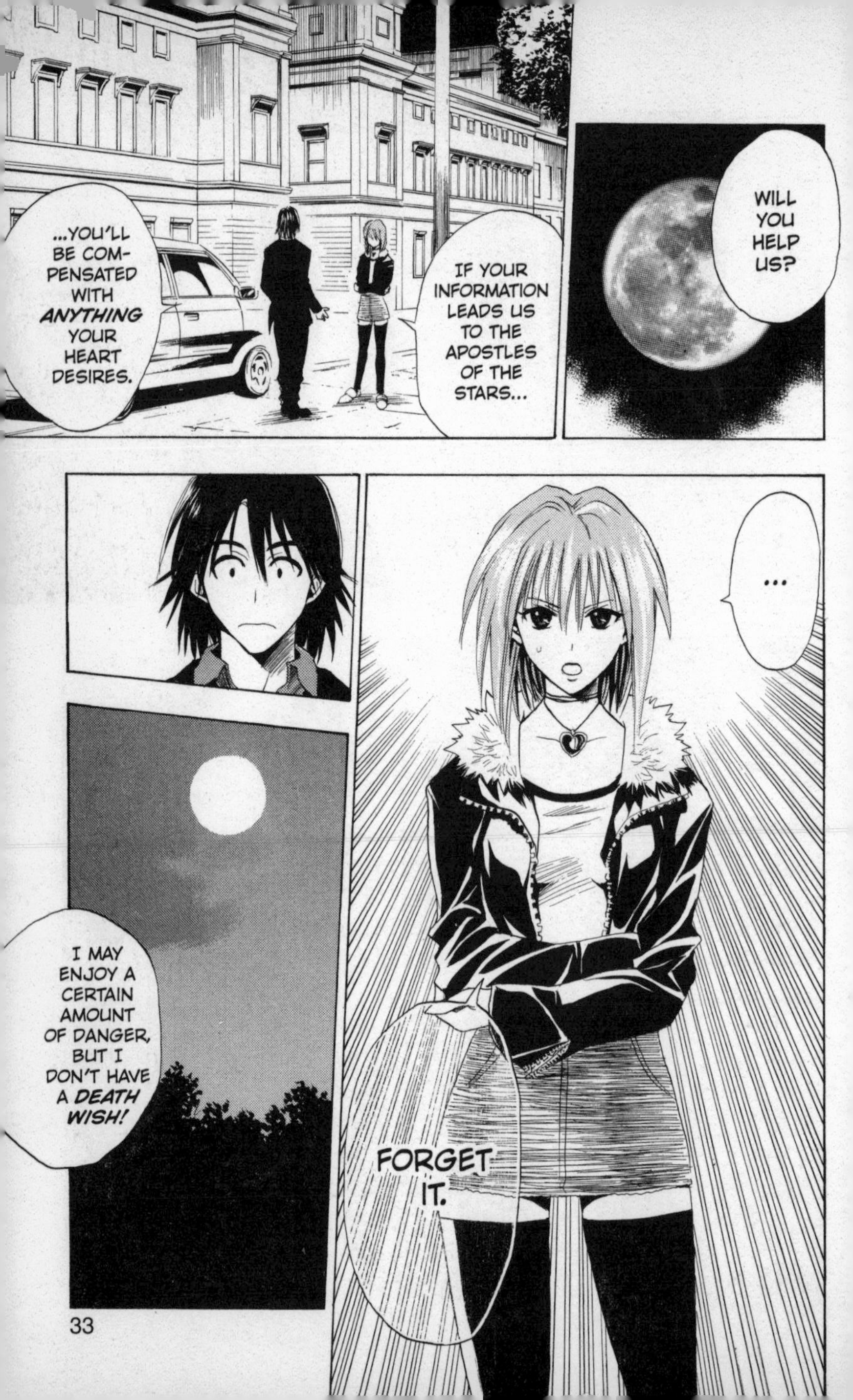
WILL YOU HELP US?
IF YOUR INFORMATION LEADS US TO THE APOSTLES OF THE STARS...
...YOU'LL BE COM-PENSATED WITH *ANYTHING* YOUR HEART DESIRES.
...
FORGET IT.
I MAY ENJOY A CERTAIN AMOUNT OF DANGER, BUT I DON'T HAVE A *DEATH WISH!*

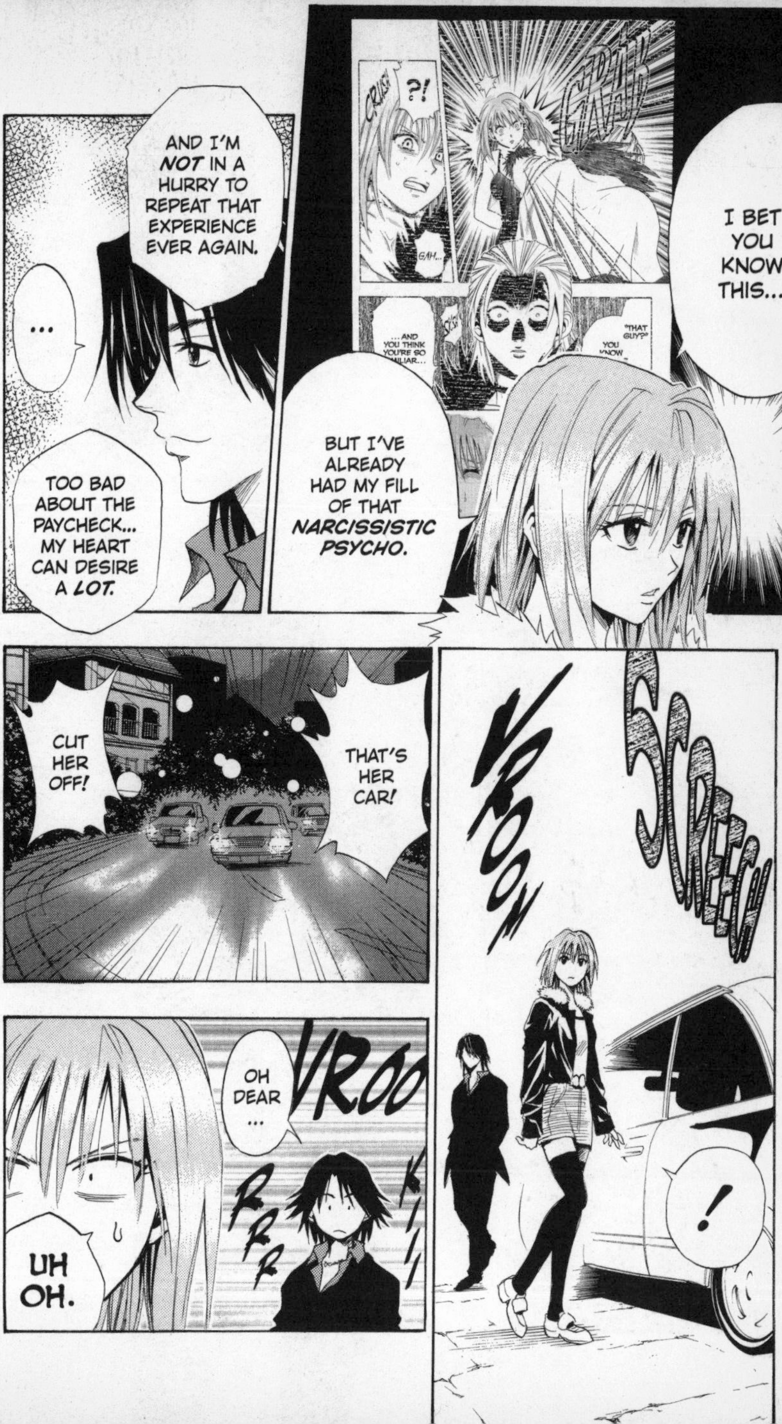
I BET YOU KNOW THIS...
?!
GAH...
BUT I'VE ALREADY HAD MY FILL OF THAT NARCISSISTIC PSYCHO.
AND I'M NOT IN A HURRY TO REPEAT THAT EXPERIENCE EVER AGAIN.
...
TOO BAD ABOUT THE PAYCHECK... MY HEART CAN DESIRE A LOT.
SCREECH
VROOOM
!
THAT'S HER CAR!
CUT HER OFF!
OH DEAR...
VROO
RRRR
KIII
UH OH.

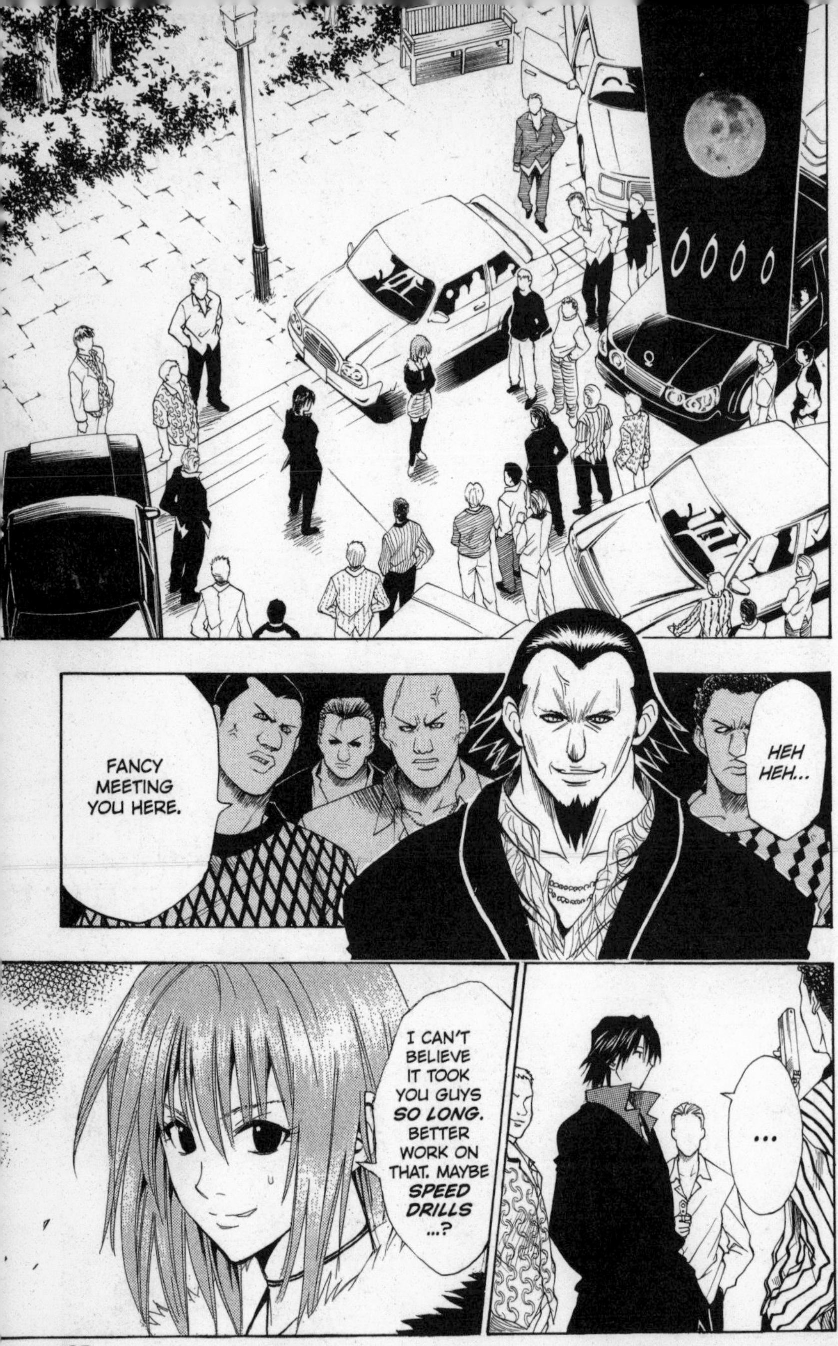
HEH HEH...
FANCY MEETING YOU HERE.
...
I CAN'T BELIEVE IT TOOK YOU GUYS SO LONG. BETTER WORK ON THAT. MAYBE SPEED DRILLS ...?

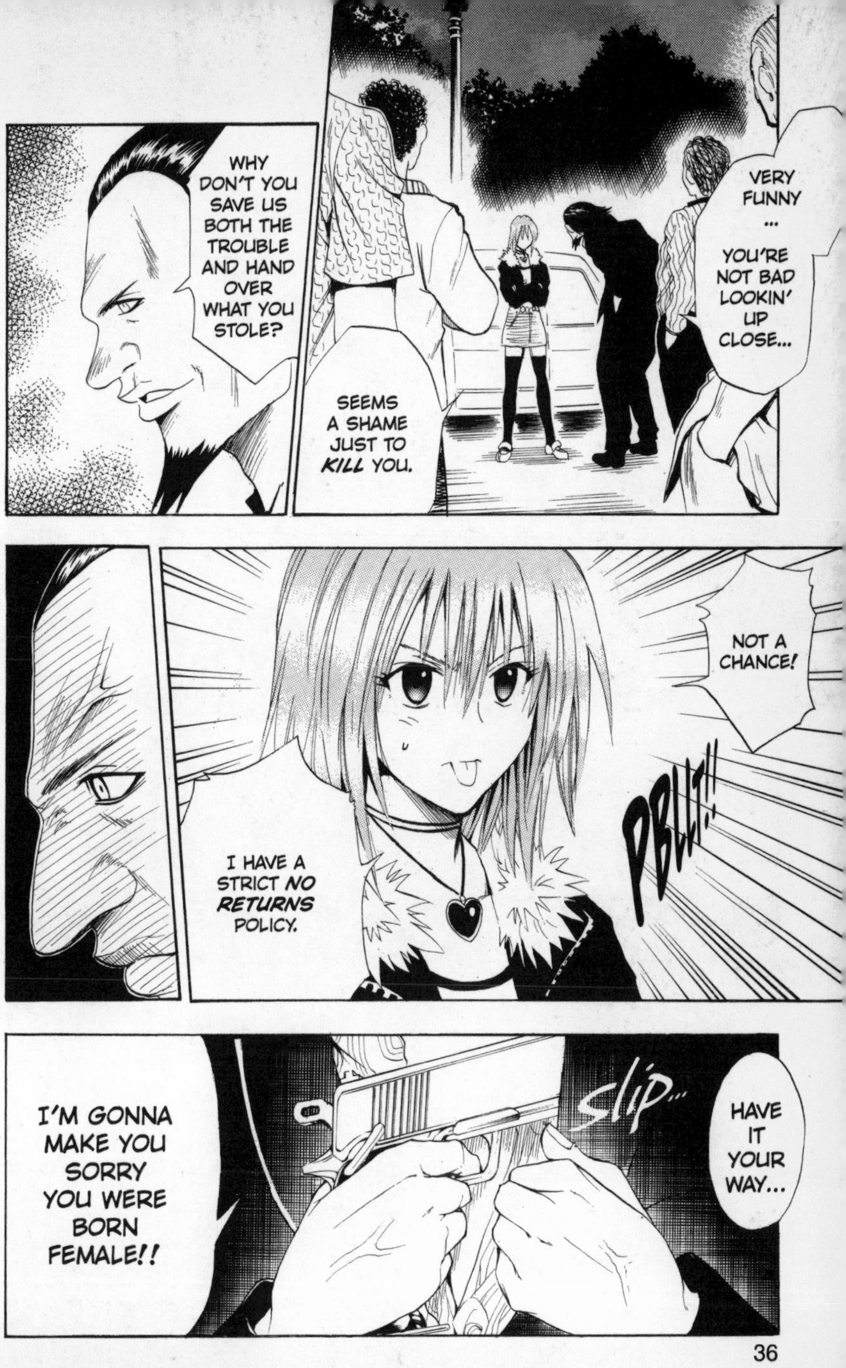
VERY FUNNY ... YOU'RE NOT BAD LOOKIN' UP CLOSE...
SEEMS A SHAME JUST TO *KILL* YOU.
WHY DON'T YOU SAVE US BOTH THE TROUBLE AND HAND OVER WHAT YOU STOLE?
NOT A CHANCE!
PBLLT!!
I HAVE A STRICT *NO RETURNS* POLICY.
HAVE IT YOUR WAY...
SLIP...
I'M GONNA MAKE YOU SORRY YOU WERE BORN FEMALE!!

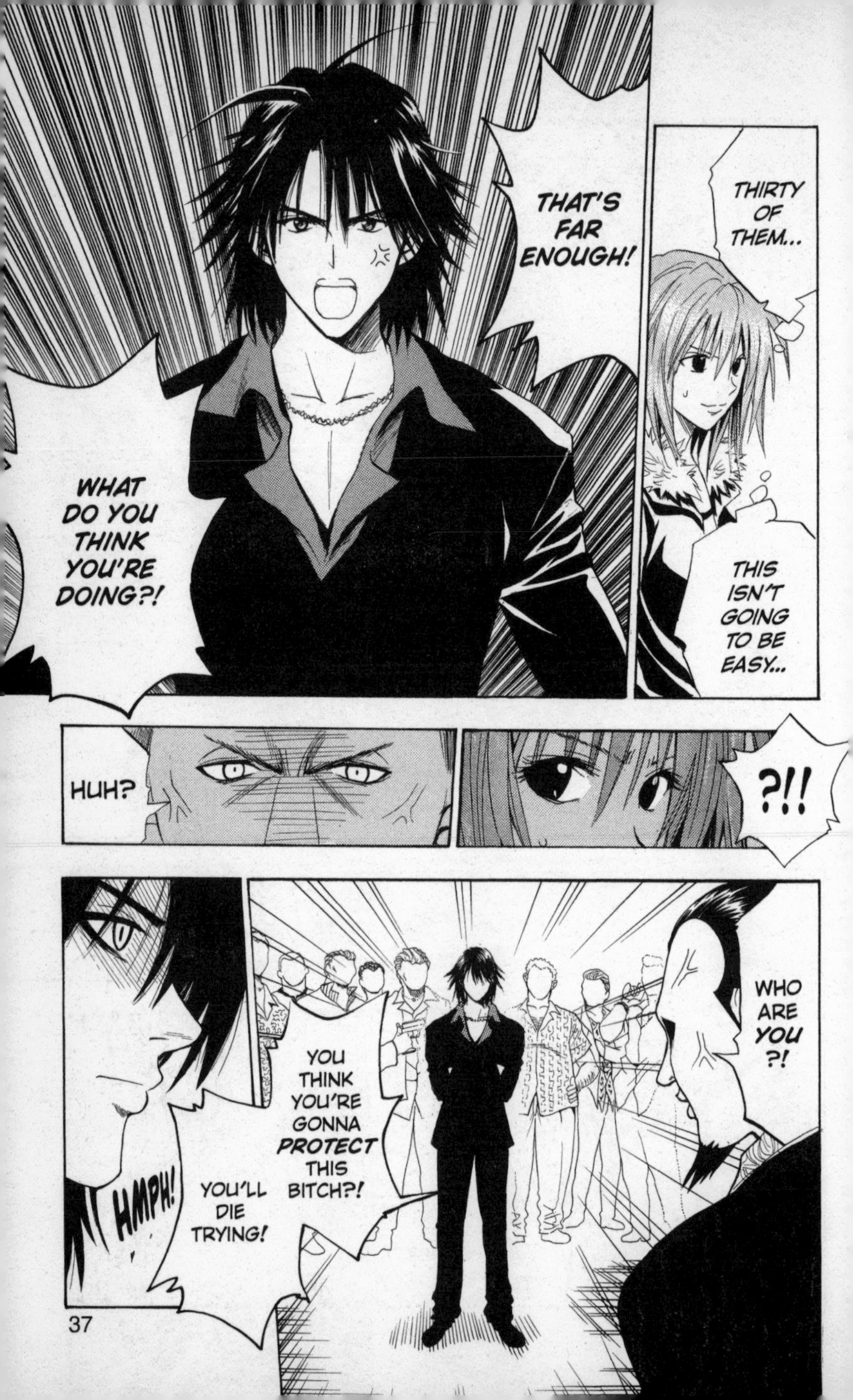
THIRTY OF THEM...
THIS ISN'T GOING TO BE EASY...
THAT'S FAR ENOUGH!
WHAT DO YOU THINK YOU'RE DOING?!
?!!
HUH?
WHO ARE YOU?!
YOU THINK YOU'RE GONNA PROTECT THIS BITCH?!
YOU'LL DIE TRYING!
HMPH!

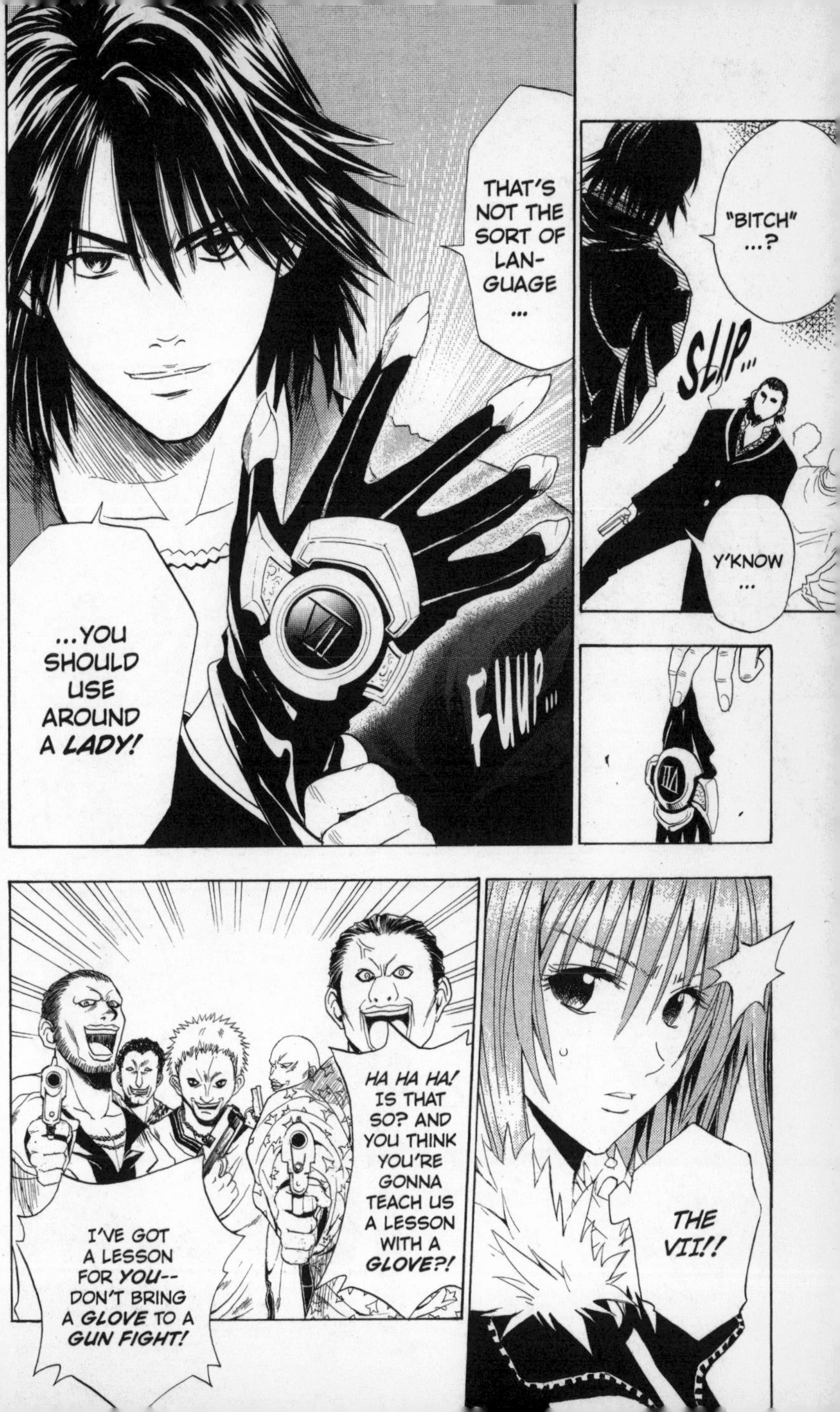
"BITCH" ...?
SLIP...
Y'KNOW ...
THAT'S NOT THE SORT OF LAN-GUAGE ...
FUUP...
...YOU SHOULD USE AROUND A *LADY!*
THE VII!!
HA HA HA! IS THAT SO? AND YOU THINK YOU'RE GONNA TEACH US A LESSON WITH A *GLOVE?!*
I'VE GOT A LESSON FOR *YOU--* DON'T BRING A *GLOVE* TO A *GUN FIGHT!*

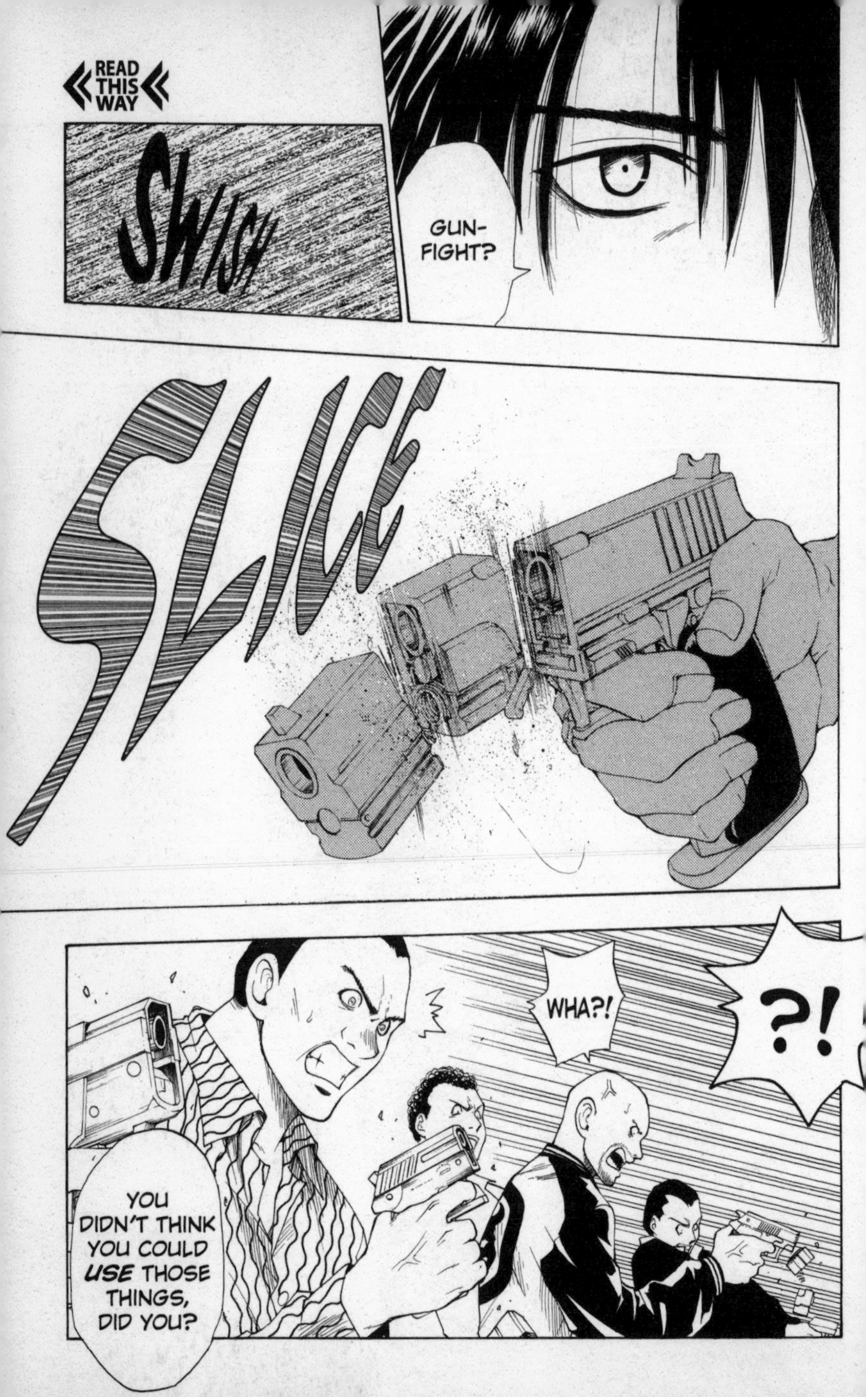
READ THIS WAY
GUN-FIGHT?
SWISH
SLICE
?!
WHA?!
YOU DIDN'T THINK YOU COULD *USE* THOSE THINGS, DID YOU?

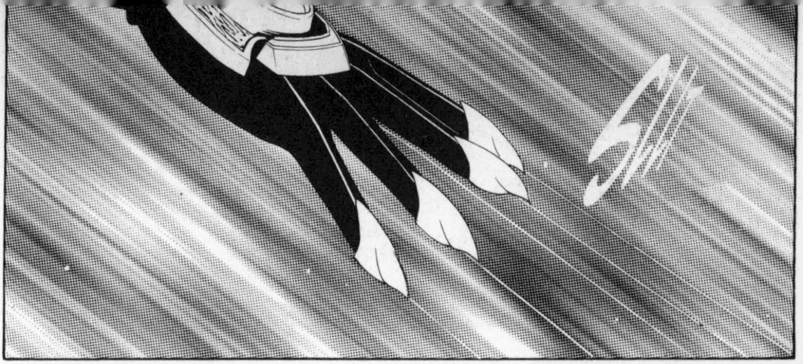

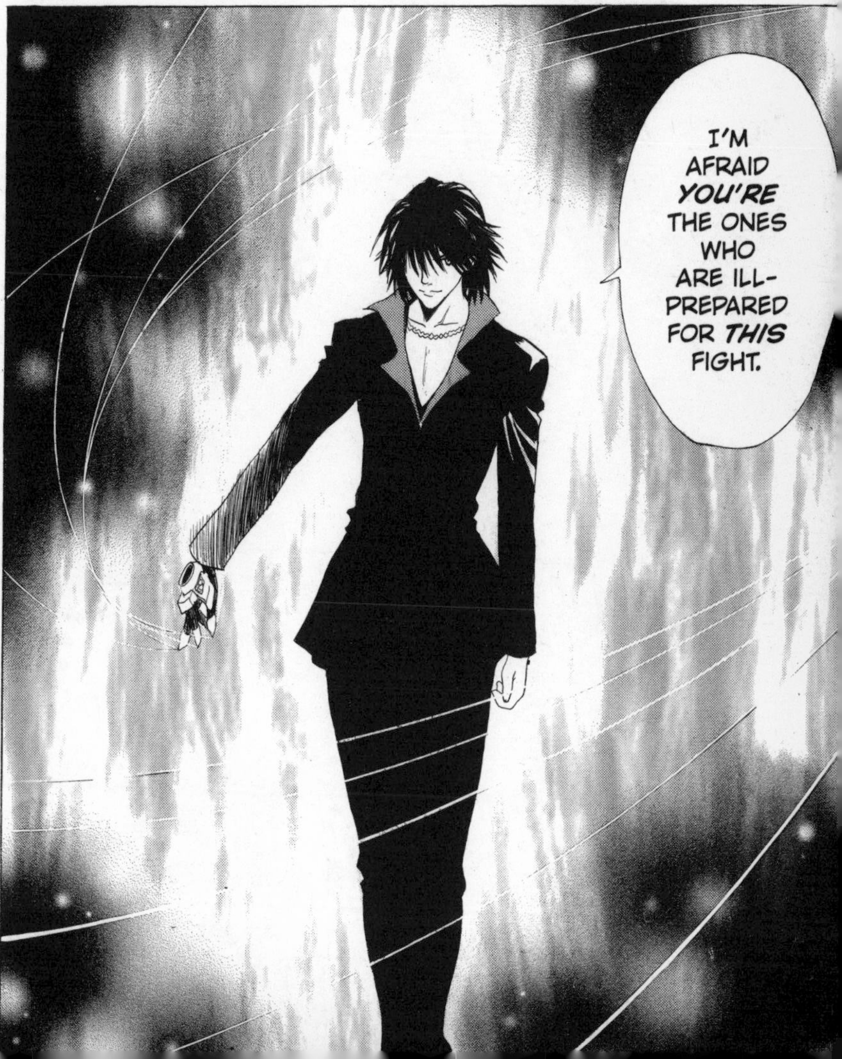
I'M AFRAID YOU'RE THE ONES WHO ARE ILL-PREPARED FOR THIS FIGHT.

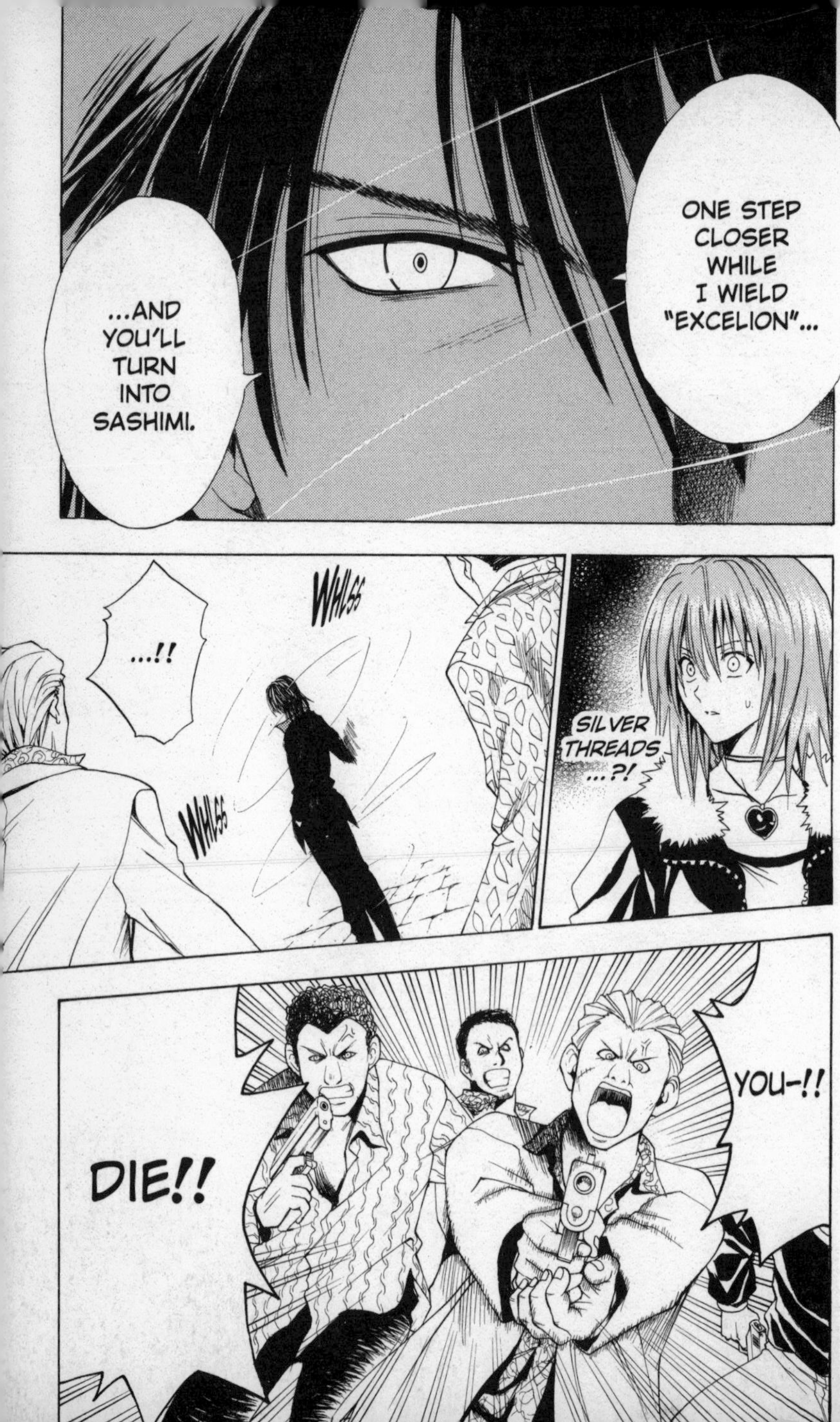
ONE STEP CLOSER WHILE I WIELD "EXCELION"...
...AND YOU'LL TURN INTO SASHIMI.
SILVER THREADS ...?!
WHLSS
...!!
WHLSS
YOU-!!
DIE!!

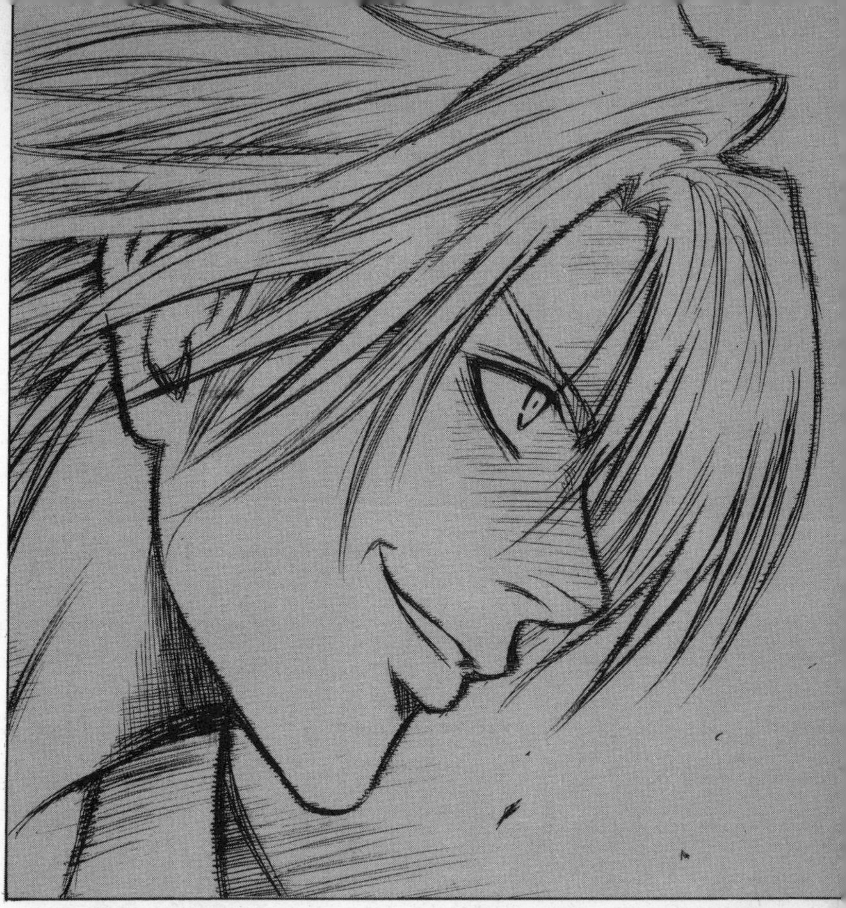
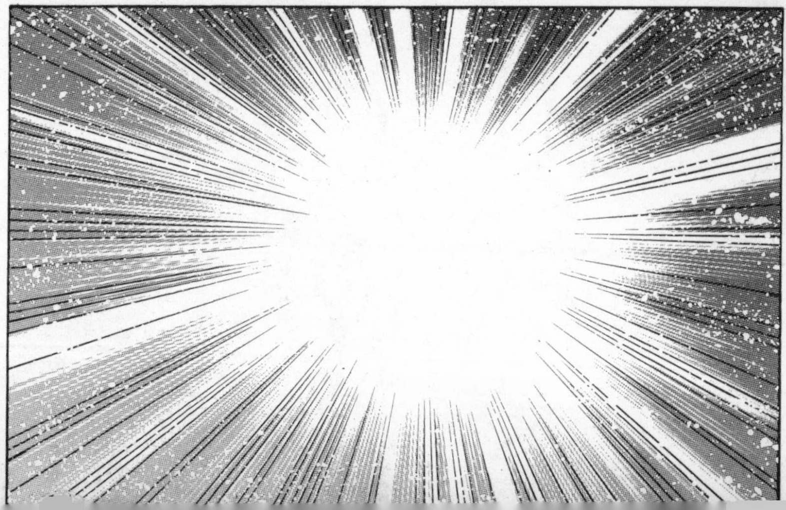

READ THIS WAY

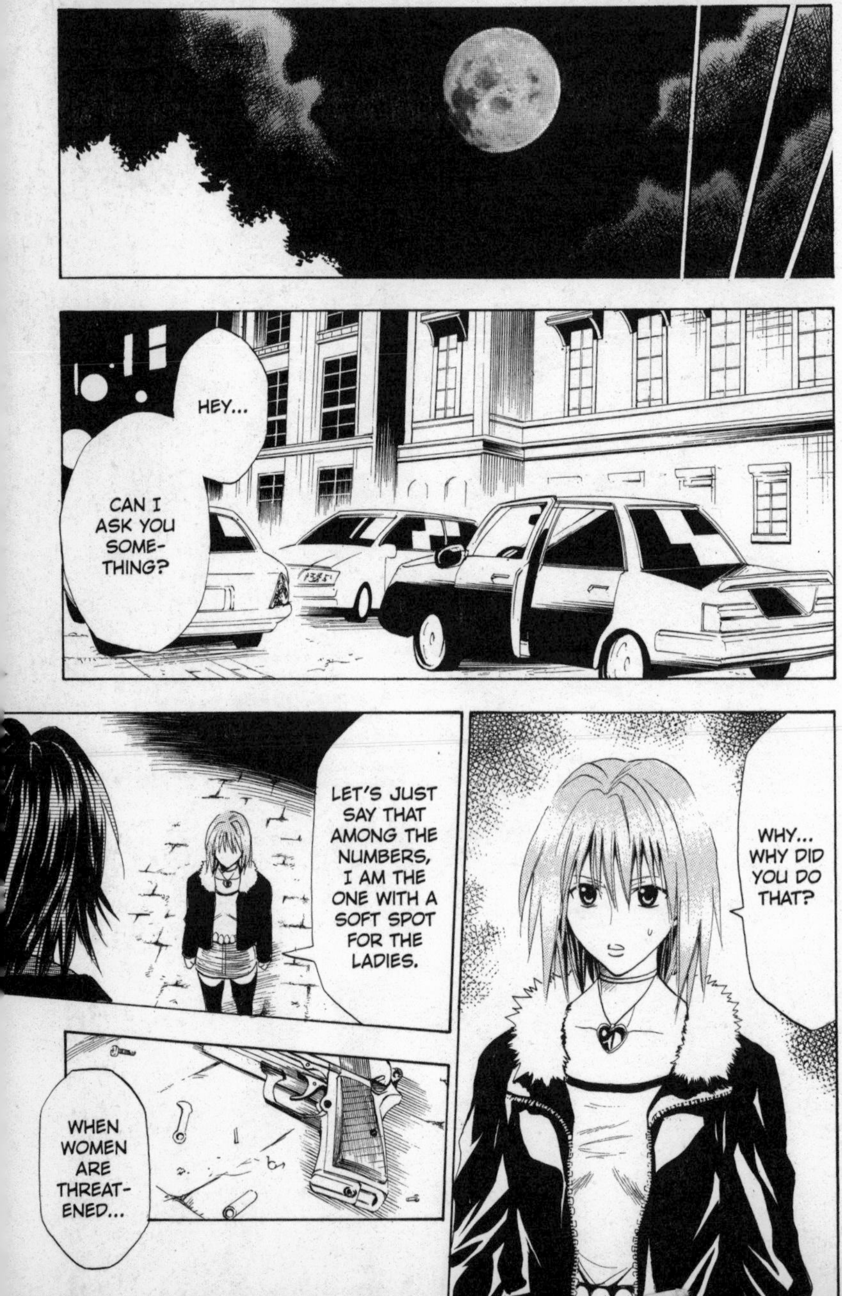
HEY...
CAN I ASK YOU SOME-THING?
WHY... WHY DID YOU DO THAT?
LET'S JUST SAY THAT AMONG THE NUMBERS, I AM THE ONE WITH A SOFT SPOT FOR THE LADIES.
WHEN WOMEN ARE THREAT-ENED...

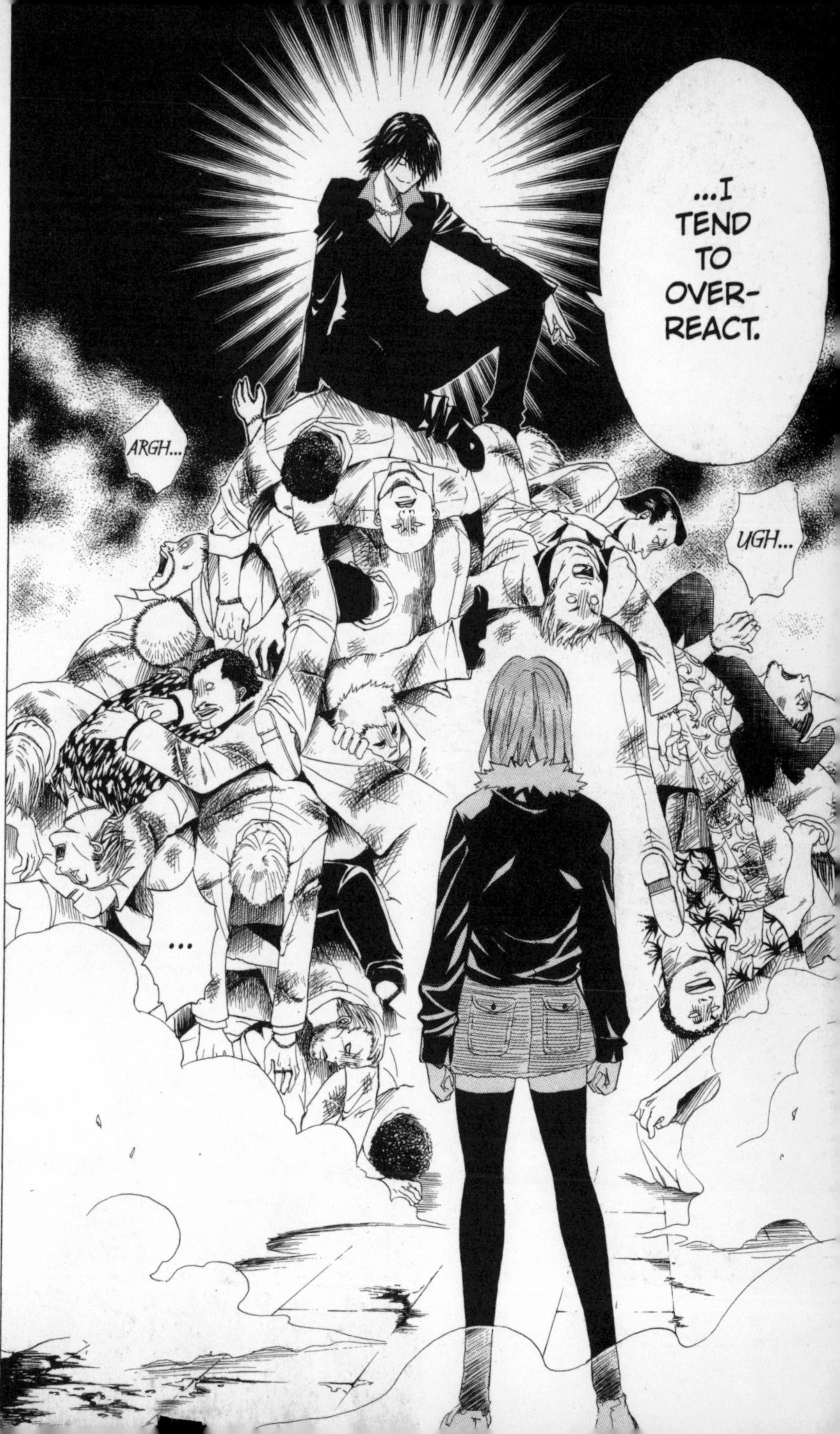
...I TEND TO OVER-REACT.
ARGH...
UGH...
...

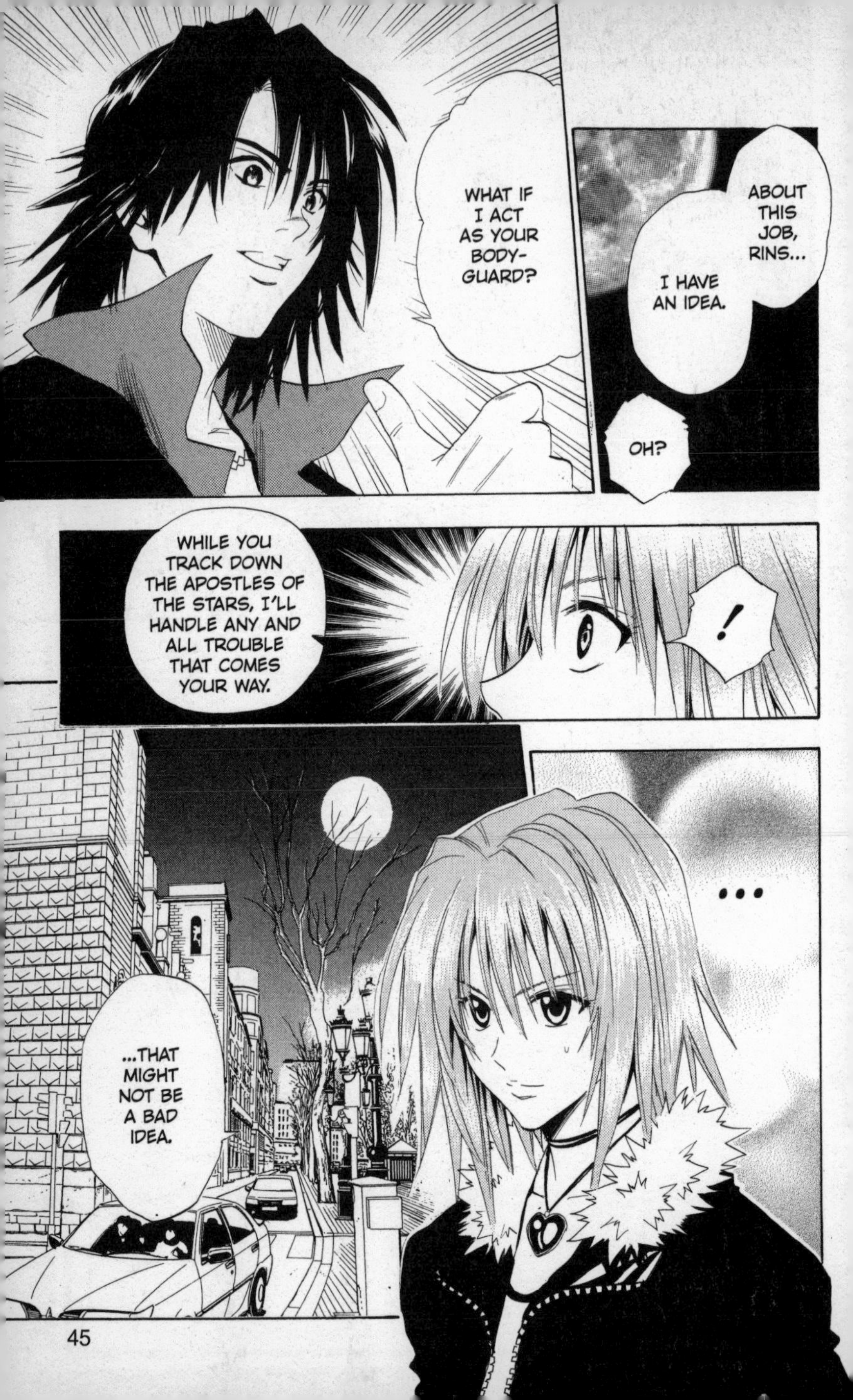
ABOUT THIS JOB, RINS...
I HAVE AN IDEA.
OH?
WHAT IF I ACT AS YOUR BODY-GUARD?
WHILE YOU TRACK DOWN THE APOSTLES OF THE STARS, I'LL HANDLE ANY AND ALL TROUBLE THAT COMES YOUR WAY.
!
...
...THAT MIGHT NOT BE A BAD IDEA.

BLACK CAT

profile

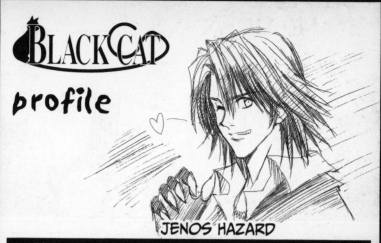

JENOS HAZARD

DATA	
BIRTHDATE:	JULY 7
AGE:	25
BLOOD TYPE:	B
HEIGHT:	179 CM
WEIGHT:	80 KG
WEAPON:	EXCELION
INTEREST:	PICKING UP GIRLS (HIS SUCCESS RATE ISN'T ACTUALLY ALL THAT GREAT.)
COMMENTS:	AGENT VII USES WIRES AS WEAPONS. HE'S BEEN A MEMBER OF THE NUMBERS FOR A NUMBER OF YEARS, BUT HE'S NEVER MET TRAIN. THE NUMBERED AGENTS OFTEN TRAVEL THE WORLD SOLO, SO IT'S COMMON FOR THEM NOT TO KNOW THEIR COMRADES BY SIGHT.

Chapter 60: Champais Town

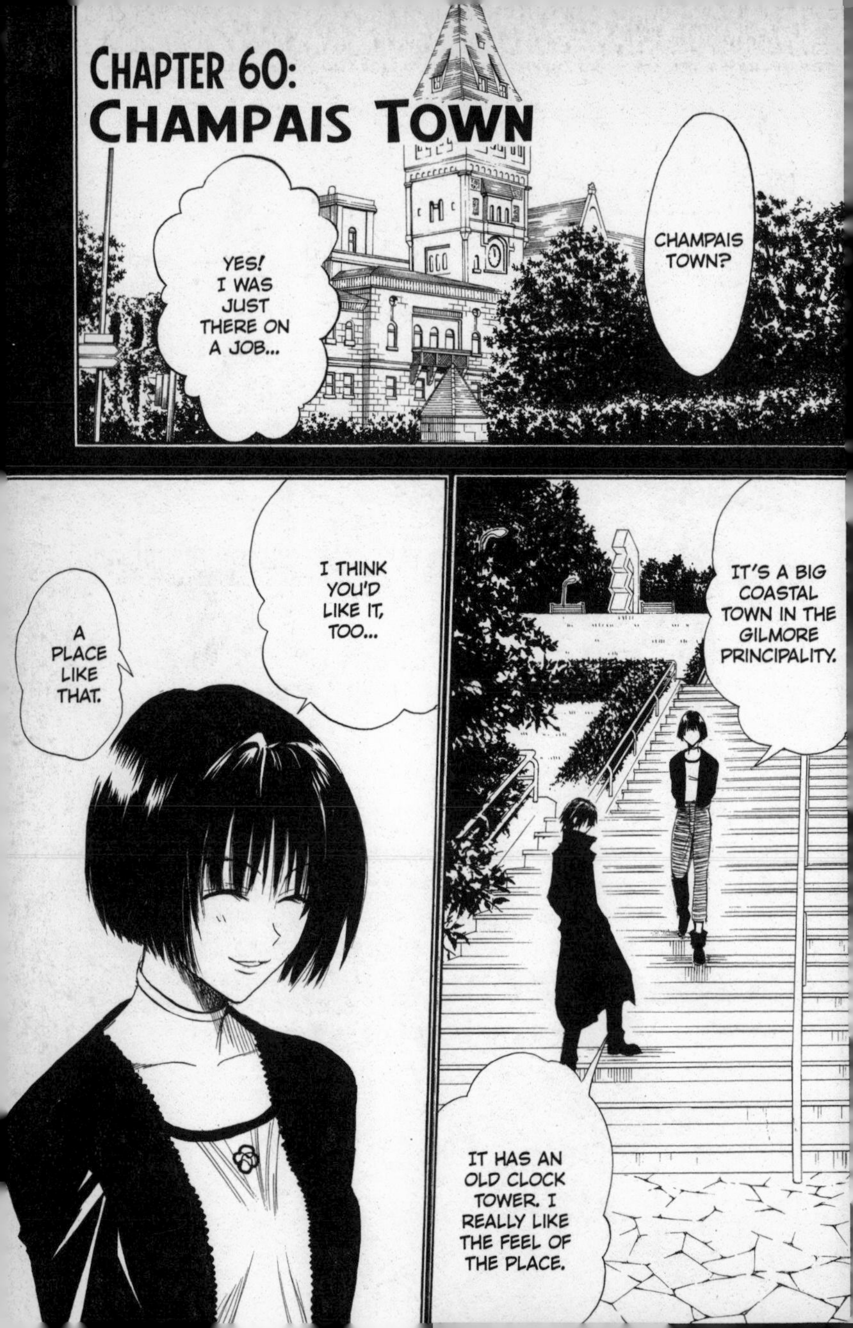
CHAMPAIS TOWN?
YES! I WAS JUST THERE ON A JOB...
IT'S A BIG COASTAL TOWN IN THE GILMORE PRINCIPALITY.
IT HAS AN OLD CLOCK TOWER. I REALLY LIKE THE FEEL OF THE PLACE.
I THINK YOU'D LIKE IT, TOO...
A PLACE LIKE THAT.

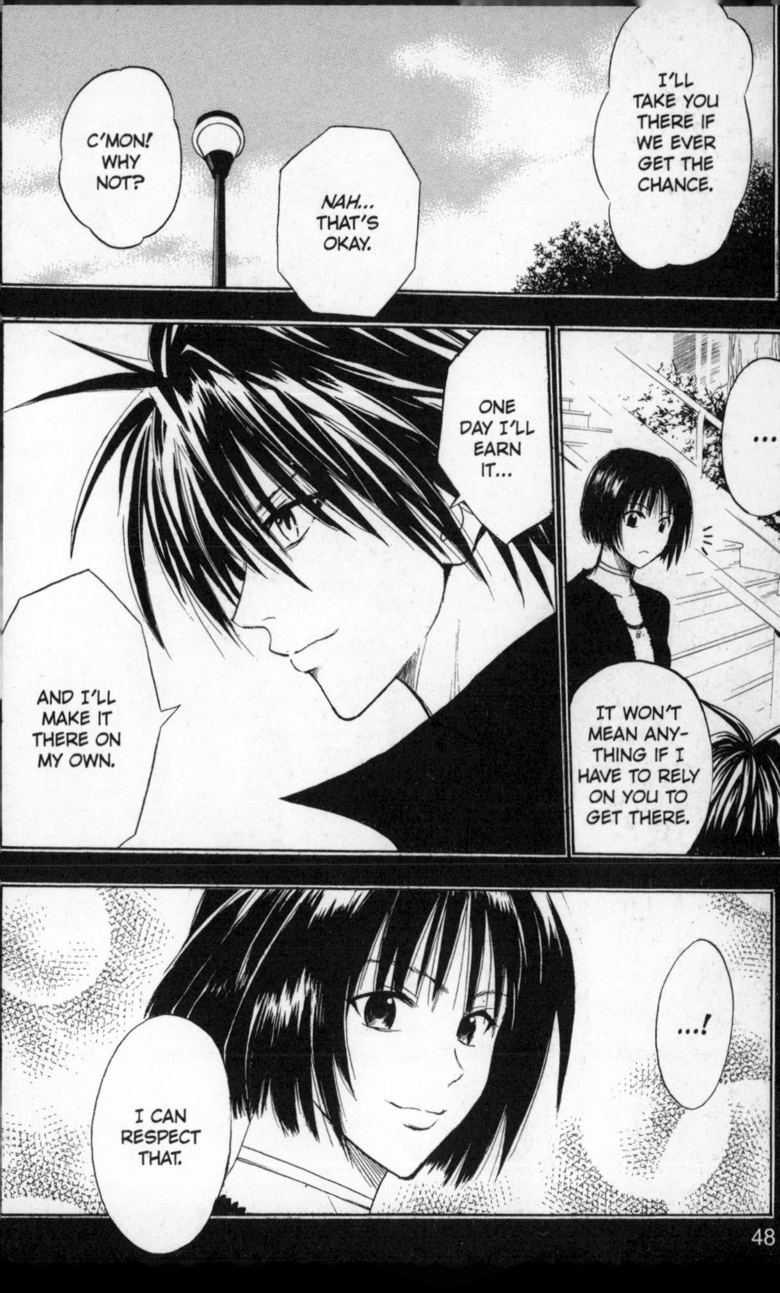
I'LL TAKE YOU THERE IF WE EVER GET THE CHANCE.
NAH... THAT'S OKAY.
C'MON! WHY NOT?
...
IT WON'T MEAN ANY-THING IF I HAVE TO RELY ON YOU TO GET THERE.
ONE DAY I'LL EARN IT...
AND I'LL MAKE IT THERE ON MY OWN.
...!
I CAN RESPECT THAT.

CHAPTER 60: CHAMPAIS TOWN

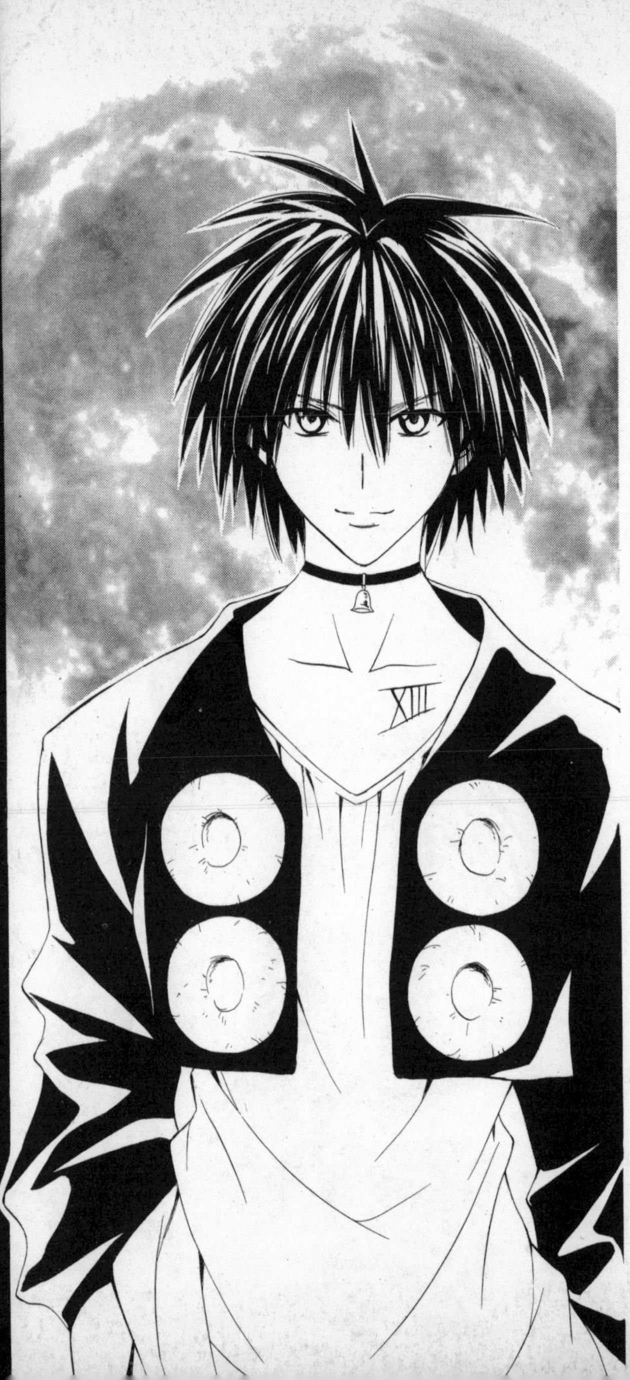
XIII

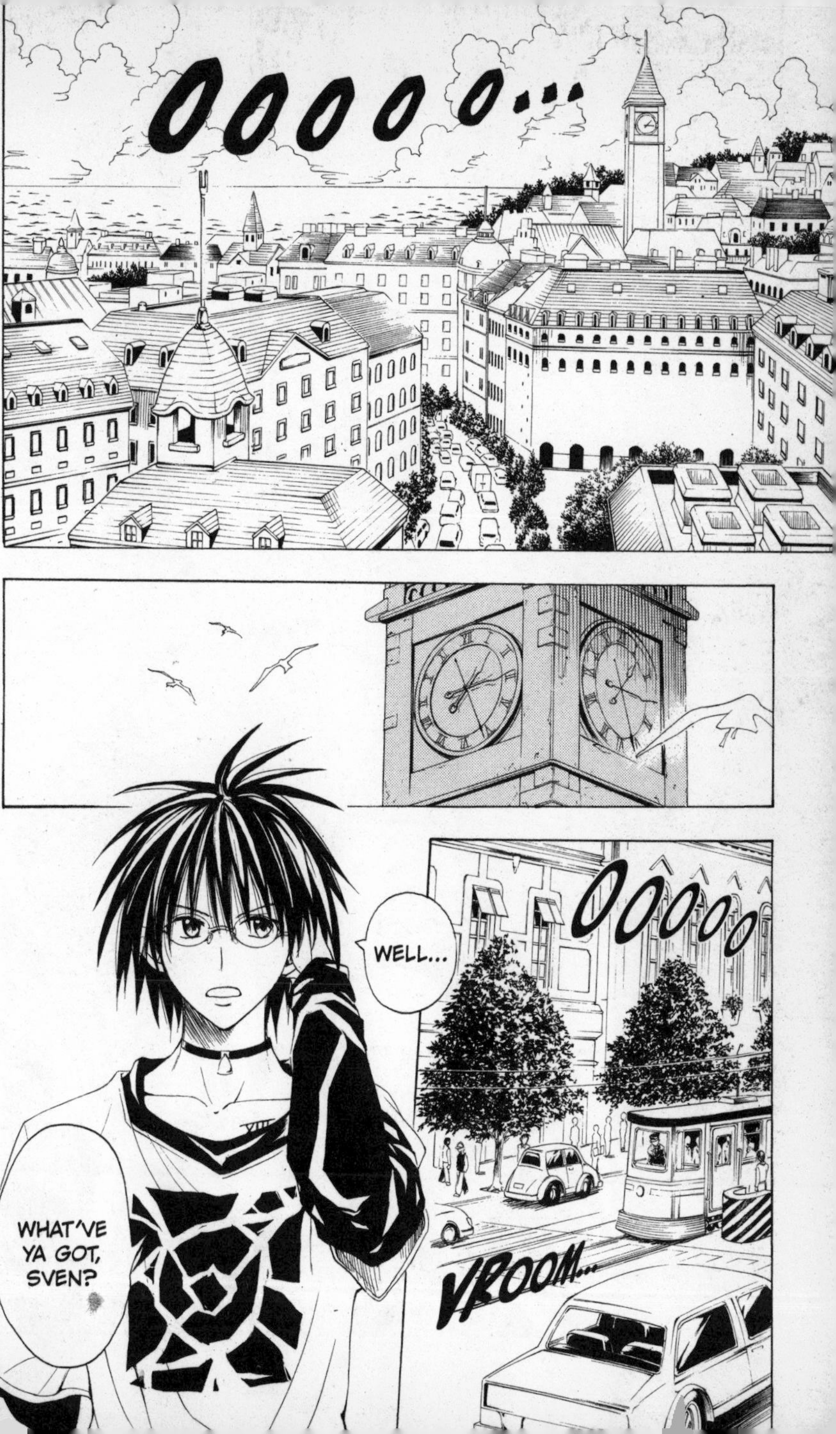
OOOOO...
OOOOO
VROOM...
WELL...
WHAT'VE YA GOT, SVEN?

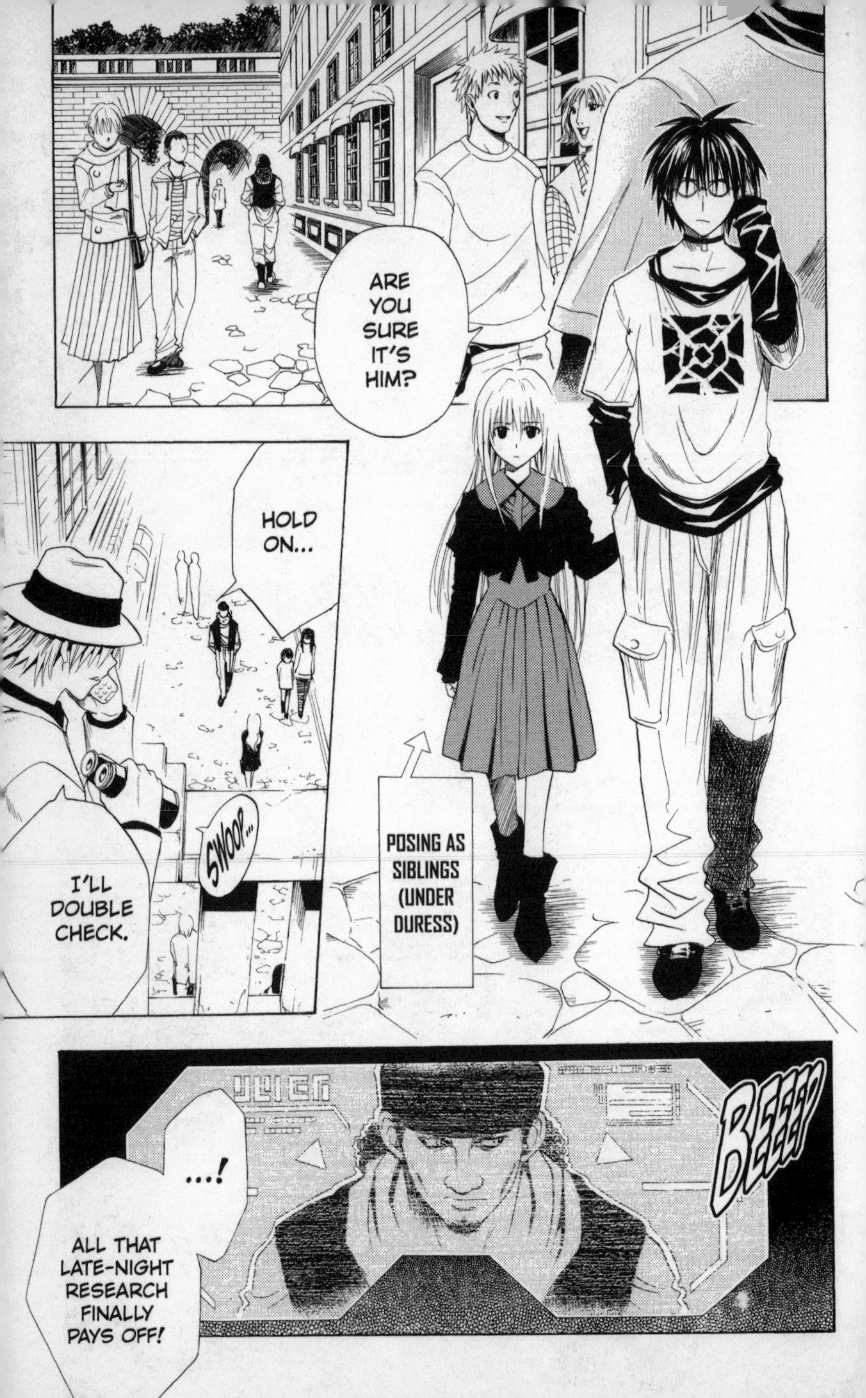
ARE YOU SURE IT'S HIM?
POSING AS SIBLINGS (UNDER DURESS)
HOLD ON...
SWOOP...
I'LL DOUBLE CHECK.
BLEEEP
...!
ALL THAT LATE-NIGHT RESEARCH FINALLY PAYS OFF!

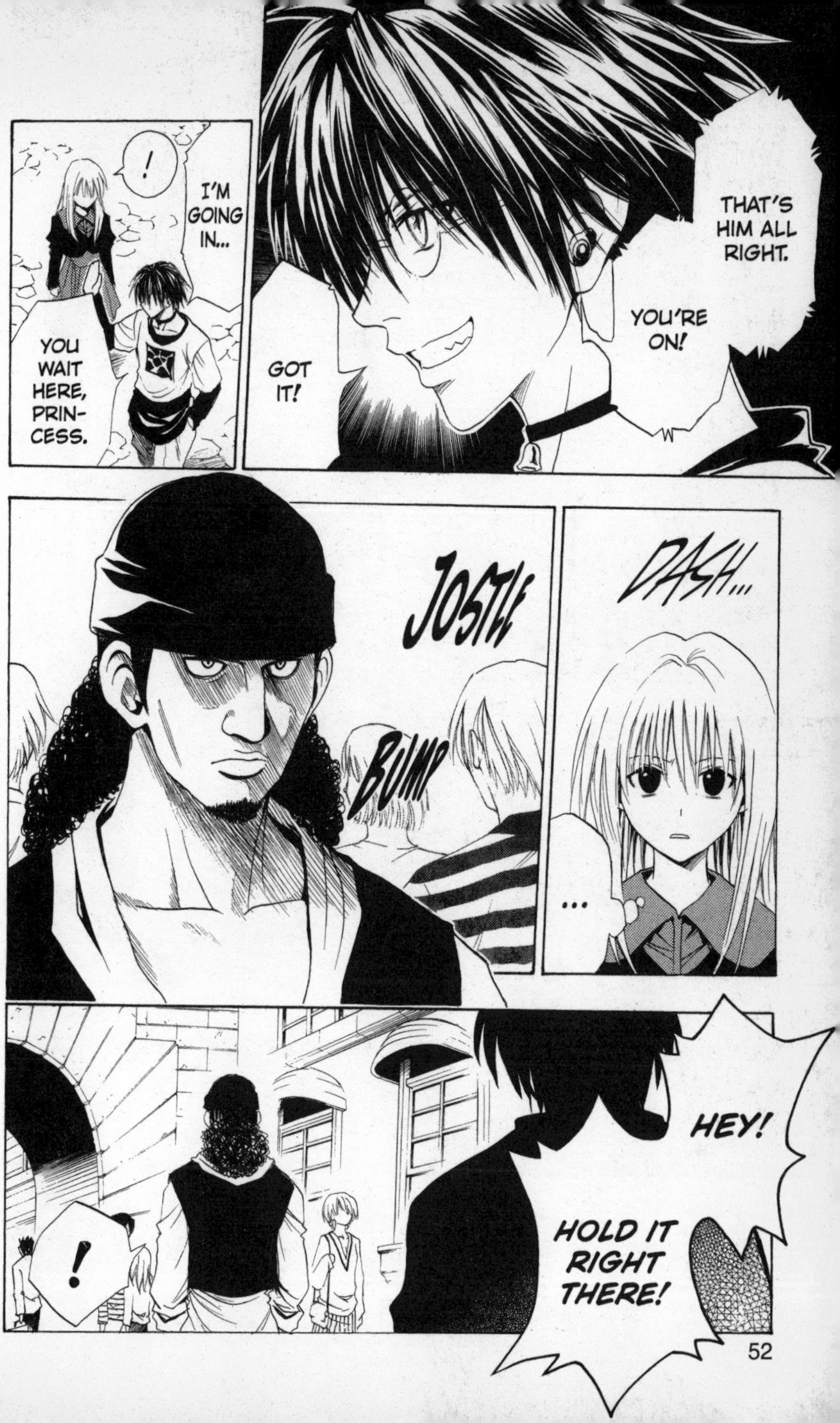
THAT'S HIM ALL RIGHT.
YOU'RE ON!
GOT IT!
!
I'M GOING IN...
YOU WAIT HERE, PRINCESS.
DASH...
...
JOSTLE
BUMP
HEY!
HOLD IT RIGHT THERE!
!

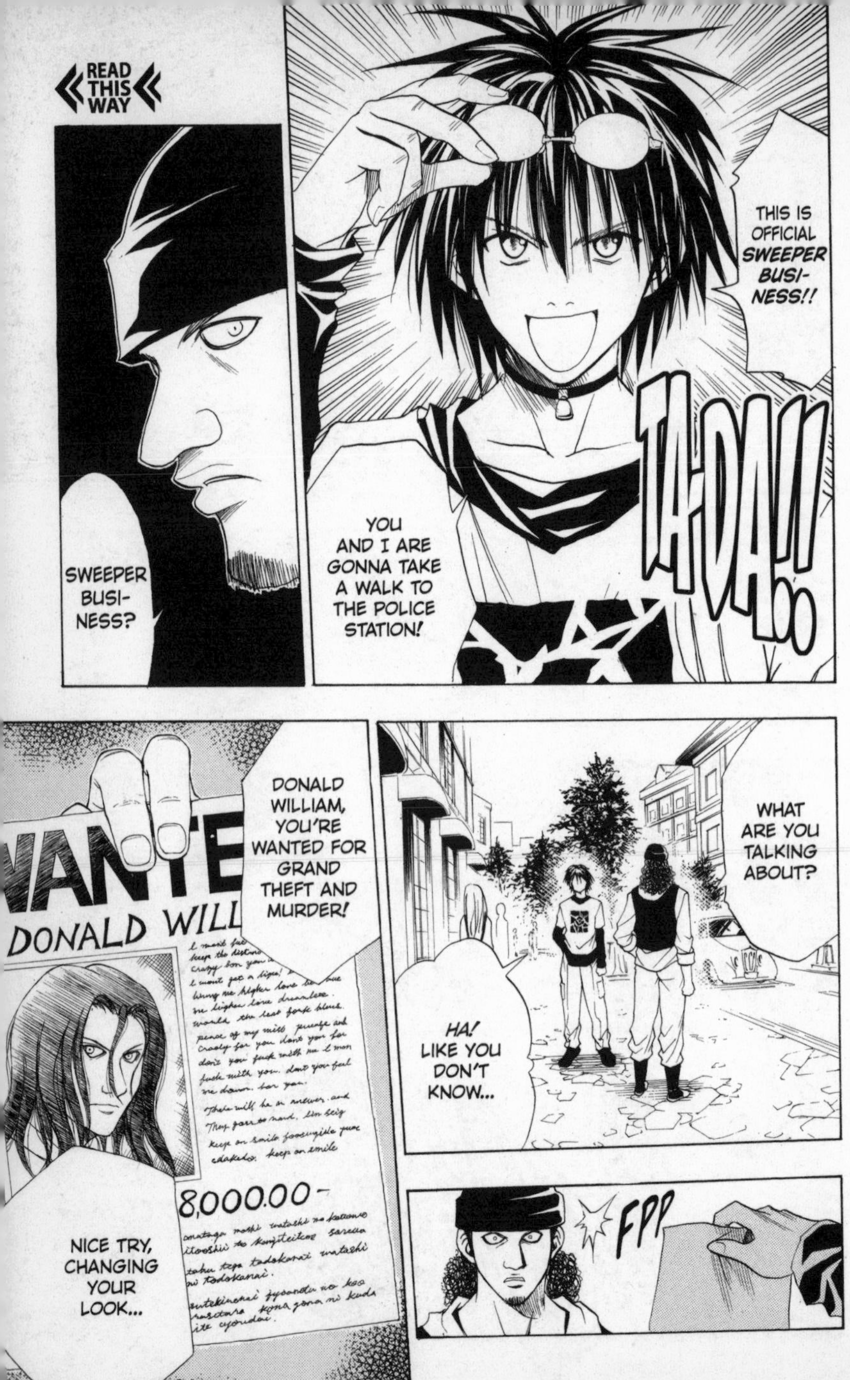
READ THIS WAY
THIS IS OFFICIAL SWEEPER BUSINESS!!
TA-DA!!
YOU AND I ARE GONNA TAKE A WALK TO THE POLICE STATION!
SWEEPER BUSINESS?
WHAT ARE YOU TALKING ABOUT?
HA! LIKE YOU DON'T KNOW...
FPP
WANTE
DONALD WILL
8,000.00-
DONALD WILLIAM, YOU'RE WANTED FOR GRAND THEFT AND MURDER!
NICE TRY, CHANGING YOUR LOOK...

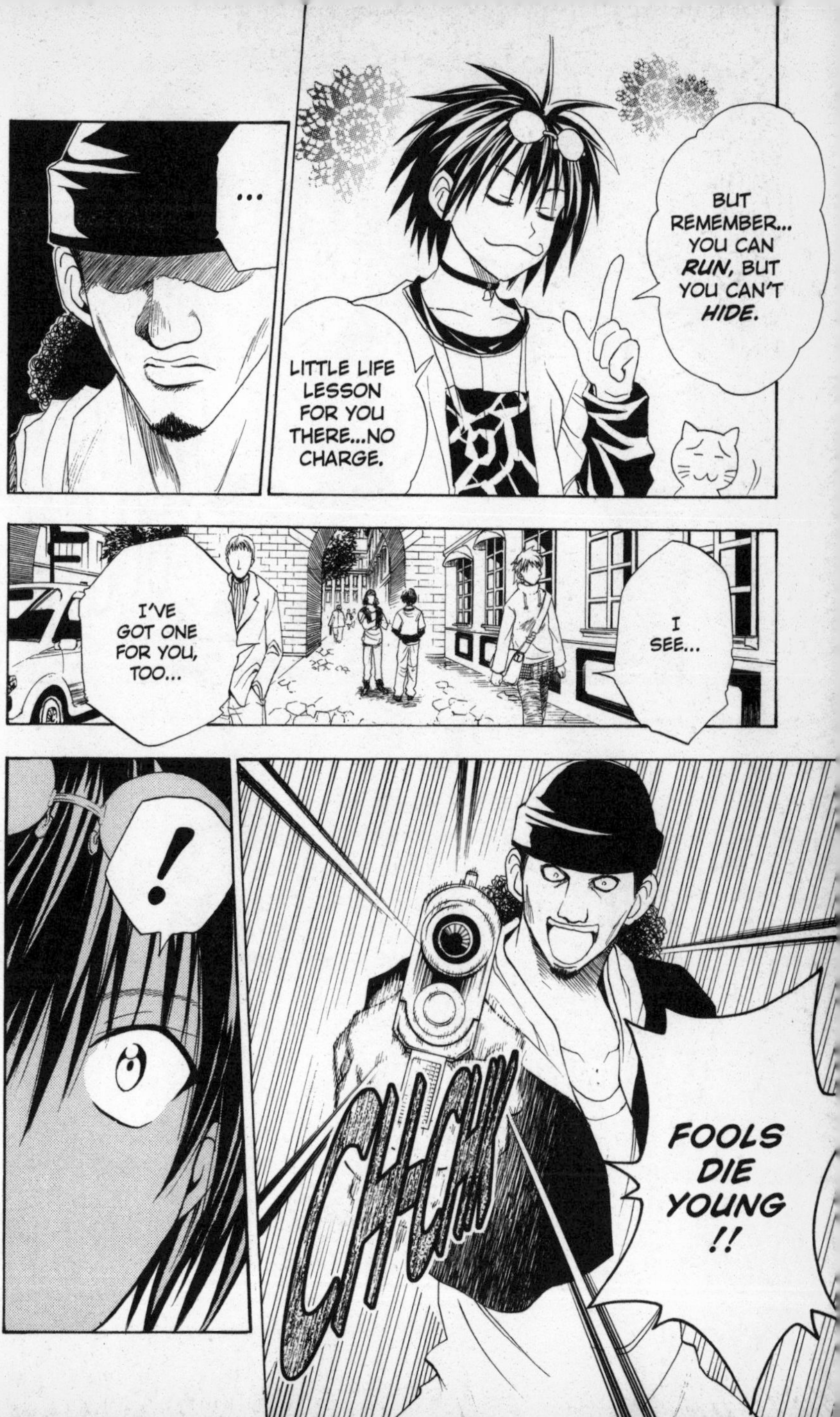
BUT REMEMBER... YOU CAN *RUN*, BUT YOU CAN'T *HIDE*.
LITTLE LIFE LESSON FOR YOU THERE...NO CHARGE.
...
I SEE...
I'VE GOT ONE FOR YOU, TOO...
FOOLS DIE YOUNG !!
!

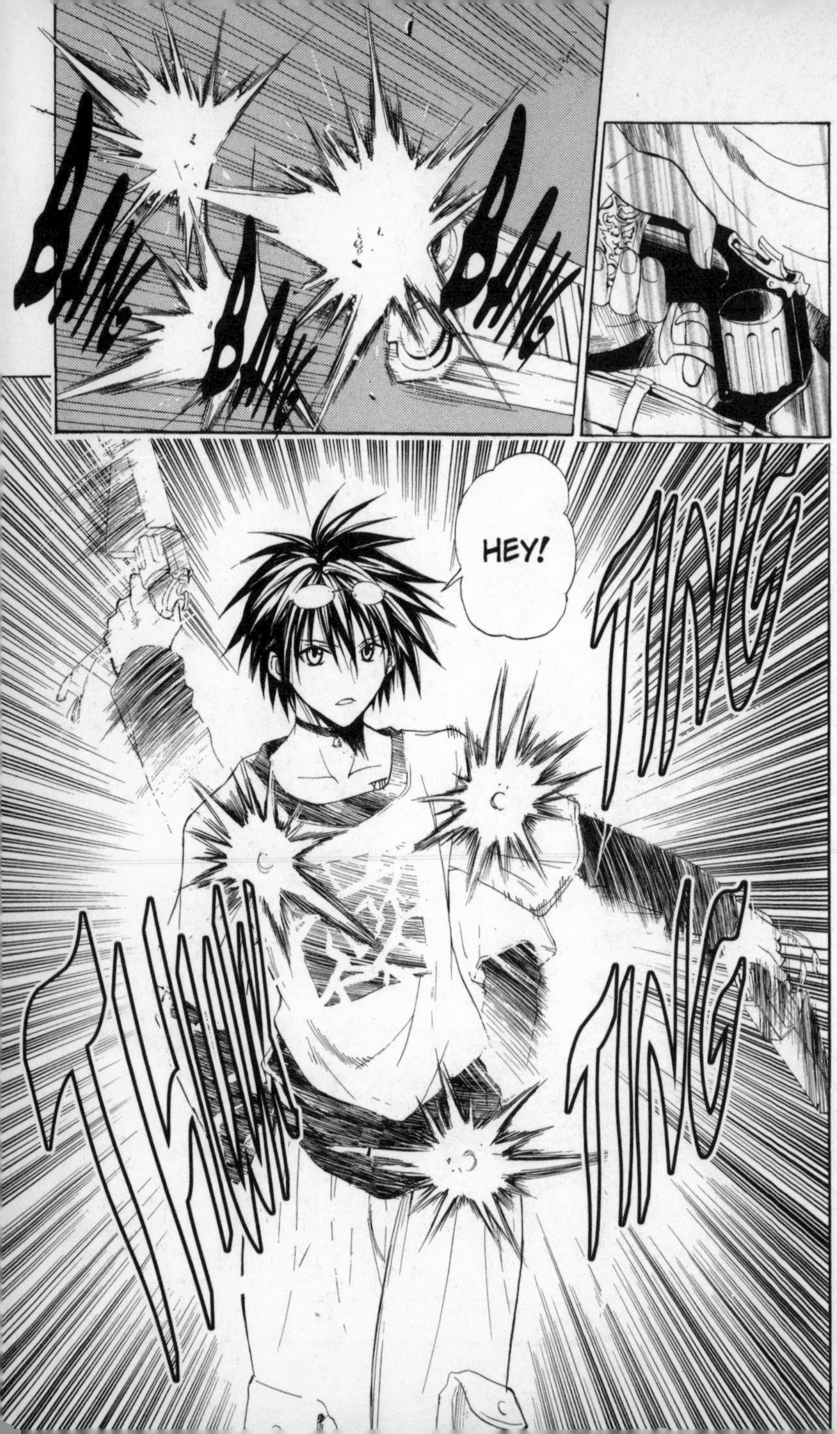
BANG
BANG
BANG
TING
HEY!
TING

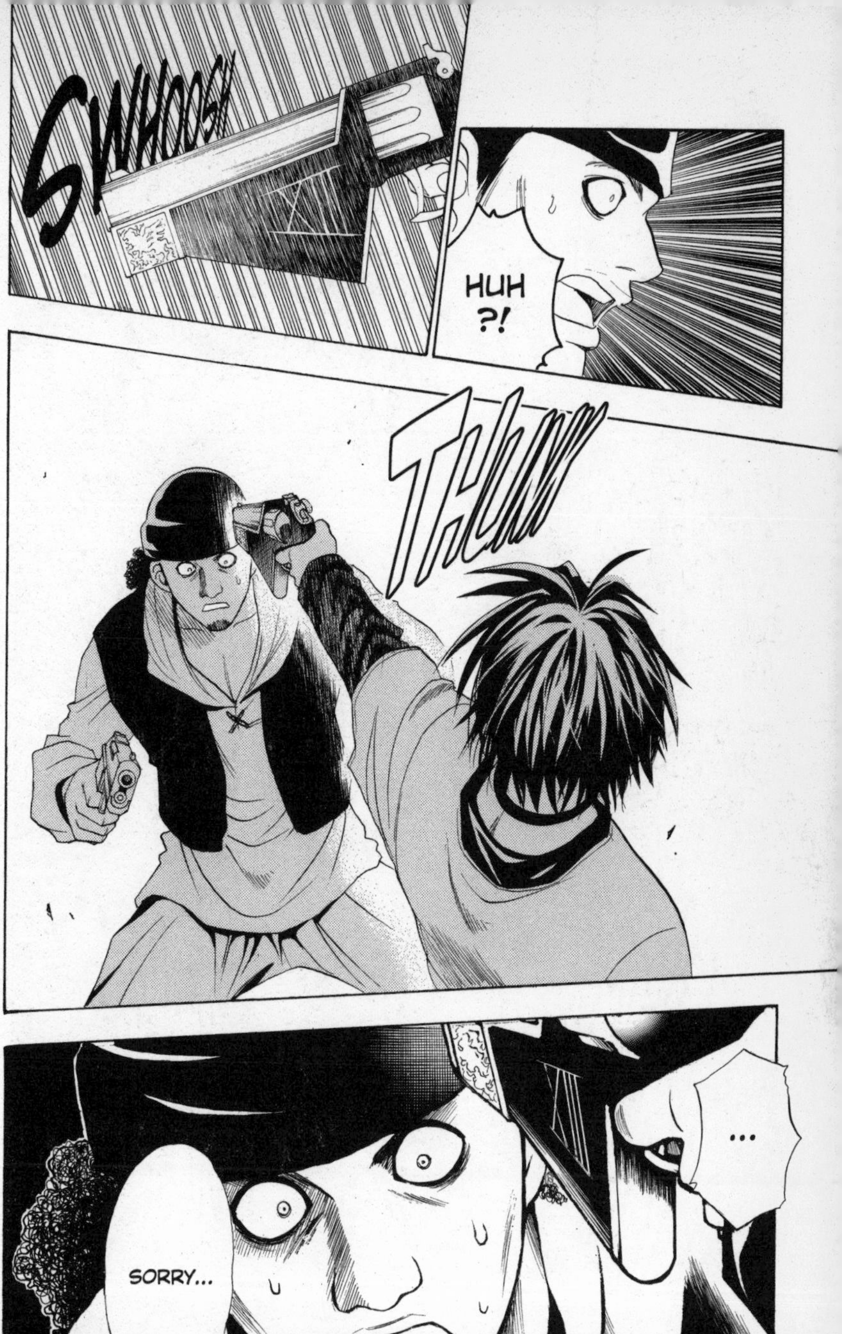
HUH ?!
SWHOOSH
T-CLIK
...
SORRY...

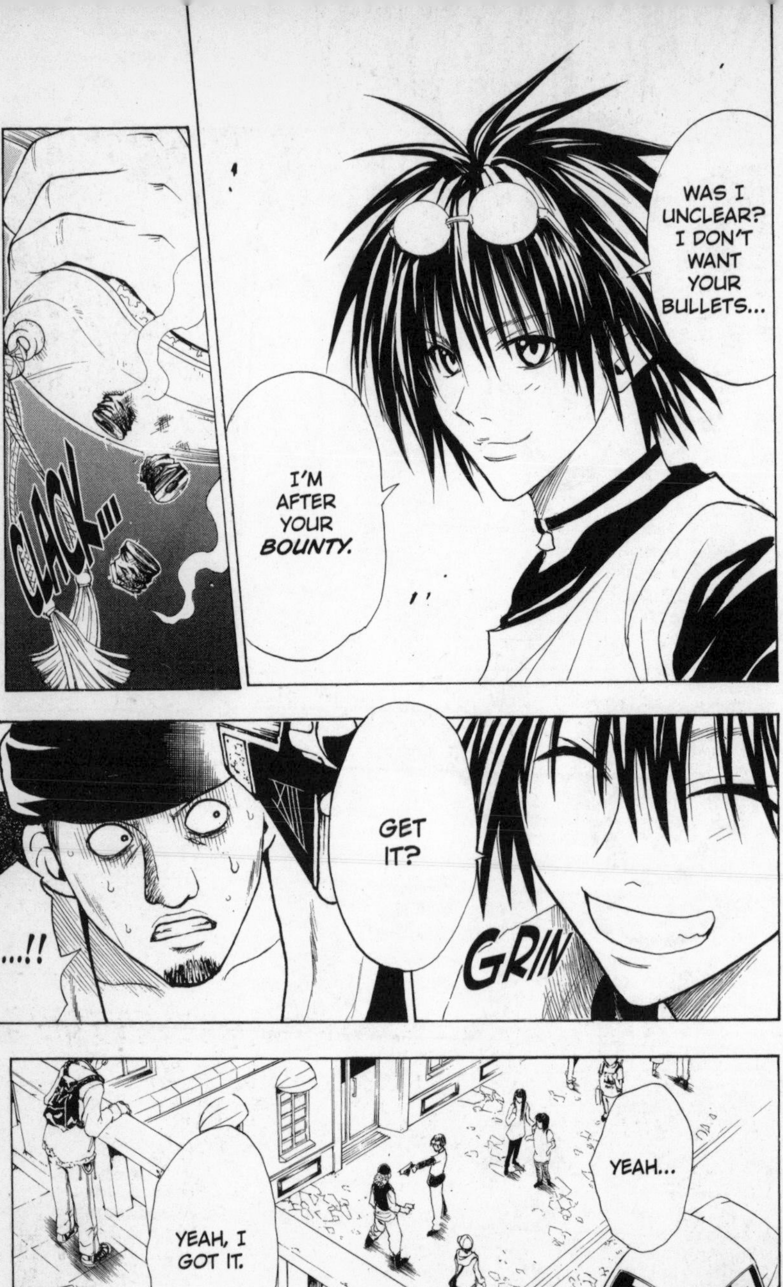
WAS I UNCLEAR? I DON'T WANT YOUR BULLETS...
I'M AFTER YOUR *BOUNTY.*
CLACK...
GET IT?
GRIN
...!!
YEAH...
YEAH, I GOT IT.

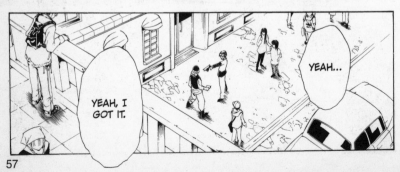

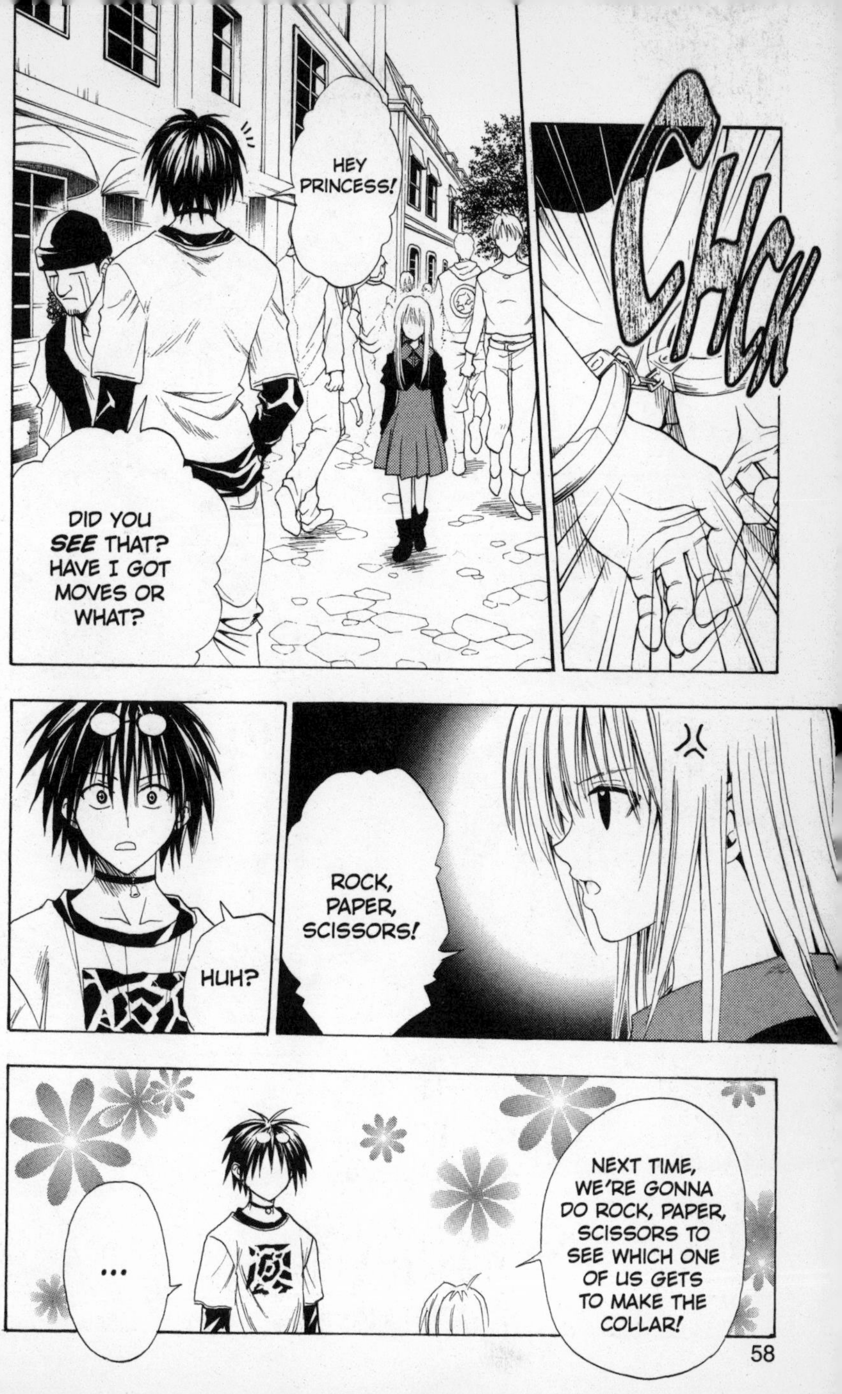
CHCK
HEY PRINCESS!
DID YOU SEE THAT? HAVE I GOT MOVES OR WHAT?
ROCK, PAPER, SCISSORS!
HUH?
NEXT TIME, WE'RE GONNA DO ROCK, PAPER, SCISSORS TO SEE WHICH ONE OF US GETS TO MAKE THE COLLAR!
...

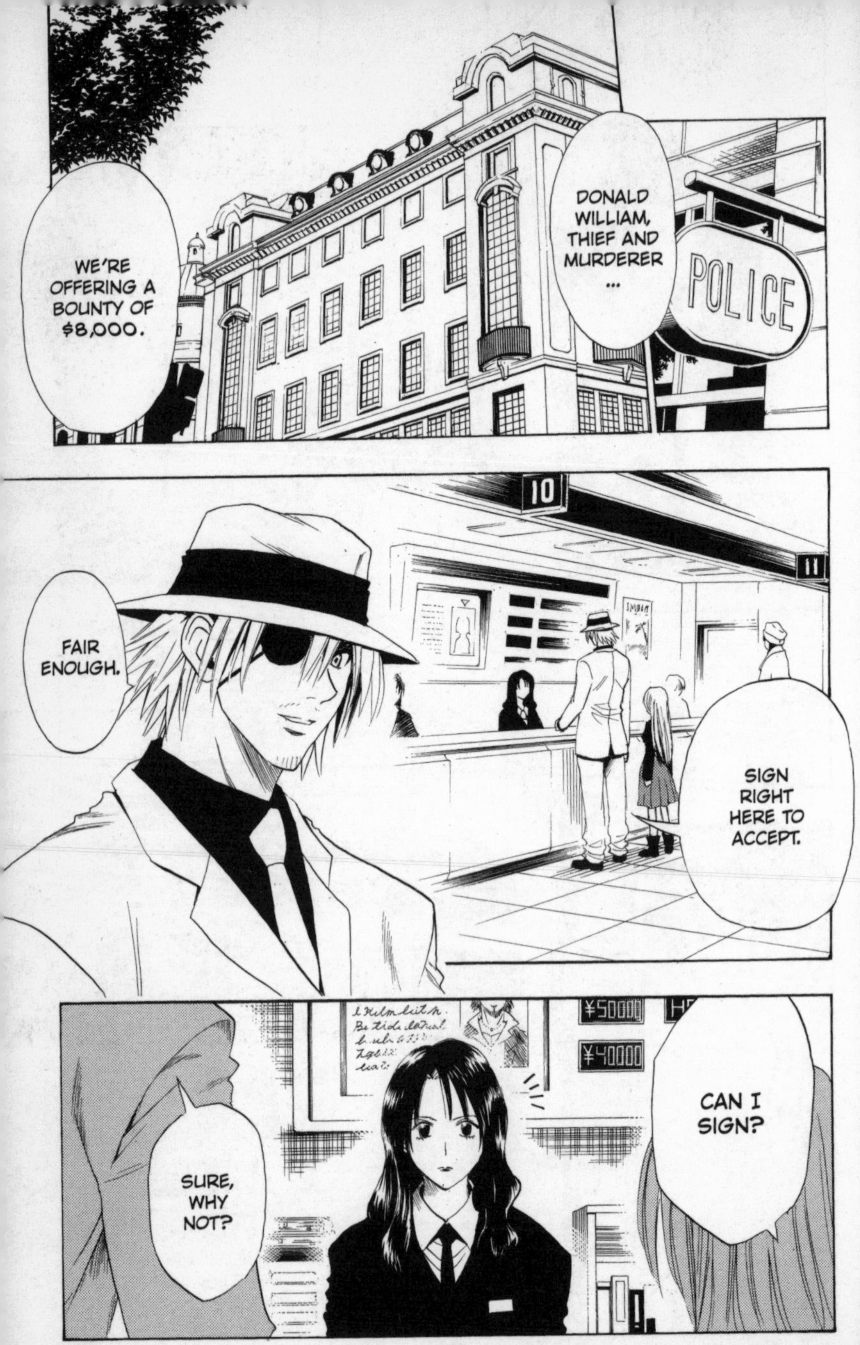
POLICE
DONALD WILLIAM, THIEF AND MURDERER ...
WE'RE OFFERING A BOUNTY OF $8,000.
10
11
SIGN RIGHT HERE TO ACCEPT.
FAIR ENOUGH.
¥40000
CAN I SIGN?
SURE, WHY NOT?

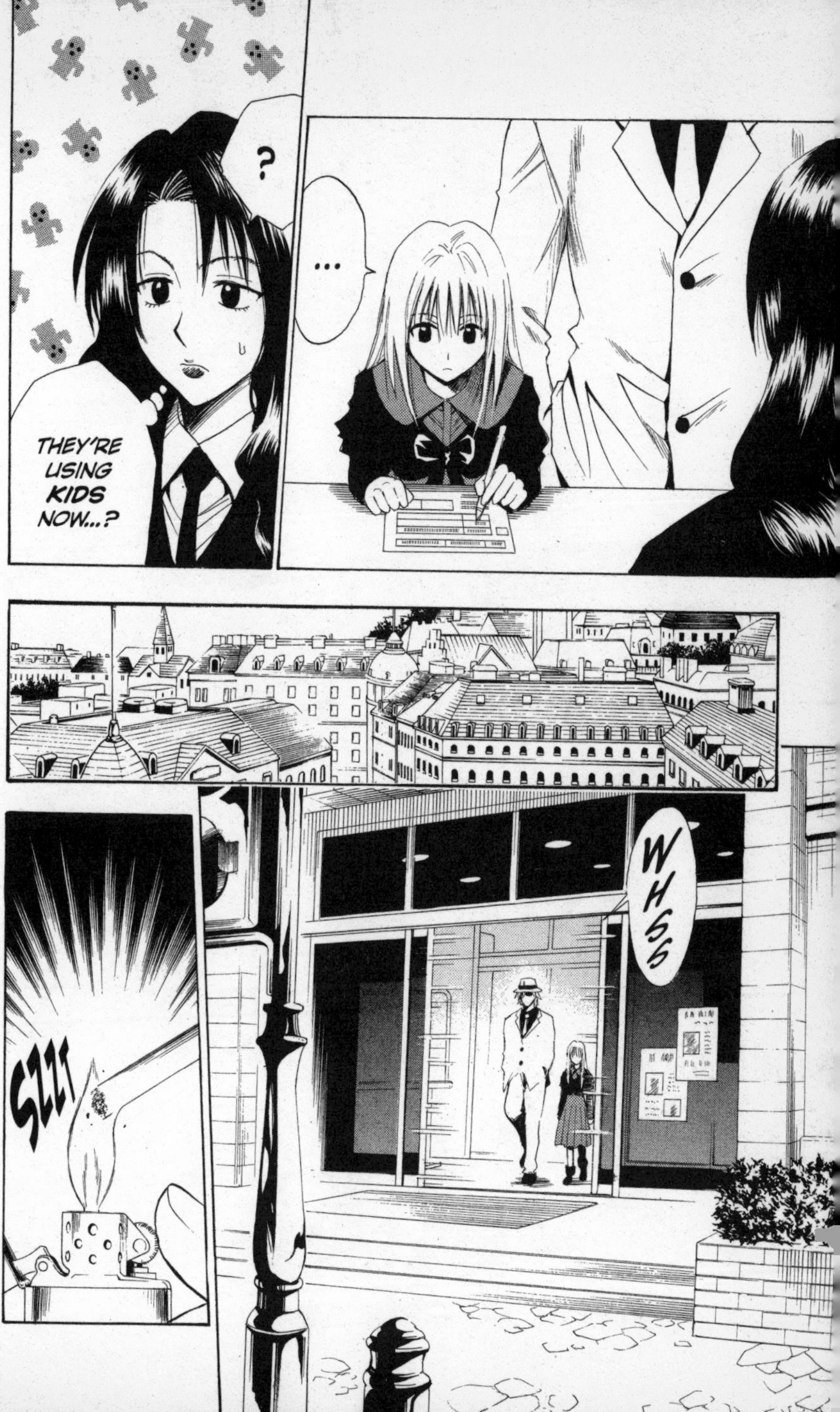
...
?
THEY'RE USING KIDS NOW...?
WHSS
SZZT

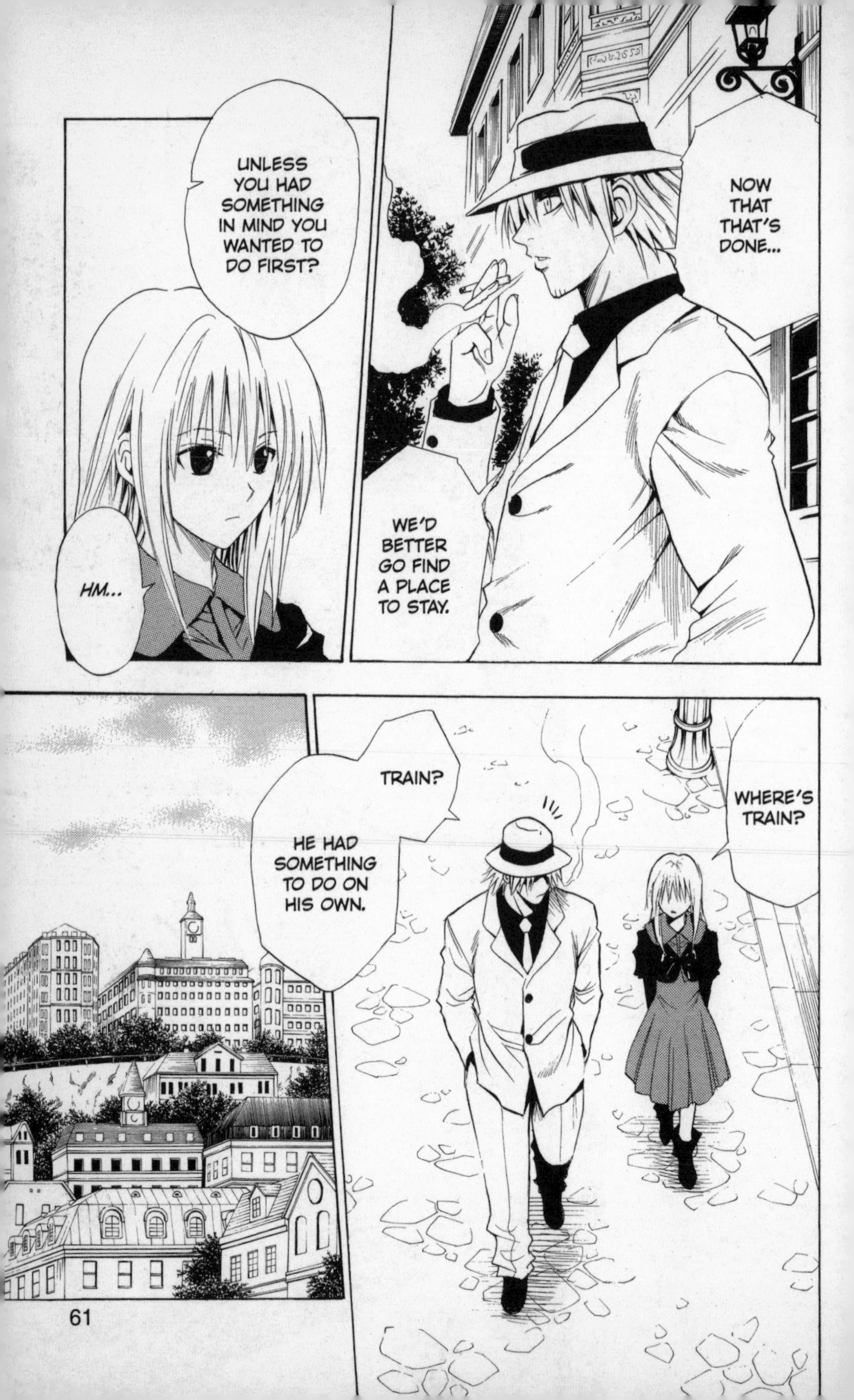
NOW THAT THAT'S DONE...
WE'D BETTER GO FIND A PLACE TO STAY.
UNLESS YOU HAD SOMETHING IN MIND YOU WANTED TO DO FIRST?
HM...
WHERE'S TRAIN?
TRAIN?
HE HAD SOMETHING TO DO ON HIS OWN.

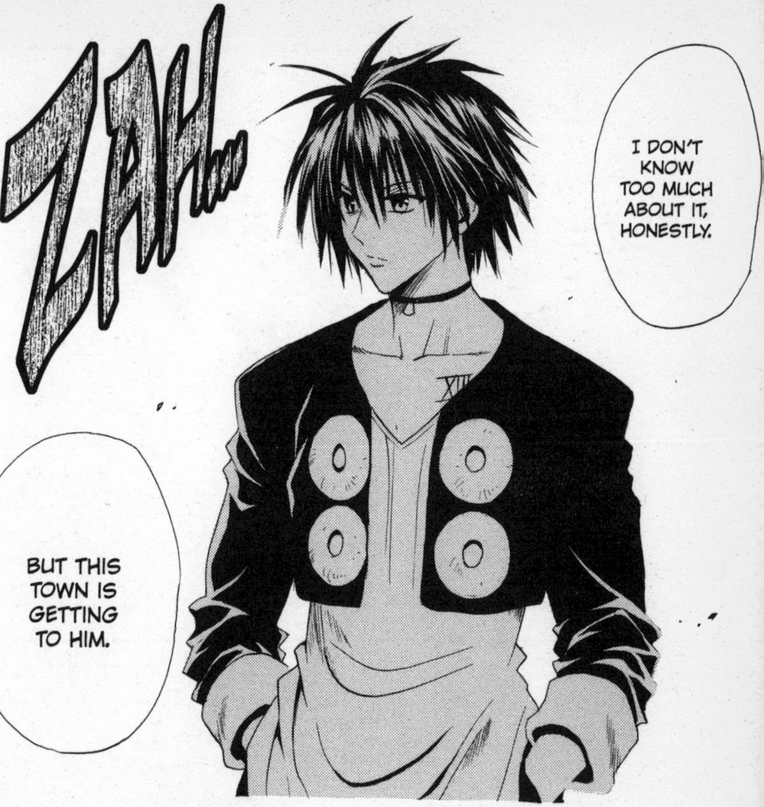
I DON'T KNOW TOO MUCH ABOUT IT, HONESTLY.
ZAH...
BUT THIS TOWN IS GETTING TO HIM.
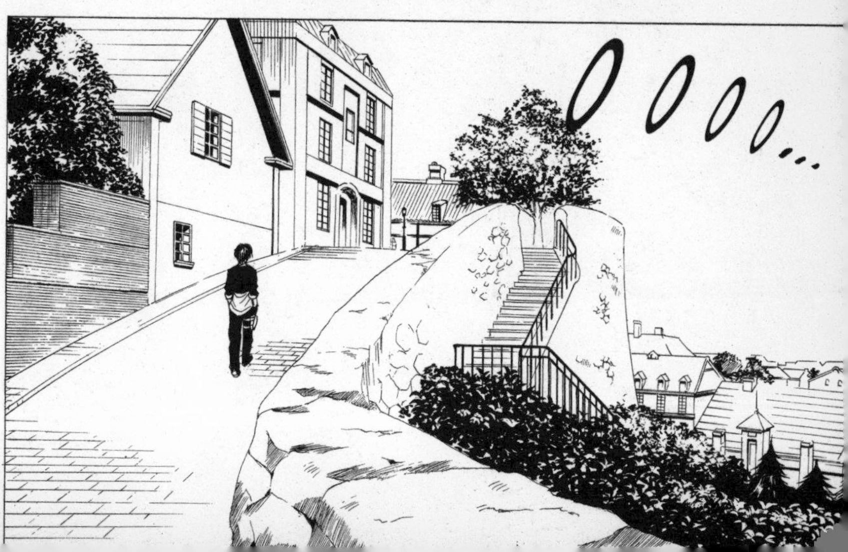
OOOO...

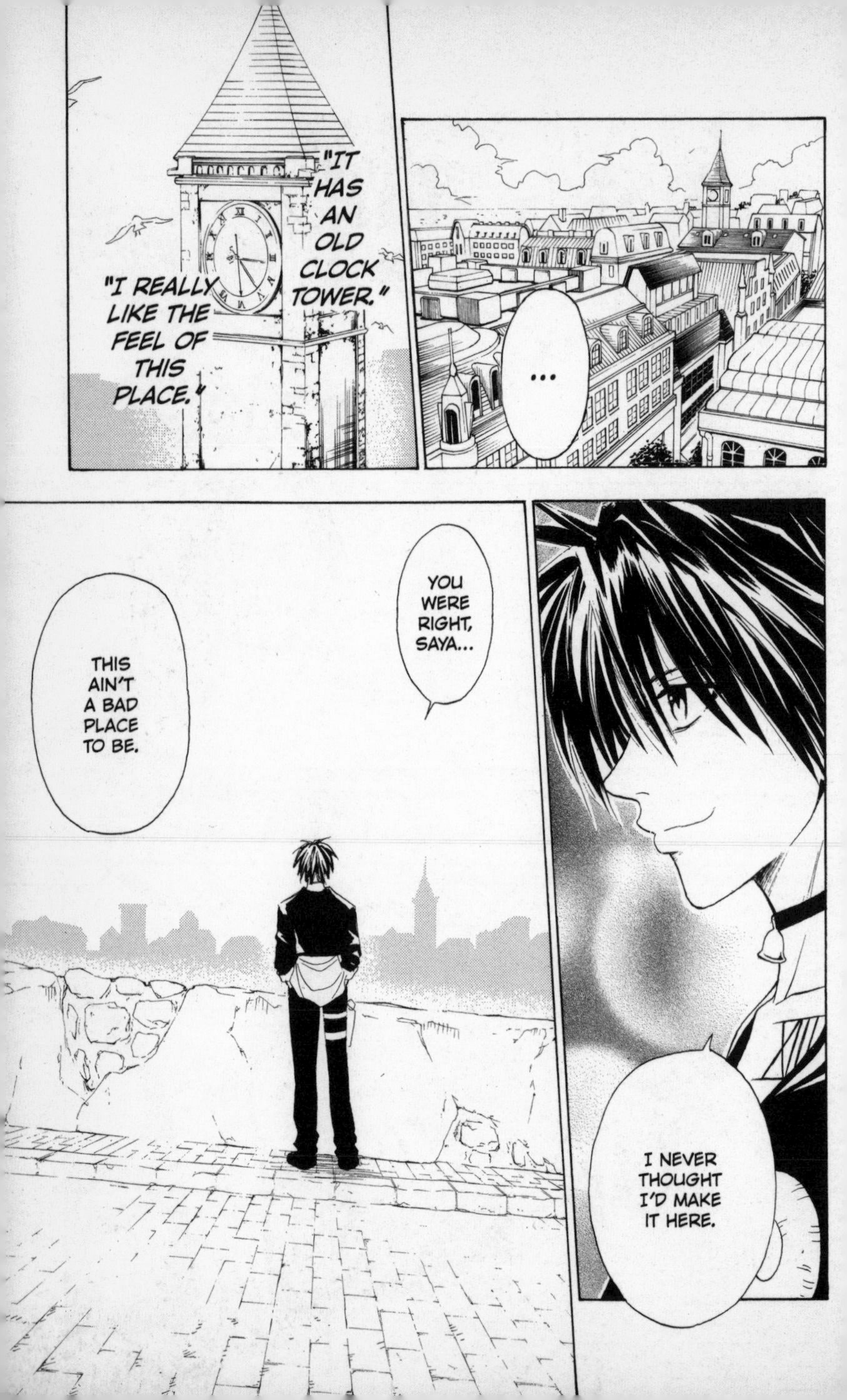
...
"IT HAS AN OLD CLOCK TOWER."
"I REALLY LIKE THE FEEL OF THIS PLACE."
I NEVER THOUGHT I'D MAKE IT HERE.
YOU WERE RIGHT, SAYA...
THIS AIN'T A BAD PLACE TO BE.

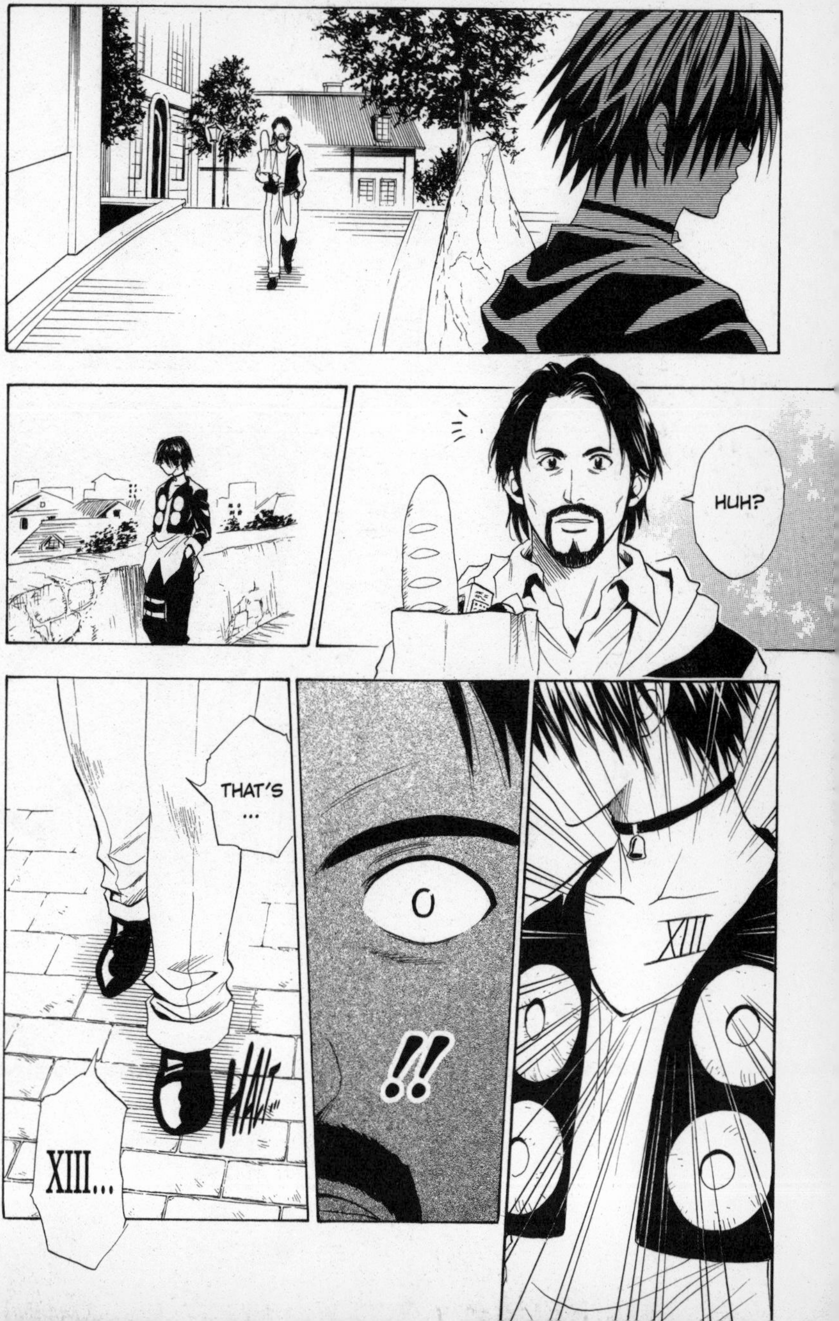
HUH?
!!
THAT'S ...
XIII...

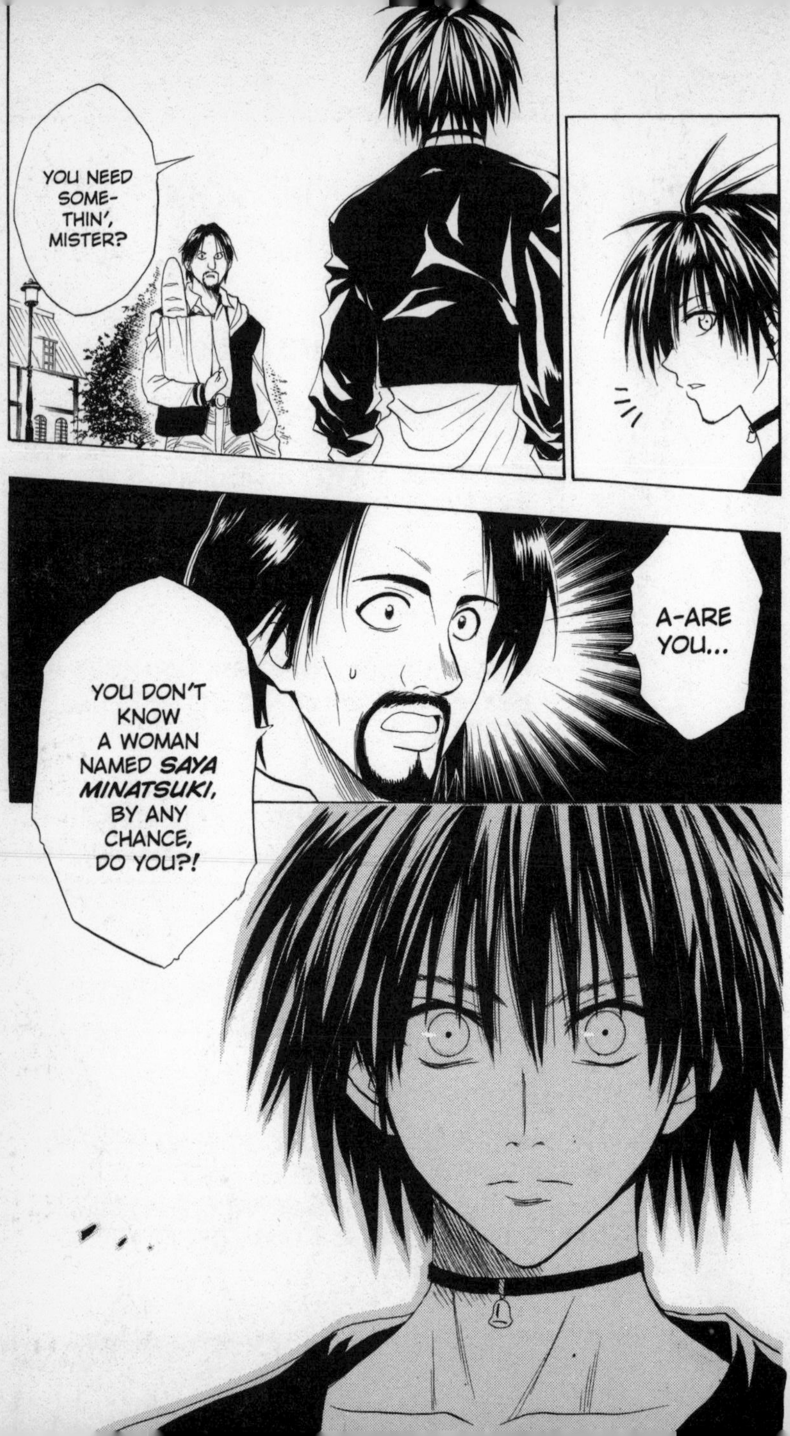
YOU NEED SOME-THIN', MISTER?
A-ARE YOU...
YOU DON'T KNOW A WOMAN NAMED *SAYA MINATSUKI*, BY ANY CHANCE, DO YOU?!
...

BLACK CAT

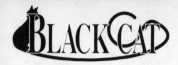

ONE POINT

THE ORIGINS OF THE NAMES

Train 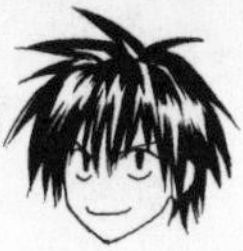 ······ I LIKED THE FEEL OF IT. IT CONJURES THE IMAGE OF HIM TRAVELING FROM PLACE TO PLACE ON THE RAILS.

Sven 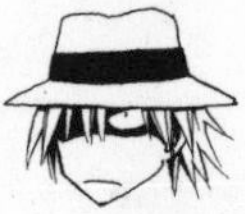 ······ IT'S THE NAME OF A VERY MINOR CHARACTER IN A BIG BLOCKBUSTER FILM THAT I LIKE.

Eve 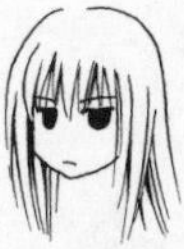 ······ I WAS LOOKING FOR A NAME THAT EVOKED PURITY AND INNOCENCE. I AGONIZED AND AGONIZED BEFORE FINALLY SETTLING ON "EVE."

Rinslet 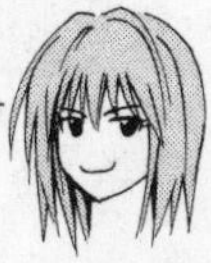 ······ THIS NAME EVOKES THE IMAGE OF A SILKY-HAIRED BEAUTY.

Saya 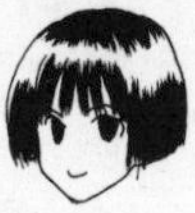 ······ I LOOKED AT HER FACE AND THE NAME JUST POPPED INTO MY HEAD OUT OF NOWHERE.

◎ I USE VARIOUS METHODS TO NAME MY CHARACTERS. SOMETIMES I BORROW FROM SOMETHING I'VE SEEN OR READ; SOMETIMES THE NAMES JUST COME TO ME AS I DRAW; SOMETIMES I LOOK AT LISTS OF FOREIGN NAMES AND TRY TO PICK ONE THAT I THINK FITS. FOR MY MAIN CHARACTERS, I TRY TO PICK NAMES THAT ARE EASY TO REMEMBER!

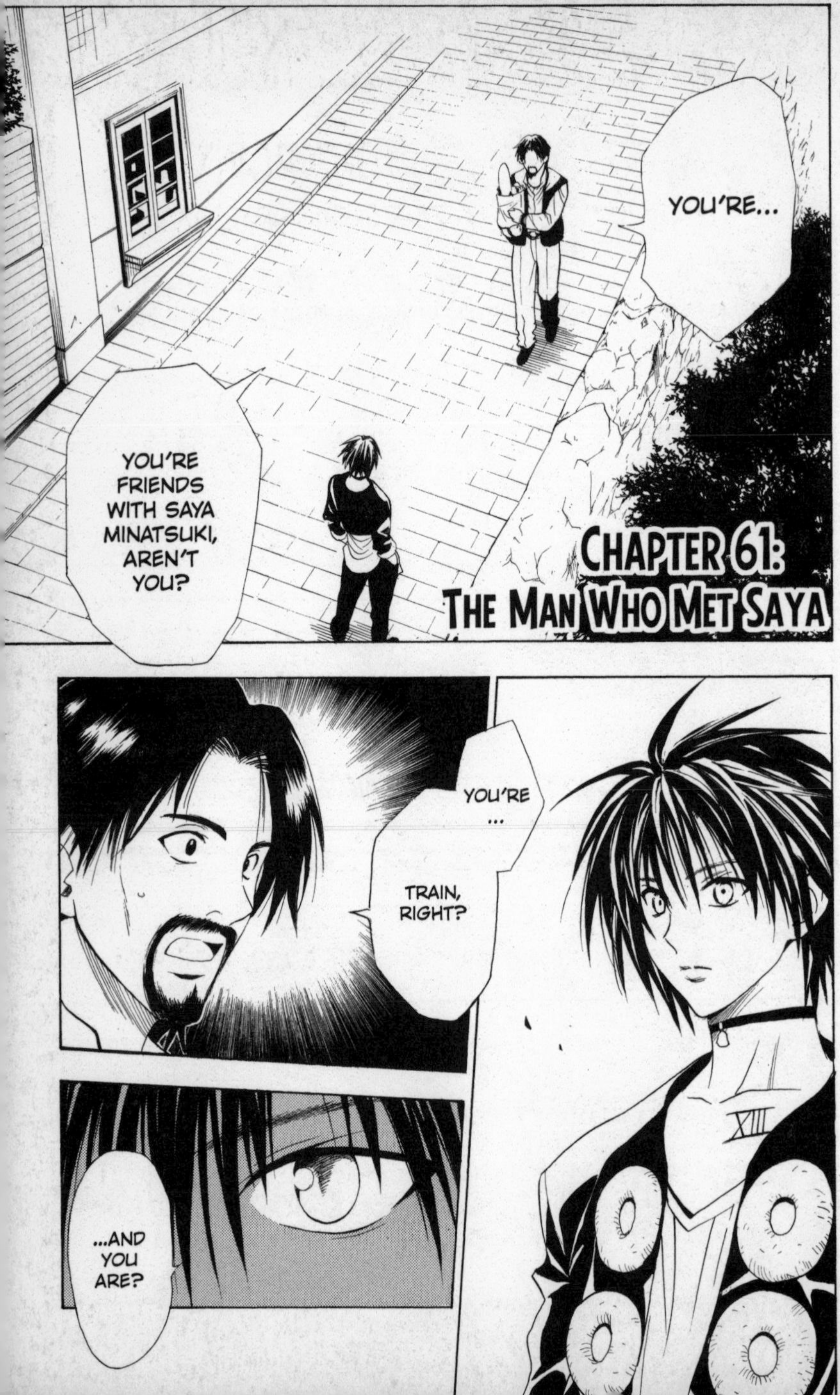
YOU'RE...
YOU'RE FRIENDS WITH SAYA MINATSUKI, AREN'T YOU?
CHAPTER 61: THE MAN WHO MET SAYA
YOU'RE ...
TRAIN, RIGHT?
...AND YOU ARE?

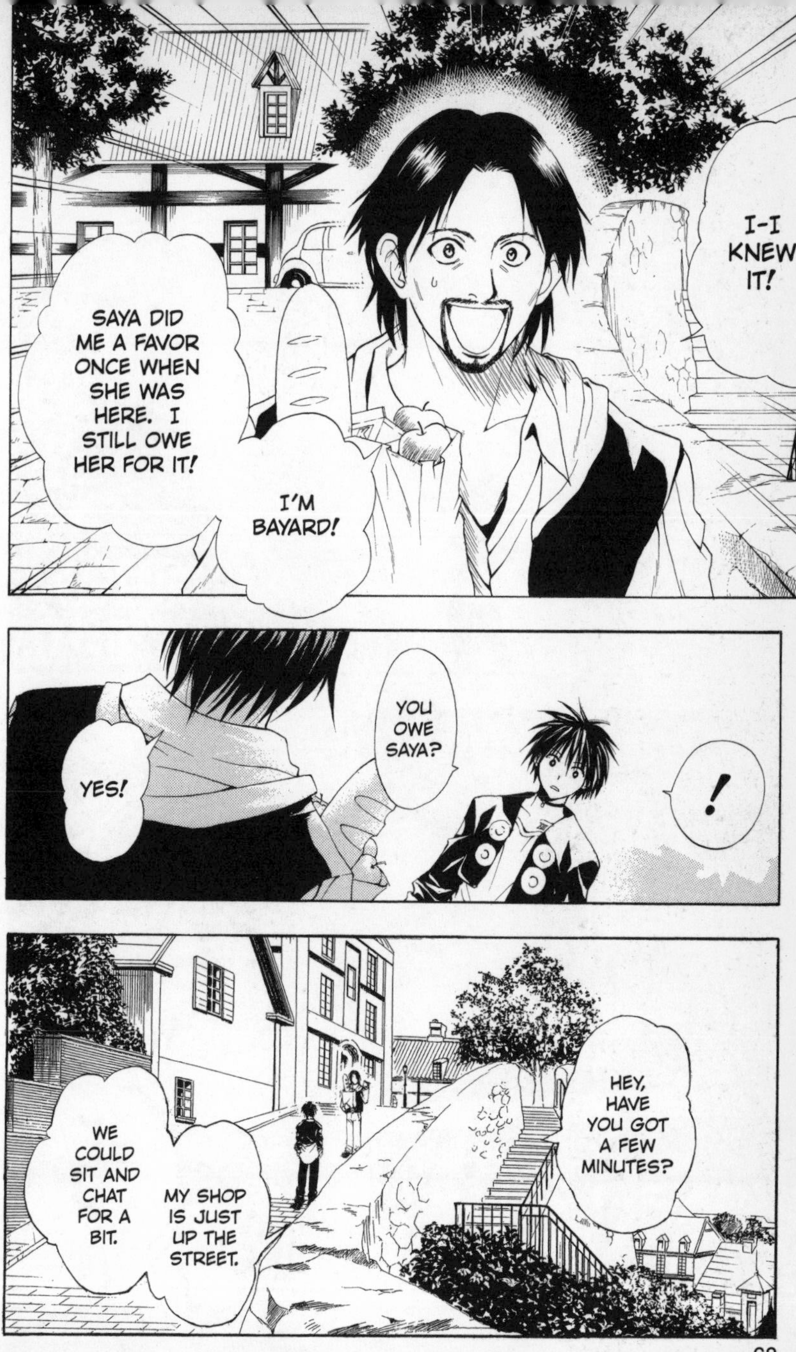
I-I KNEW IT!
I'M BAYARD!
SAYA DID ME A FAVOR ONCE WHEN SHE WAS HERE. I STILL OWE HER FOR IT!
!
YOU OWE SAYA?
YES!
HEY, HAVE YOU GOT A FEW MINUTES?
MY SHOP IS JUST UP THE STREET.
WE COULD SIT AND CHAT FOR A BIT.

CHAPTER 61: THE MAN WHO MET SAYA

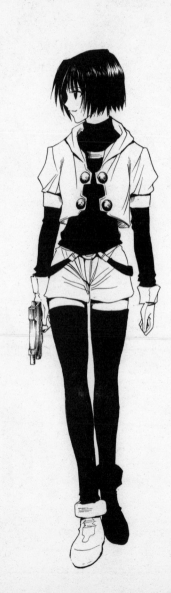

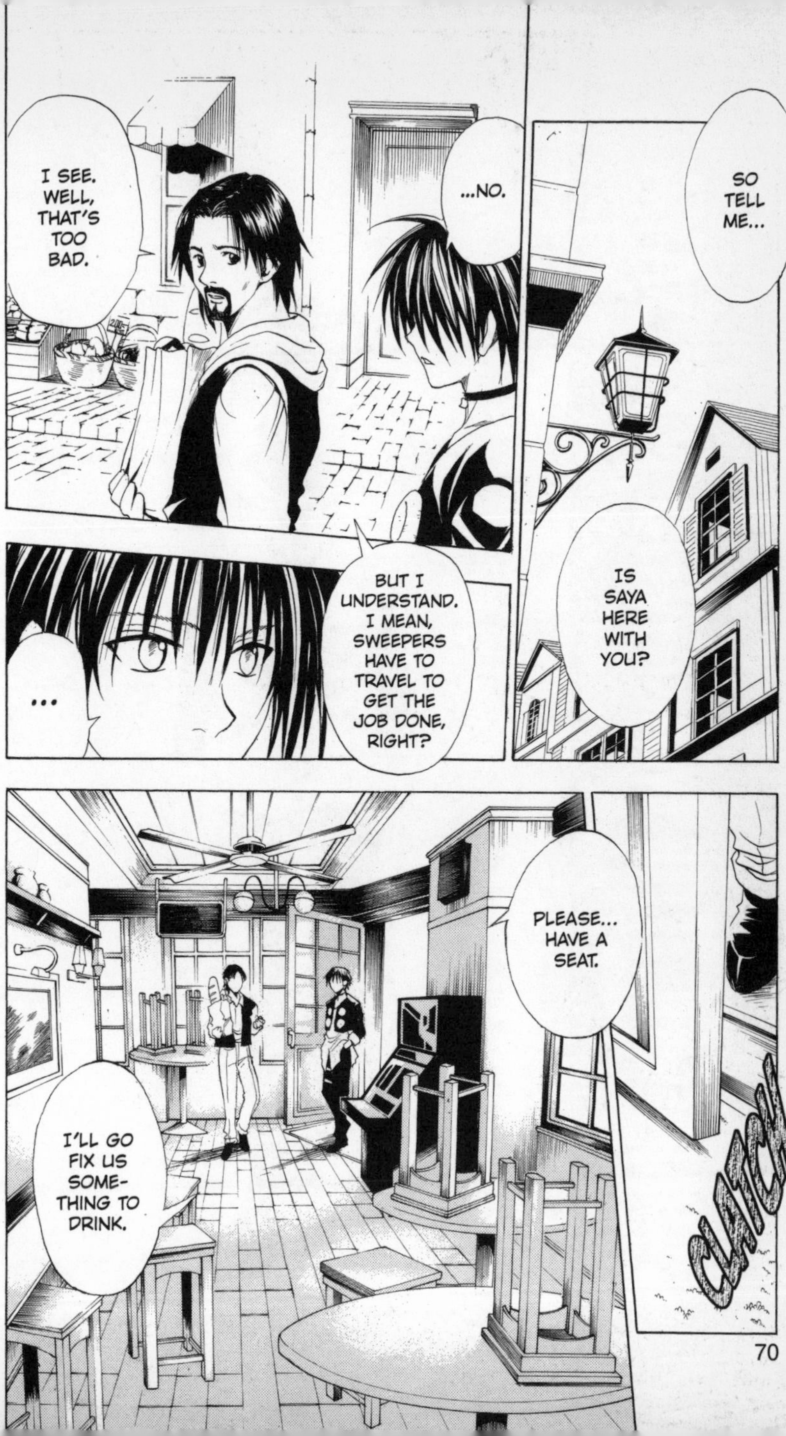
SO TELL ME...
IS SAYA HERE WITH YOU?
...NO.
I SEE. WELL, THAT'S TOO BAD.
BUT I UNDERSTAND. I MEAN, SWEEPERS HAVE TO TRAVEL TO GET THE JOB DONE, RIGHT?
...
PLEASE... HAVE A SEAT.
CLATCH...
I'LL GO FIX US SOME-THING TO DRINK.

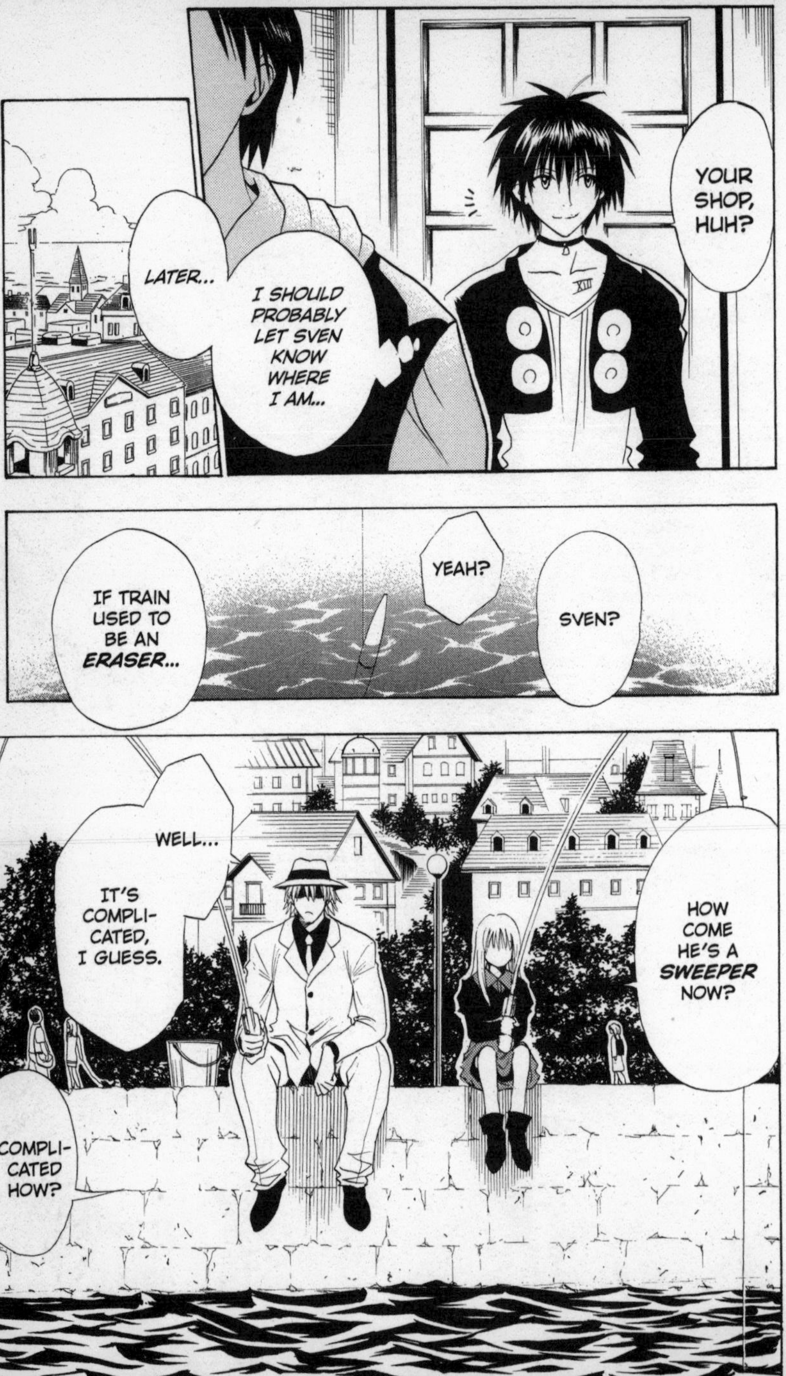
YOUR SHOP, HUH?
I SHOULD PROBABLY LET SVEN KNOW WHERE I AM...
LATER...
SVEN?
YEAH?
IF TRAIN USED TO BE AN ERASER...
HOW COME HE'S A SWEEPER NOW?
WELL...
IT'S COMPLICATED, I GUESS.
COMPLICATED HOW?

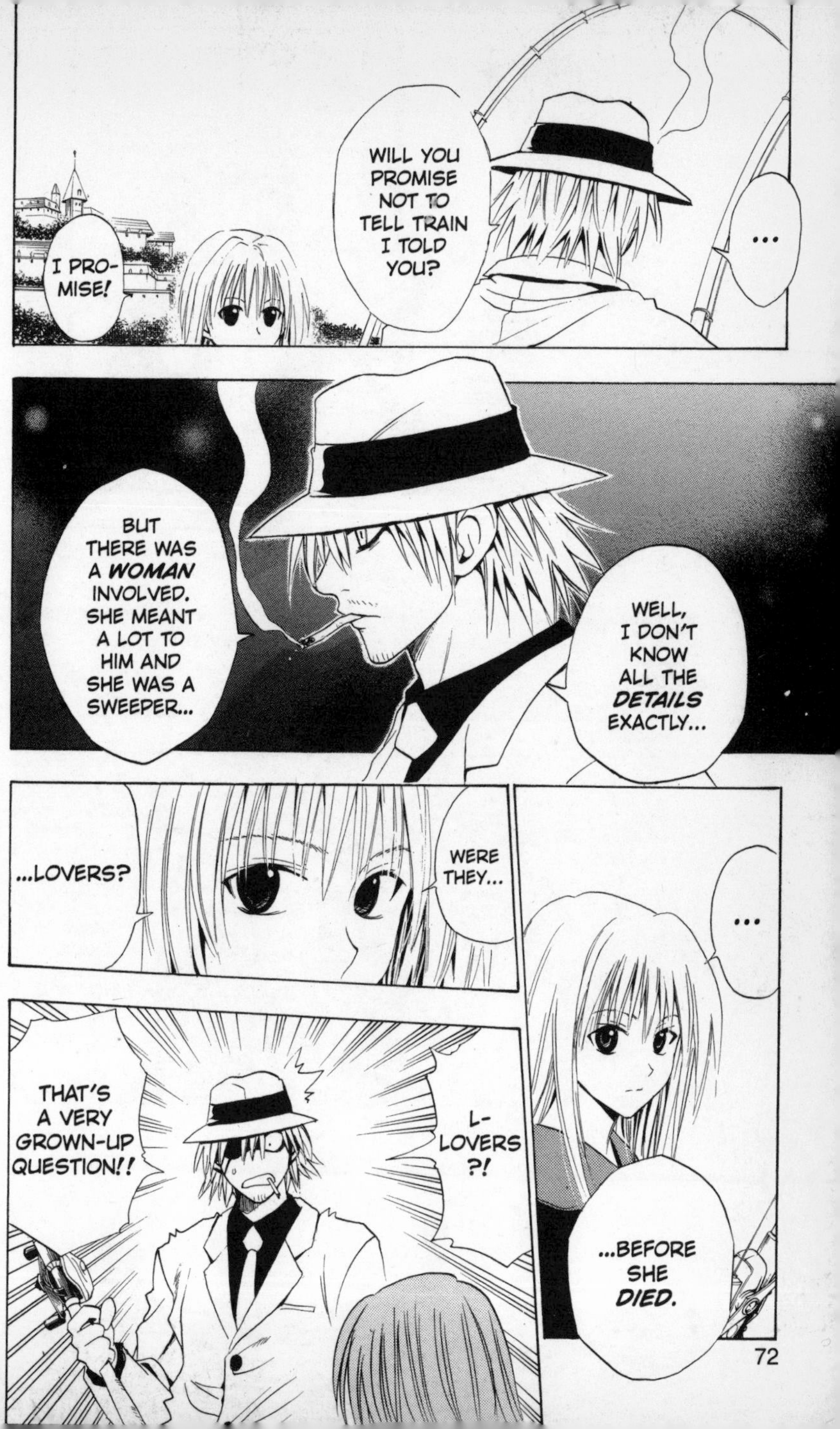
...
WILL YOU PROMISE NOT TO TELL TRAIN I TOLD YOU?
I PRO-MISE!
WELL, I DON'T KNOW ALL THE *DETAILS* EXACTLY...
BUT THERE WAS A *WOMAN* INVOLVED. SHE MEANT A LOT TO HIM AND SHE WAS A SWEEPER...
...
...BEFORE SHE *DIED.*
WERE THEY...
...LOVERS?
L-LOVERS?!
THAT'S A VERY GROWN-UP QUESTION!!

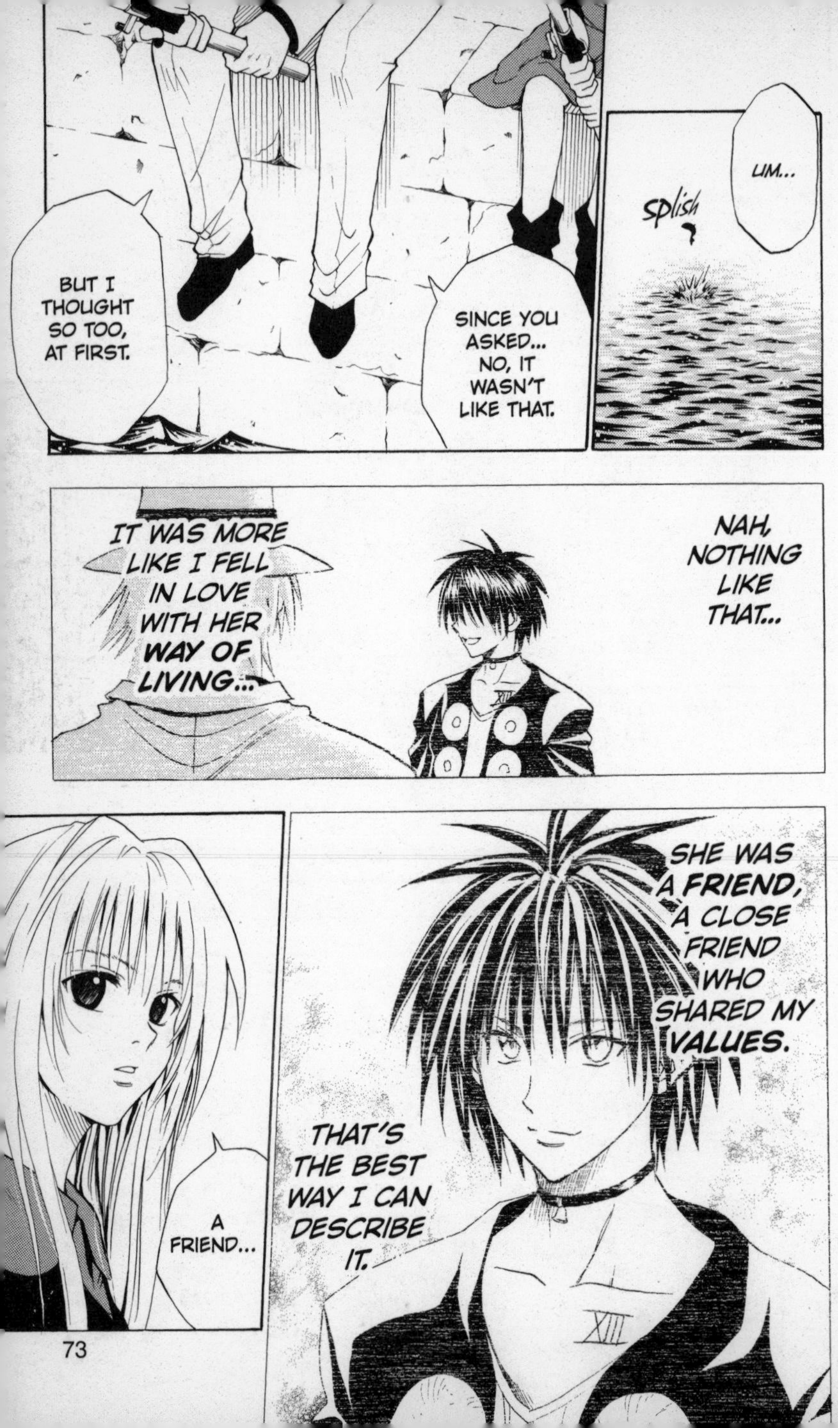
UM...
SPLISH
SINCE YOU ASKED... NO, IT WASN'T LIKE THAT.
BUT I THOUGHT SO TOO, AT FIRST.
NAH, NOTHING LIKE THAT...
IT WAS MORE LIKE I FELL IN LOVE WITH HER WAY OF LIVING...
SHE WAS A FRIEND, A CLOSE FRIEND WHO SHARED MY VALUES.
THAT'S THE BEST WAY I CAN DESCRIBE IT.
A FRIEND...

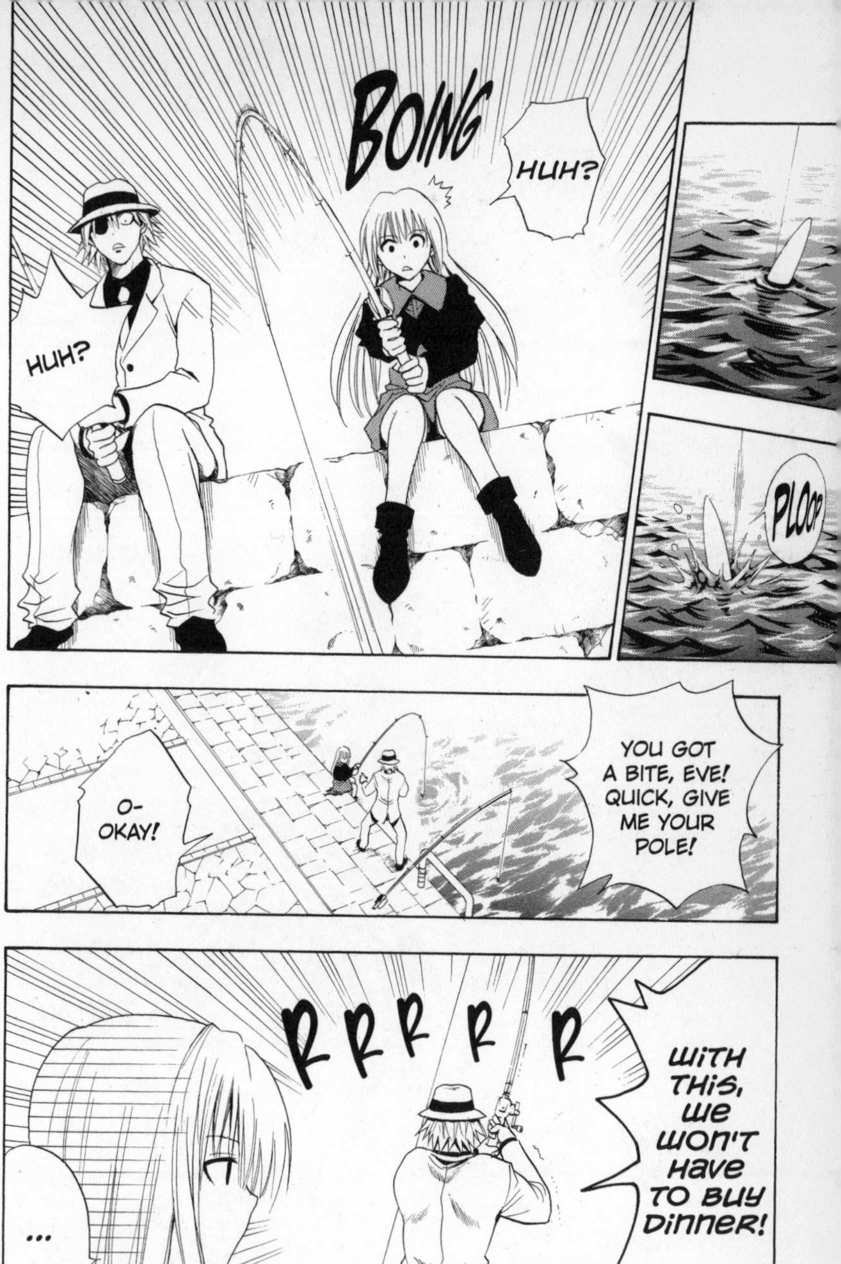
PLOOP
BOING
HUH?
HUH?
YOU GOT A BITE, EVE! QUICK, GIVE ME YOUR POLE!
O-OKAY!
WITH THIS, WE WON'T HAVE TO BUY DINNER!
RRRRR
...

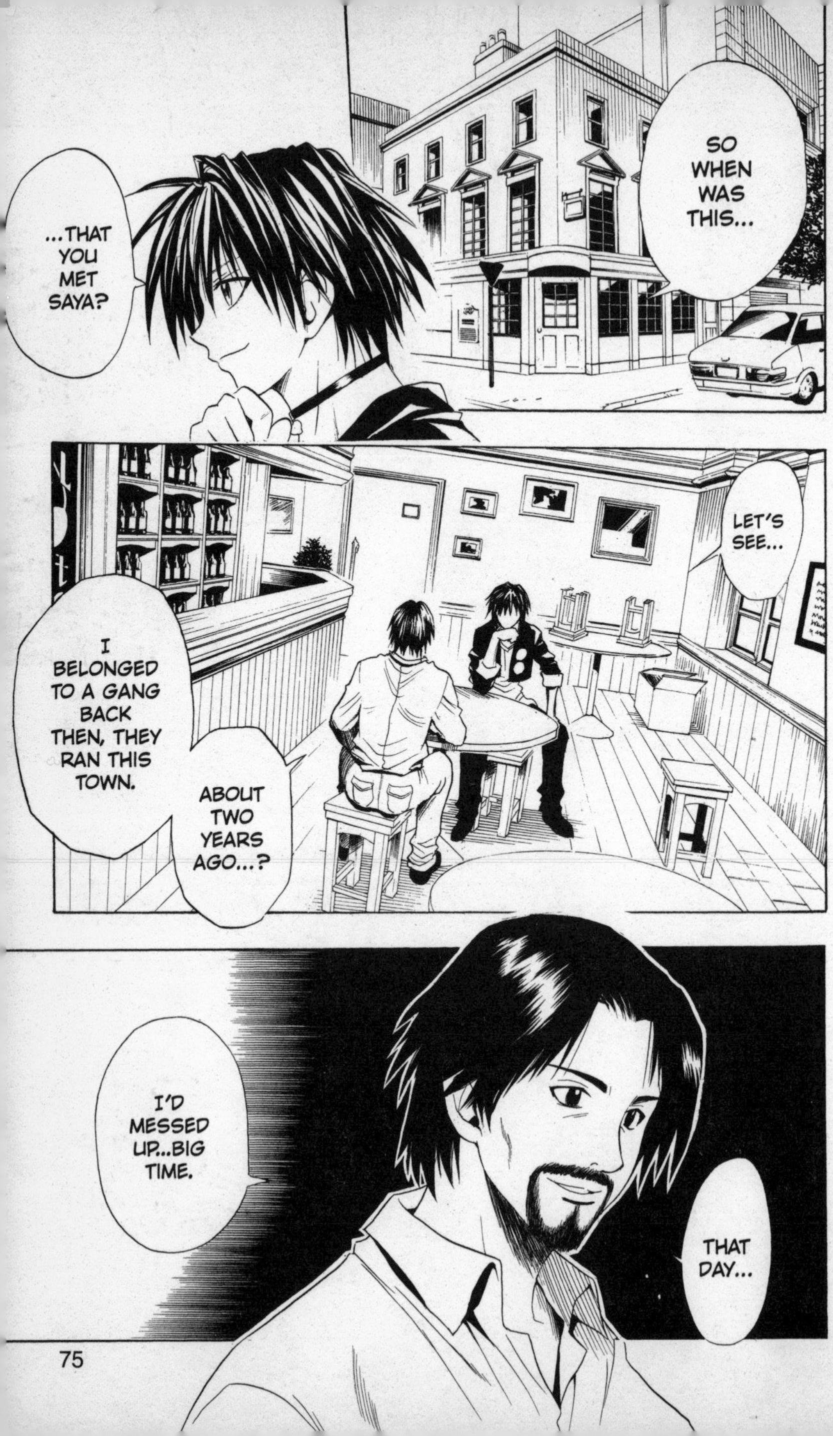
SO WHEN WAS THIS...
...THAT YOU MET SAYA?
LET'S SEE...
ABOUT TWO YEARS AGO...?
I BELONGED TO A GANG BACK THEN, THEY RAN THIS TOWN.
THAT DAY...
I'D MESSED UP...BIG TIME.

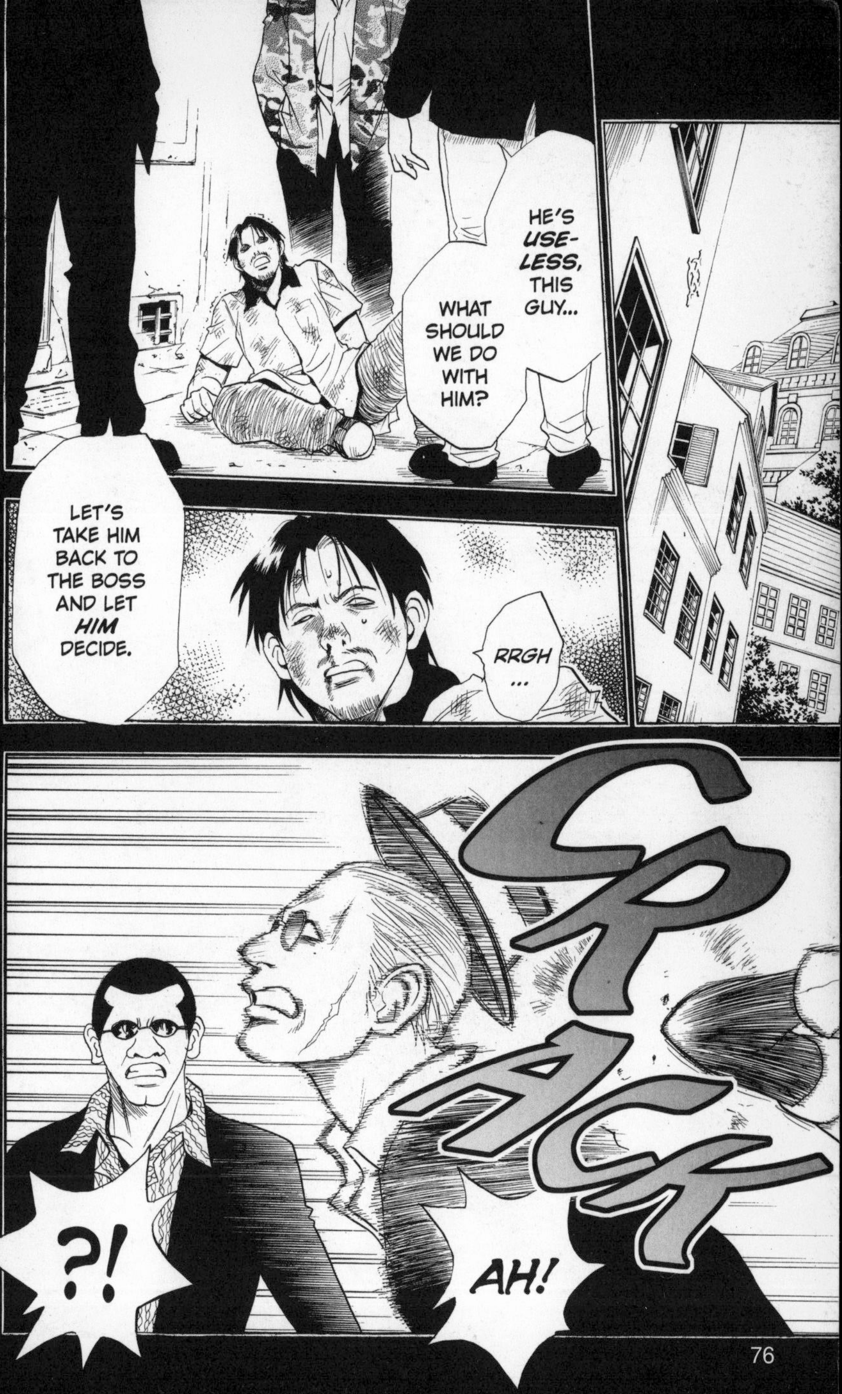
HE'S *USE-LESS,* THIS GUY...
WHAT SHOULD WE DO WITH HIM?
LET'S TAKE HIM BACK TO THE BOSS AND LET ***HIM*** DECIDE.
RRGH ...
CRACK
AH!
?!

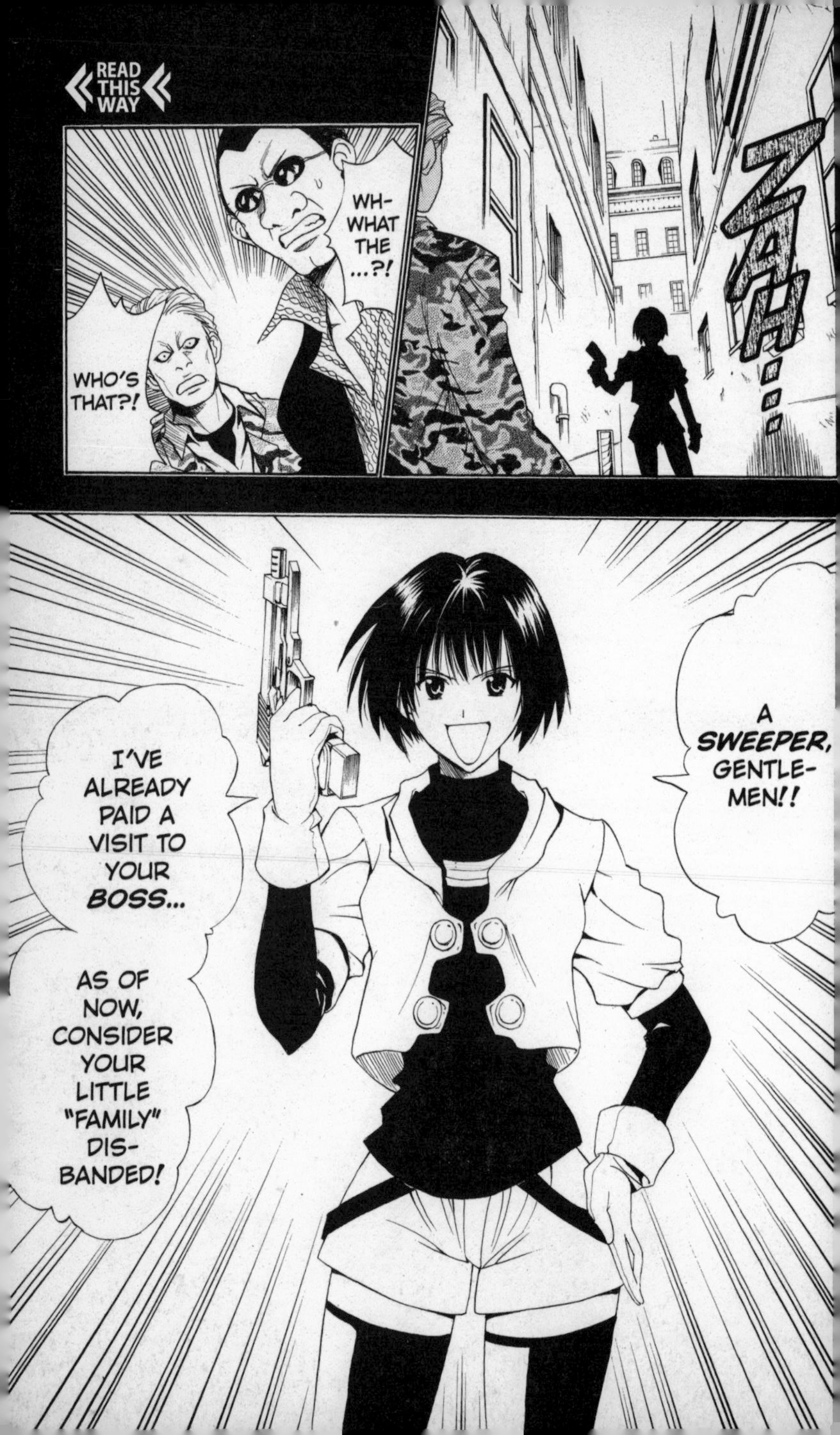
READ THIS WAY
ZAH!!
WH-WHAT THE ...?!
WHO'S THAT?!
A SWEEPER, GENTLEMEN!!
I'VE ALREADY PAID A VISIT TO YOUR BOSS...
AS OF NOW, CONSIDER YOUR LITTLE "FAMILY" DISBANDED!

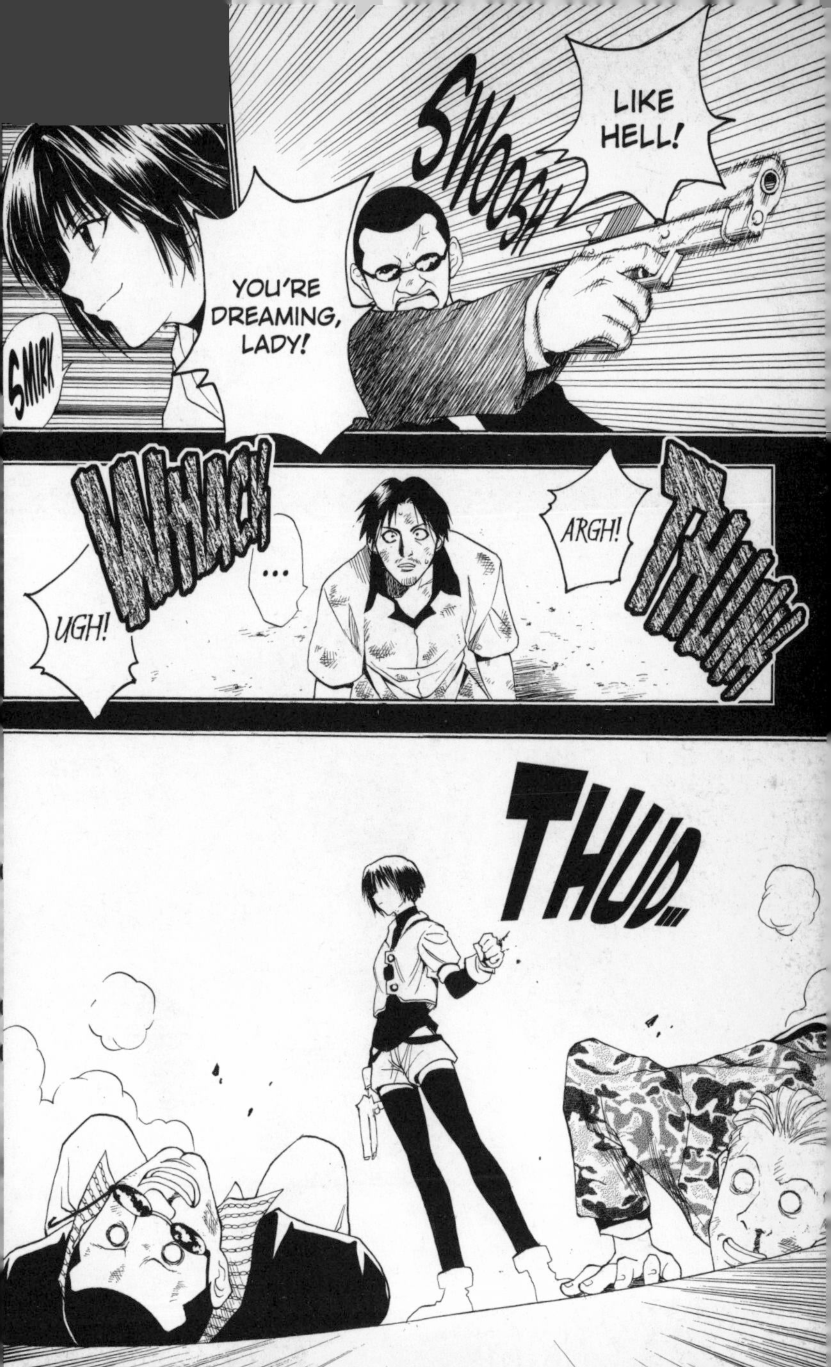
LIKE HELL!
SWOOSH
YOU'RE DREAMING, LADY!
SMIRK
ARGH!
...
WHACK!
UGH!
THUD...

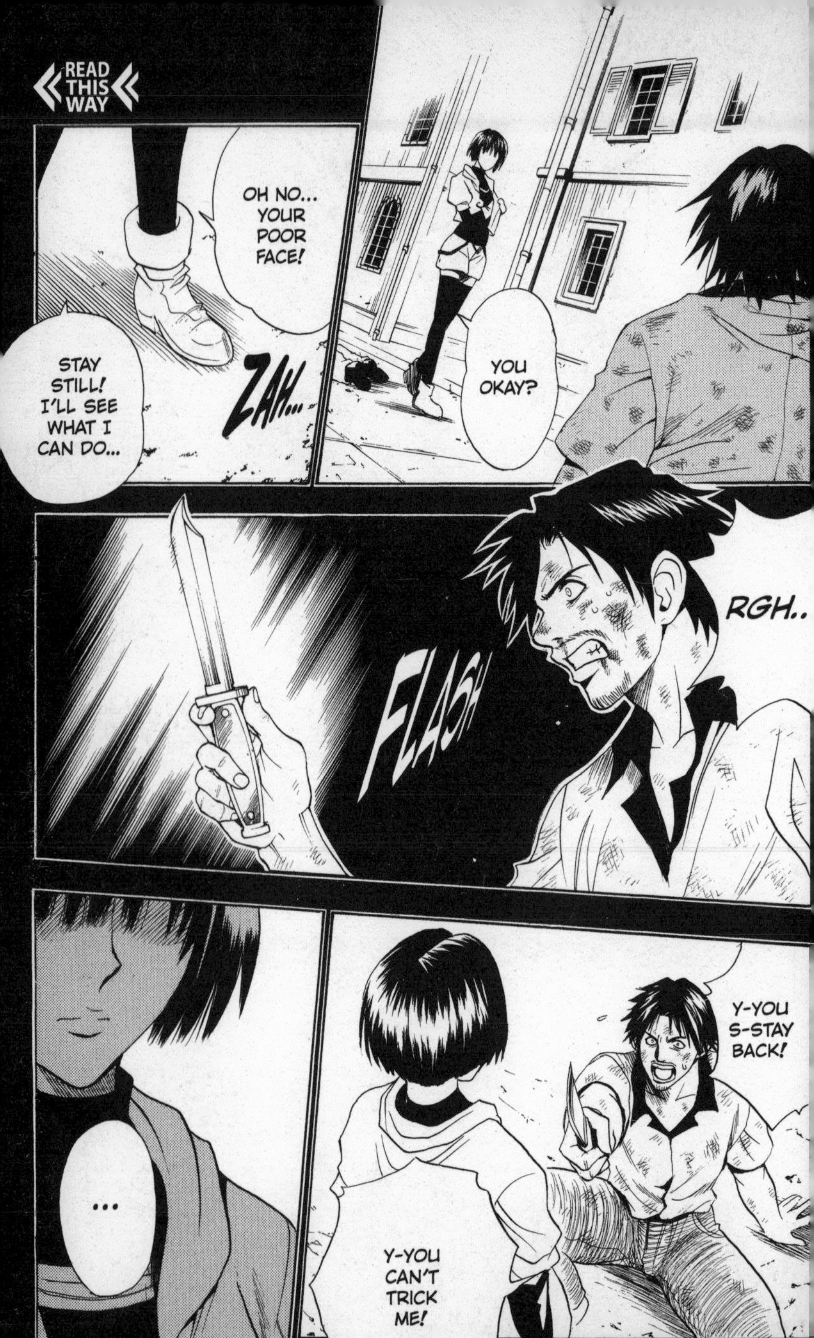
READ THIS WAY
YOU OKAY?
OH NO... YOUR POOR FACE!
STAY STILL! I'LL SEE WHAT I CAN DO...
ZAH...
RGH..
FLASH
Y-YOU S-STAY BACK!
Y-YOU CAN'T TRICK ME!
...

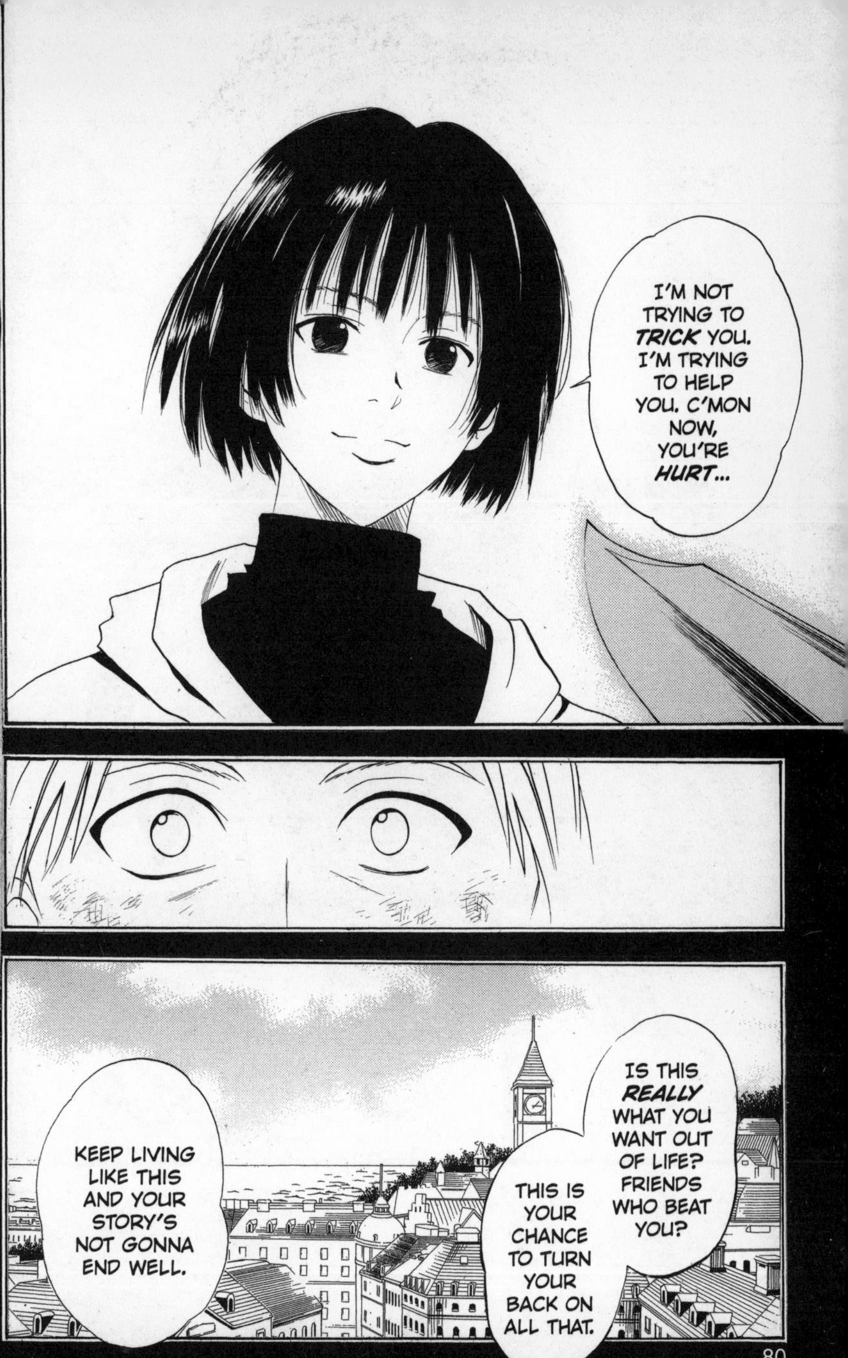
I'M NOT TRYING TO *TRICK* YOU. I'M TRYING TO HELP YOU. C'MON NOW, YOU'RE *HURT*...
IS THIS *REALLY* WHAT YOU WANT OUT OF LIFE? FRIENDS WHO BEAT YOU?
THIS IS YOUR CHANCE TO TURN YOUR BACK ON ALL THAT.
KEEP LIVING LIKE THIS AND YOUR STORY'S NOT GONNA END WELL.

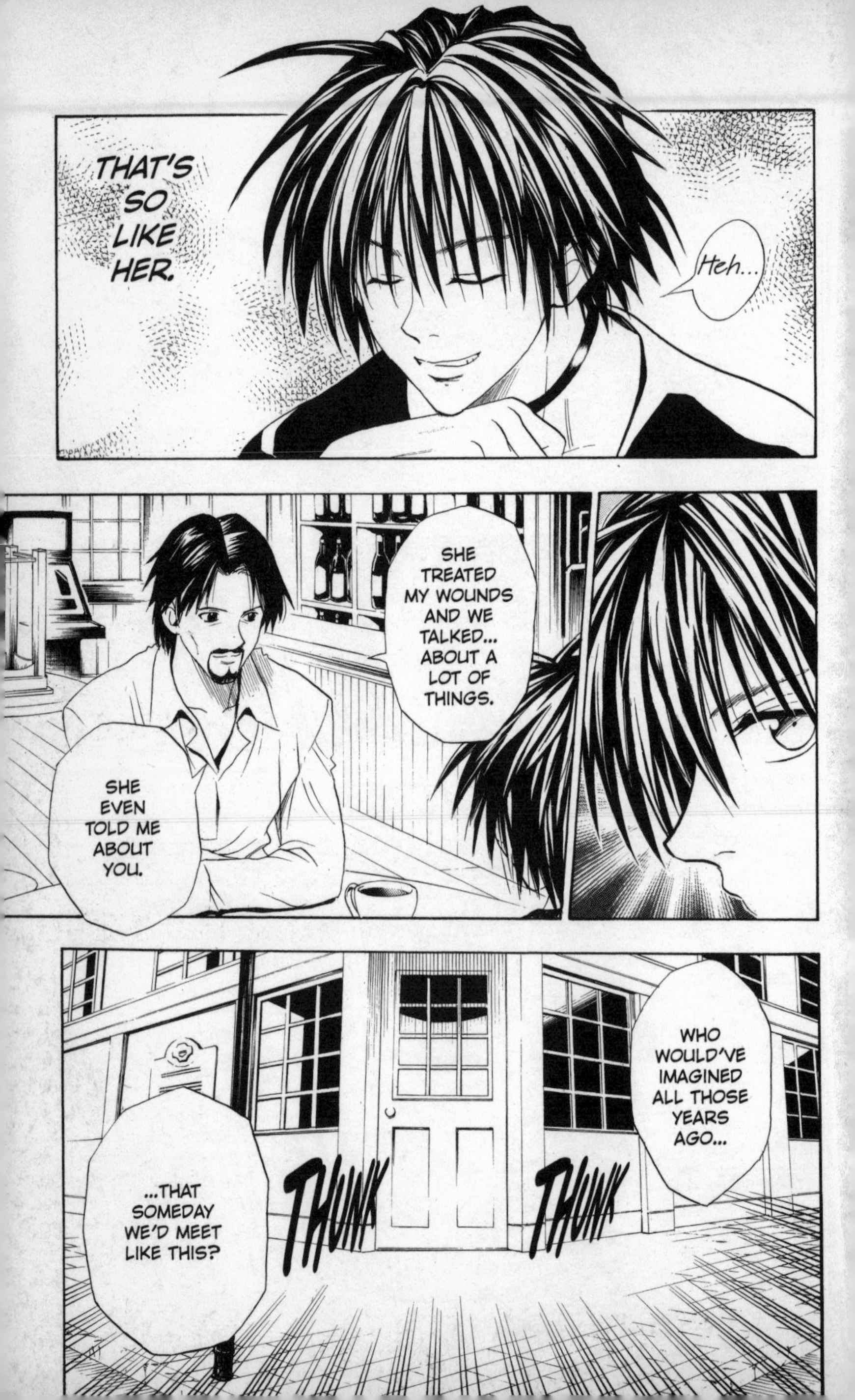
Heh...
THAT'S SO LIKE HER.
SHE TREATED MY WOUNDS AND WE TALKED... ABOUT A LOT OF THINGS.
SHE EVEN TOLD ME ABOUT YOU.
WHO WOULD'VE IMAGINED ALL THOSE YEARS AGO...
THUNK
THUNK
...THAT SOMEDAY WE'D MEET LIKE THIS?

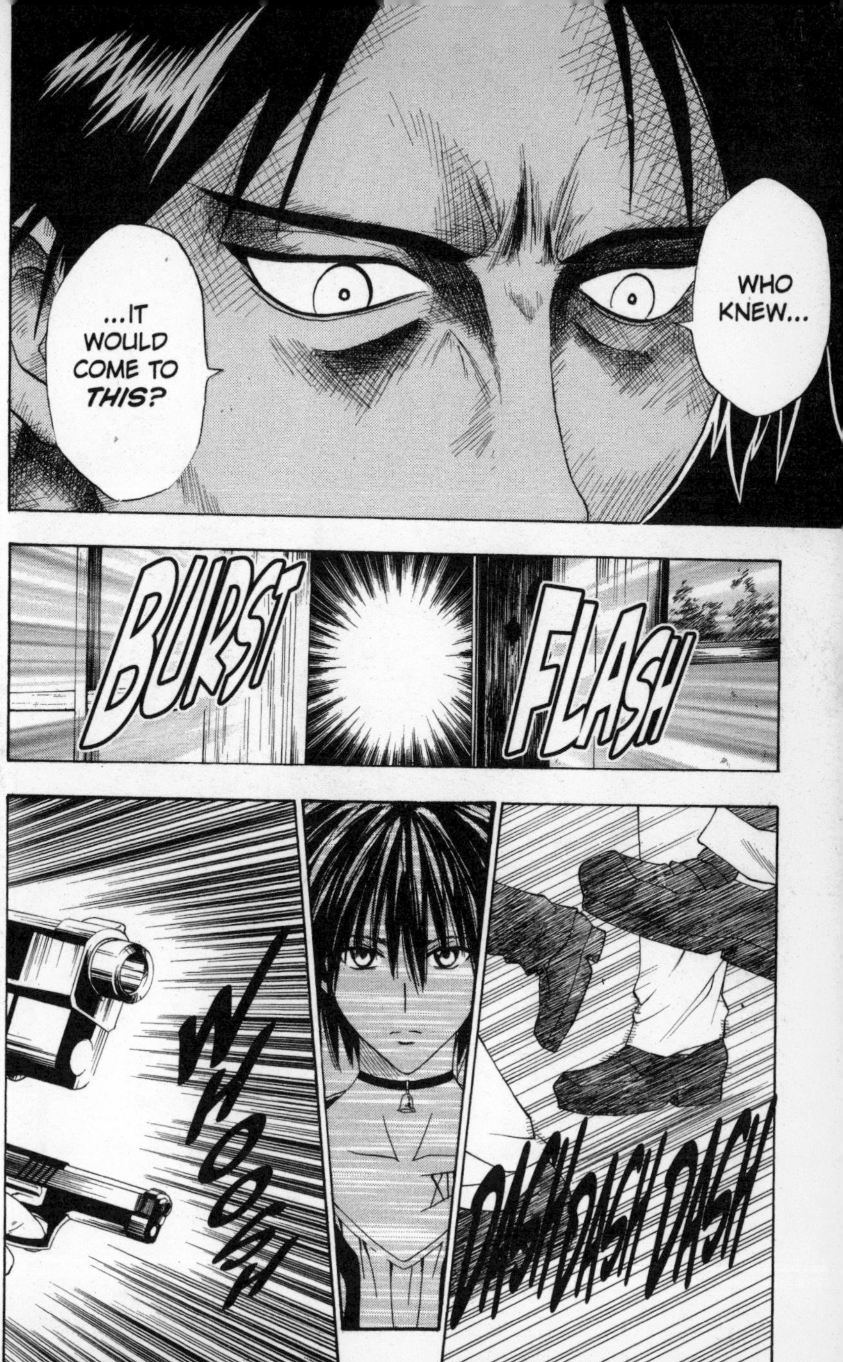
WHO KNEW...
...IT WOULD COME TO THIS?
FLASH
BURST
DASH DASH DASH
WHOOSH

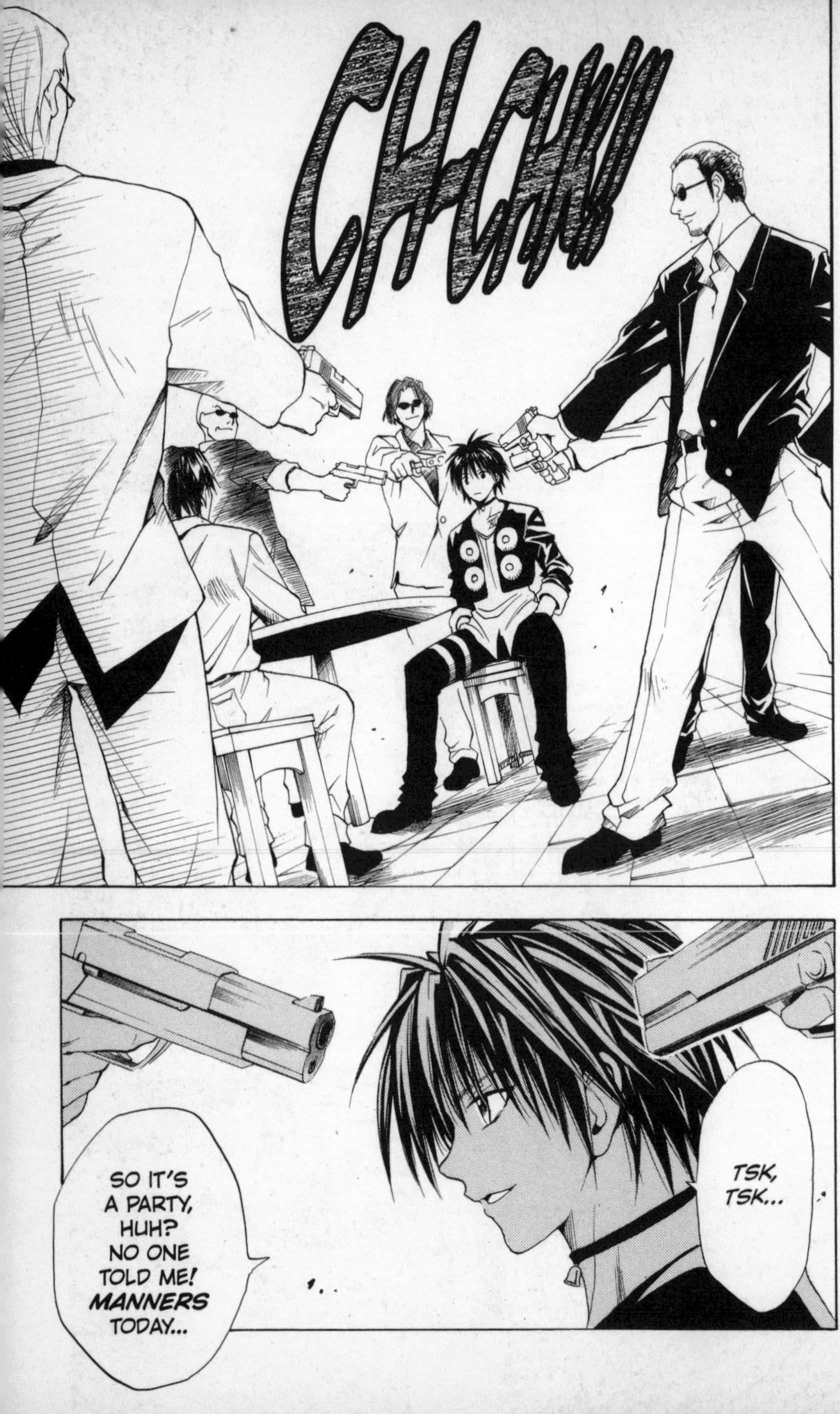
CH-CHK!!
TSK, TSK...
SO IT'S A PARTY, HUH? NO ONE TOLD ME! *MANNERS* TODAY...

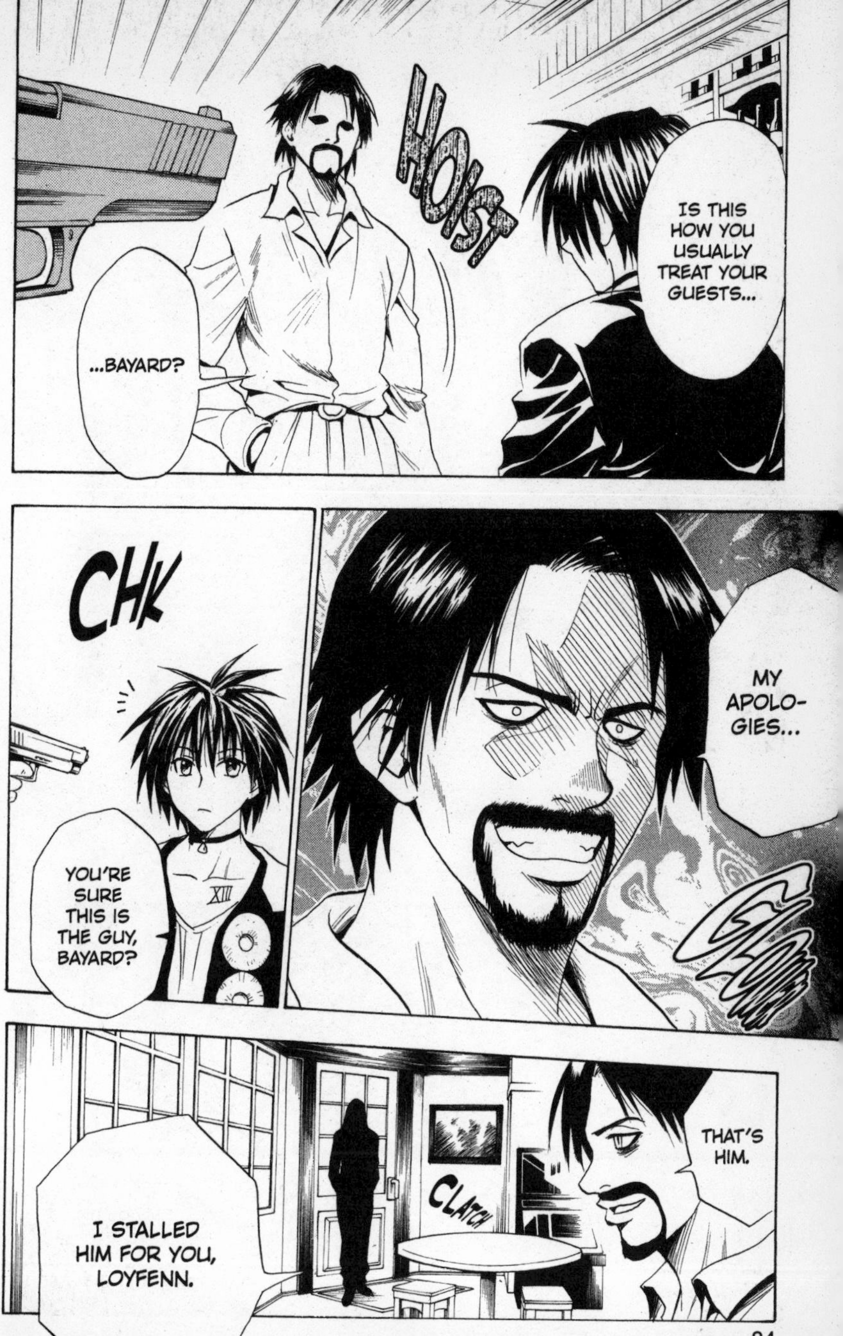
IS THIS HOW YOU USUALLY TREAT YOUR GUESTS...
HOIST
...BAYARD?
MY APOLOGIES...
CHK
YOU'RE SURE THIS IS THE GUY, BAYARD?
THAT'S HIM.
CLATCH
I STALLED HIM FOR YOU, LOYFENN.

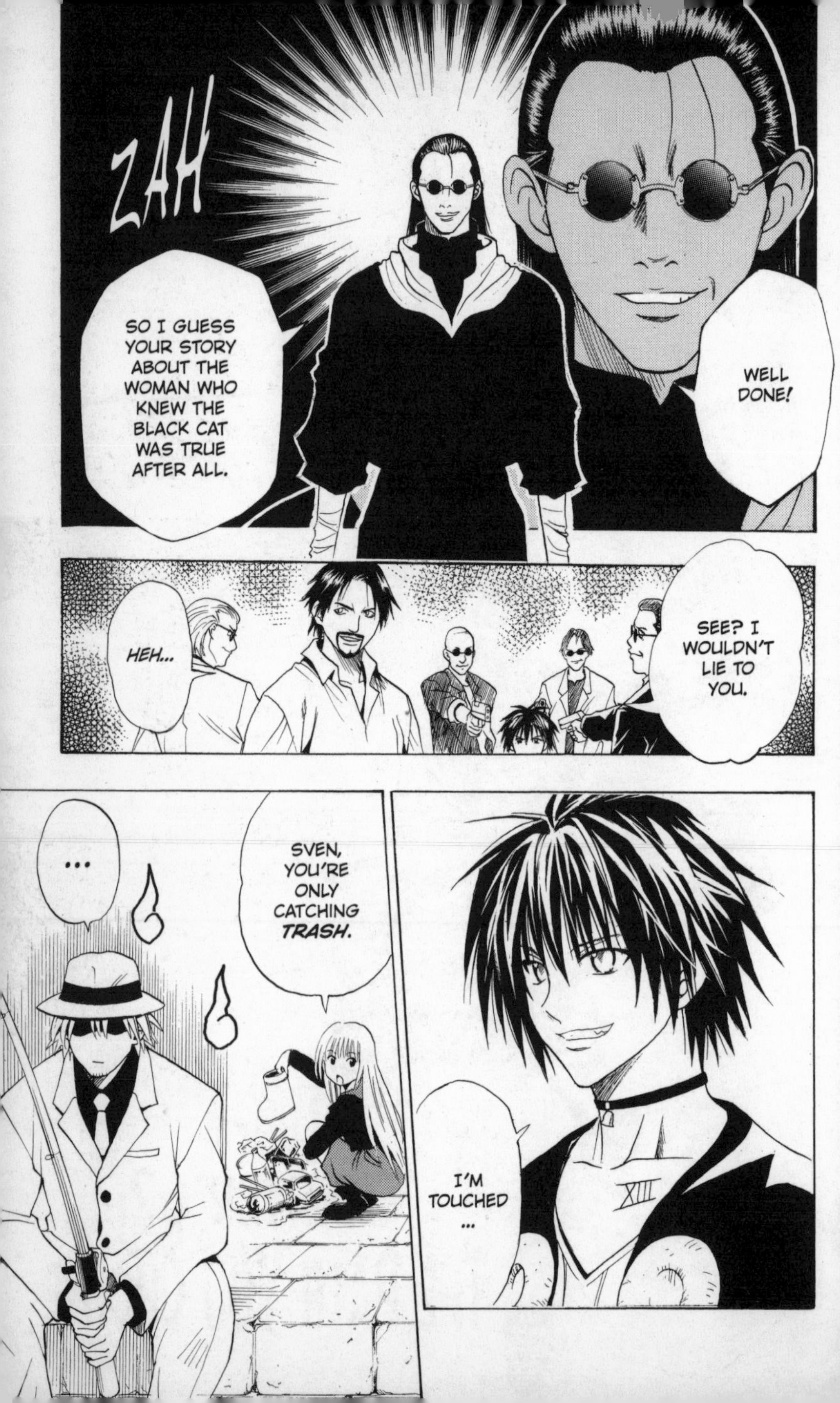
ZAH
WELL DONE!
SO I GUESS YOUR STORY ABOUT THE WOMAN WHO KNEW THE BLACK CAT WAS TRUE AFTER ALL.
SEE? I WOULDN'T LIE TO YOU.
HEH...
I'M TOUCHED ...
SVEN, YOU'RE ONLY CATCHING *TRASH*.
...

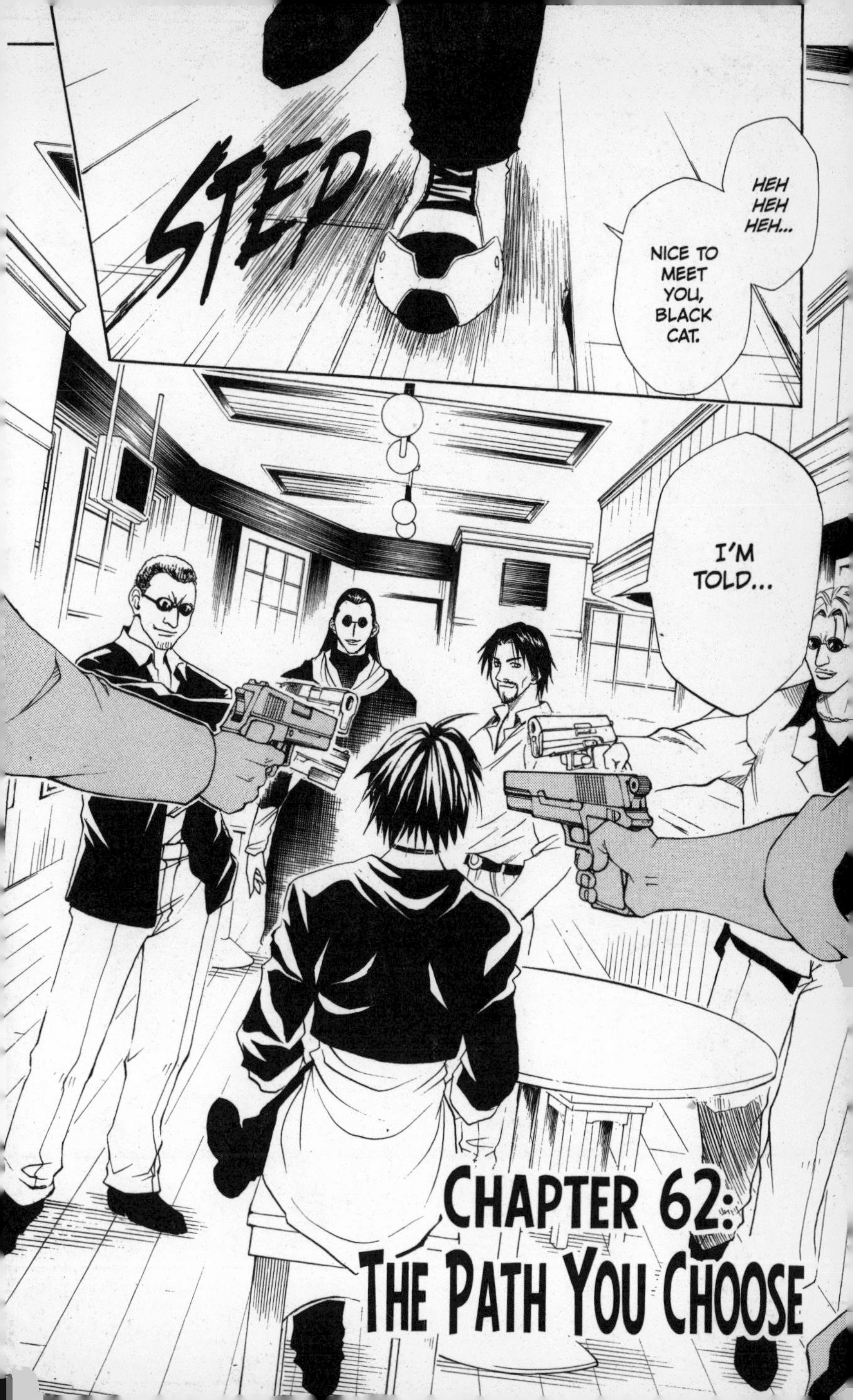
STEP
HEH HEH HEH...
NICE TO MEET YOU, BLACK CAT.
I'M TOLD...
CHAPTER 62:
THE PATH YOU CHOOSE

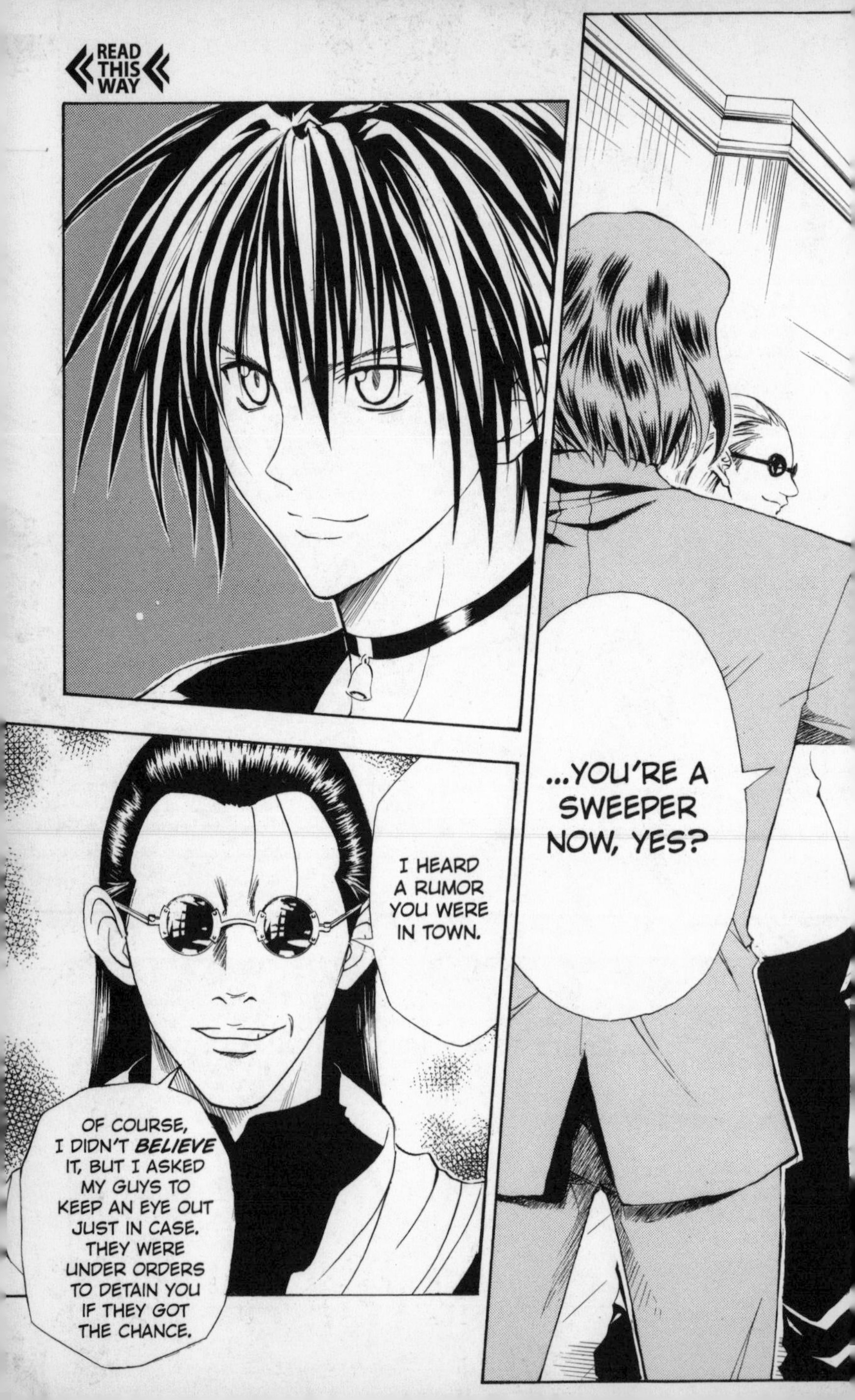
READ THIS WAY
...YOU'RE A SWEEPER NOW, YES?
I HEARD A RUMOR YOU WERE IN TOWN.
OF COURSE, I DIDN'T *BELIEVE* IT, BUT I ASKED MY GUYS TO KEEP AN EYE OUT JUST IN CASE. THEY WERE UNDER ORDERS TO DETAIN YOU IF THEY GOT THE CHANCE.

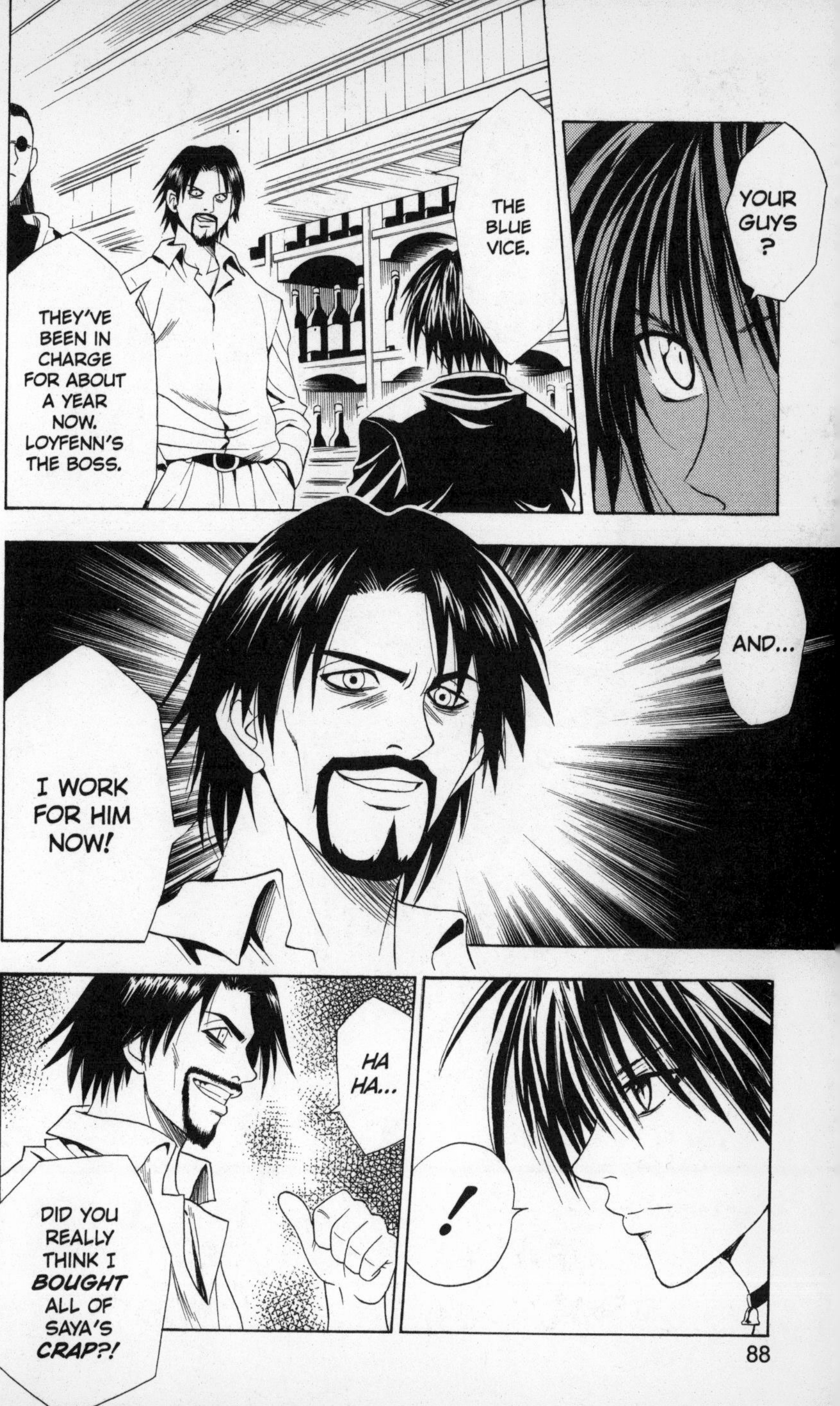
YOUR GUYS ?
THE BLUE VICE.
THEY'VE BEEN IN CHARGE FOR ABOUT A YEAR NOW. LOYFENN'S THE BOSS.
AND...
I WORK FOR HIM NOW!
!
HA HA...
DID YOU REALLY THINK I *BOUGHT* ALL OF SAYA'S *CRAP?!*

READ THIS WAY

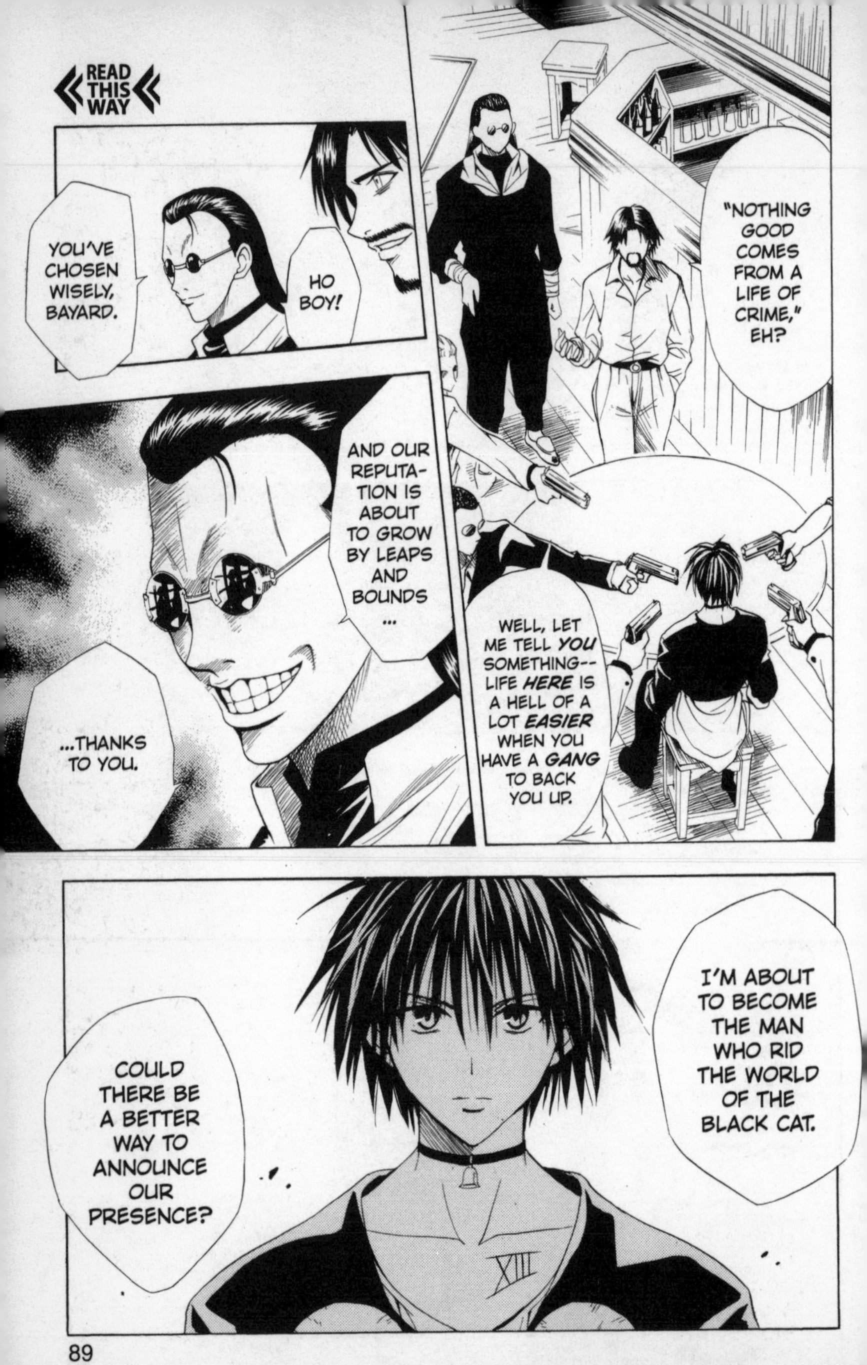
"NOTHING GOOD COMES FROM A LIFE OF CRIME," EH?
WELL, LET ME TELL *YOU* SOMETHING-- LIFE *HERE* IS A HELL OF A LOT *EASIER* WHEN YOU HAVE A *GANG* TO BACK YOU UP.
HO BOY!
YOU'VE CHOSEN WISELY, BAYARD.
AND OUR REPUTATION IS ABOUT TO GROW BY LEAPS AND BOUNDS ...
...THANKS TO YOU.
I'M ABOUT TO BECOME THE MAN WHO RID THE WORLD OF THE BLACK CAT.
COULD THERE BE A BETTER WAY TO ANNOUNCE OUR PRESENCE?

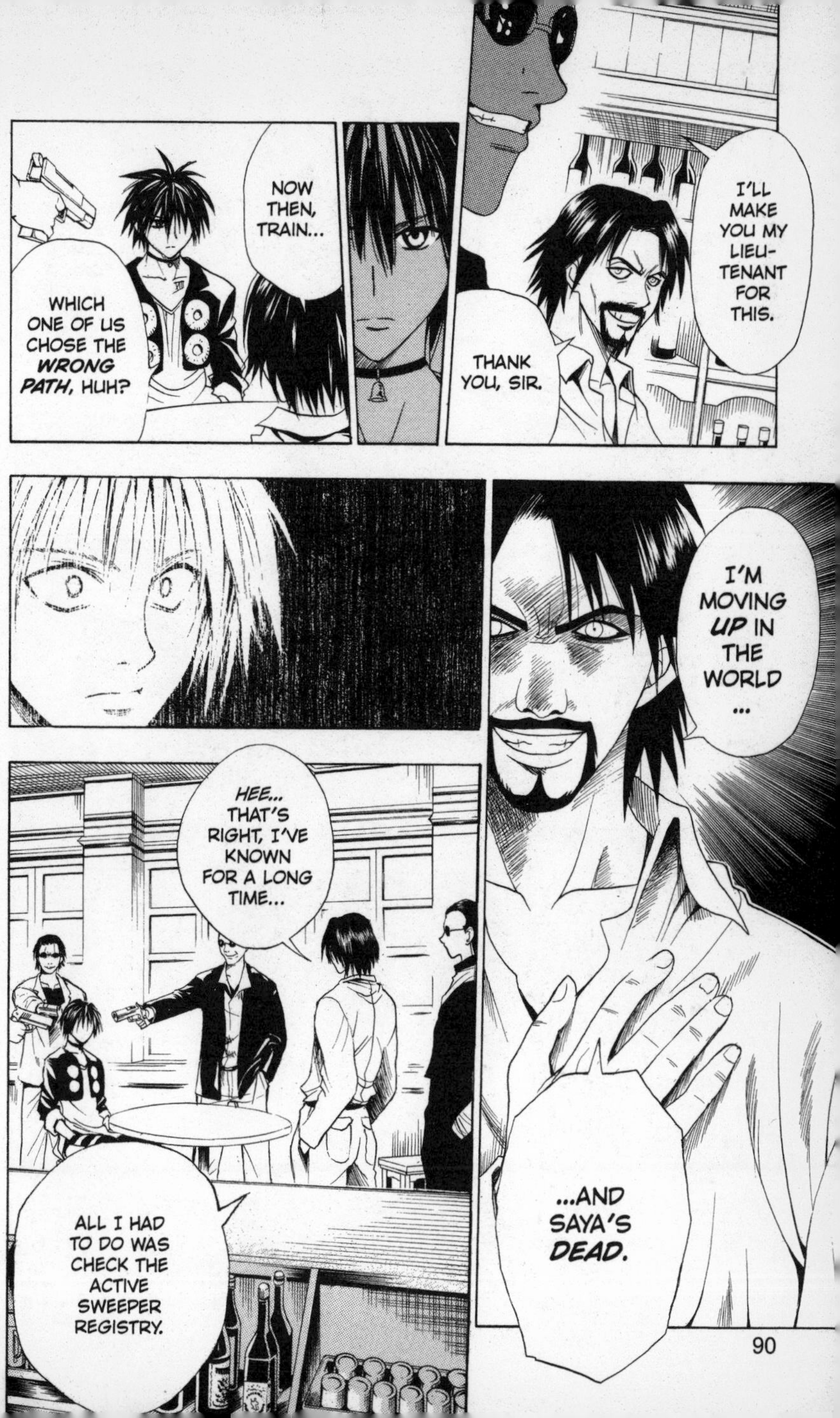
I'LL MAKE YOU MY LIEUTENANT FOR THIS.
THANK YOU, SIR.
NOW THEN, TRAIN...
WHICH ONE OF US CHOSE THE WRONG PATH, HUH?
I'M MOVING UP IN THE WORLD ...
...AND SAYA'S DEAD.
HEE... THAT'S RIGHT, I'VE KNOWN FOR A LONG TIME...
ALL I HAD TO DO WAS CHECK THE ACTIVE SWEEPER REGISTRY.

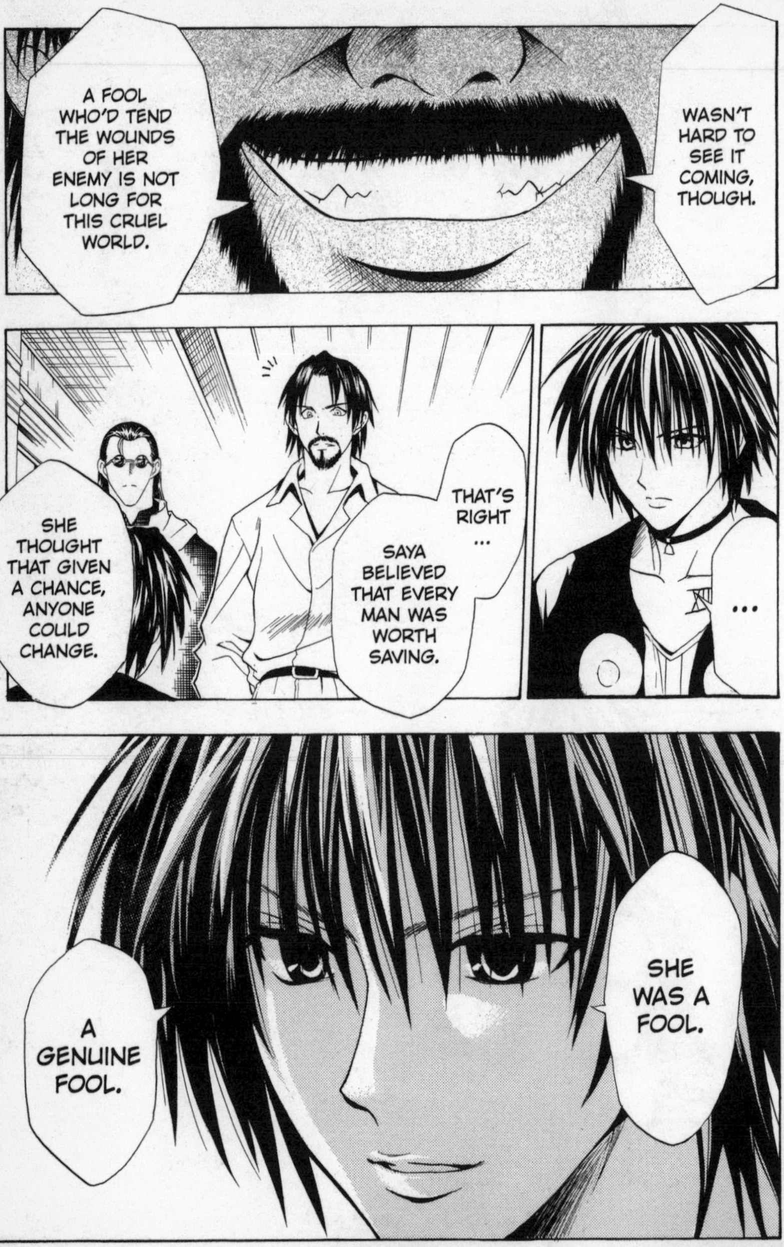

WASN'T HARD TO SEE IT COMING, THOUGH.
A FOOL WHO'D TEND THE WOUNDS OF HER ENEMY IS NOT LONG FOR THIS CRUEL WORLD.
...
THAT'S RIGHT ...
SAYA BELIEVED THAT EVERY MAN WAS WORTH SAVING.
SHE THOUGHT THAT GIVEN A CHANCE, ANYONE COULD CHANGE.
SHE WAS A FOOL.
A GENUINE FOOL.

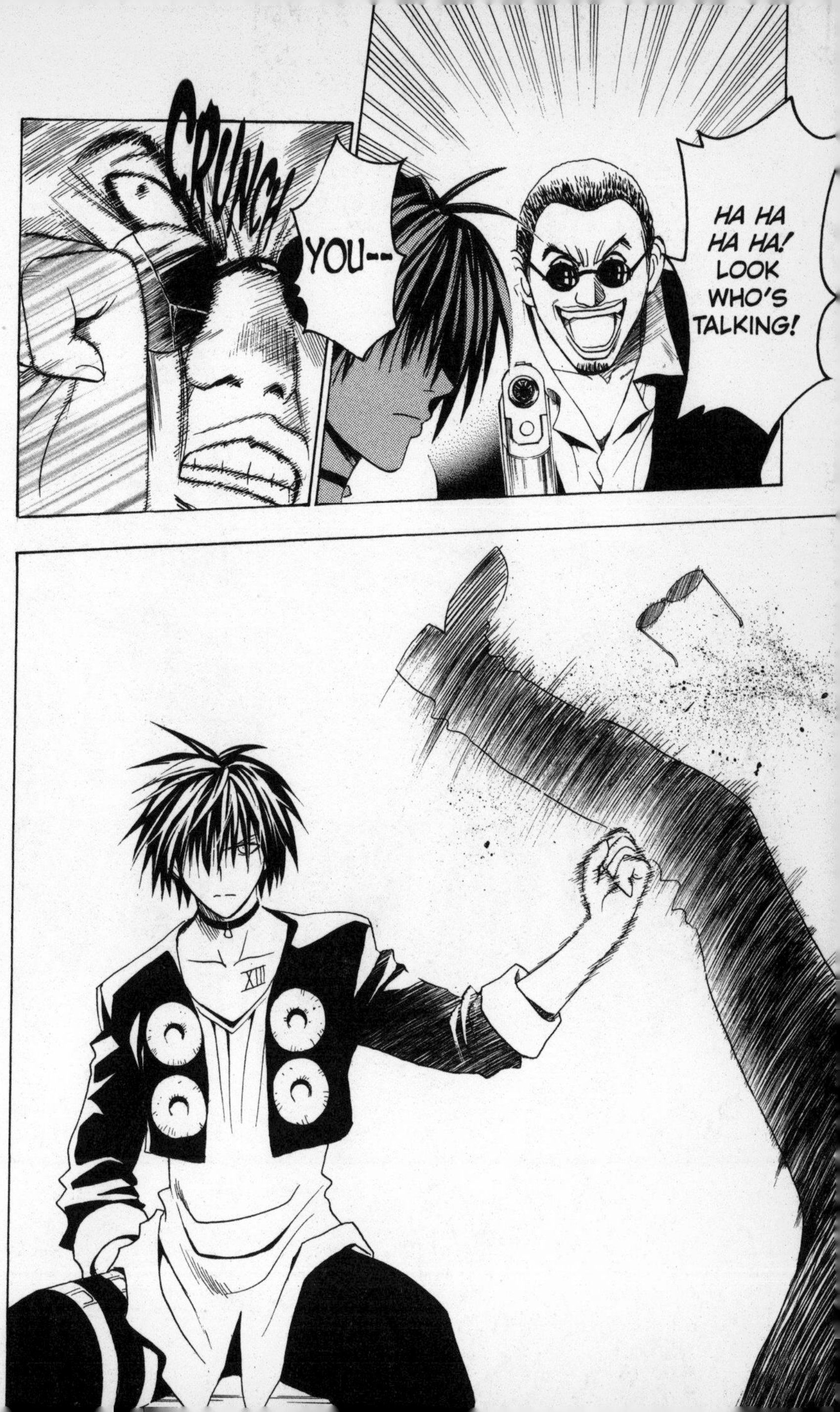
YOU--
HA HA HA HA! LOOK WHO'S TALKING!
CRUNCH

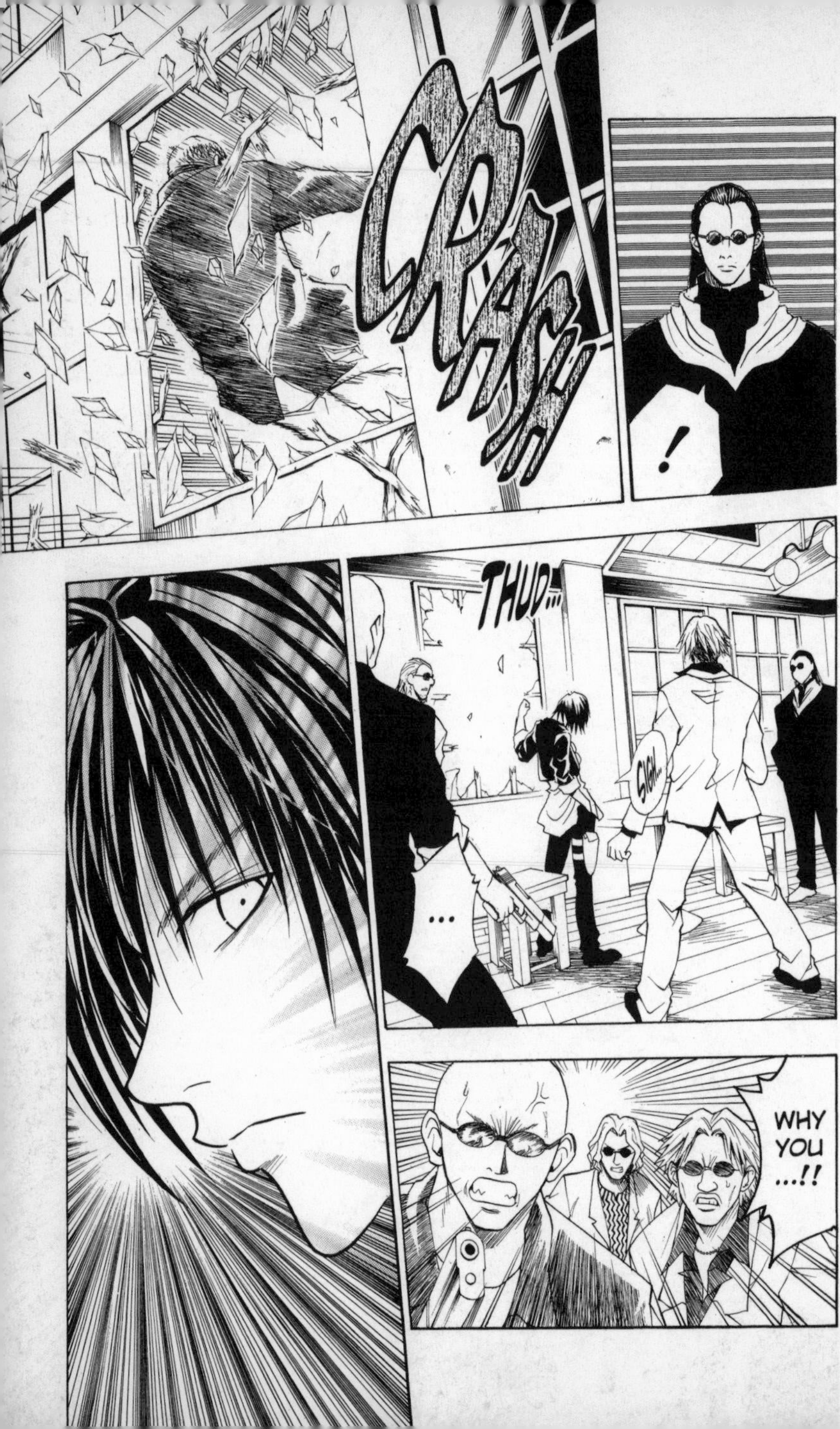
!
CRASH
THUD...
SIGH...
...
WHY YOU ...!!

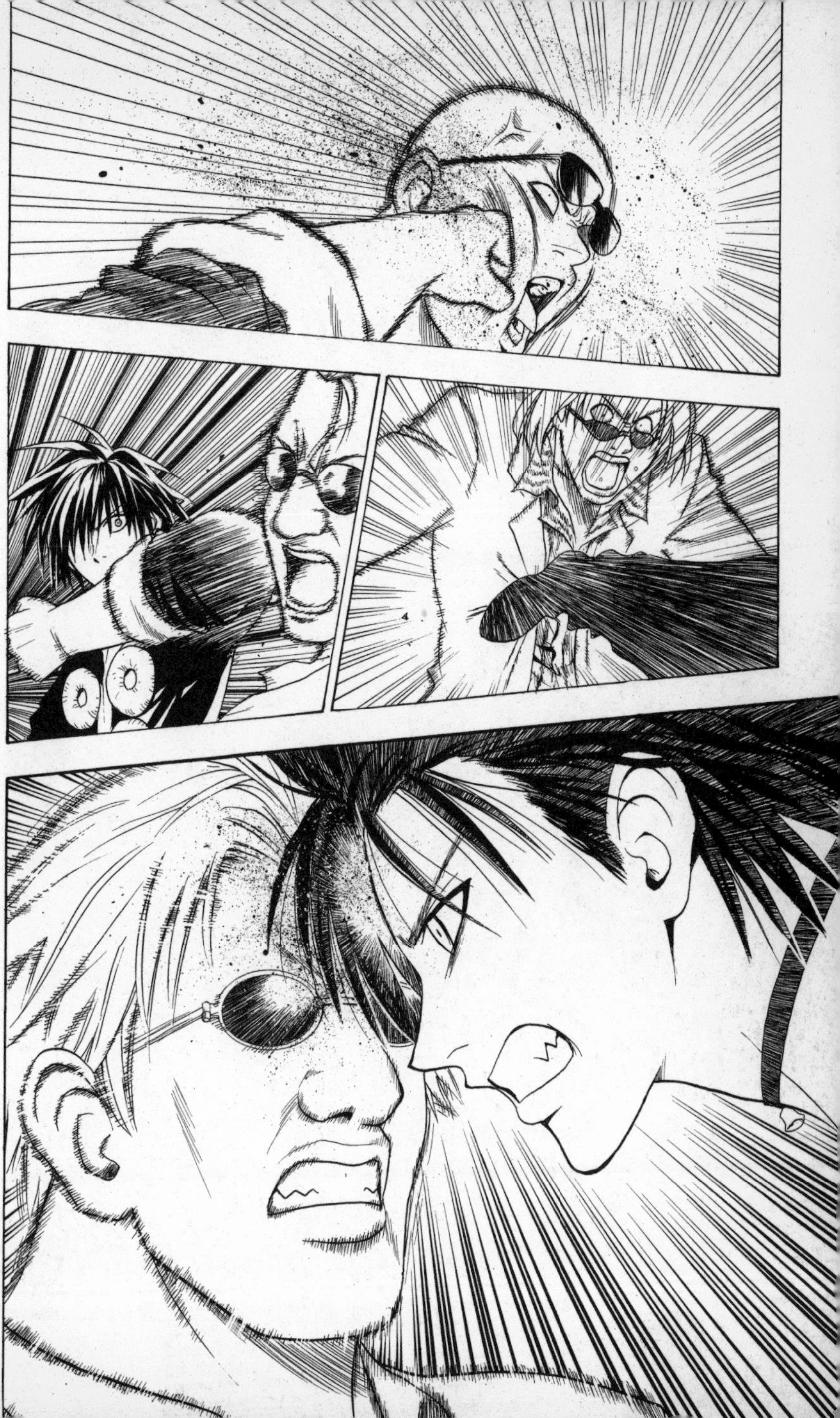

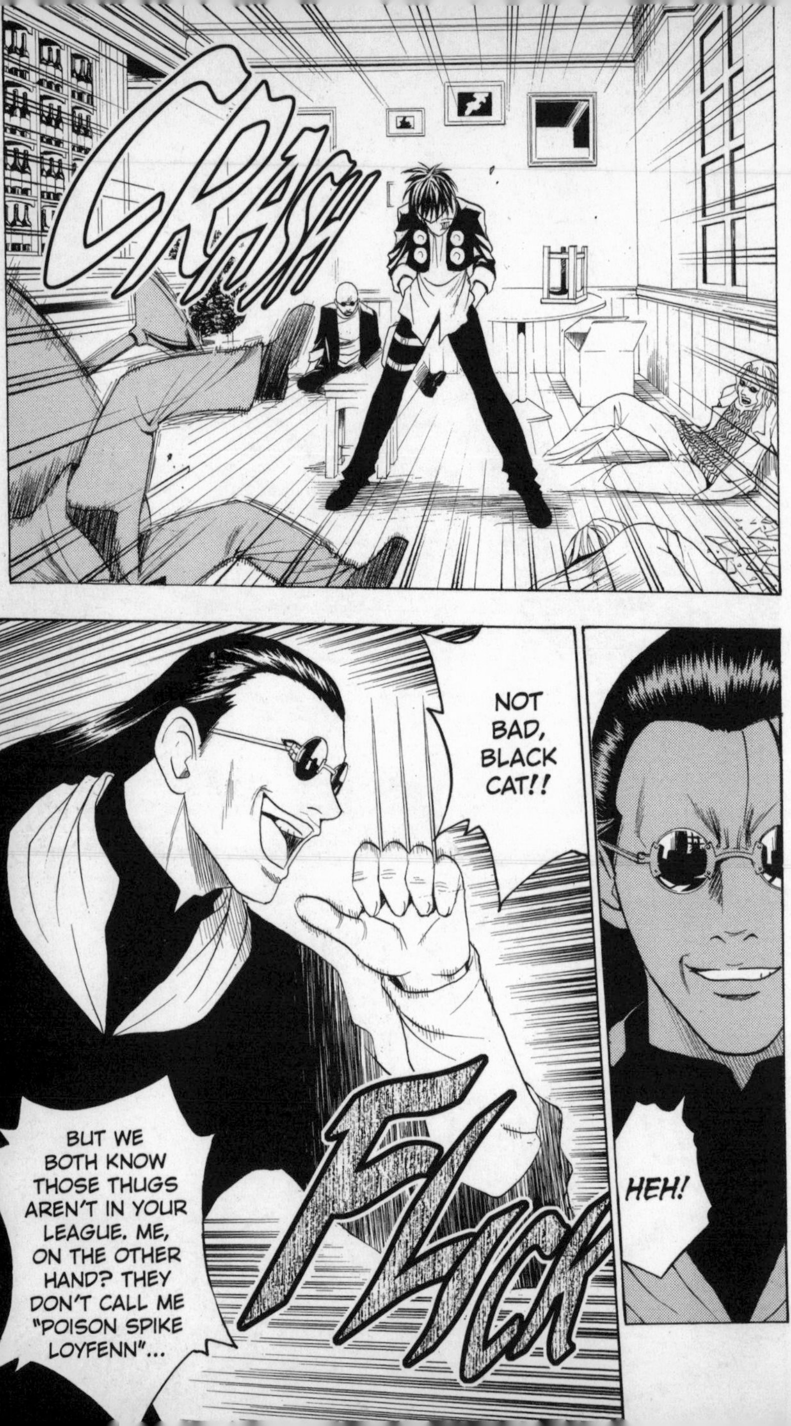
CRASH
HEH!
NOT BAD, BLACK CAT!!
BUT WE BOTH KNOW THOSE THUGS AREN'T IN YOUR LEAGUE. ME, ON THE OTHER HAND? THEY DON'T CALL ME "POISON SPIKE LOYFENN"...

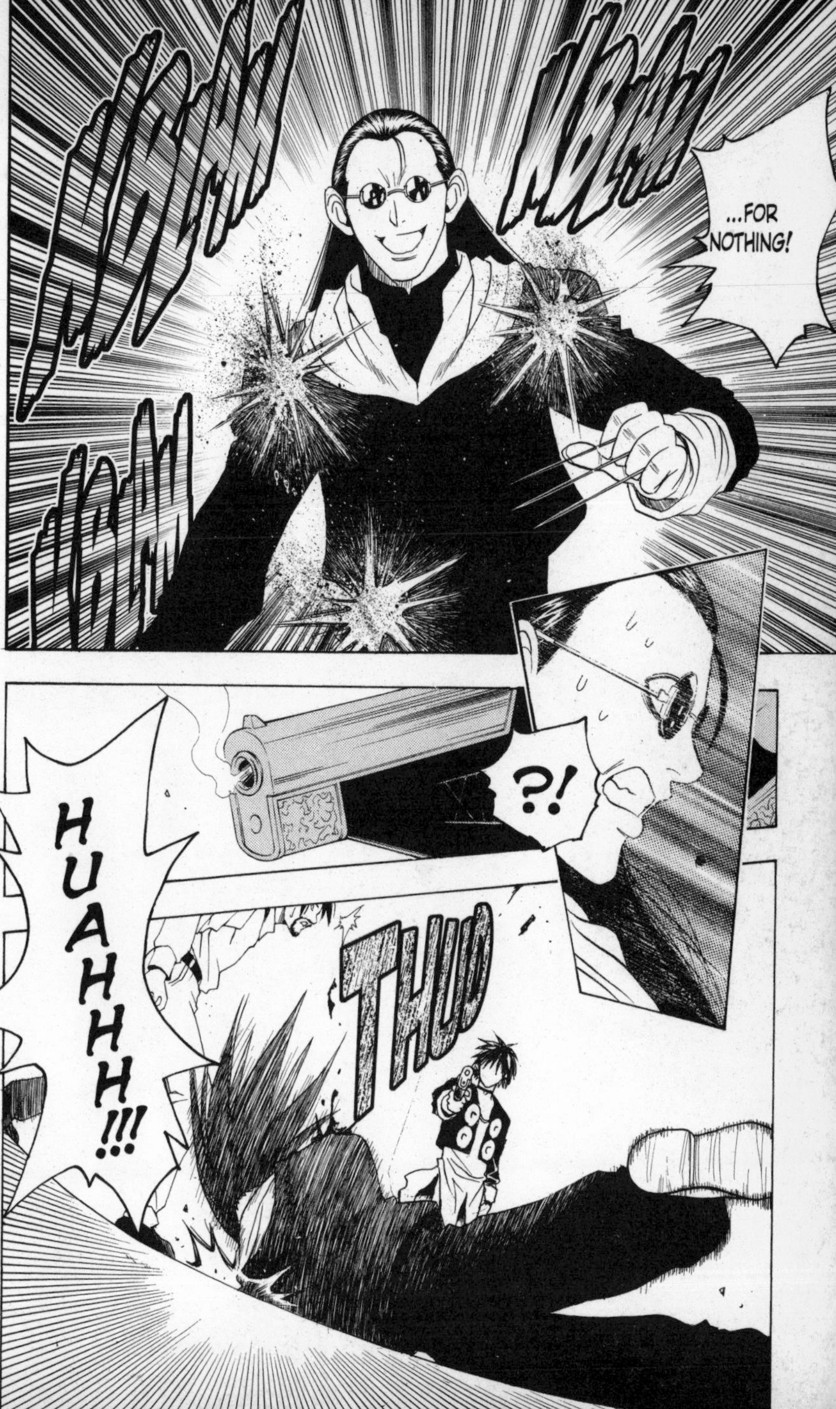

...FOR NOTHING!
?!
HUAHHH!!!
THUD

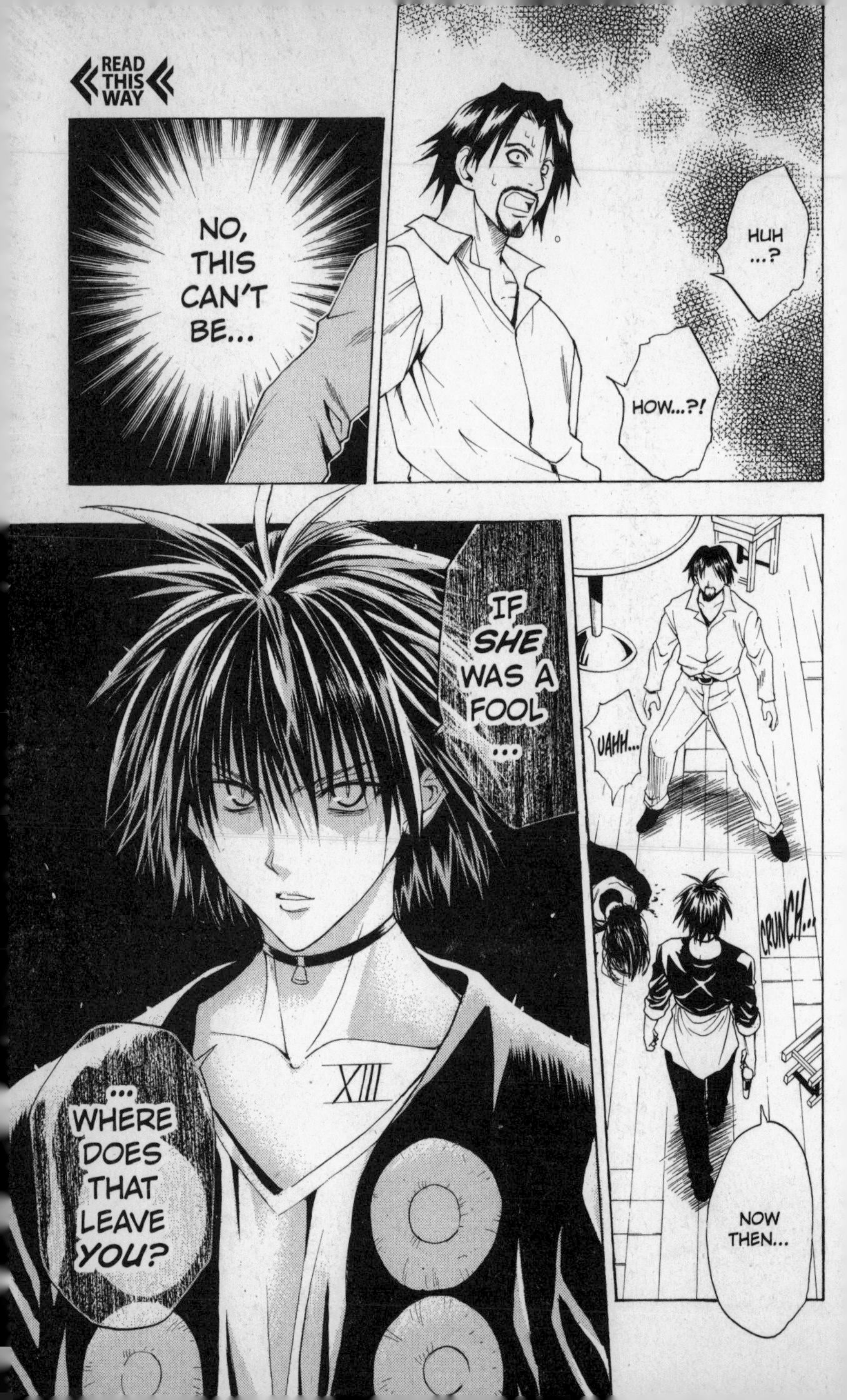
READ THIS WAY
HUH ...?
HOW...?!
NO, THIS CAN'T BE...
UAHH...
CRUNCH...
NOW THEN...
IF SHE WAS A FOOL ...
...WHERE DOES THAT LEAVE YOU?

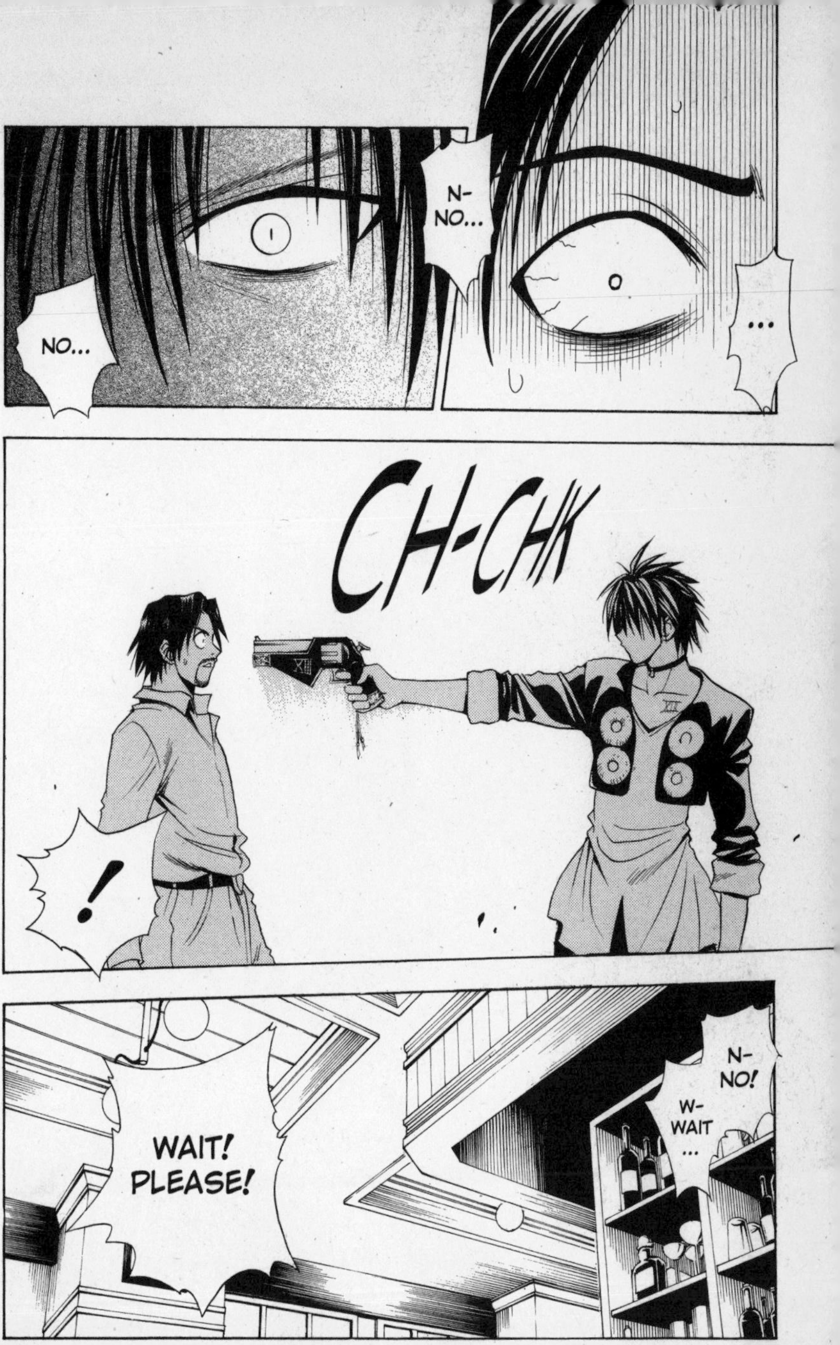

N- NO...
...
NO...
CH-CHK
!
N- NO!
W- WAIT ...
WAIT! PLEASE!

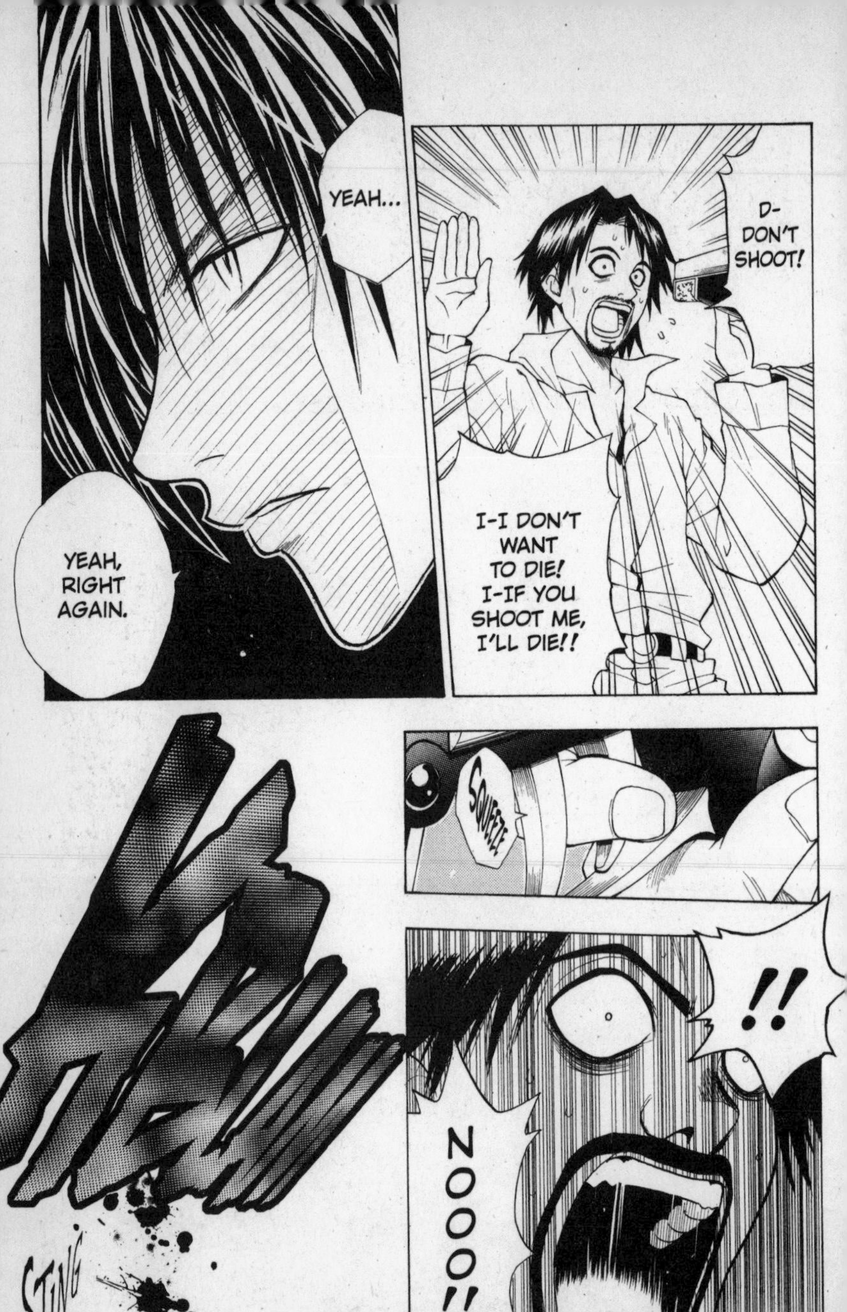
D-DON'T SHOOT!
I-I DON'T WANT TO DIE! I-IF YOU SHOOT ME, I'LL DIE!!
YEAH...
YEAH, RIGHT AGAIN.
SQUEEZE
!!
NOOOO!!
STING

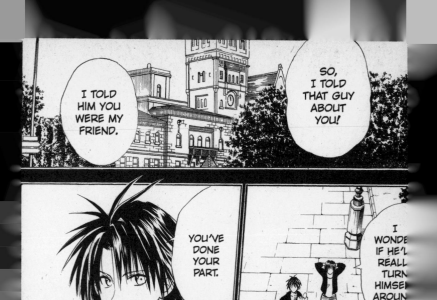

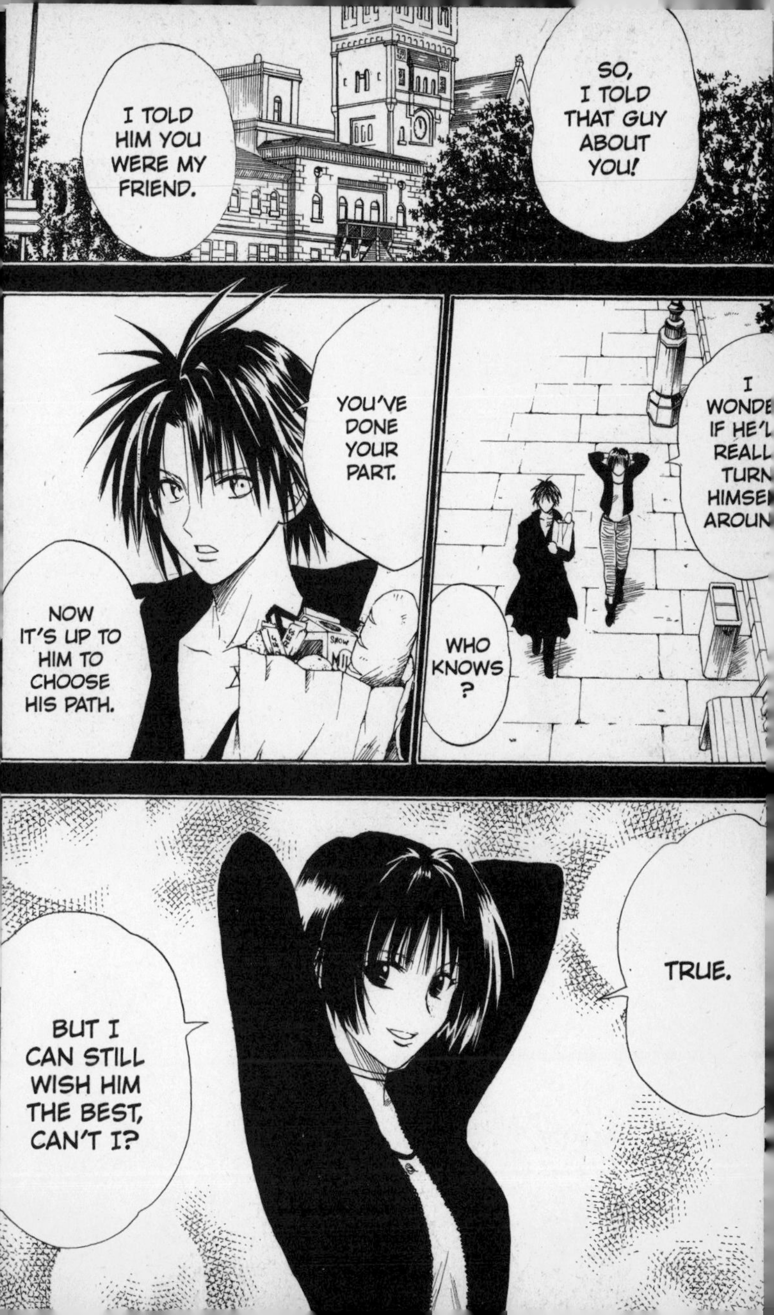
SO, I TOLD THAT GUY ABOUT YOU!
I TOLD HIM YOU WERE MY FRIEND.
I WONDE IF HE'L REALL TURN HIMSE AROUN
WHO KNOWS?
YOU'VE DONE YOUR PART.
NOW IT'S UP TO HIM TO CHOOSE HIS PATH.
TRUE.
BUT I CAN STILL WISH HIM THE BEST, CAN'T I?

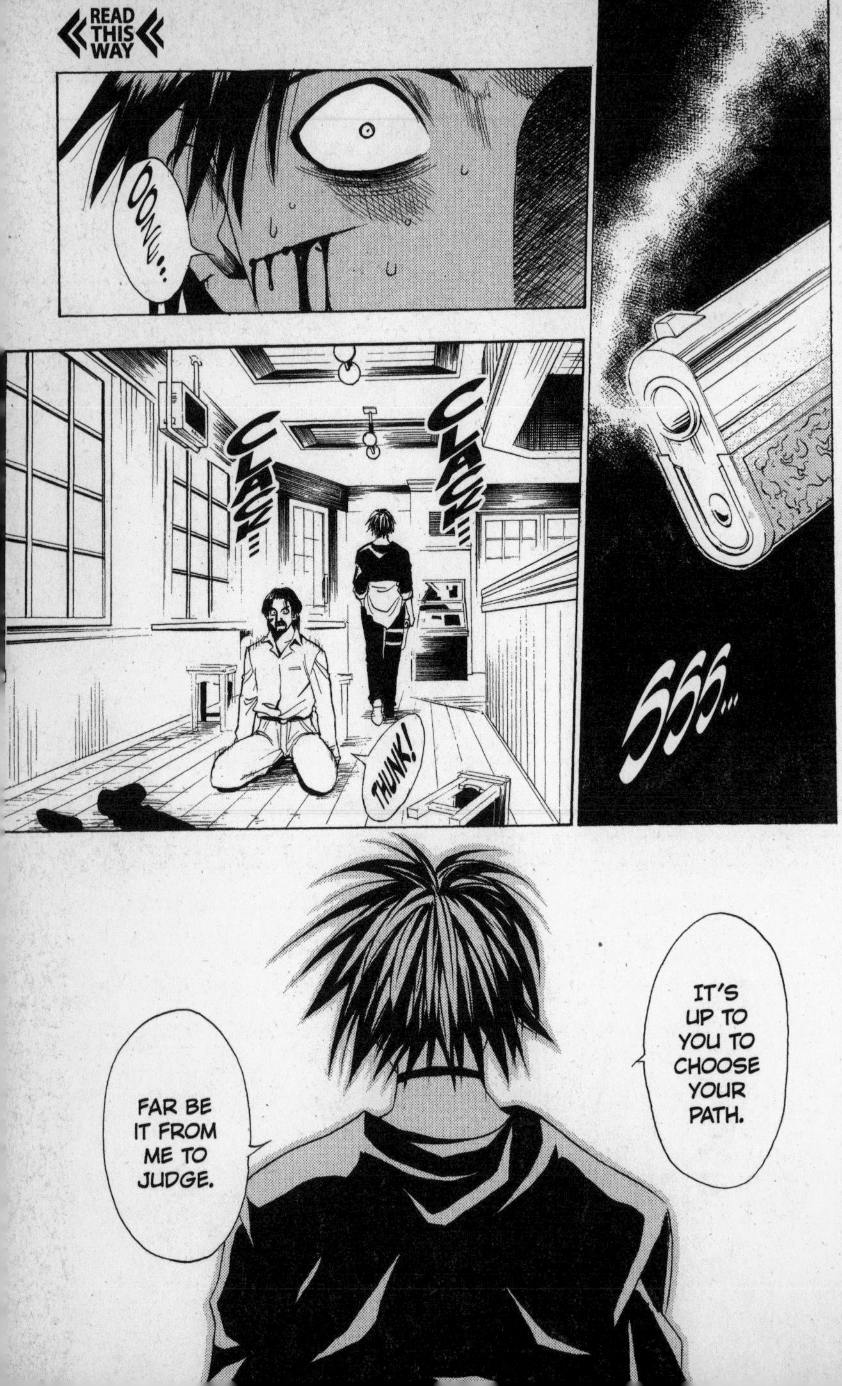
READ THIS WAY
SSS...
OONU...
CLACK...
CLACK...
THUNK!
IT'S UP TO YOU TO CHOOSE YOUR PATH.
FAR BE IT FROM ME TO JUDGE.

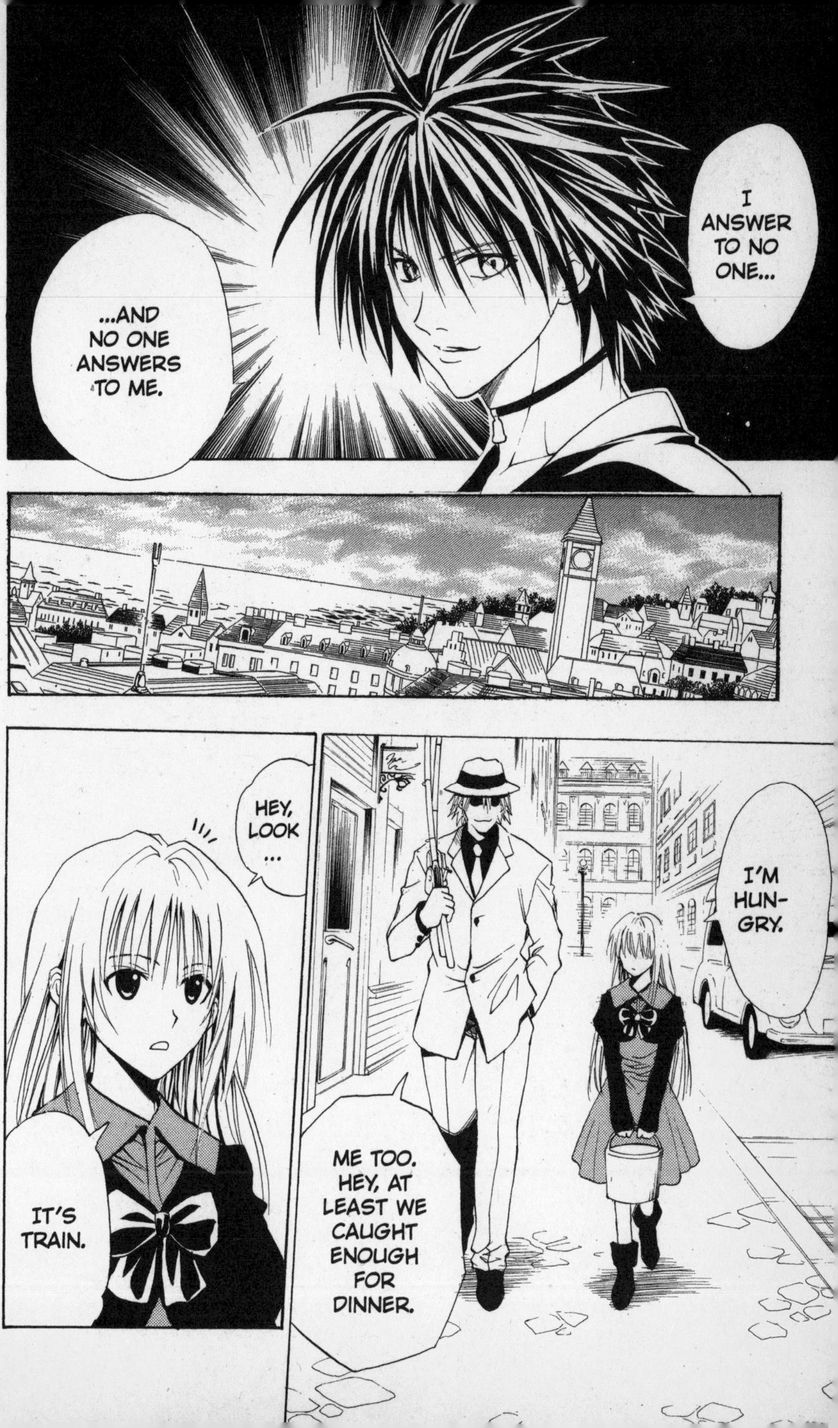
I ANSWER TO NO ONE...
...AND NO ONE ANSWERS TO ME.
I'M HUN-GRY.
ME TOO. HEY, AT LEAST WE CAUGHT ENOUGH FOR DINNER.
HEY, LOOK ...
IT'S TRAIN.

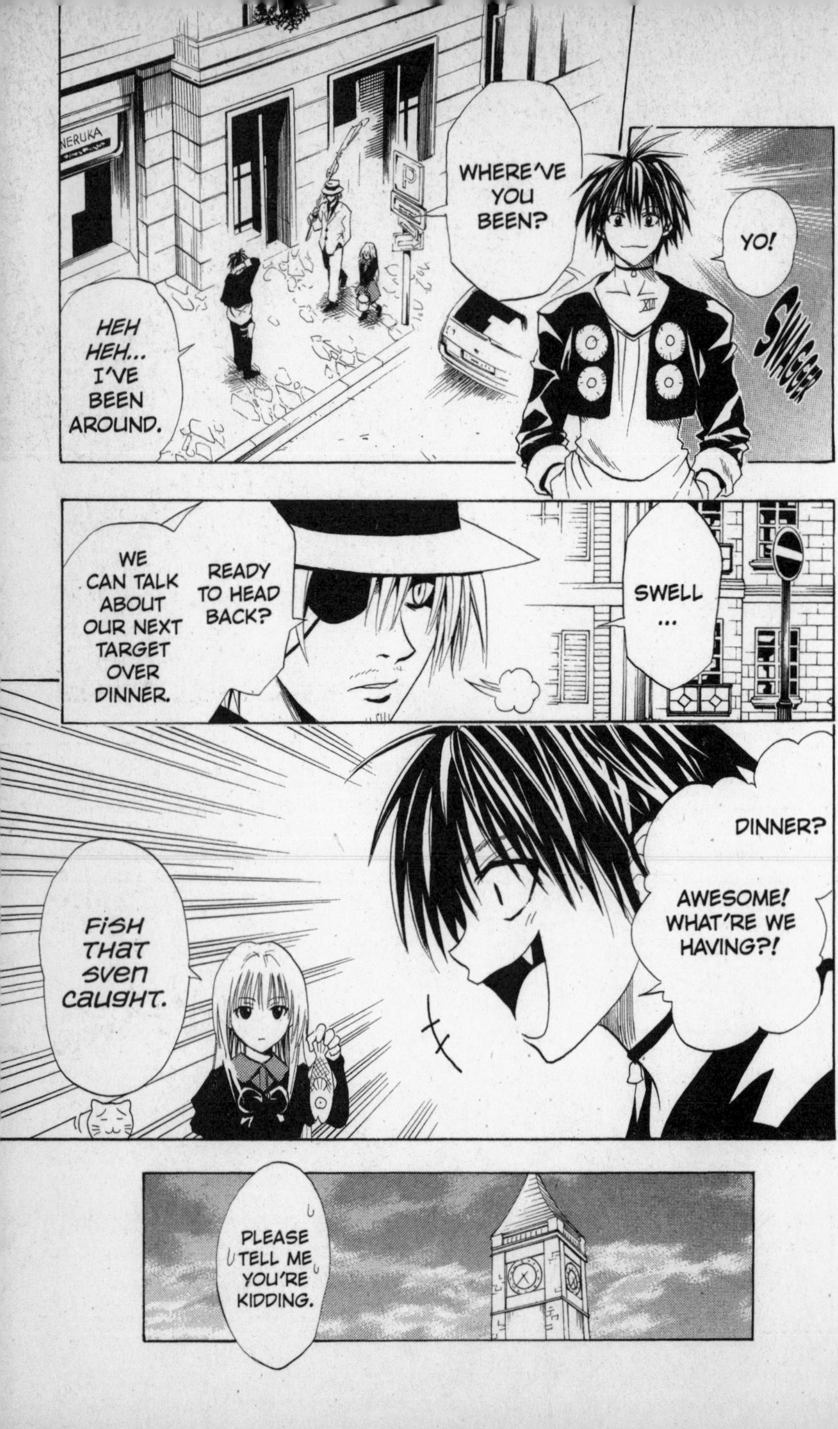
YO!
SWAGGER
WHERE'VE YOU BEEN?
NERUKA
HEH HEH... I'VE BEEN AROUND.
SWELL ...
READY TO HEAD BACK?
WE CAN TALK ABOUT OUR NEXT TARGET OVER DINNER.
DINNER?
AWESOME! WHAT'RE WE HAVING?!
FISH THAT SVEN CAUGHT.
PLEASE TELL ME YOU'RE KIDDING.

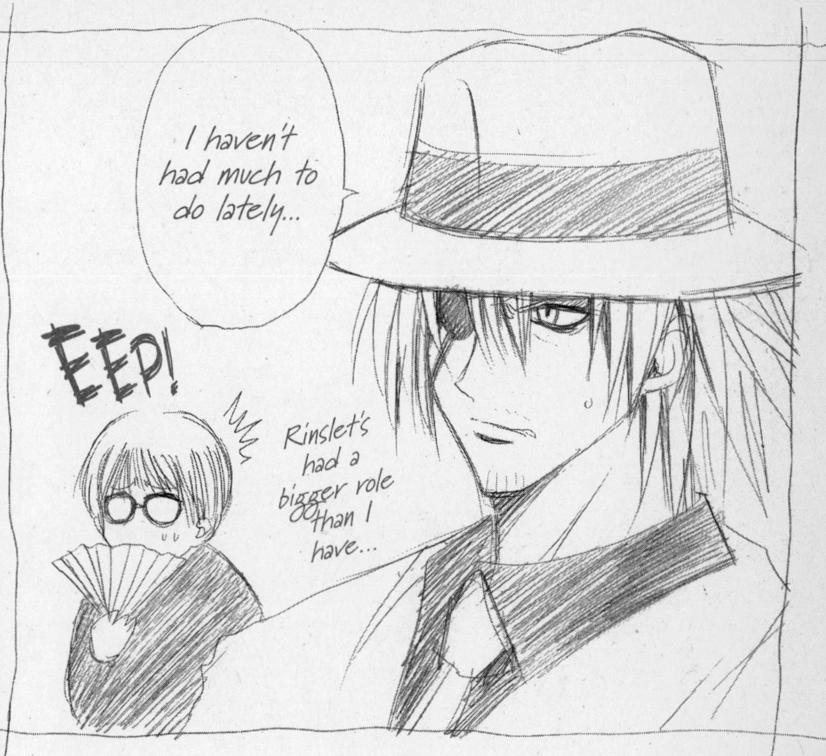
I haven't had much to do lately...
EEP!
Rinslet's had a bigger role than I have...

...He's right.

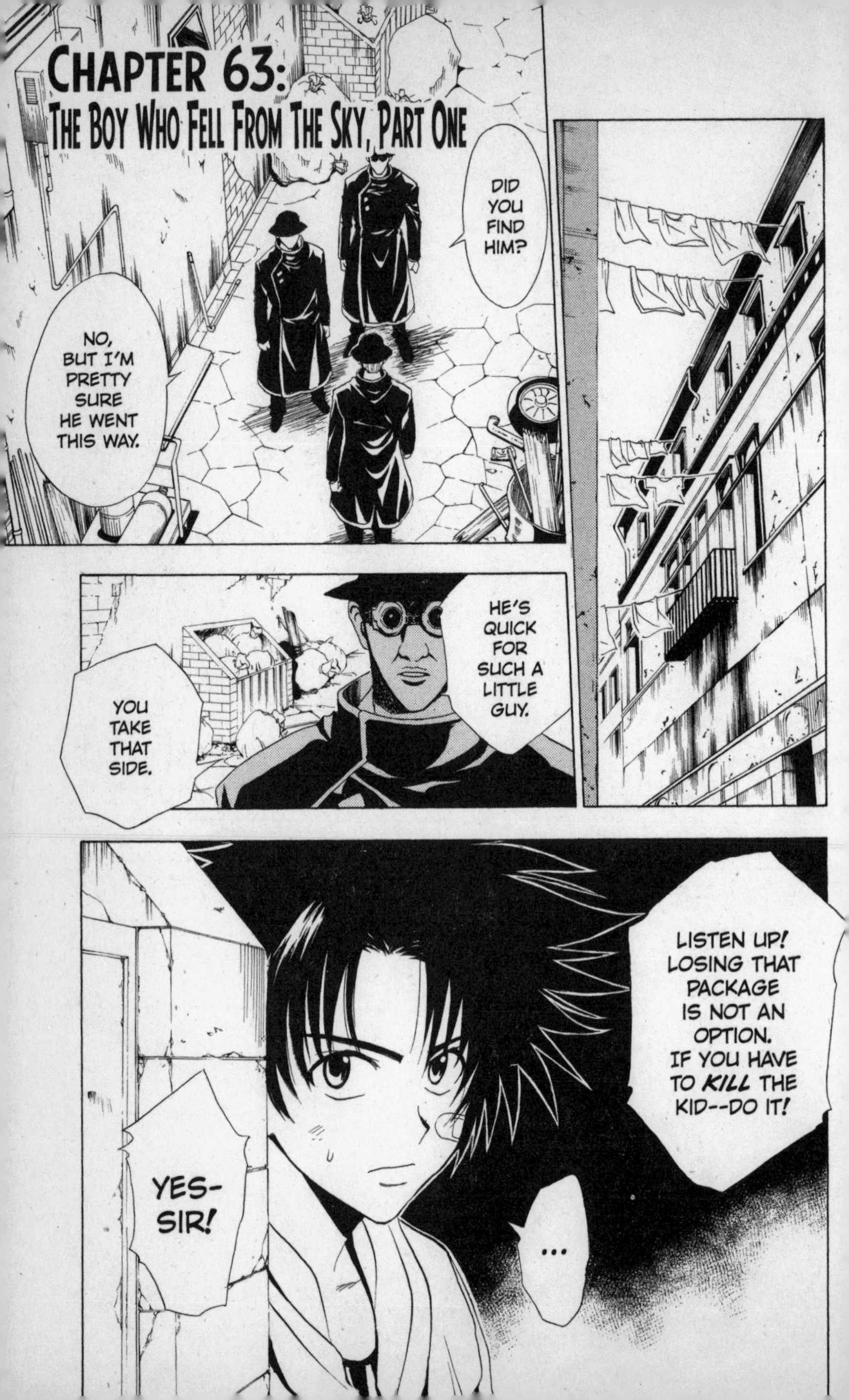
CHAPTER 63:
THE BOY WHO FELL FROM THE SKY, PART ONE
DID YOU FIND HIM?
NO, BUT I'M PRETTY SURE HE WENT THIS WAY.
HE'S QUICK FOR SUCH A LITTLE GUY.
YOU TAKE THAT SIDE.
LISTEN UP! LOSING THAT PACKAGE IS NOT AN OPTION. IF YOU HAVE TO *KILL* THE KID--DO IT!
YES-SIR!
...

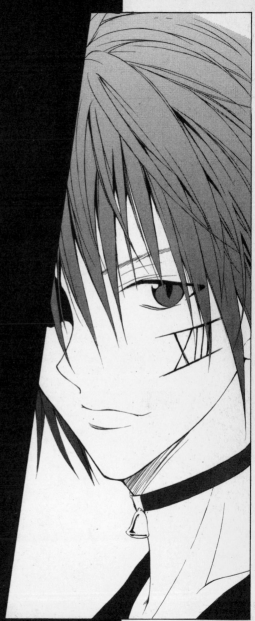

CHAPTER 63: THE BOY WHO FELL FROM THE SKY, PART ONE

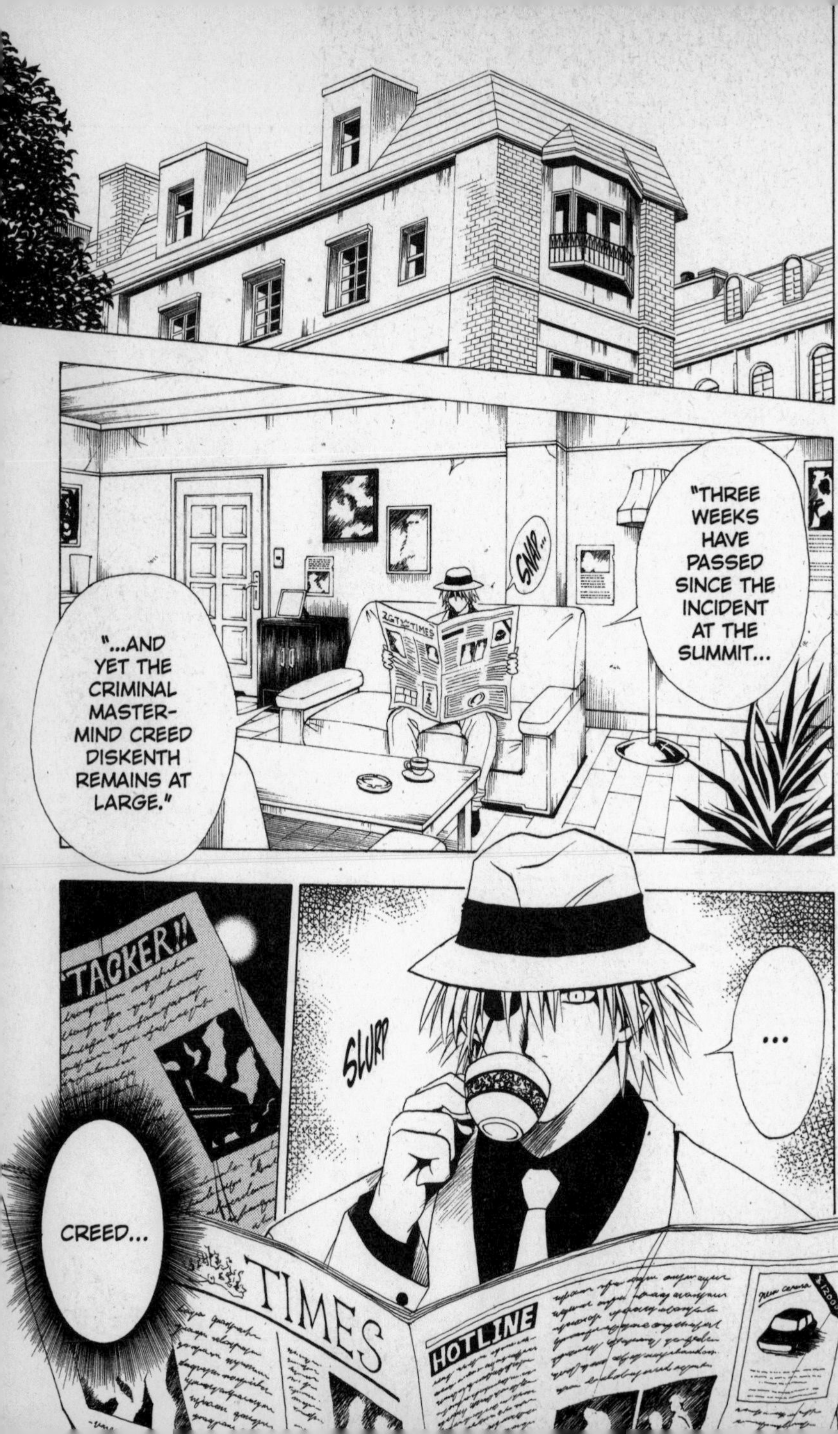
"THREE WEEKS HAVE PASSED SINCE THE INCIDENT AT THE SUMMIT...
SNAP...
"...AND YET THE CRIMINAL MASTER-MIND CREED DISKENTH REMAINS AT LARGE."
...
SLURP
TIMES
HOTLINE
TACKER!!
CREED...

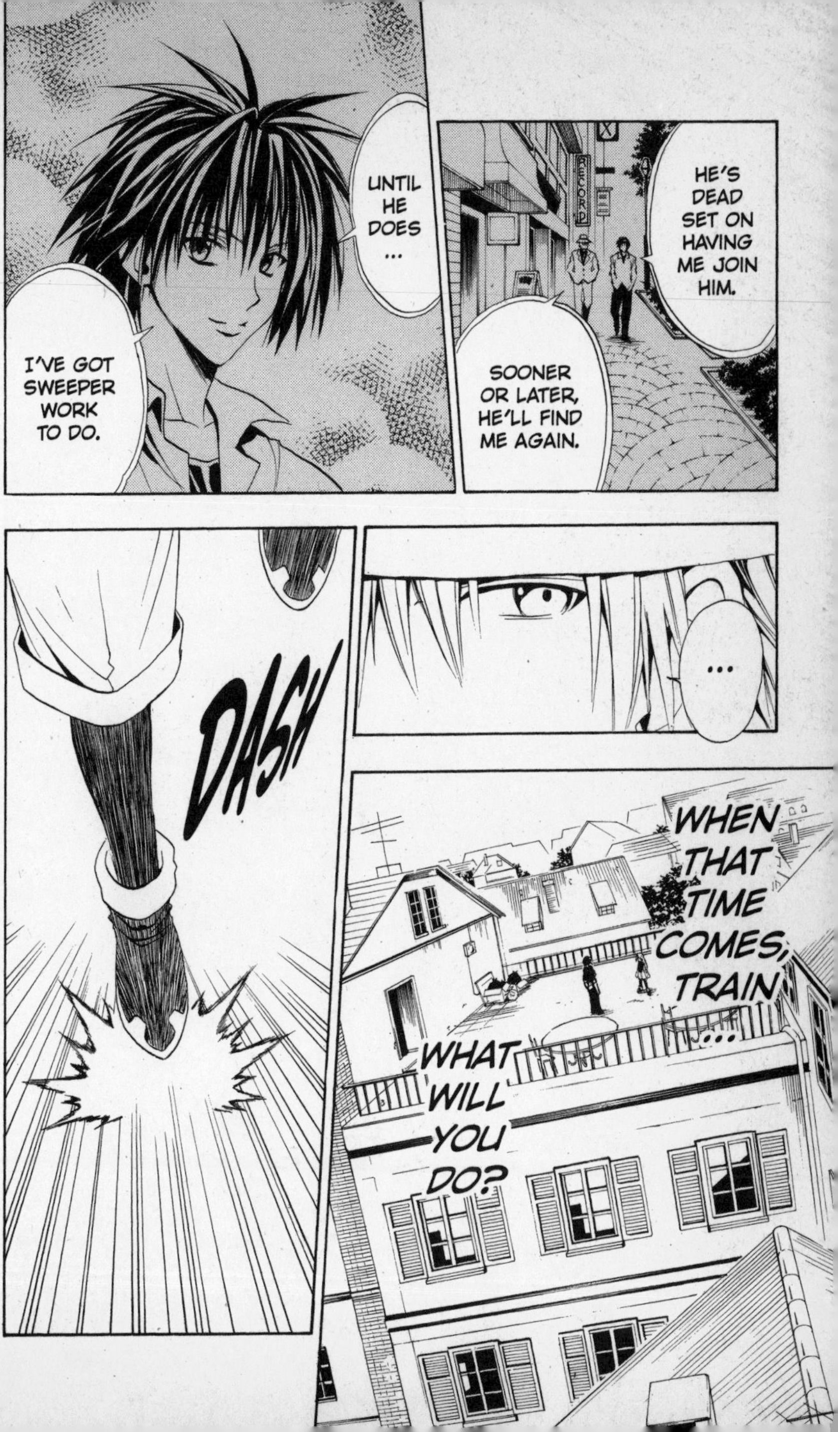
HE'S DEAD SET ON HAVING ME JOIN HIM.
SOONER OR LATER, HE'LL FIND ME AGAIN.
UNTIL HE DOES...
I'VE GOT SWEEPER WORK TO DO.
...
WHEN THAT TIME COMES, TRAIN...
WHAT WILL YOU DO?
DASH

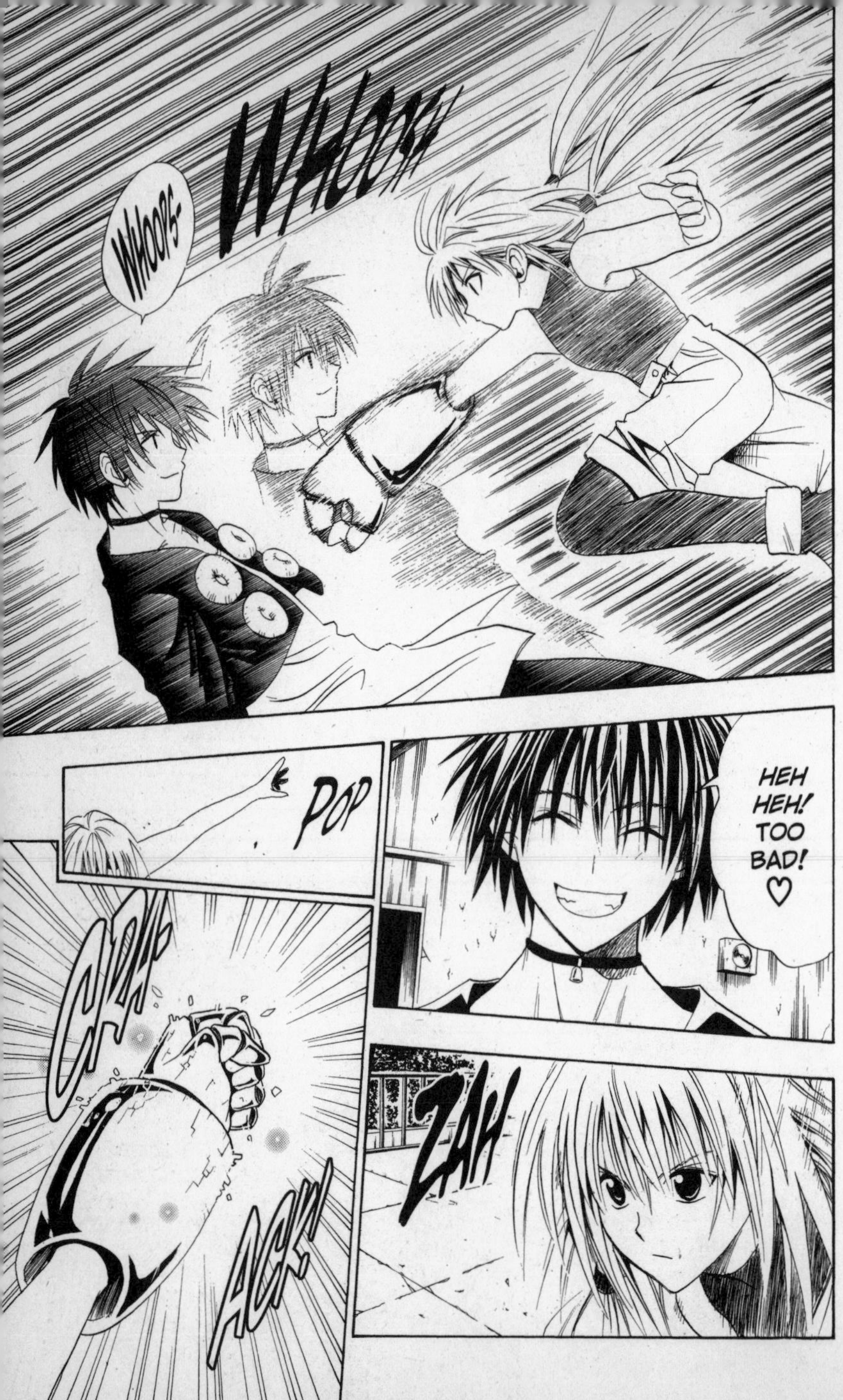
WHOOPS-
WHOOSH
HEH HEH! TOO BAD! ♥
POP
ZAH
ACK!

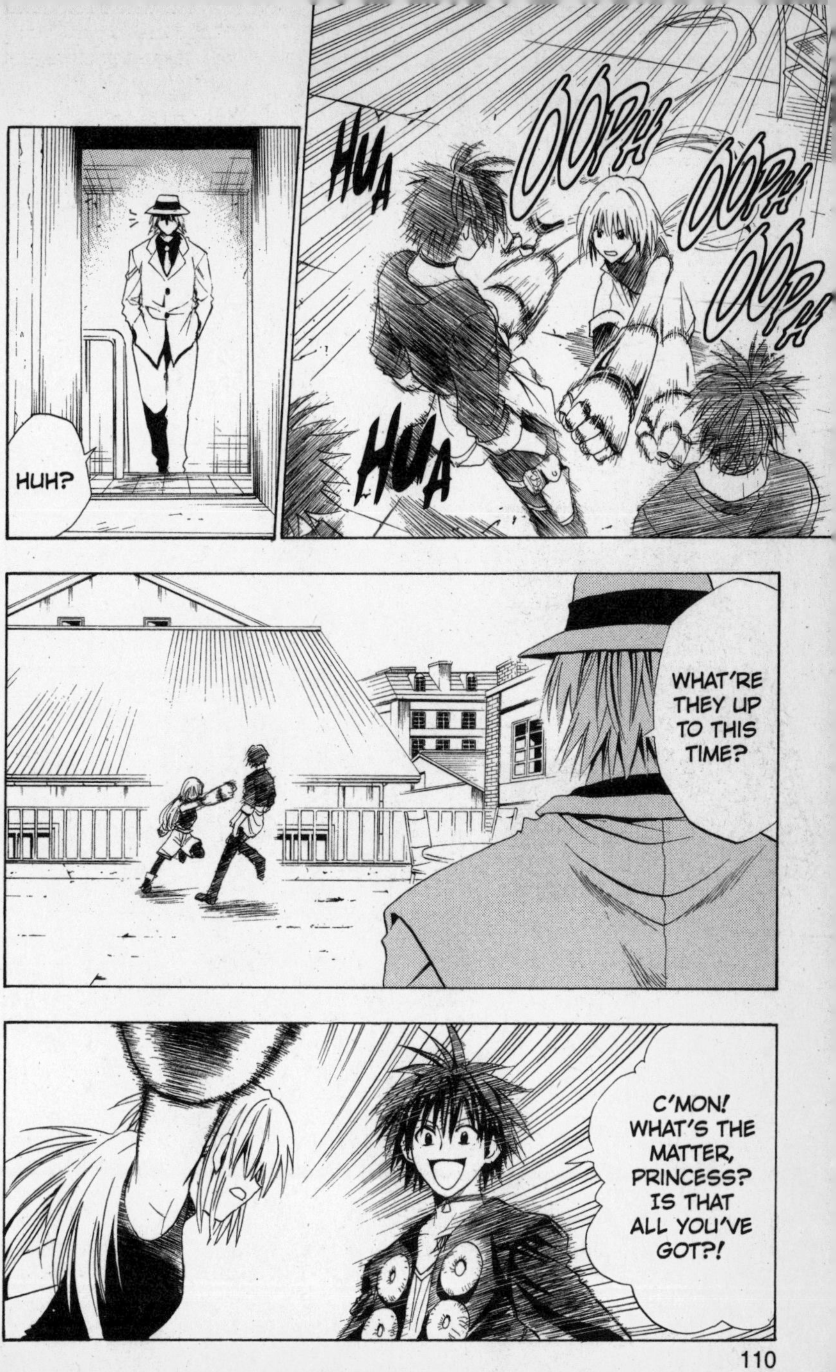
OOPAH
OOPAH
OOPAH
OOPAH
HUA
HUA
HUH?
WHAT'RE THEY UP TO THIS TIME?
C'MON! WHAT'S THE MATTER, PRINCESS? IS THAT ALL YOU'VE GOT?!

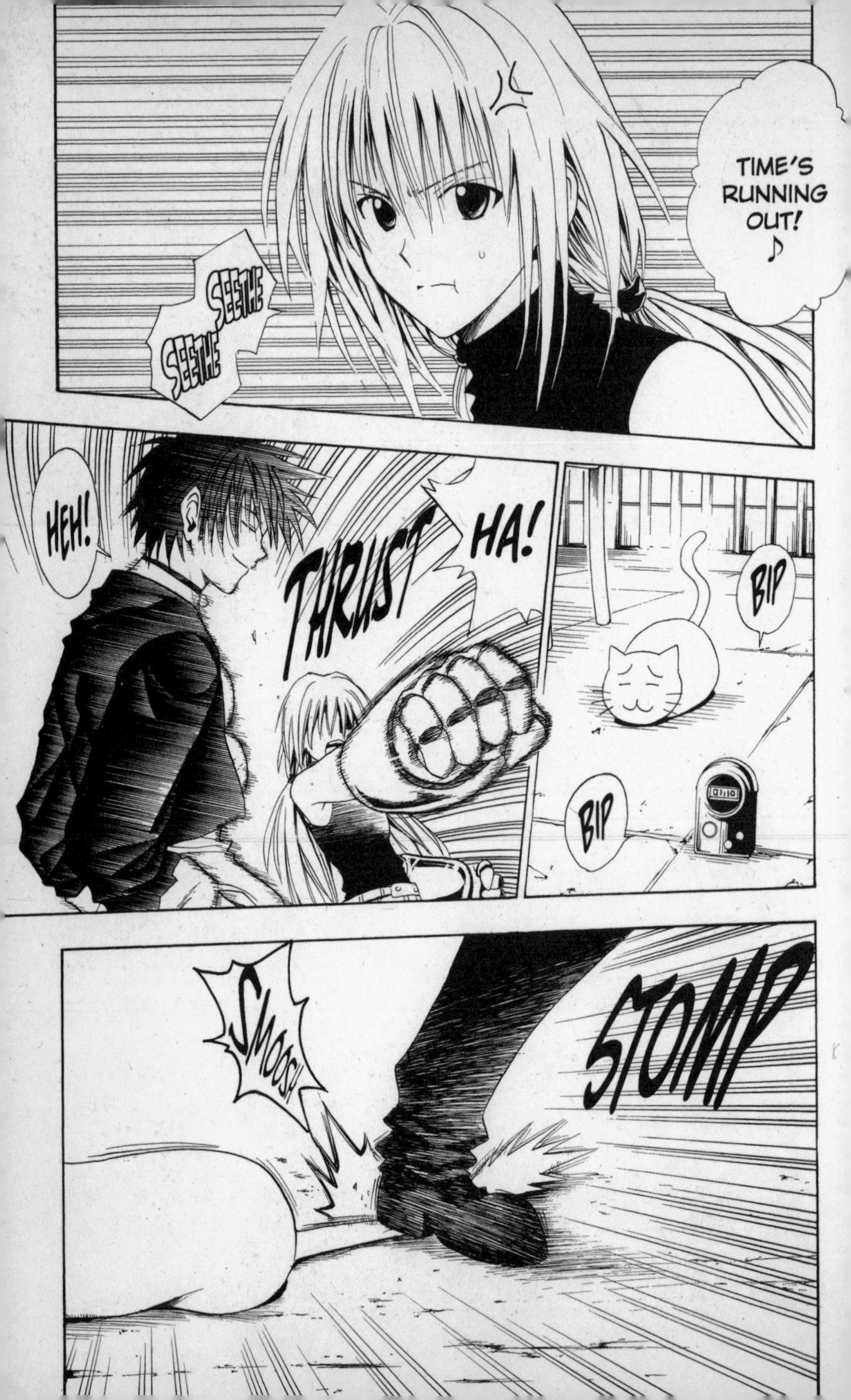
TIME'S RUNNING OUT! ♪
SEETHE SEETHE
BIP
BIP
HA!
THRUST
HEH!
STOMP
SMOOSH

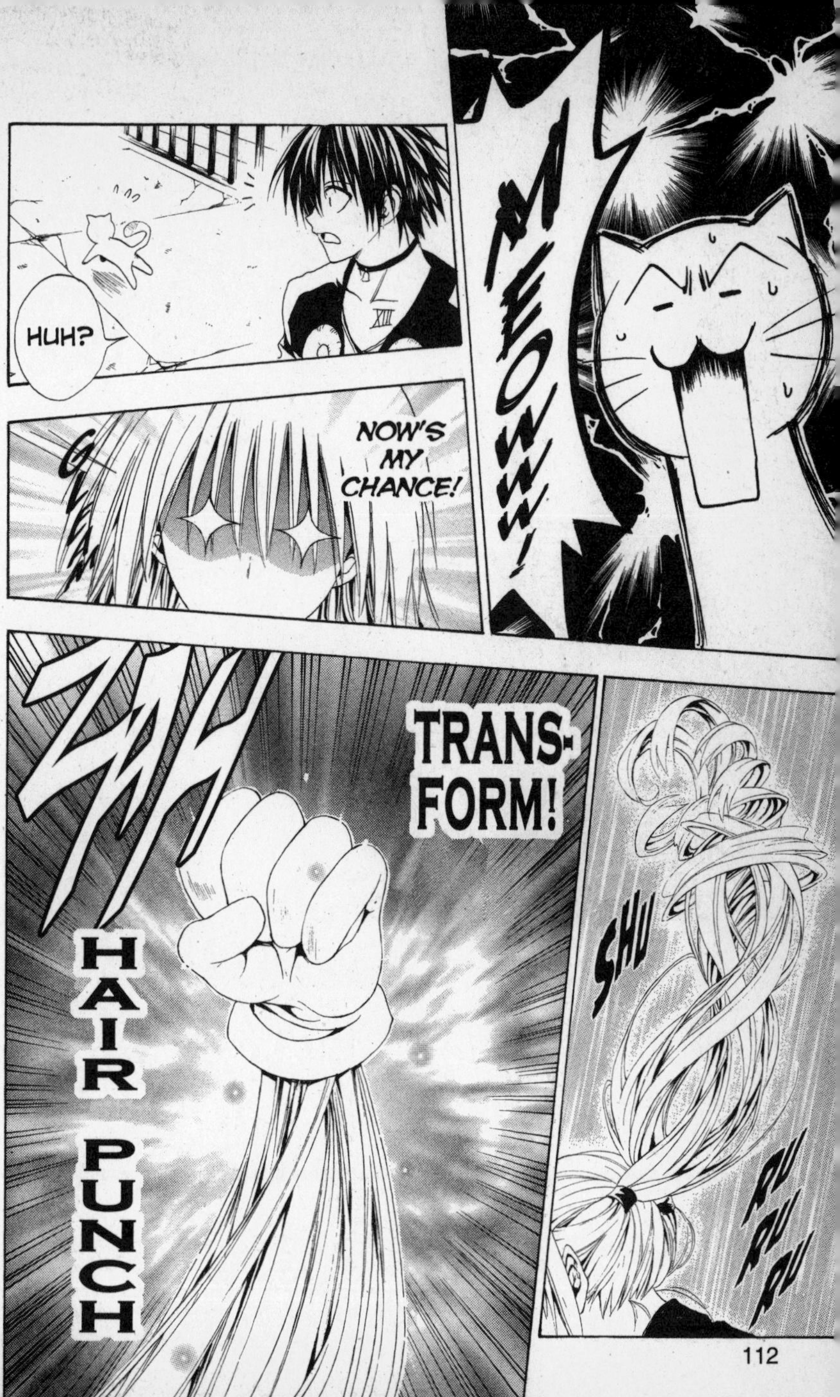
MEOWWWW!
HUH?
NOW'S MY CHANCE!
SHU
TRANS-FORM!
HAIR PUNCH

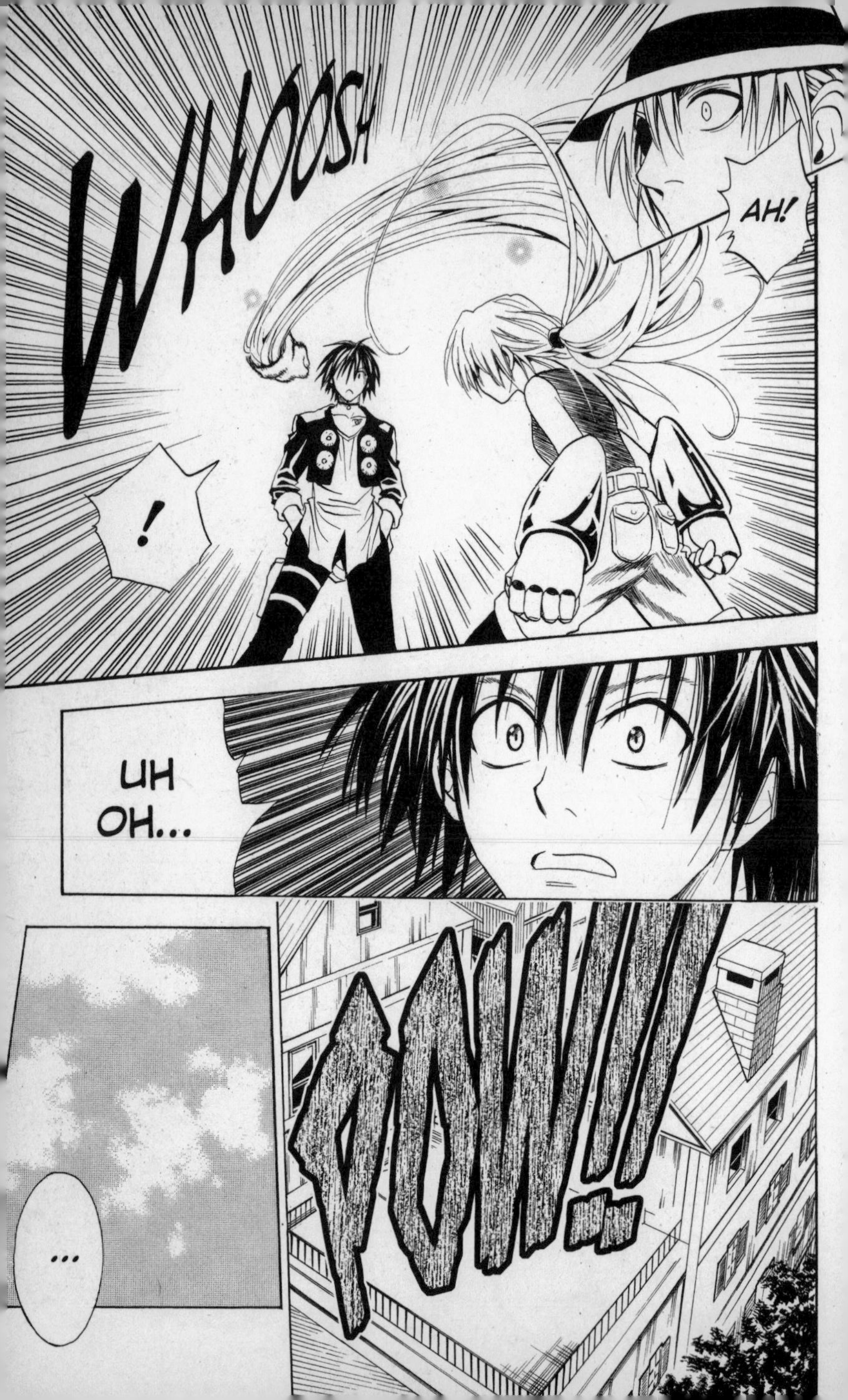
AH!
WHOOSH
!
UH OH...
POW!!
...

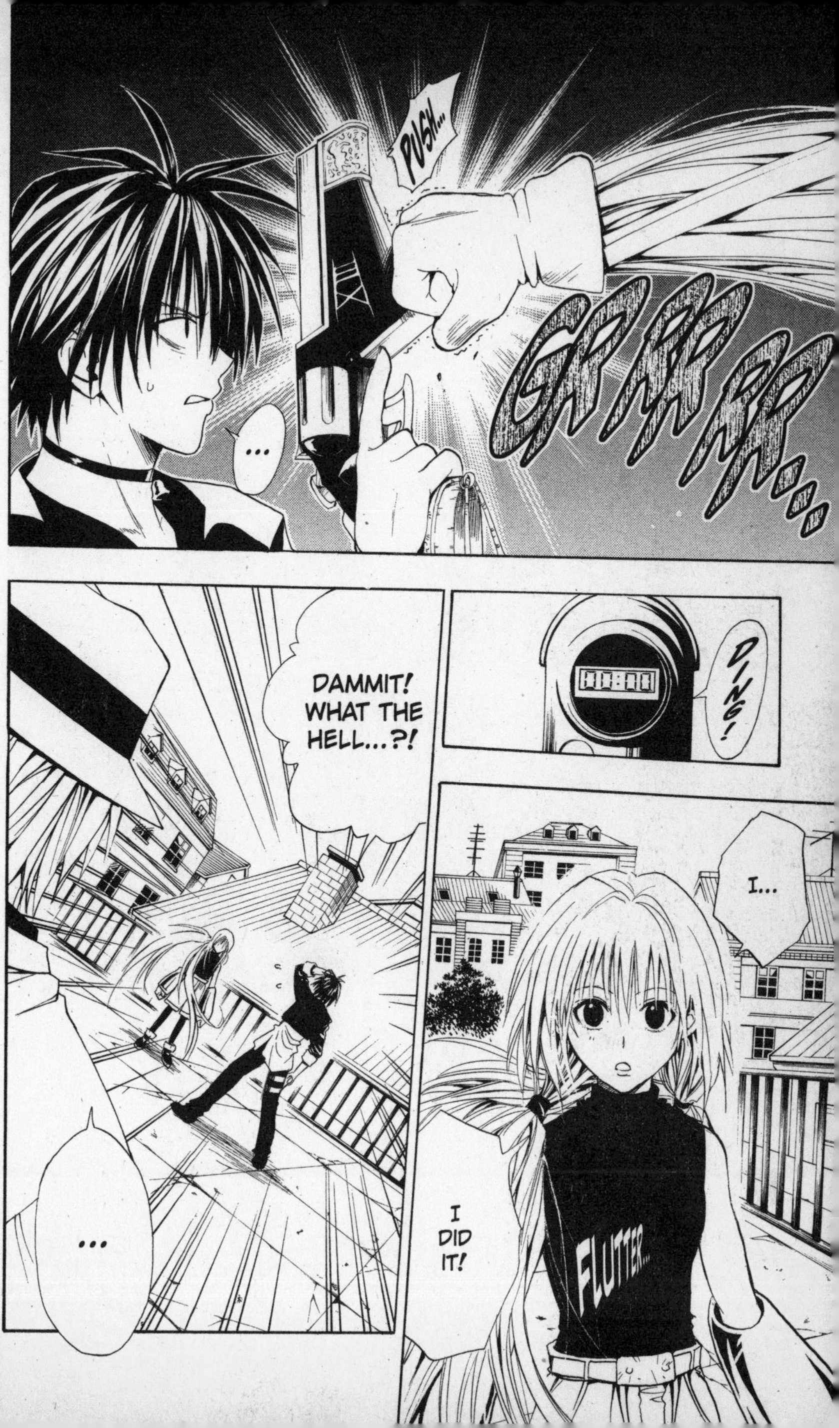
PUSH...
GRRRRR...
...
DING!
I...
I DID IT!
FLUTTER...
DAMMIT! WHAT THE HELL...?!
...

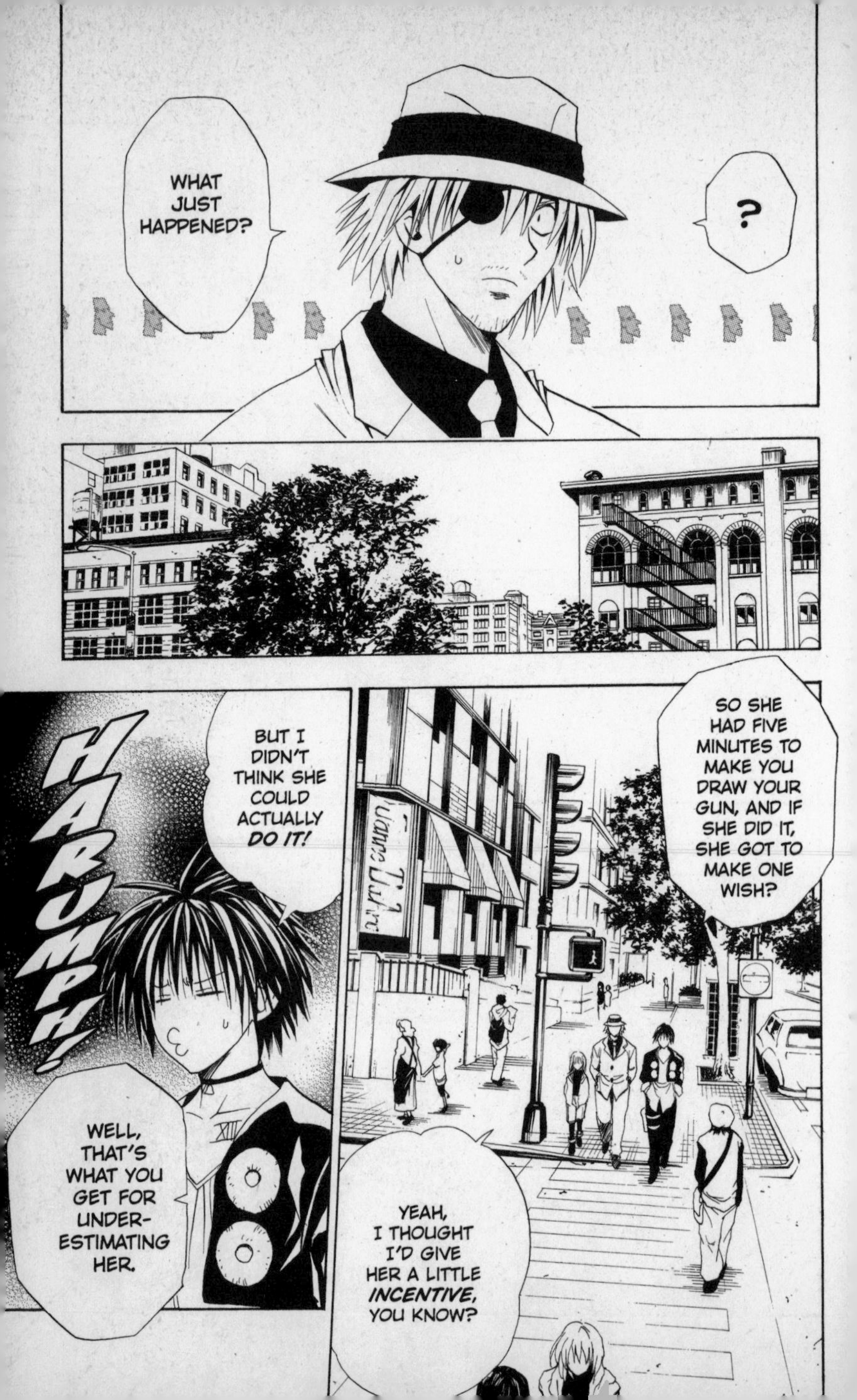
?
WHAT JUST HAPPENED?
SO SHE HAD FIVE MINUTES TO MAKE YOU DRAW YOUR GUN, AND IF SHE DID IT, SHE GOT TO MAKE ONE WISH?
YEAH, I THOUGHT I'D GIVE HER A LITTLE *INCENTIVE,* YOU KNOW?
BUT I DIDN'T THINK SHE COULD ACTUALLY *DO IT!*
HARUMPH!
WELL, THAT'S WHAT YOU GET FOR UNDER-ESTIMATING HER.

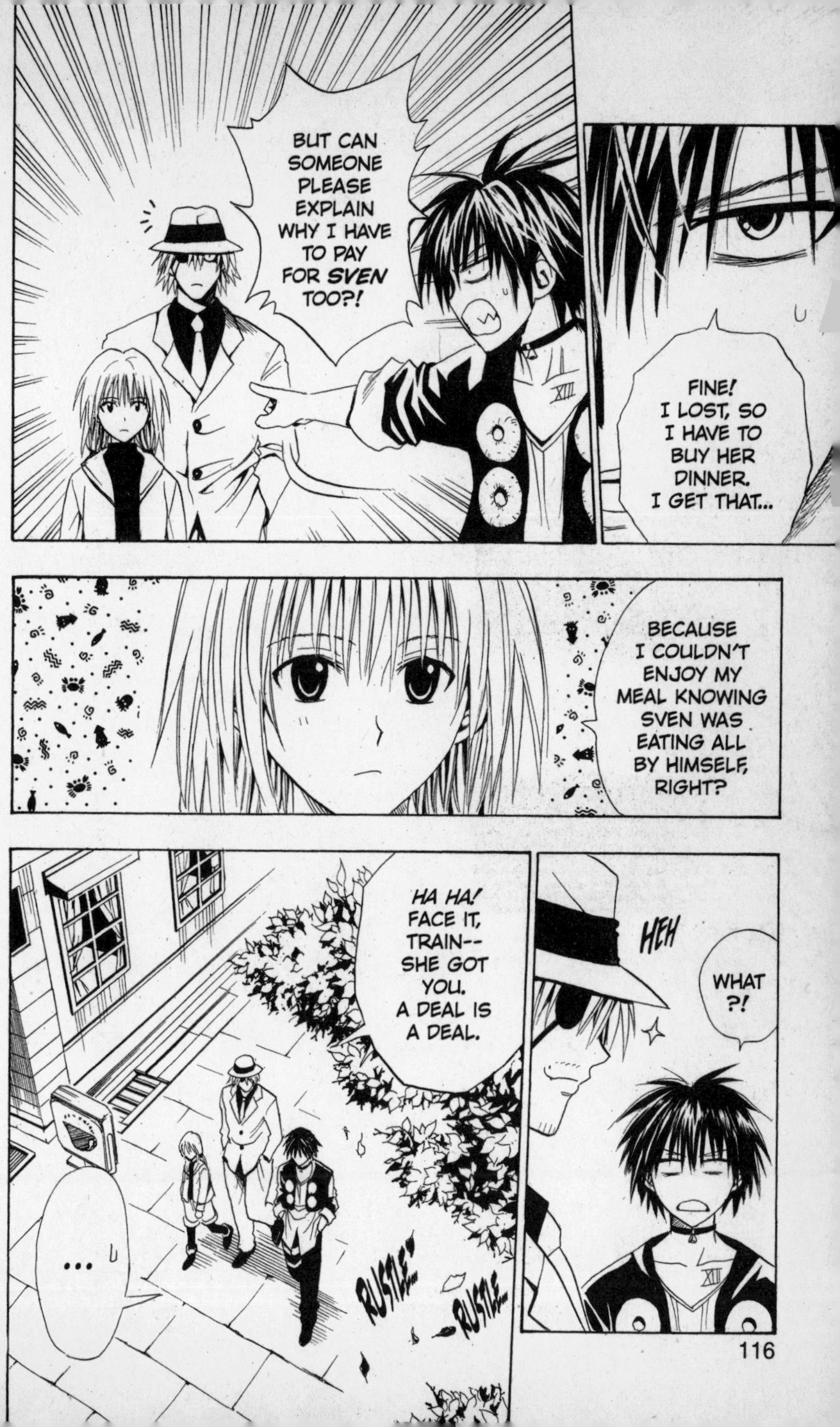
FINE! I LOST, SO I HAVE TO BUY HER DINNER. I GET THAT...
BUT CAN SOMEONE PLEASE EXPLAIN WHY I HAVE TO PAY FOR *SVEN* TOO?!
BECAUSE I COULDN'T ENJOY MY MEAL KNOWING SVEN WAS EATING ALL BY HIMSELF, RIGHT?
HEH
WHAT ?!
HA HA! FACE IT, TRAIN-- SHE GOT YOU. A DEAL IS A DEAL.
RUSTLE...
RUSTLE...
...

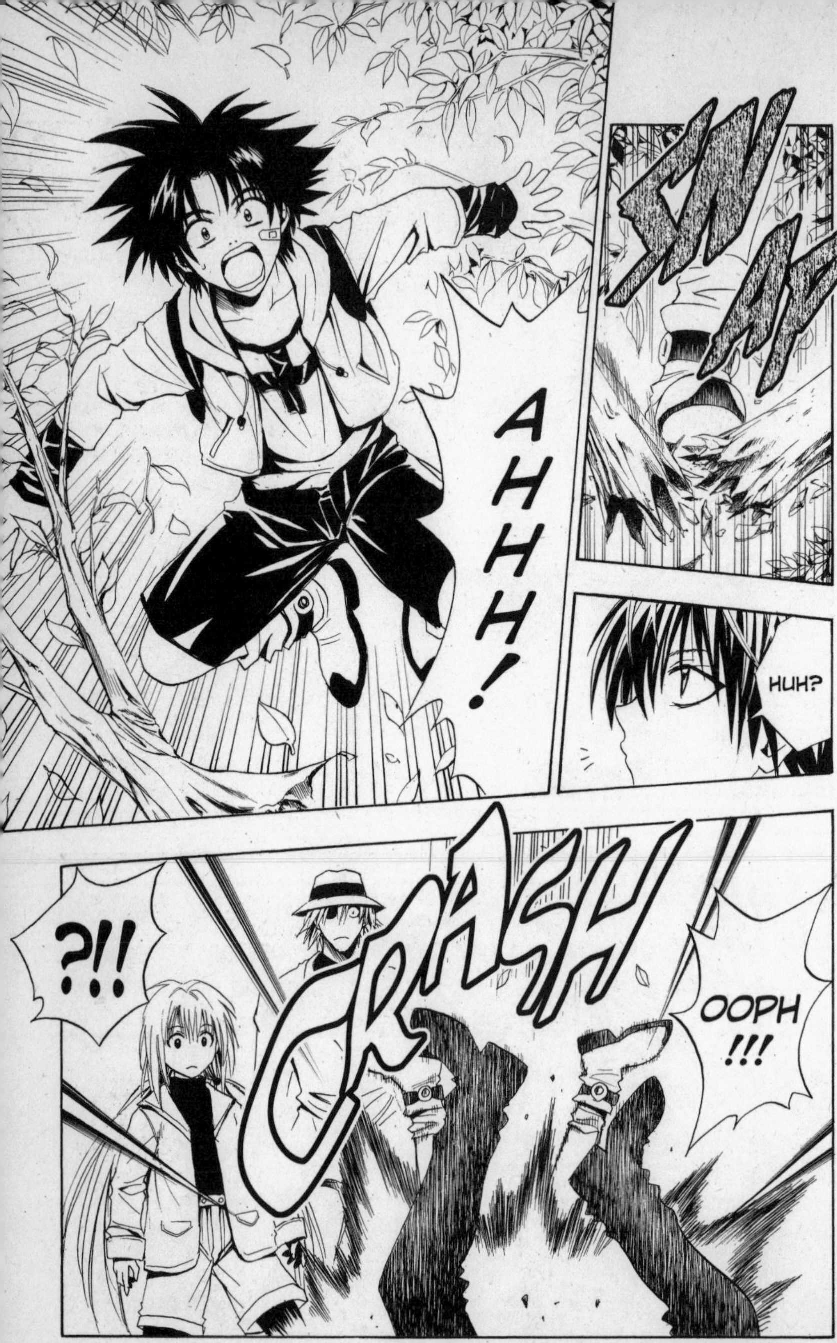
SNAP
HUH?
AHHHH!
OOPH !!!
CRASH
?!!

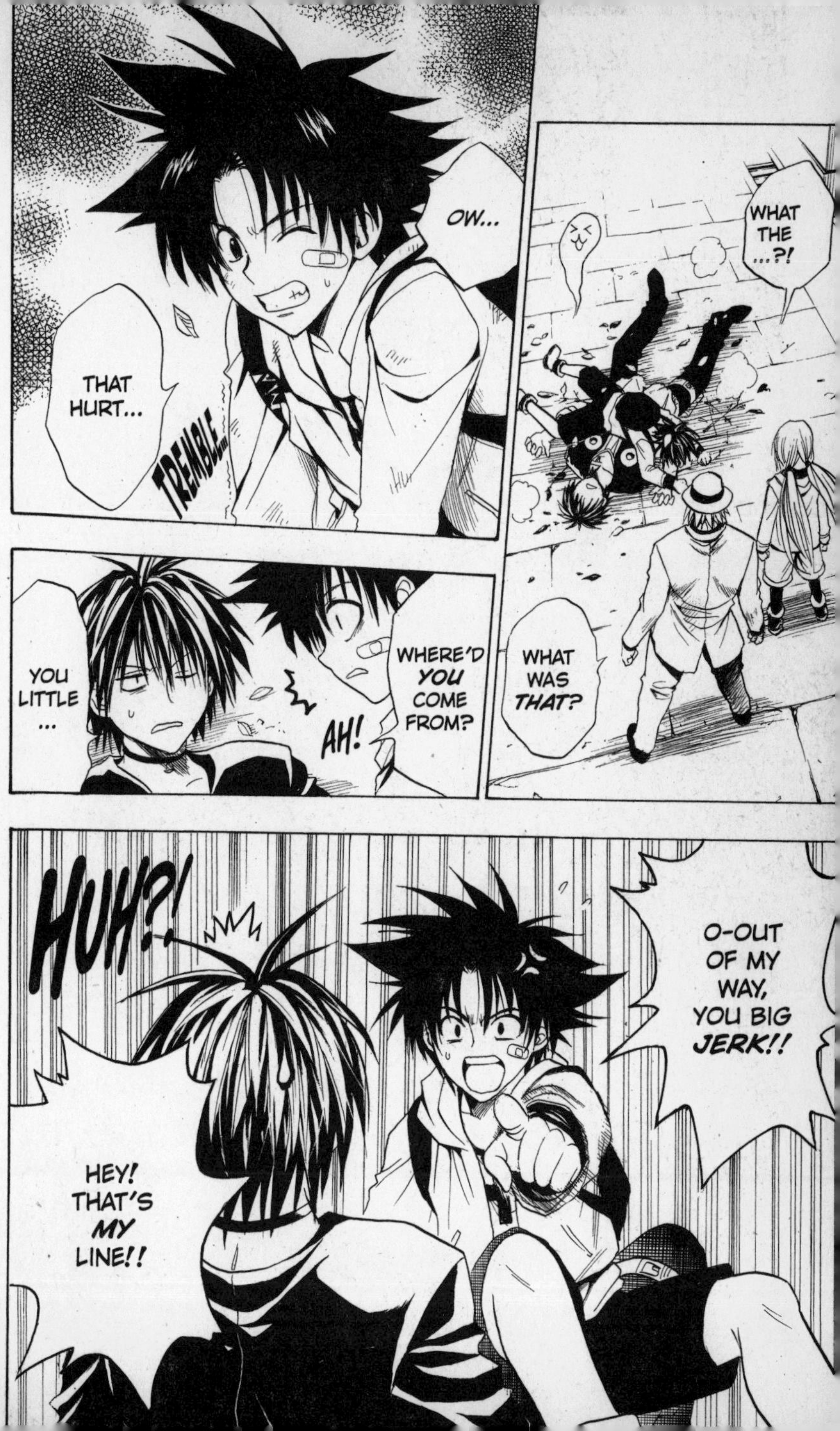
WHAT THE ...?!
WHAT WAS THAT?
OW...
THAT HURT...
TREMBLE...
WHERE'D YOU COME FROM?
AH!
YOU LITTLE ...
O-OUT OF MY WAY, YOU BIG JERK!!
HUH?!
HEY! THAT'S MY LINE!!

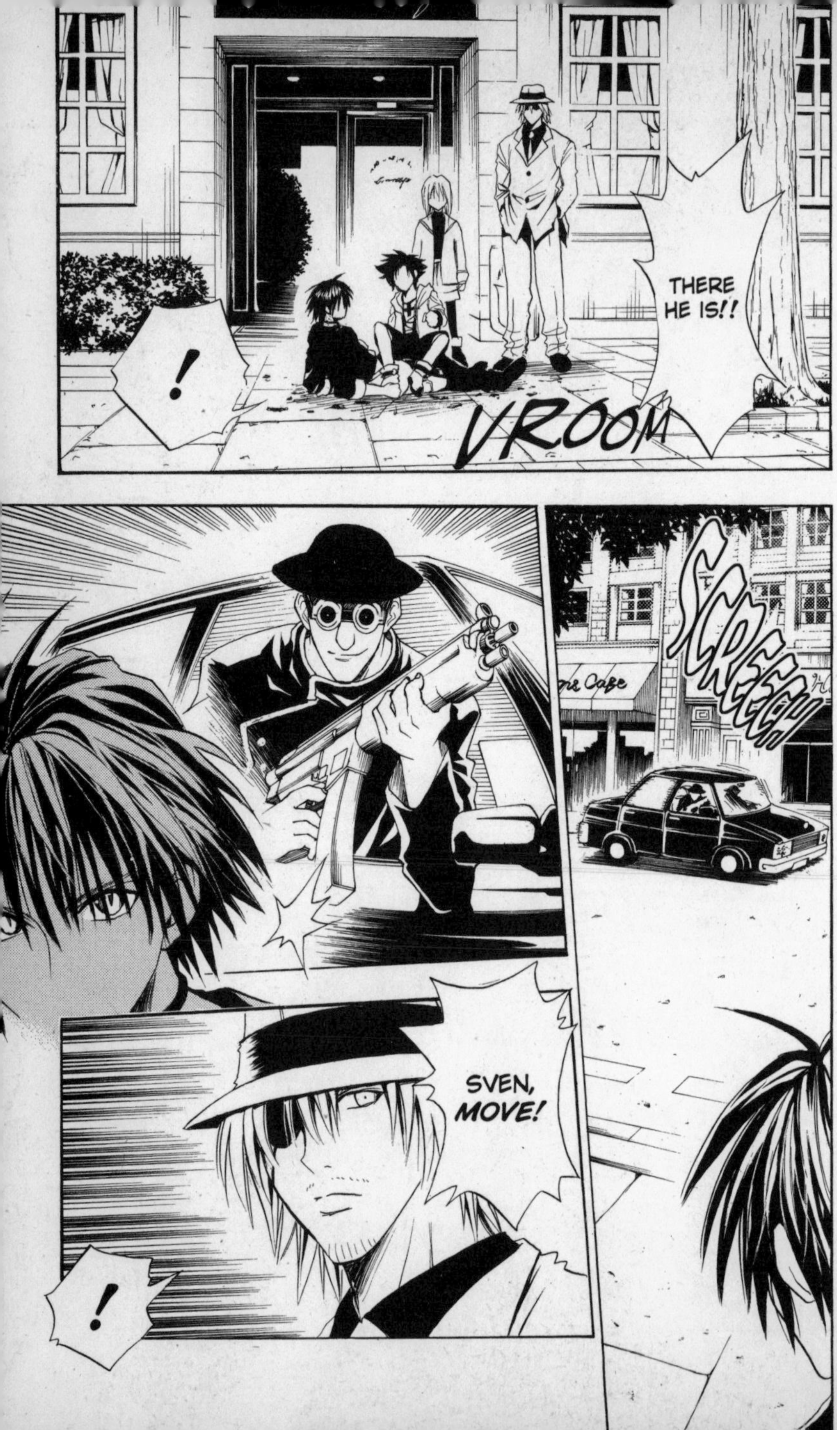
THERE HE IS!!
VROOM
!
SCREECH
SVEN, MOVE!
!

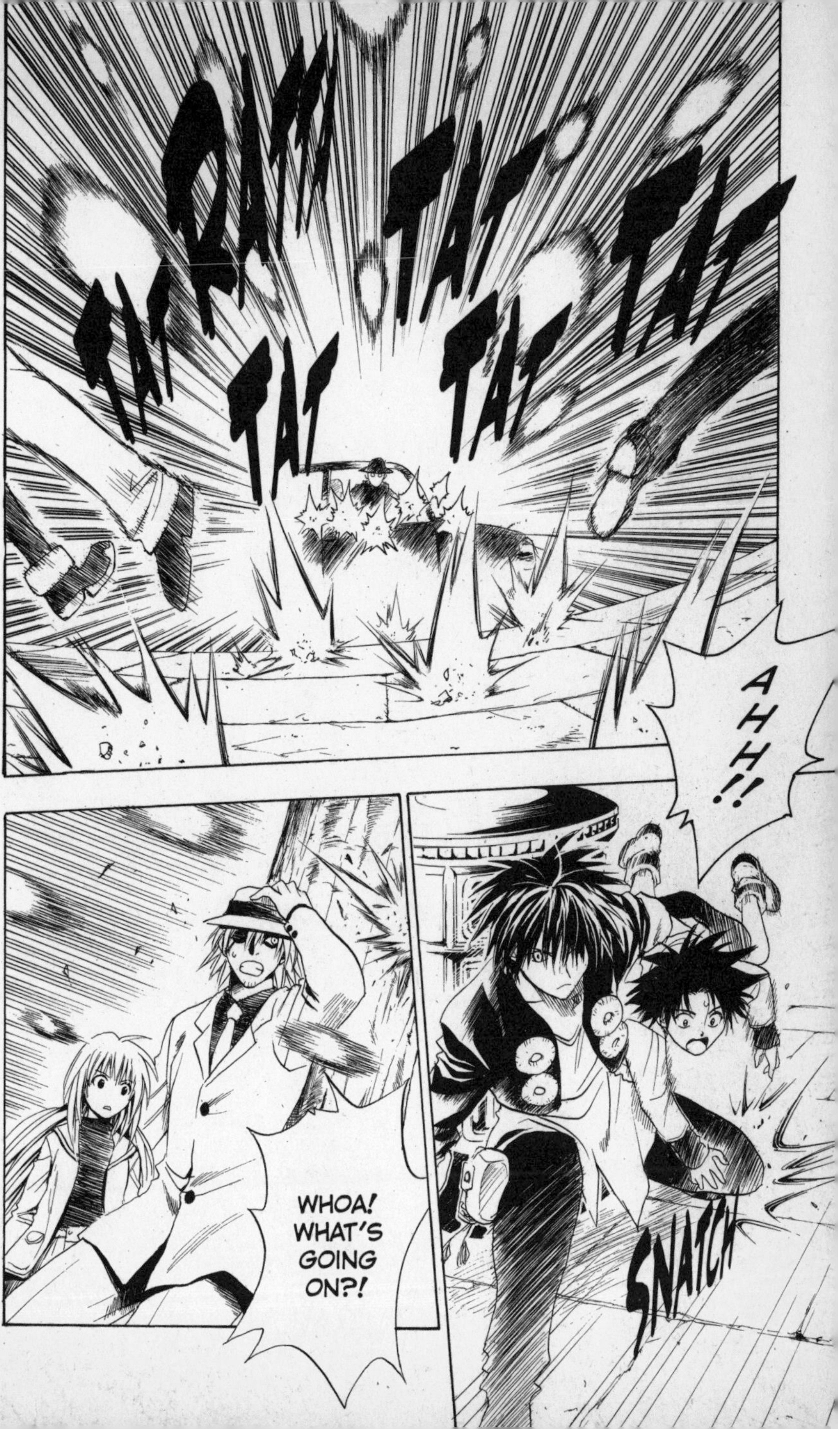

TAT
TAT
TAT
TAT
RATTA
TAT
AHH!!
SNATCH
WHOA! WHAT'S GOING ON?!

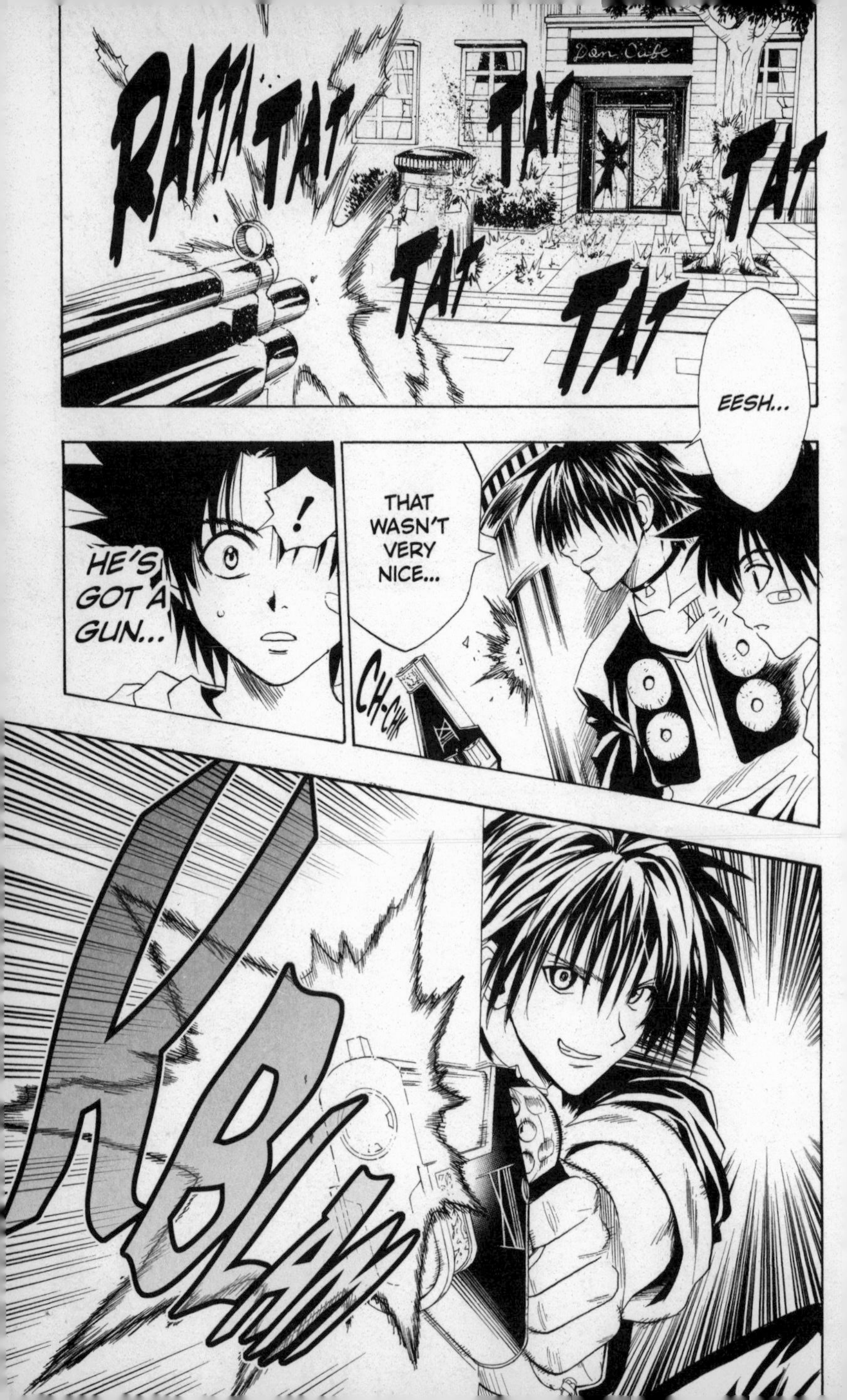
Den Cafe
TAT
TAT
TAT
TAT
RATATA TAT
EESH...
THAT WASN'T VERY NICE...
CH-CHK
!
HE'S GOT A GUN...

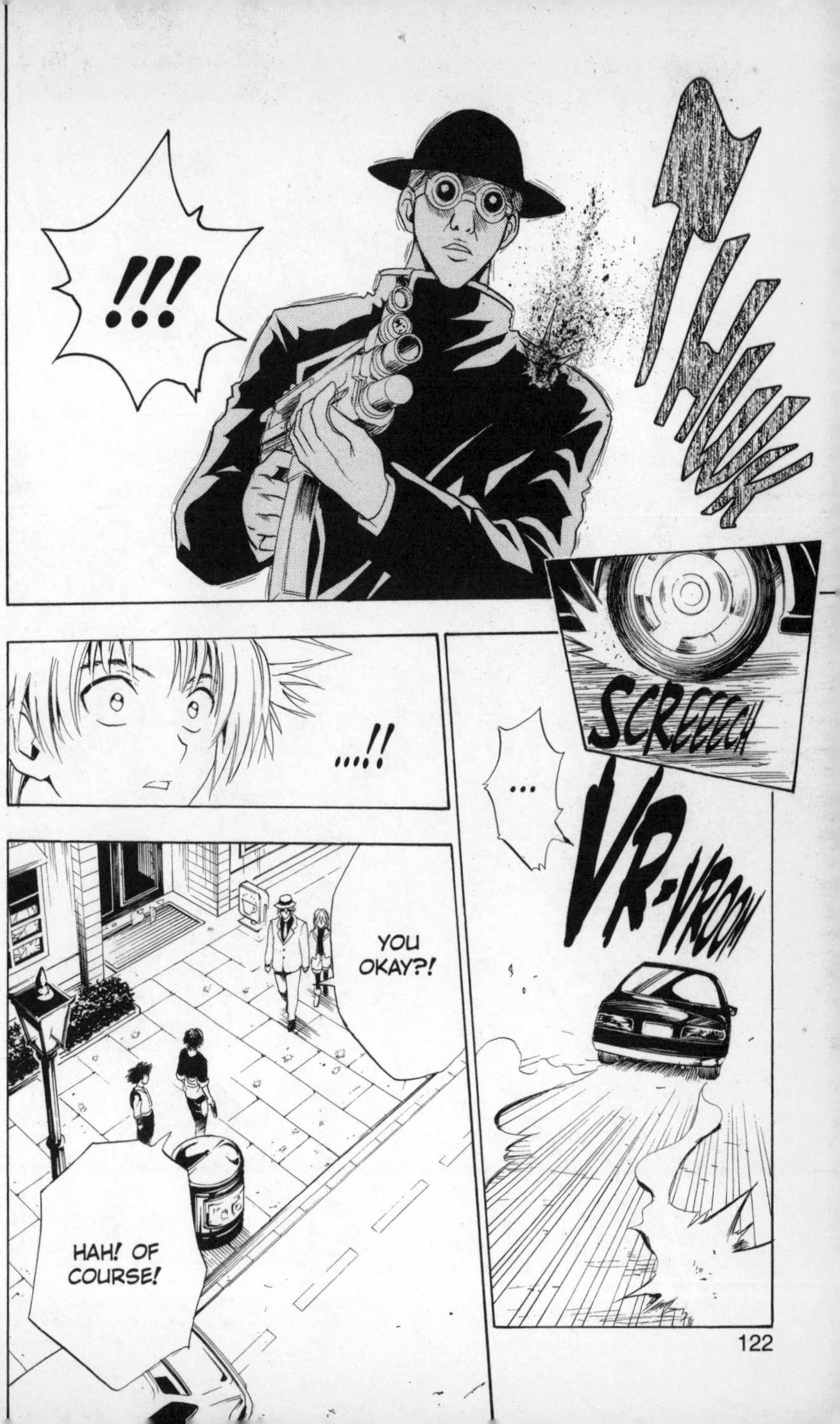
!!!
SCREEECH
...
VR-VROOM
...!!
YOU OKAY?!
HAH! OF COURSE!

READ THIS WAY

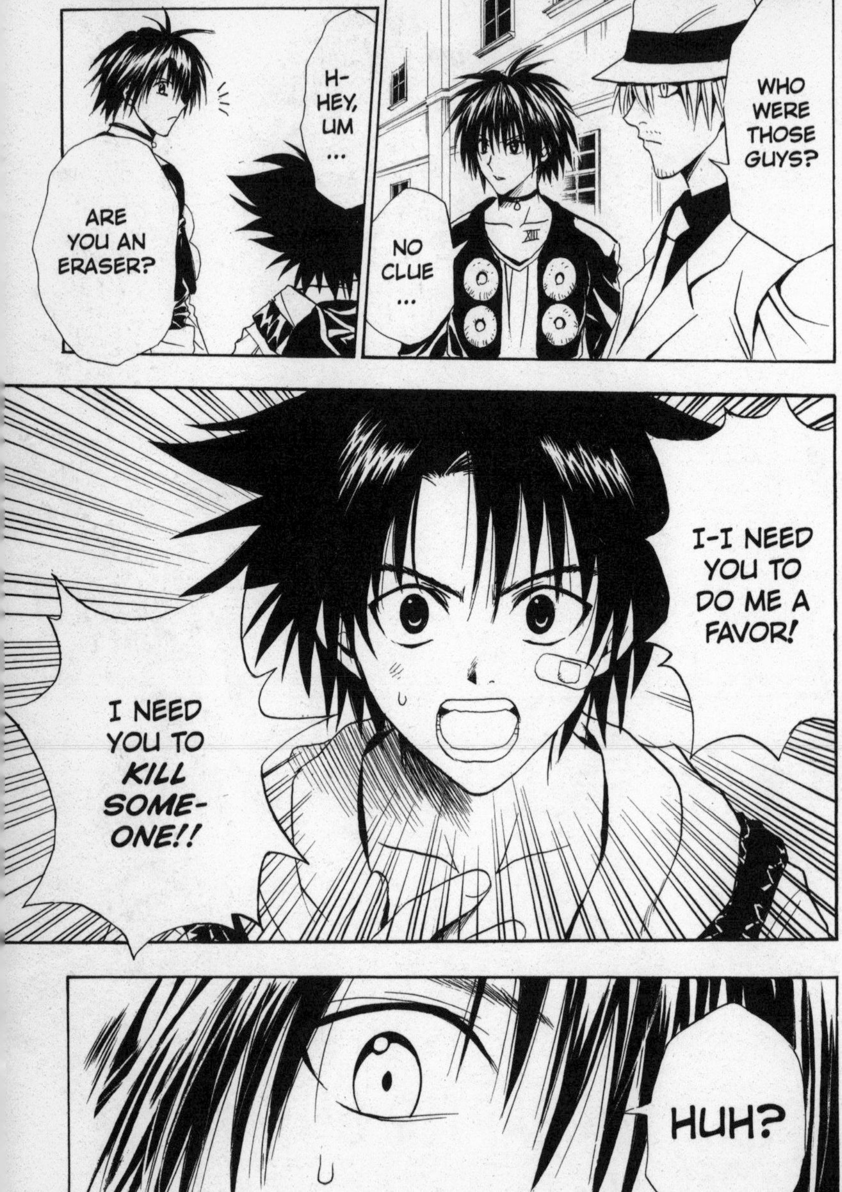
WHO WERE THOSE GUYS?
NO CLUE ...
H-HEY, UM ...
ARE YOU AN ERASER?
I-I NEED YOU TO DO ME A FAVOR!
I NEED YOU TO *KILL* SOME-ONE!!
HUH?

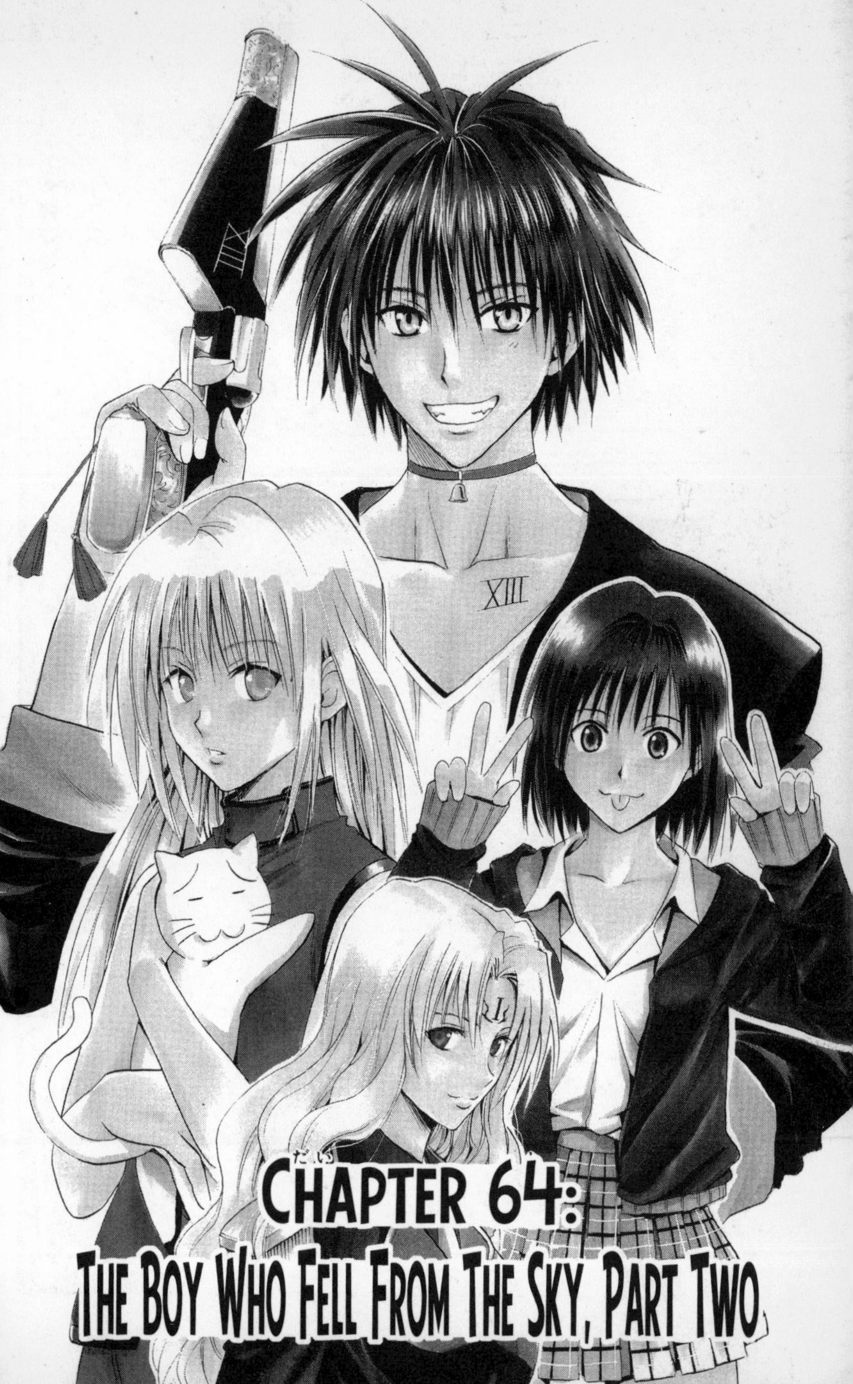
CHAPTER 64:
THE BOY WHO FELL FROM THE SKY, PART TWO

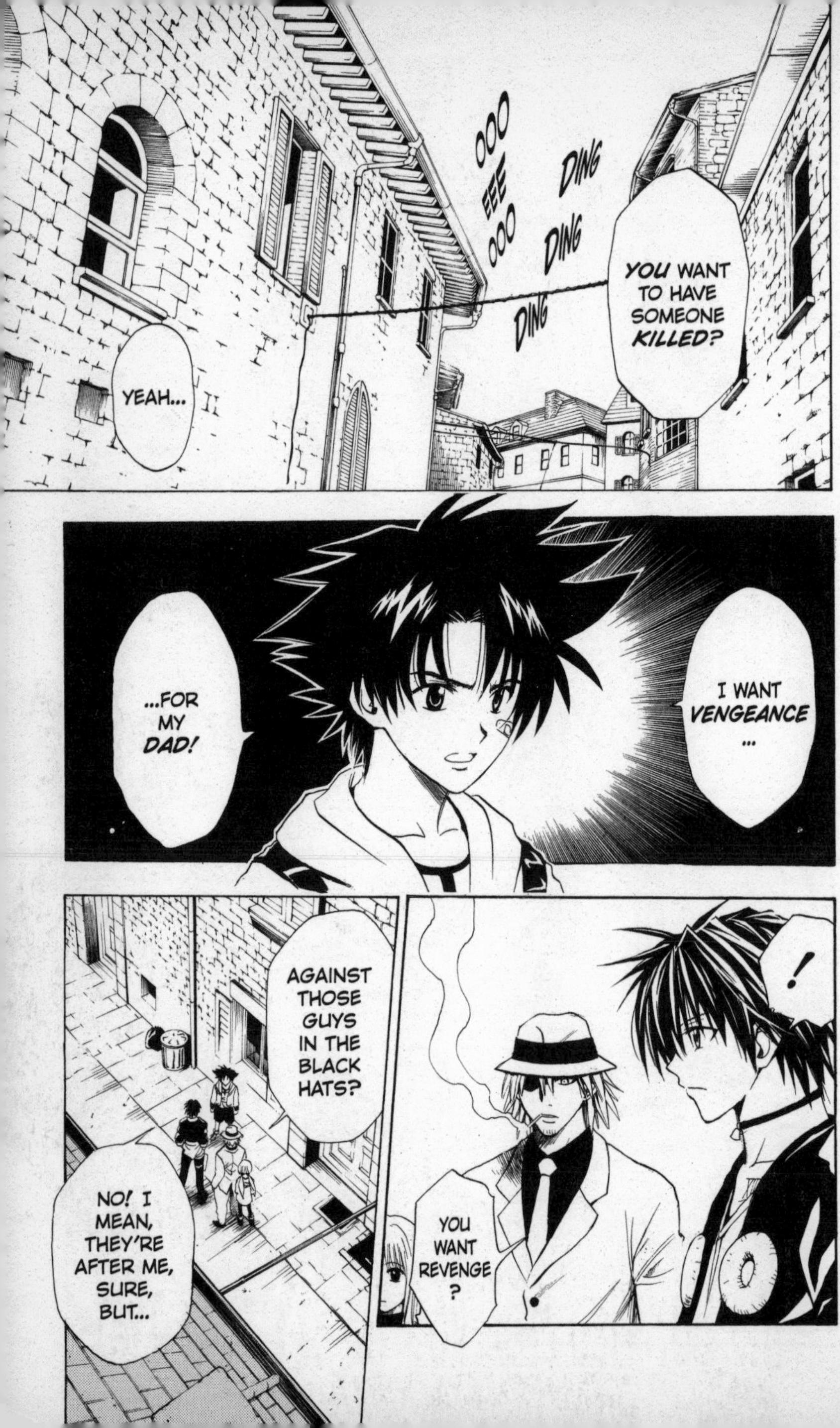
YOU WANT TO HAVE SOMEONE KILLED?
DING DING DING
OOO EEE OOO
YEAH...
I WANT VENGEANCE ...
...FOR MY DAD!
!
YOU WANT REVENGE ?
AGAINST THOSE GUYS IN THE BLACK HATS?
NO! I MEAN, THEY'RE AFTER ME, SURE, BUT...

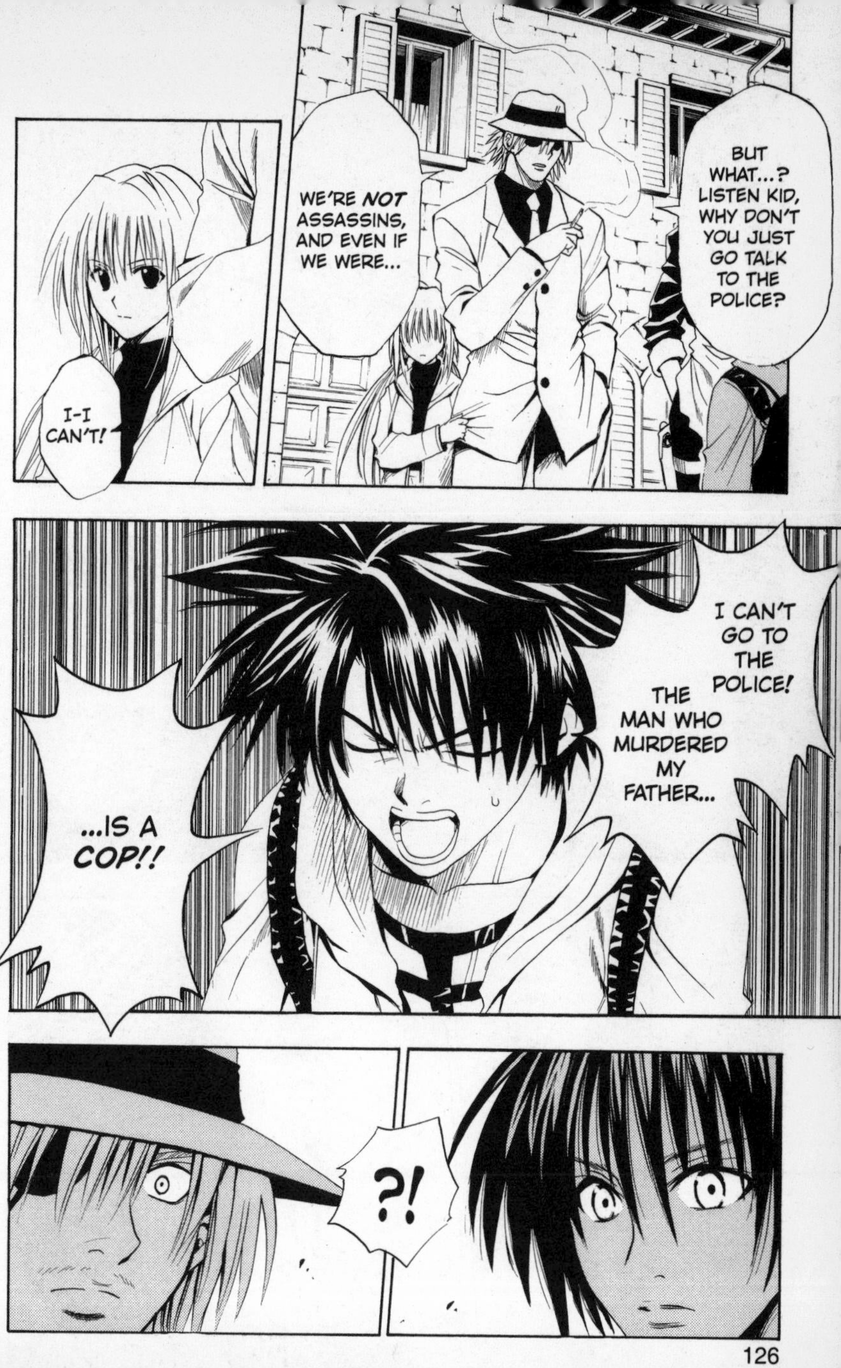
BUT WHAT...? LISTEN KID, WHY DON'T YOU JUST GO TALK TO THE POLICE?
WE'RE NOT ASSASSINS, AND EVEN IF WE WERE...
I-I CAN'T!
I CAN'T GO TO THE POLICE!
THE MAN WHO MURDERED MY FATHER...
...IS A COP!!
?!

READ THIS WAY

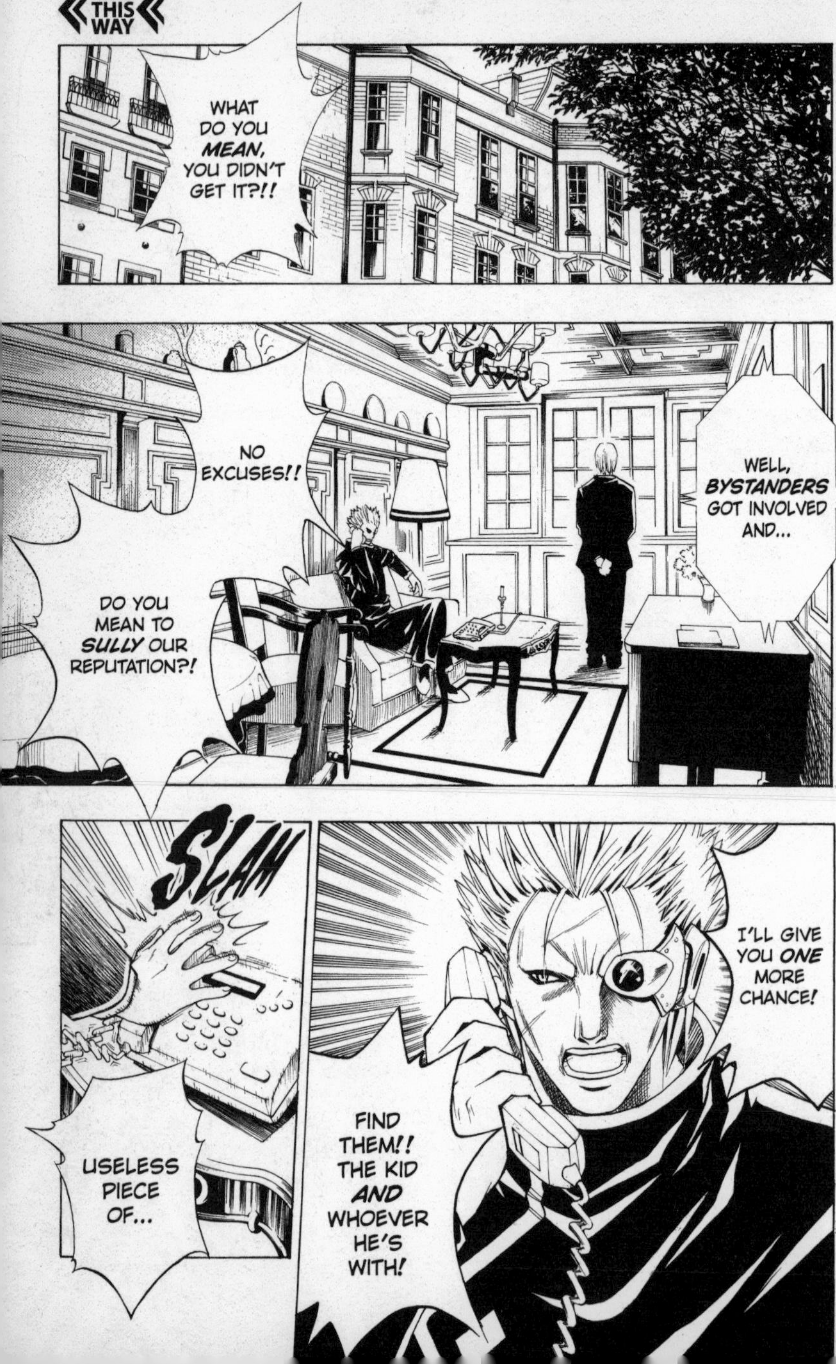
WHAT DO YOU *MEAN*, YOU DIDN'T GET IT?!!
WELL, *BYSTANDERS* GOT INVOLVED AND...
NO EXCUSES!!
DO YOU MEAN TO *SULLY* OUR REPUTATION?!
I'LL GIVE YOU *ONE* MORE CHANCE!
FIND THEM!! THE KID *AND* WHOEVER HE'S WITH!
SLAM
USELESS PIECE OF...

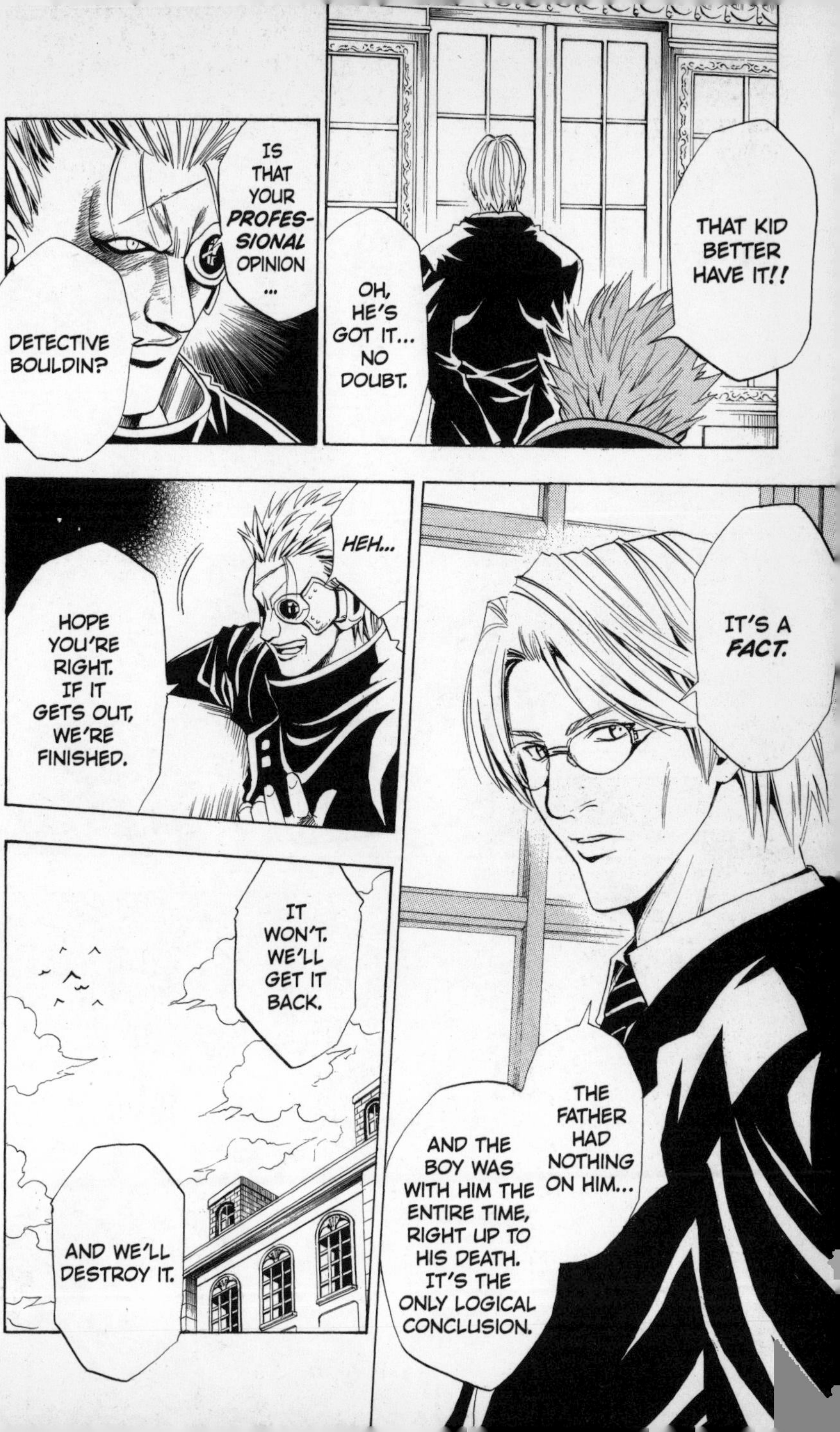
THAT KID BETTER HAVE IT!!
OH, HE'S GOT IT... NO DOUBT.
IS THAT YOUR *PROFESSIONAL* OPINION...
DETECTIVE BOULDIN?
IT'S A *FACT.*
THE FATHER HAD NOTHING ON HIM...
AND THE BOY WAS WITH HIM THE ENTIRE TIME, RIGHT UP TO HIS DEATH. IT'S THE ONLY LOGICAL CONCLUSION.
HEH...
HOPE YOU'RE RIGHT. IF IT GETS OUT, WE'RE FINISHED.
IT WON'T. WE'LL GET IT BACK.
AND WE'LL DESTROY IT.

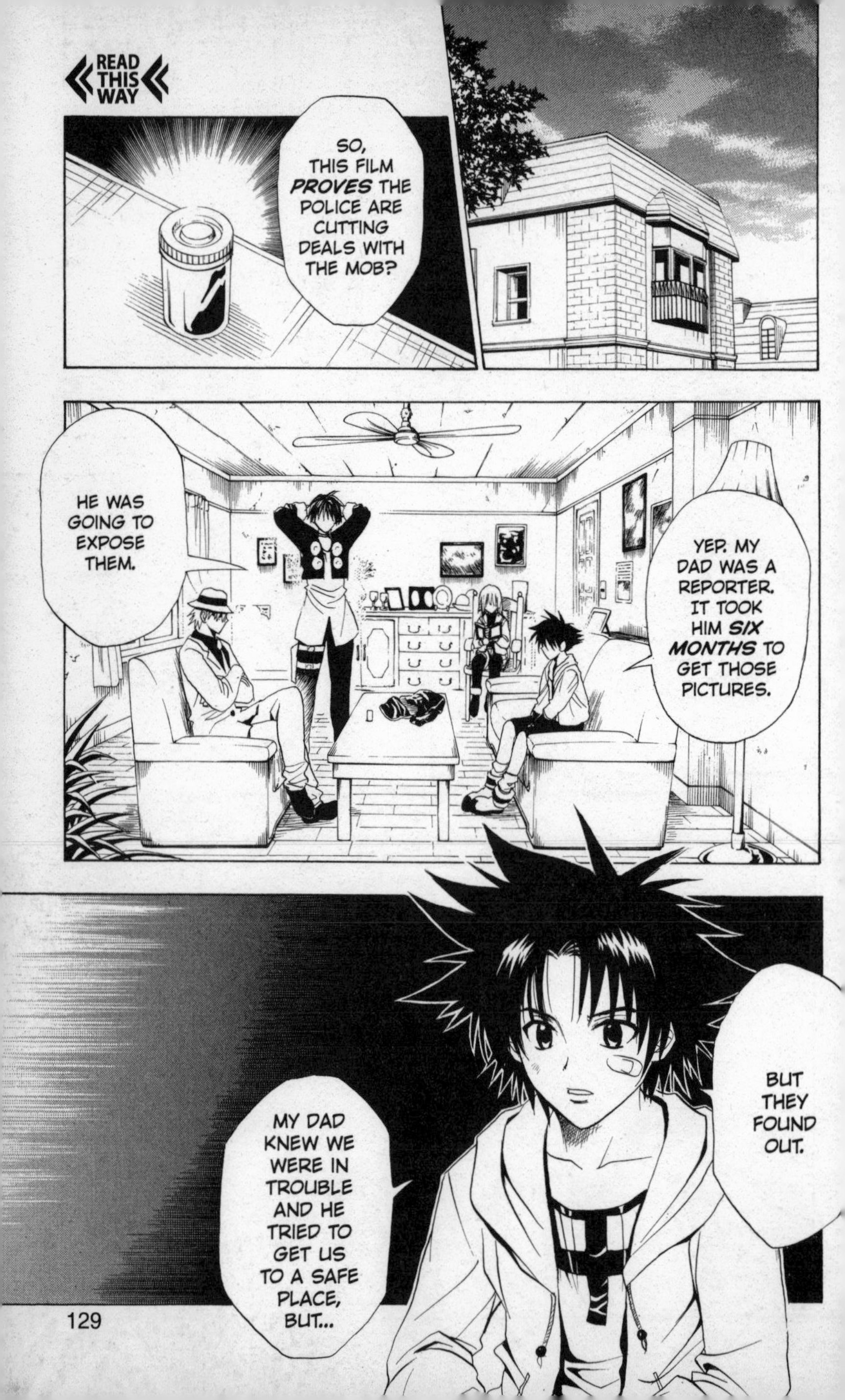
READ THIS WAY
SO, THIS FILM *PROVES* THE POLICE ARE CUTTING DEALS WITH THE MOB?
YEP. MY DAD WAS A REPORTER. IT TOOK HIM *SIX MONTHS* TO GET THOSE PICTURES.
HE WAS GOING TO EXPOSE THEM.
BUT THEY FOUND OUT.
MY DAD KNEW WE WERE IN TROUBLE AND HE TRIED TO GET US TO A SAFE PLACE, BUT...

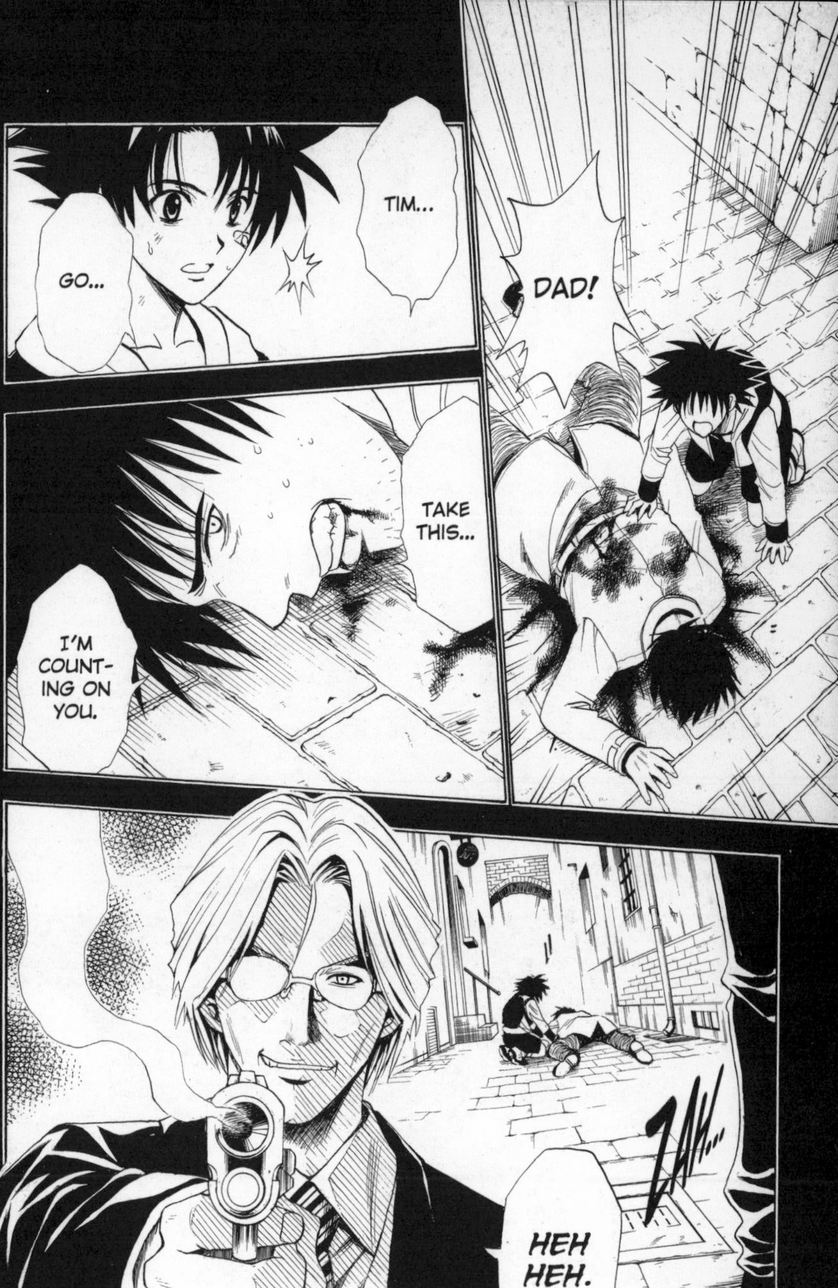
DAD!
TIM...
GO...
TAKE THIS...
I'M COUNTING ON YOU.
ZAK...
HEH HEH.

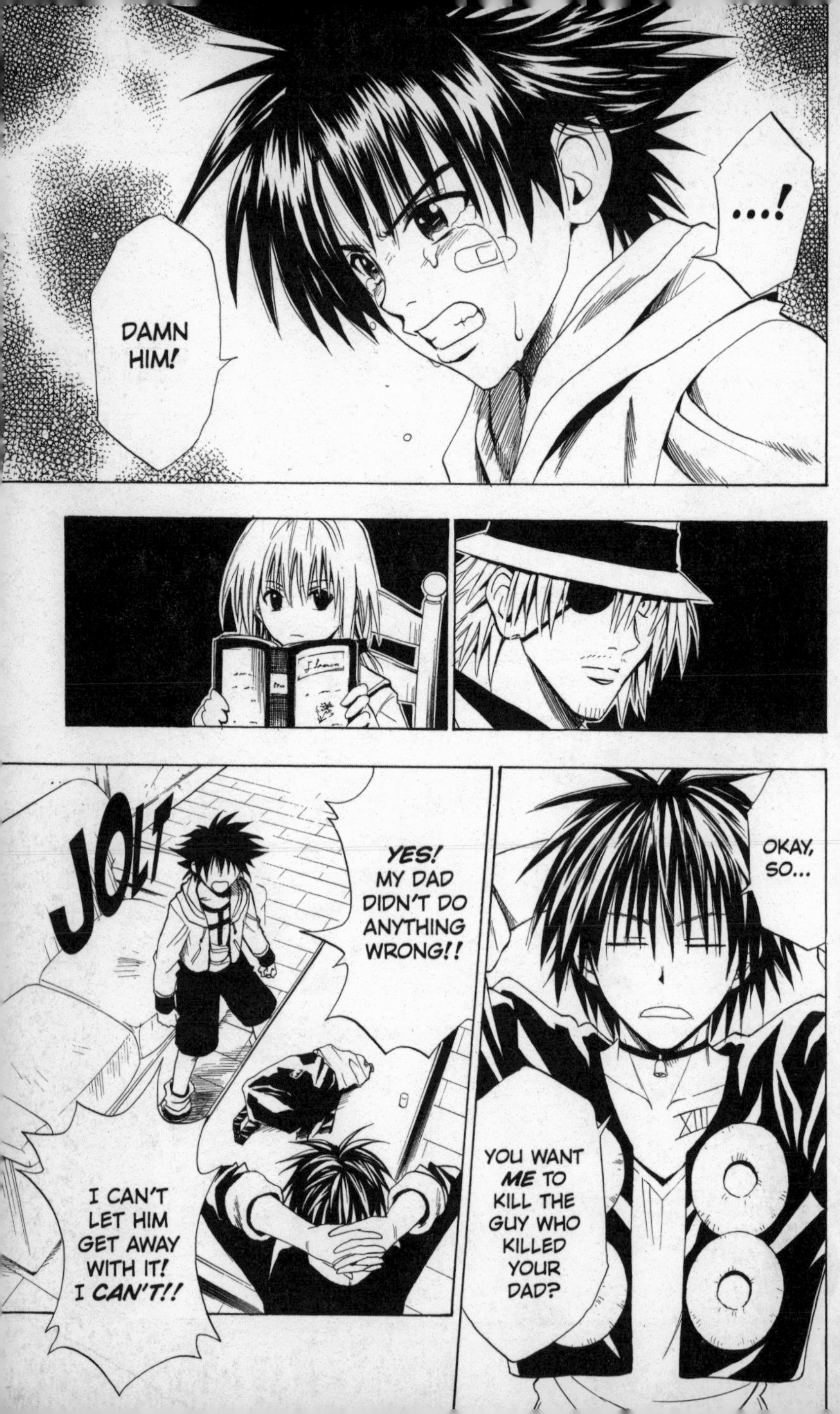
...!
DAMN HIM!
OKAY, SO...
YOU WANT *ME* TO KILL THE GUY WHO KILLED YOUR DAD?
JOLT
YES! MY DAD DIDN'T DO ANYTHING WRONG!!
I CAN'T LET HIM GET AWAY WITH IT! I *CAN'T*!!

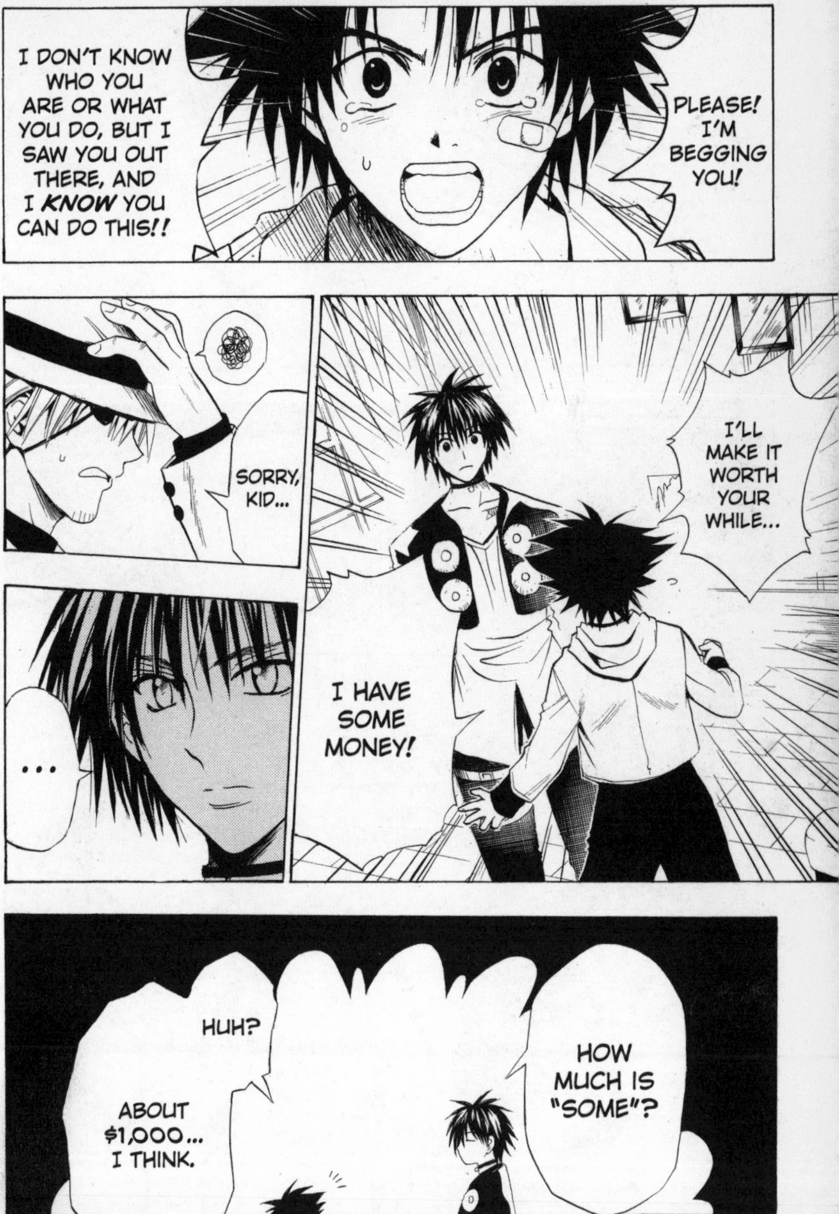
PLEASE! I'M BEGGING YOU!
I DON'T KNOW WHO YOU ARE OR WHAT YOU DO, BUT I SAW YOU OUT THERE, AND I *KNOW* YOU CAN DO THIS!!
I'LL MAKE IT WORTH YOUR WHILE...
I HAVE SOME MONEY!
SORRY, KID...
...
HOW MUCH IS "SOME"?
HUH?
ABOUT $1,000... I THINK.

READ THIS WAY

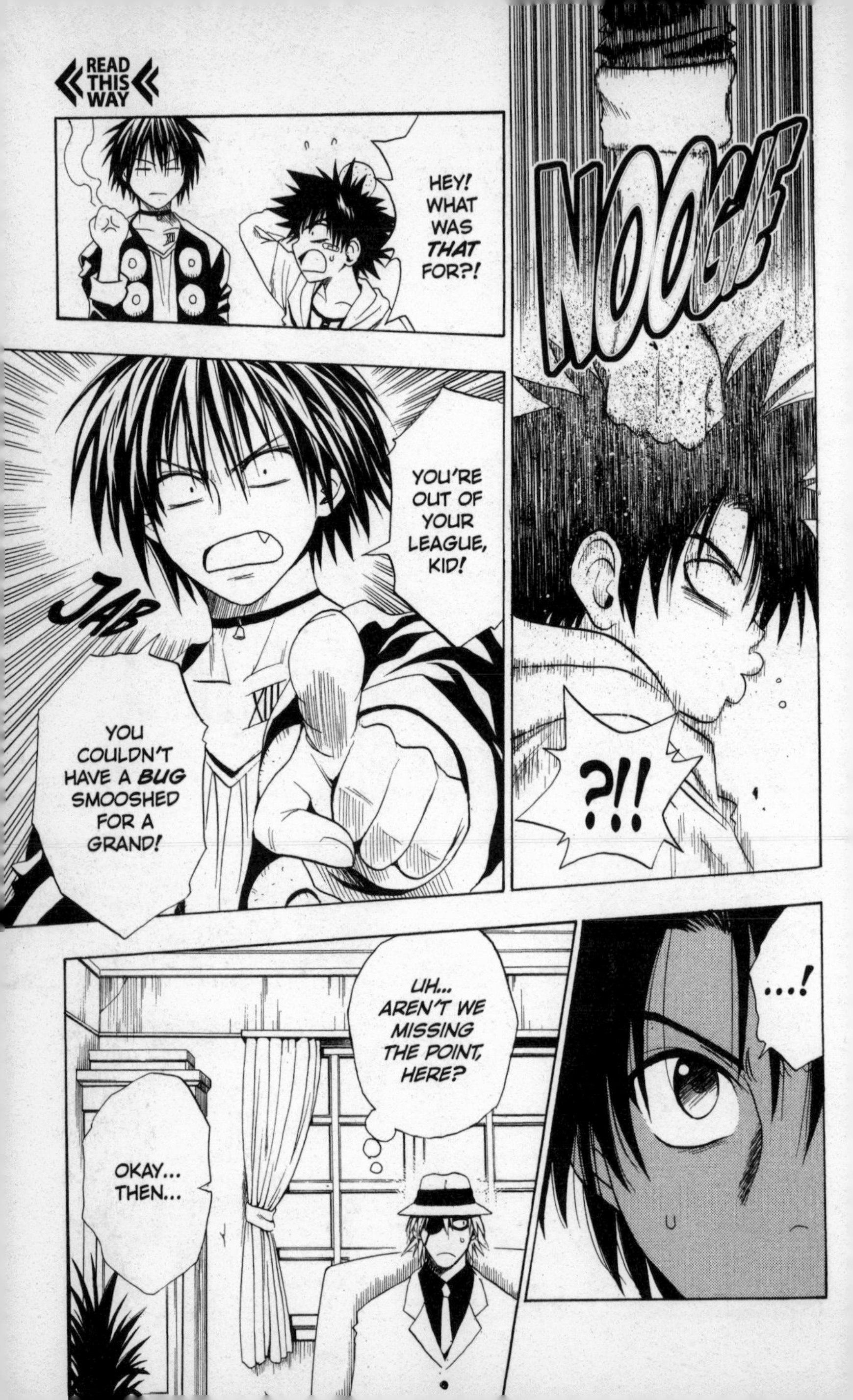

?!!
HEY! WHAT WAS *THAT* FOR?!
YOU'RE OUT OF YOUR LEAGUE, KID!
JAB
YOU COULDN'T HAVE A *BUG* SMOOSHED FOR A GRAND!
...!
UH... AREN'T WE MISSING THE POINT, HERE?
OKAY... THEN...

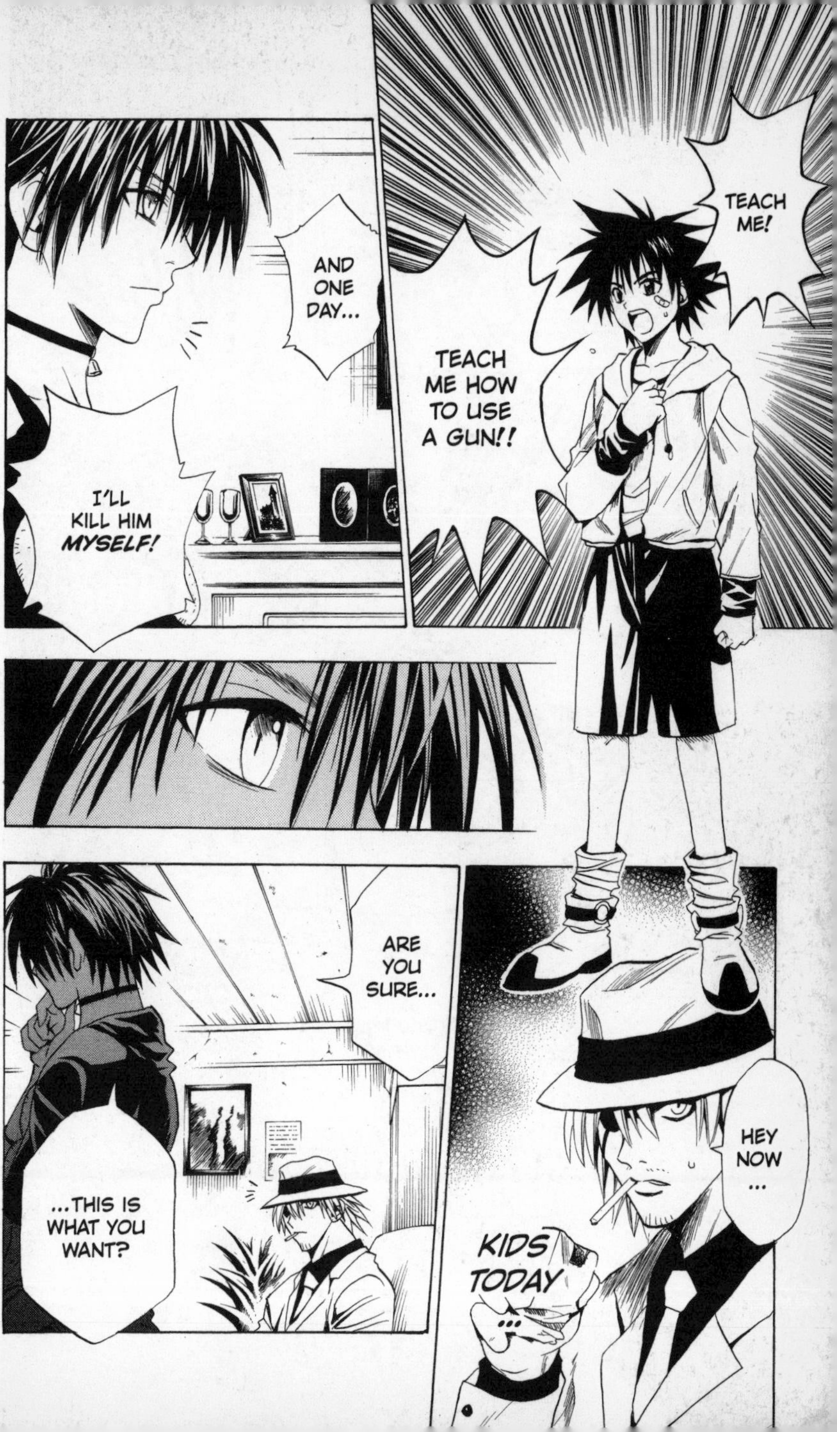
TEACH ME!
TEACH ME HOW TO USE A GUN!!
AND ONE DAY...
I'LL KILL HIM *MYSELF!*
HEY NOW ...
KIDS TODAY ...
ARE YOU SURE...
...THIS IS WHAT YOU WANT?

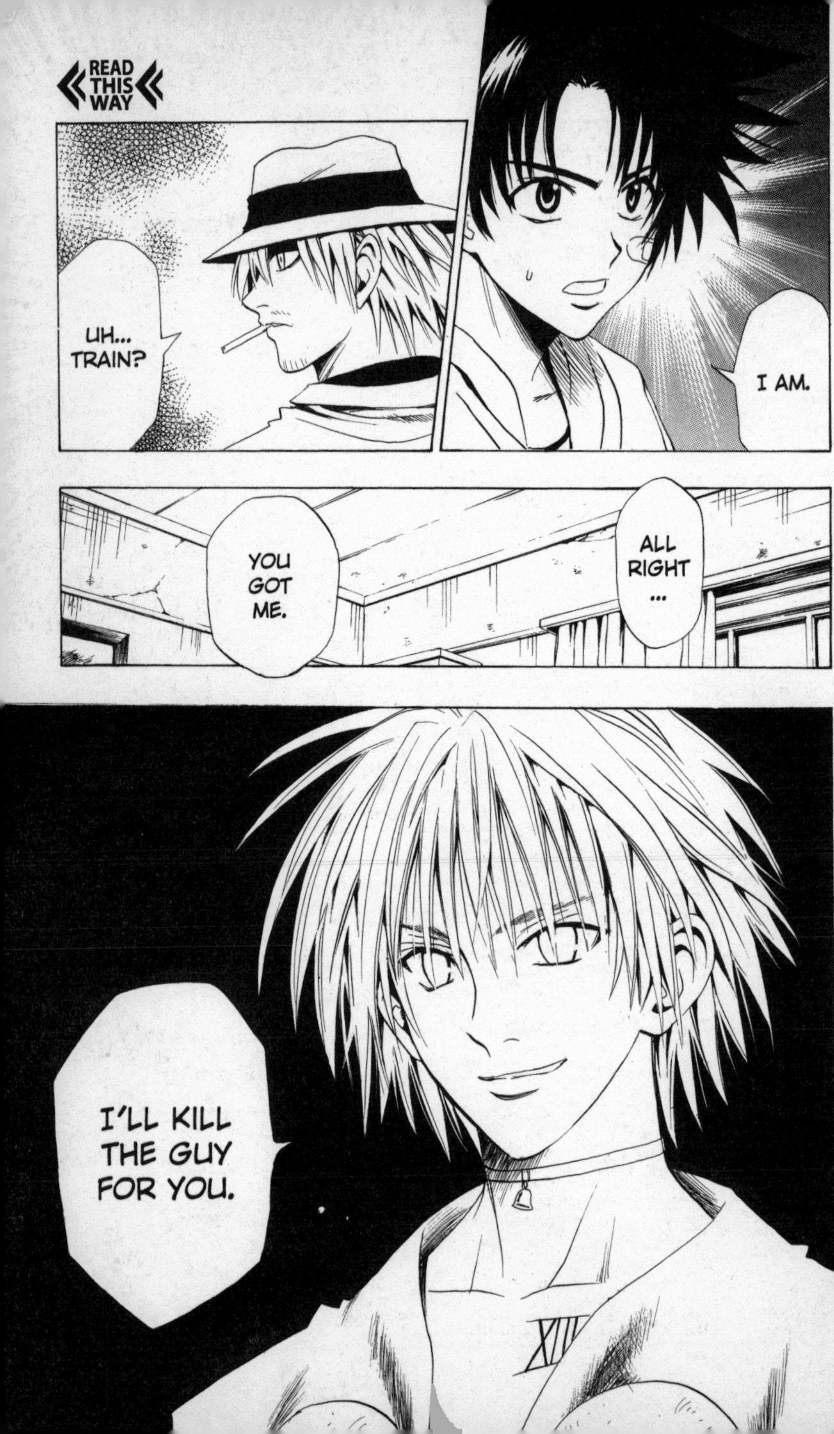
READ THIS WAY
I AM.
UH... TRAIN?
ALL RIGHT ...
YOU GOT ME.
I'LL KILL THE GUY FOR YOU.

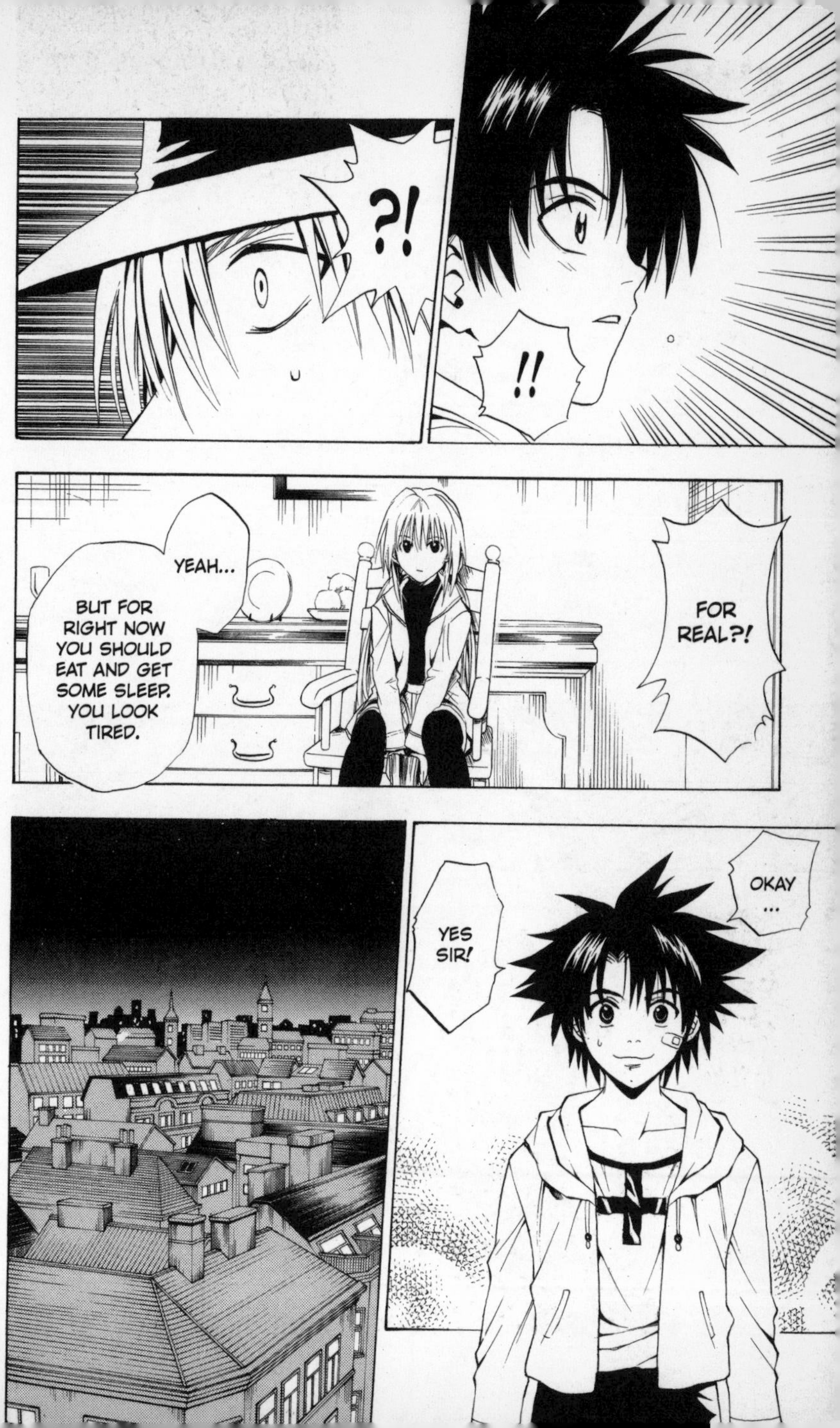
!!
?!
FOR REAL?!
YEAH...
BUT FOR RIGHT NOW YOU SHOULD EAT AND GET SOME SLEEP. YOU LOOK TIRED.
OKAY ...
YES SIR!

READ THIS WAY

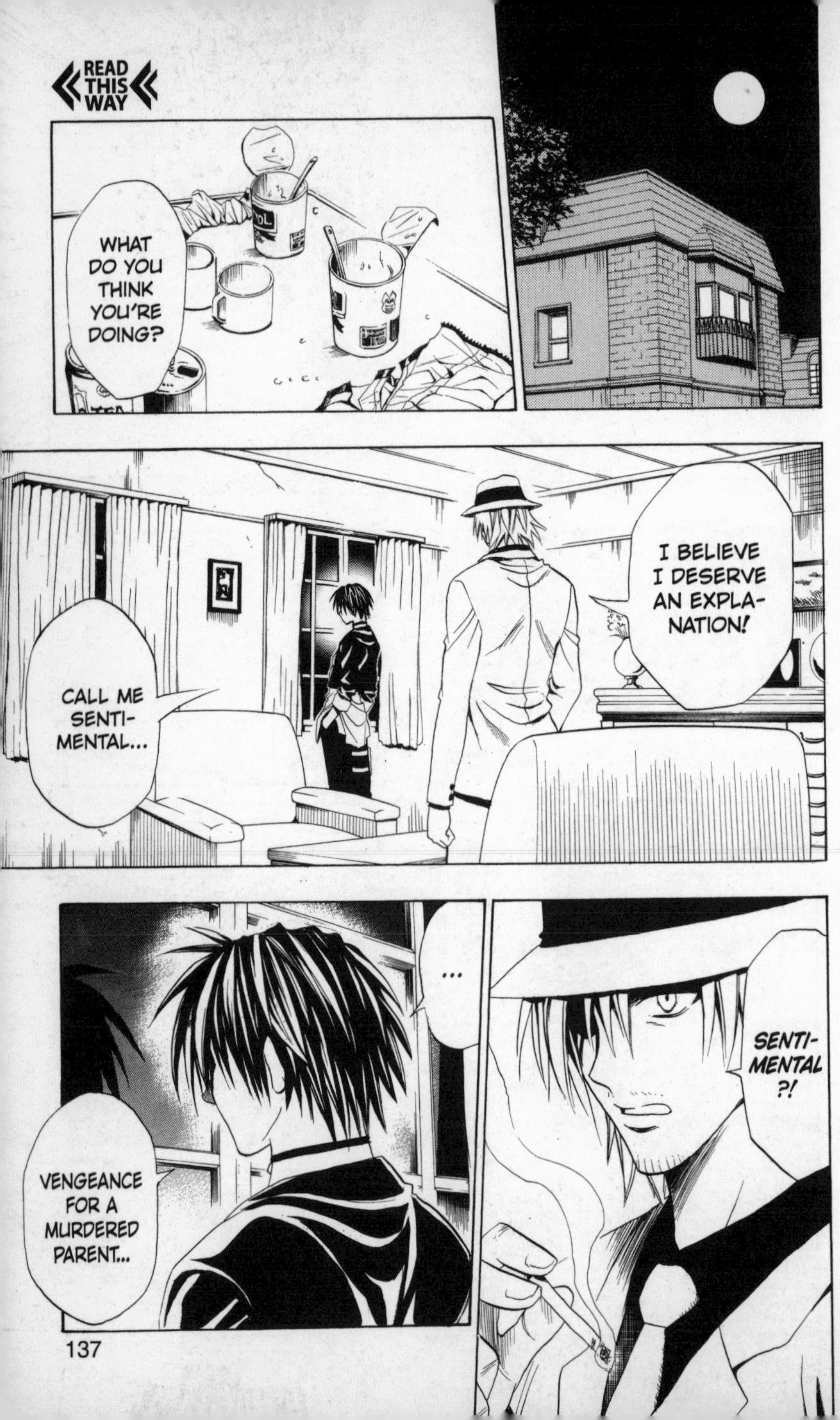

WHAT DO YOU THINK YOU'RE DOING?
I BELIEVE I DESERVE AN EXPLA-NATION!
CALL ME SENTI-MENTAL...
SENTI-MENTAL ?!
...
VENGEANCE FOR A MURDERED PARENT...

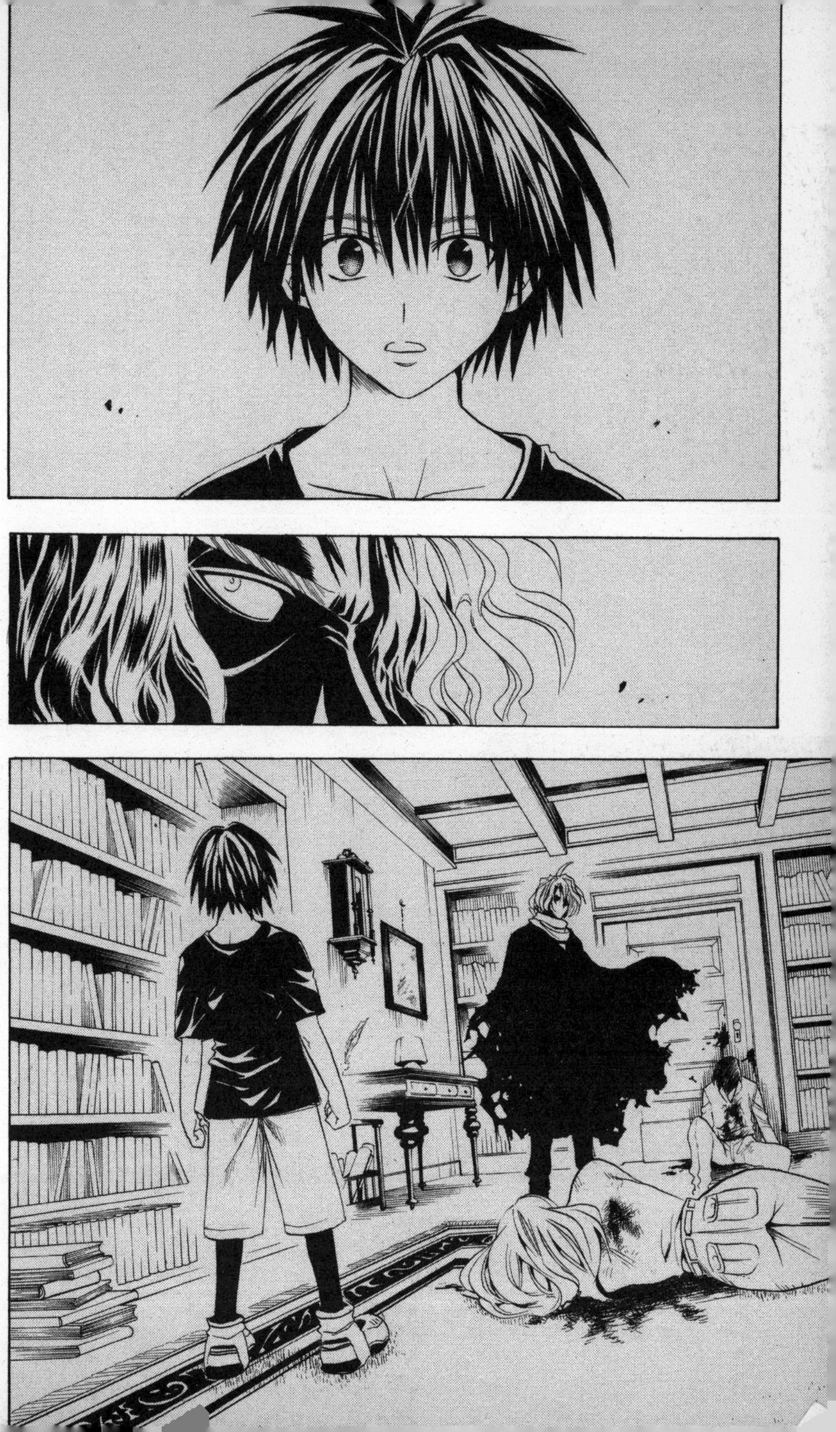

READ THIS WAY

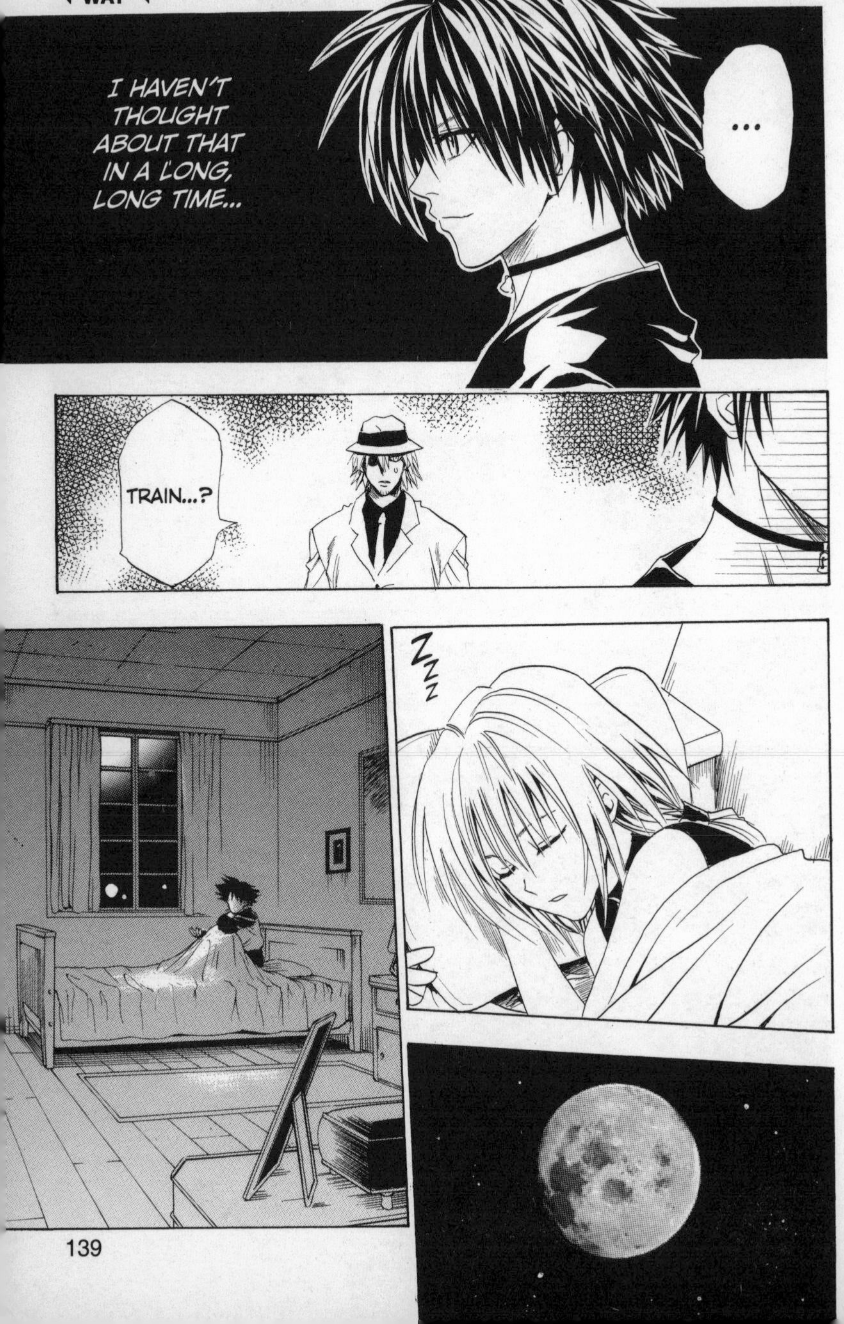

...
I HAVEN'T THOUGHT ABOUT THAT IN A LONG, LONG TIME...
TRAIN...?
ZZZ

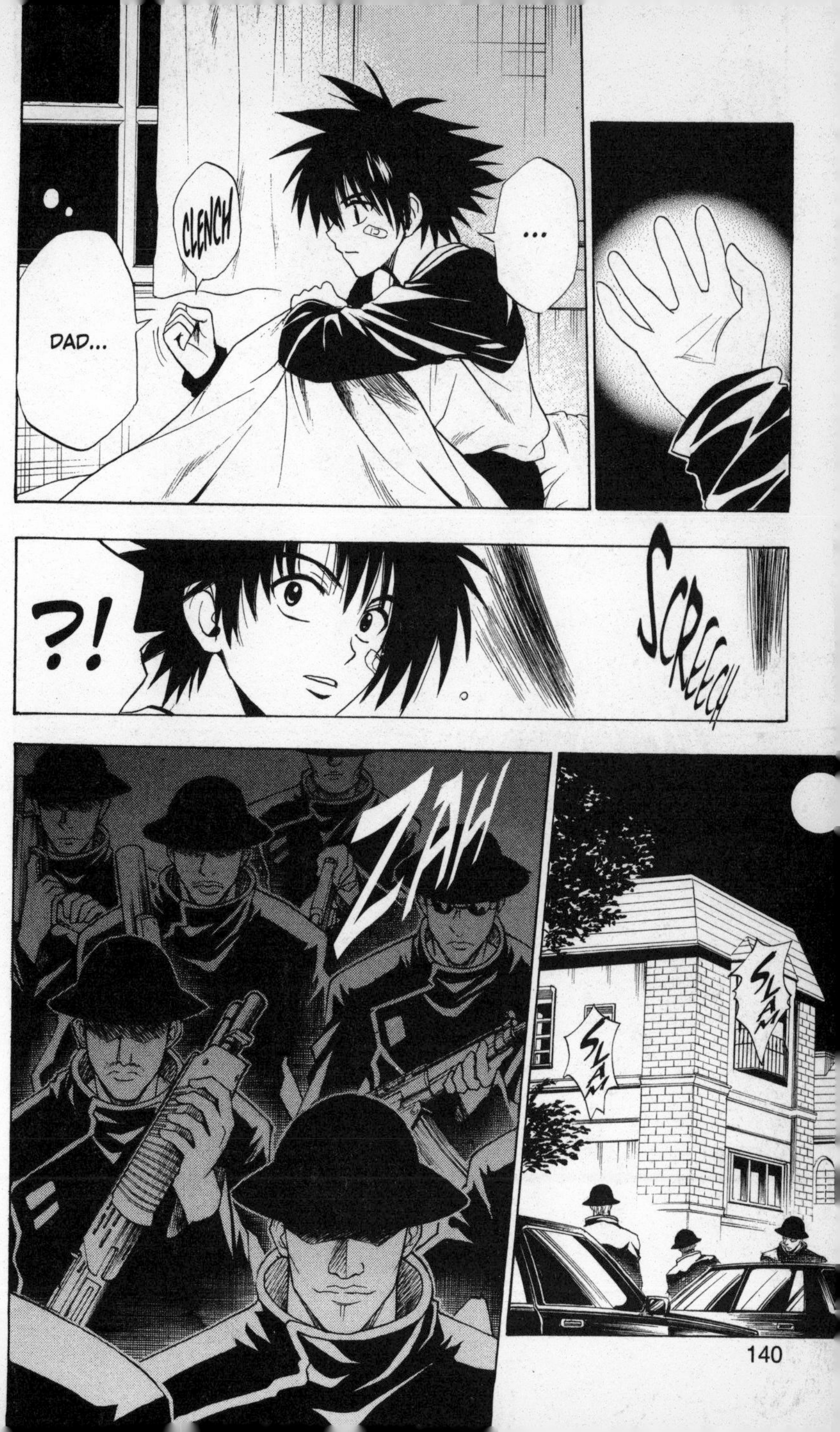
...
CLENCH
DAD...
SCREECH
?!
SLAM
SLAM
ZAH

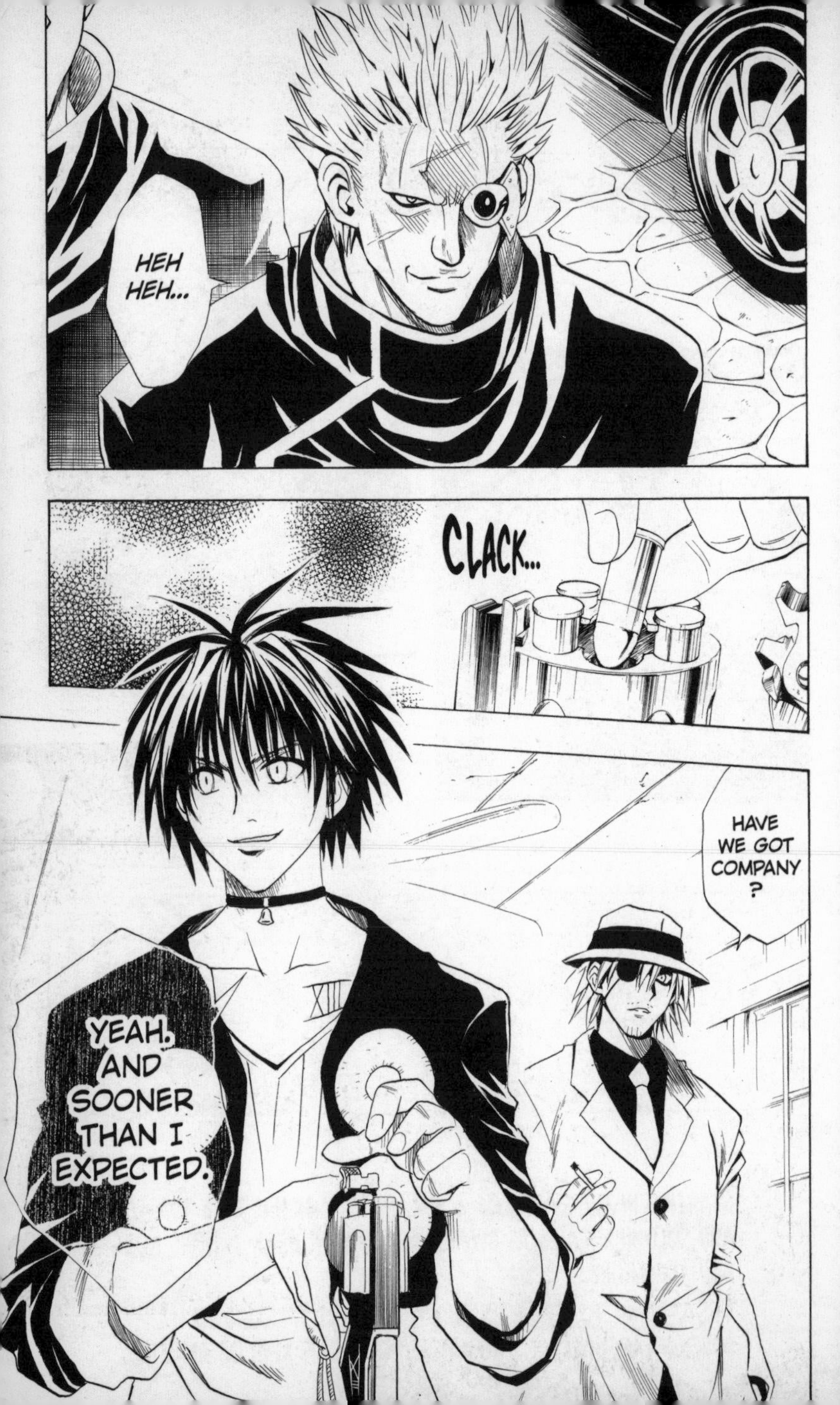
HEH HEH...
CLACK...
HAVE WE GOT COMPANY?
YEAH. AND SOONER THAN I EXPECTED.

黑貓 BLACK CAT

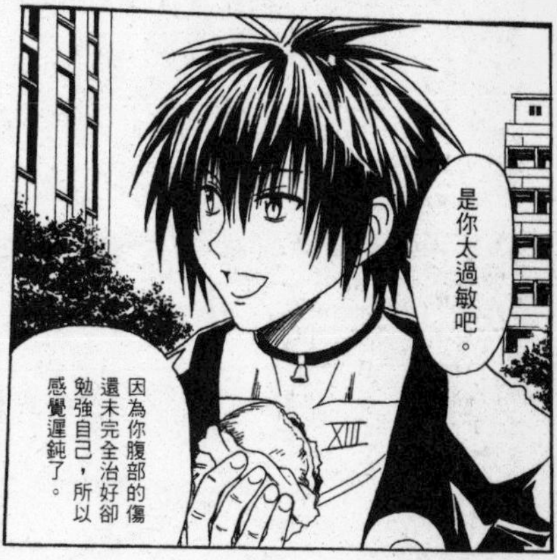
是你太過敏吧。
因為你腹部的傷還未完全治好卻勉強自己，所以感覺遲鈍了。

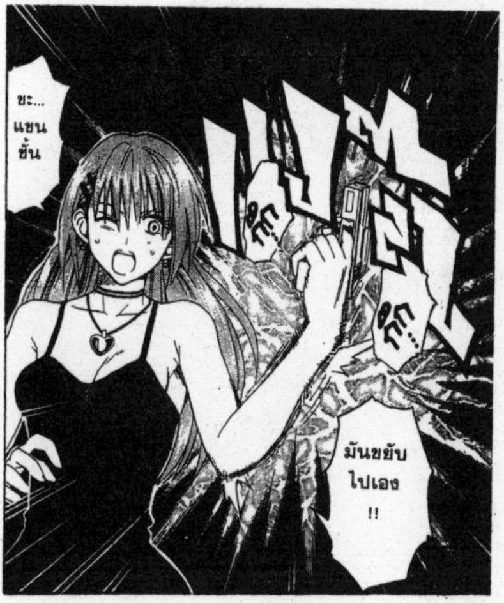
ขะ... แขน ขั้น
มันขยับ ไปเอง !!

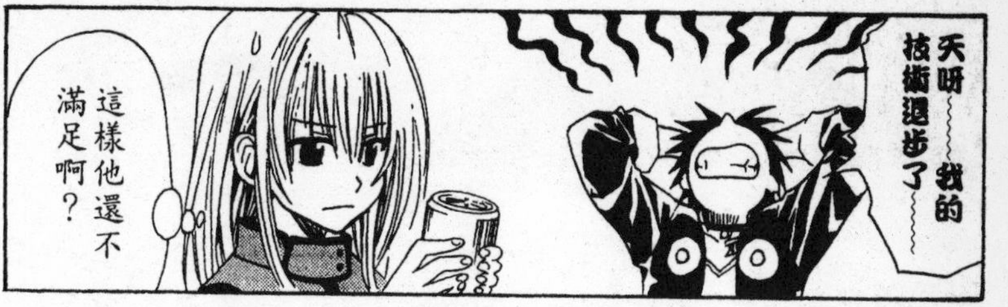
天呀～～～我的技術退步了～～～
這樣他還不滿足啊？

☆ Starting in the spring of 2002, *Black Cat* has been translated and sold in locales as diverse as Taiwan, France, Hong Kong and Singapore.

It's strange to see Train and the others speaking so many foreign languages... The whole process is kind of amazing.

Chapter 65: Attack

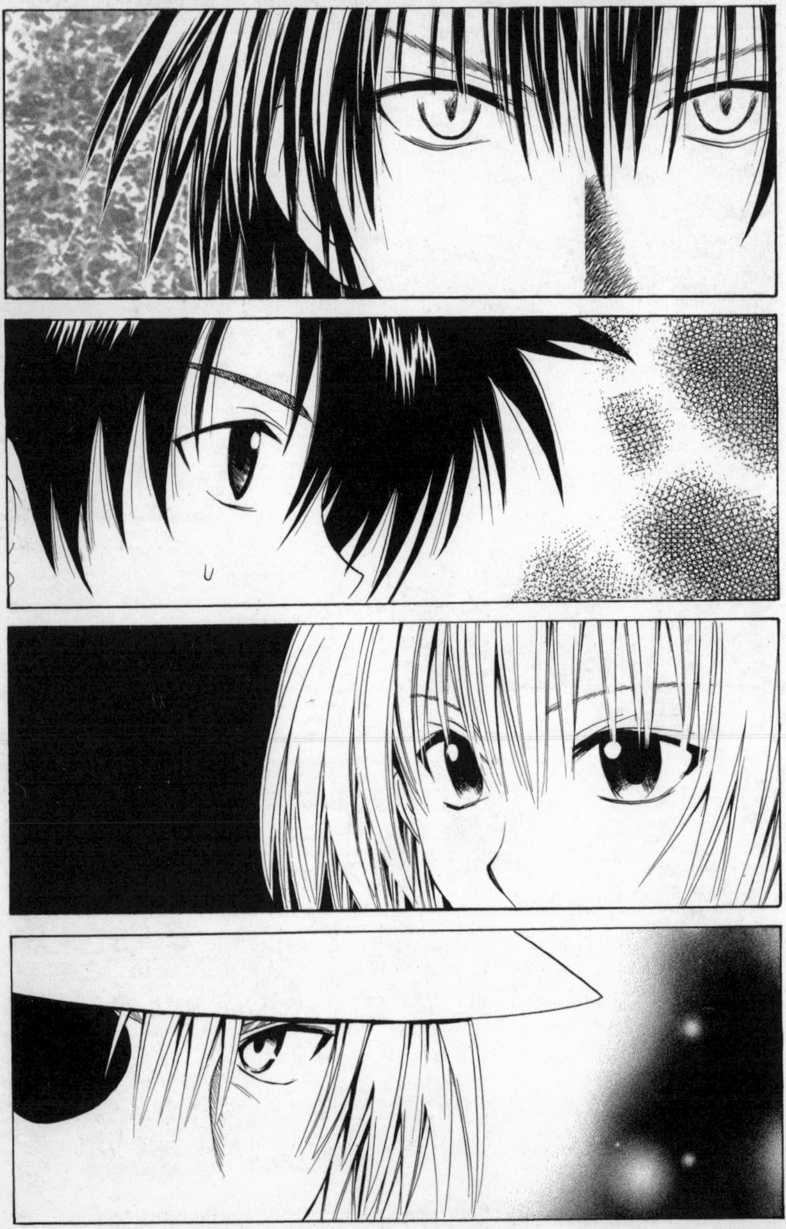

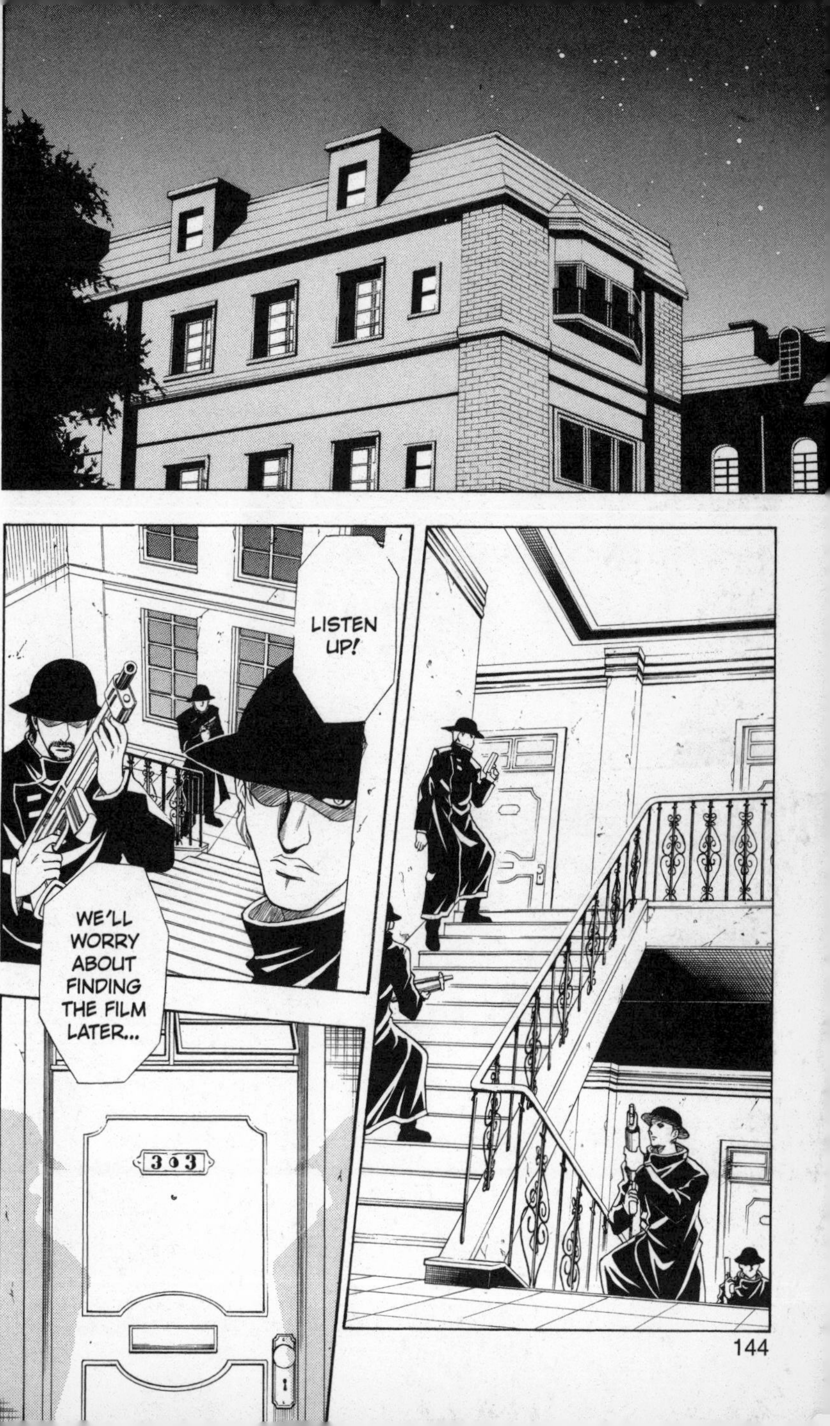
LISTEN UP!
WE'LL WORRY ABOUT FINDING THE FILM LATER...
303

READ THIS WAY

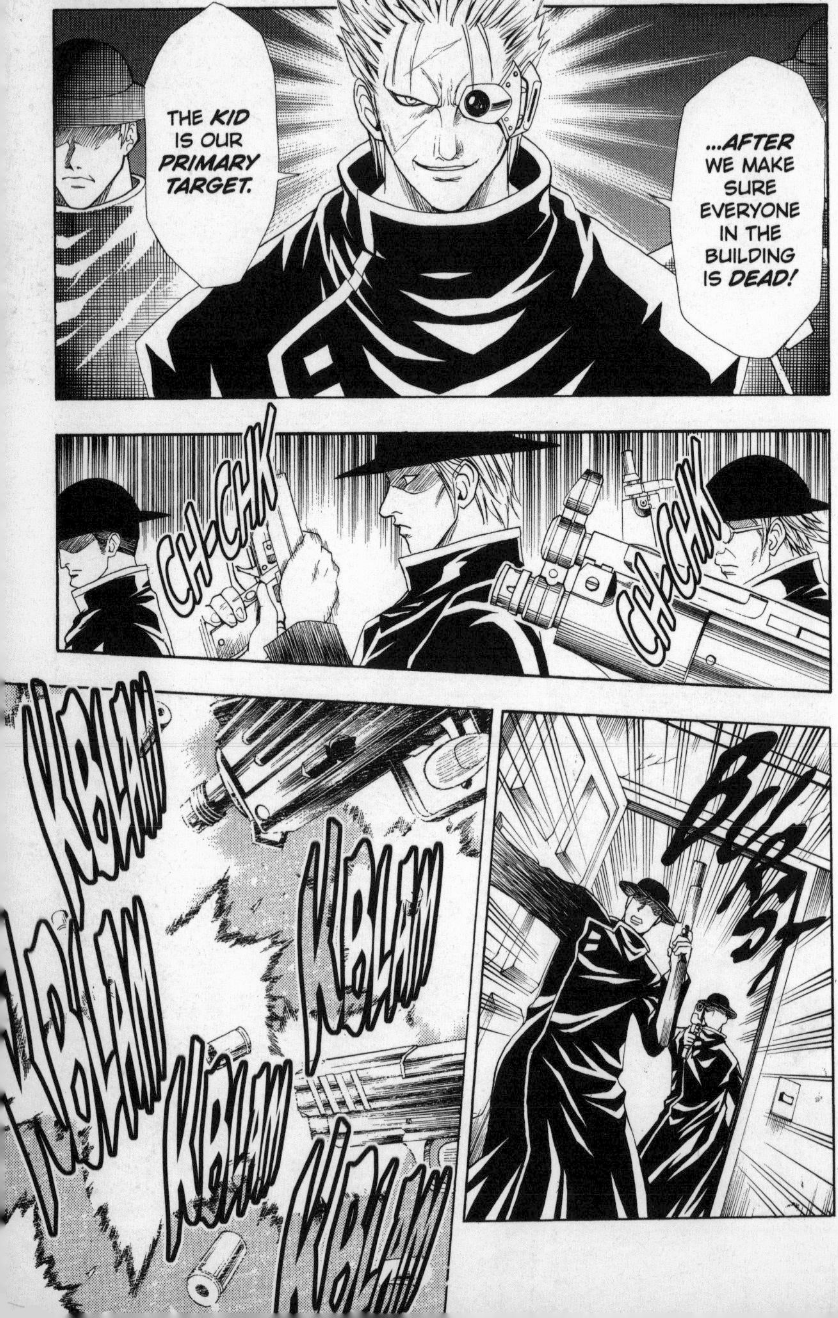
THE KID IS OUR PRIMARY TARGET.
...AFTER WE MAKE SURE EVERYONE IN THE BUILDING IS DEAD!
CH-CHK
CH-CHK
BLAST
KBLAM
KBLAM
KBLAM
KBLAM
KBLAM
KBLAM

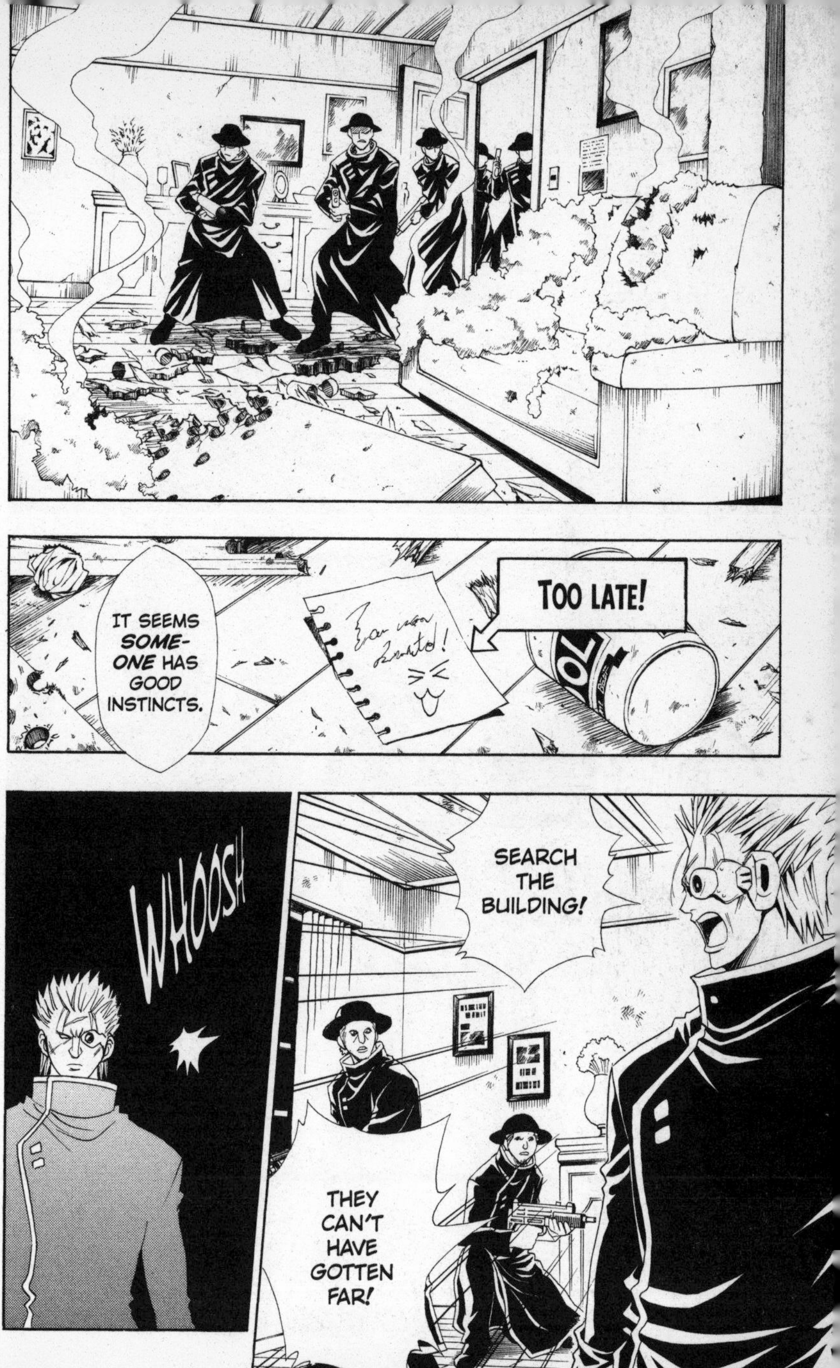
TOO LATE!
IT SEEMS SOMEONE HAS GOOD INSTINCTS.
SEARCH THE BUILDING!
THEY CAN'T HAVE GOTTEN FAR!
WHOOSH

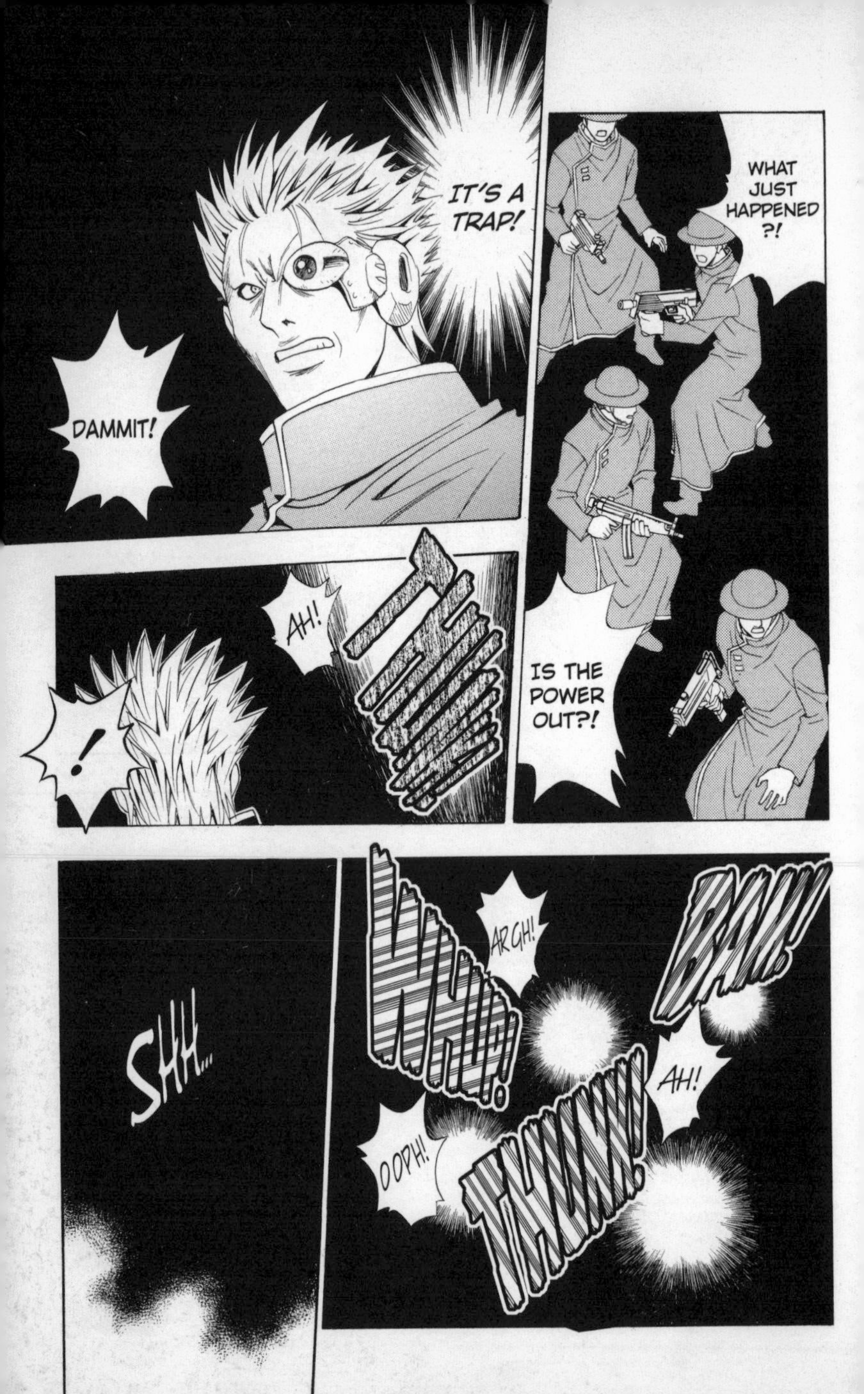
IT'S A TRAP!
DAMMIT!
WHAT JUST HAPPENED?!
IS THE POWER OUT?!
AH!
!
WHUD!
ARGH!
BAM!
AH!
THWAK!
OOPH!
SHH...

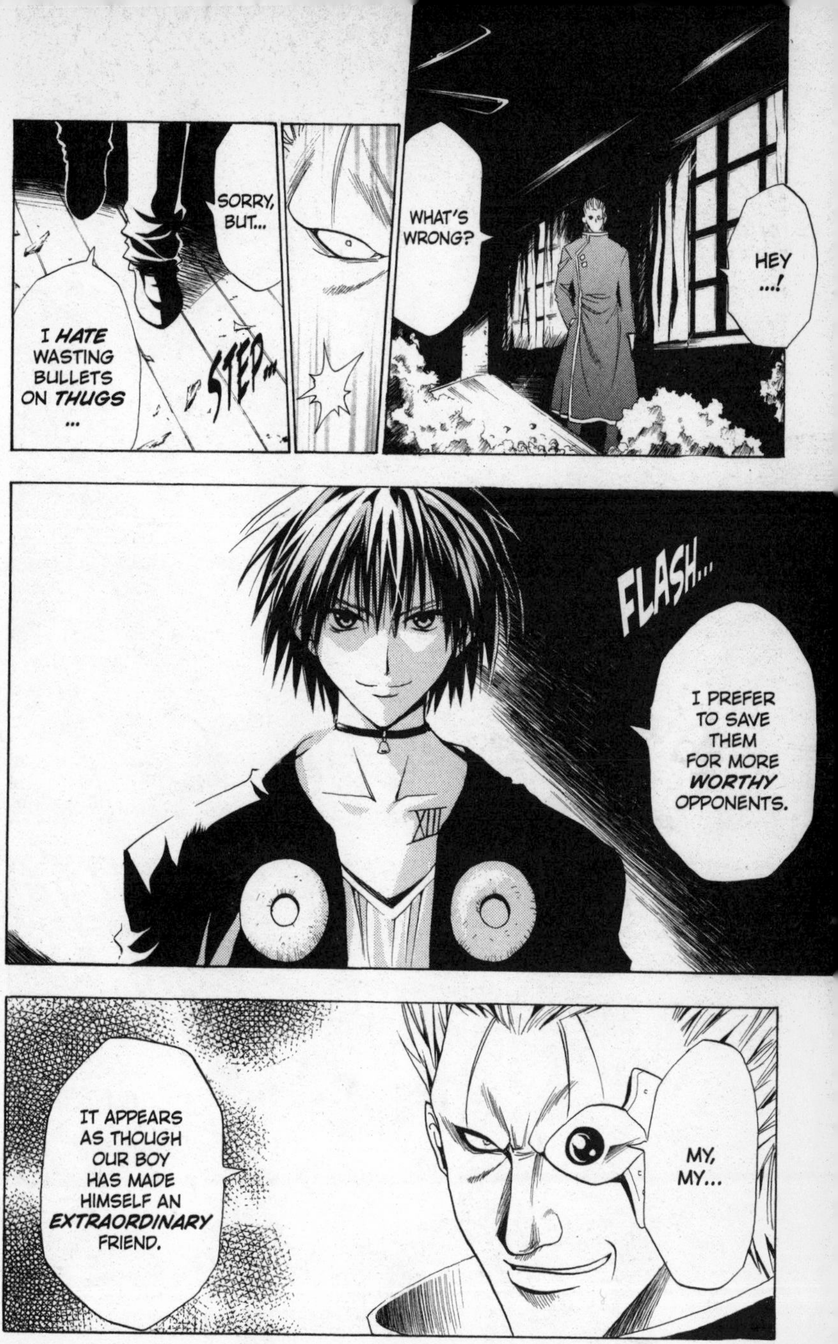
HEY ...!
WHAT'S WRONG?
SORRY, BUT...
STEP...
I HATE WASTING BULLETS ON THUGS ...
FLASH...
I PREFER TO SAVE THEM FOR MORE WORTHY OPPONENTS.
MY, MY...
IT APPEARS AS THOUGH OUR BOY HAS MADE HIMSELF AN EXTRAORDINARY FRIEND.

READ THIS WAY

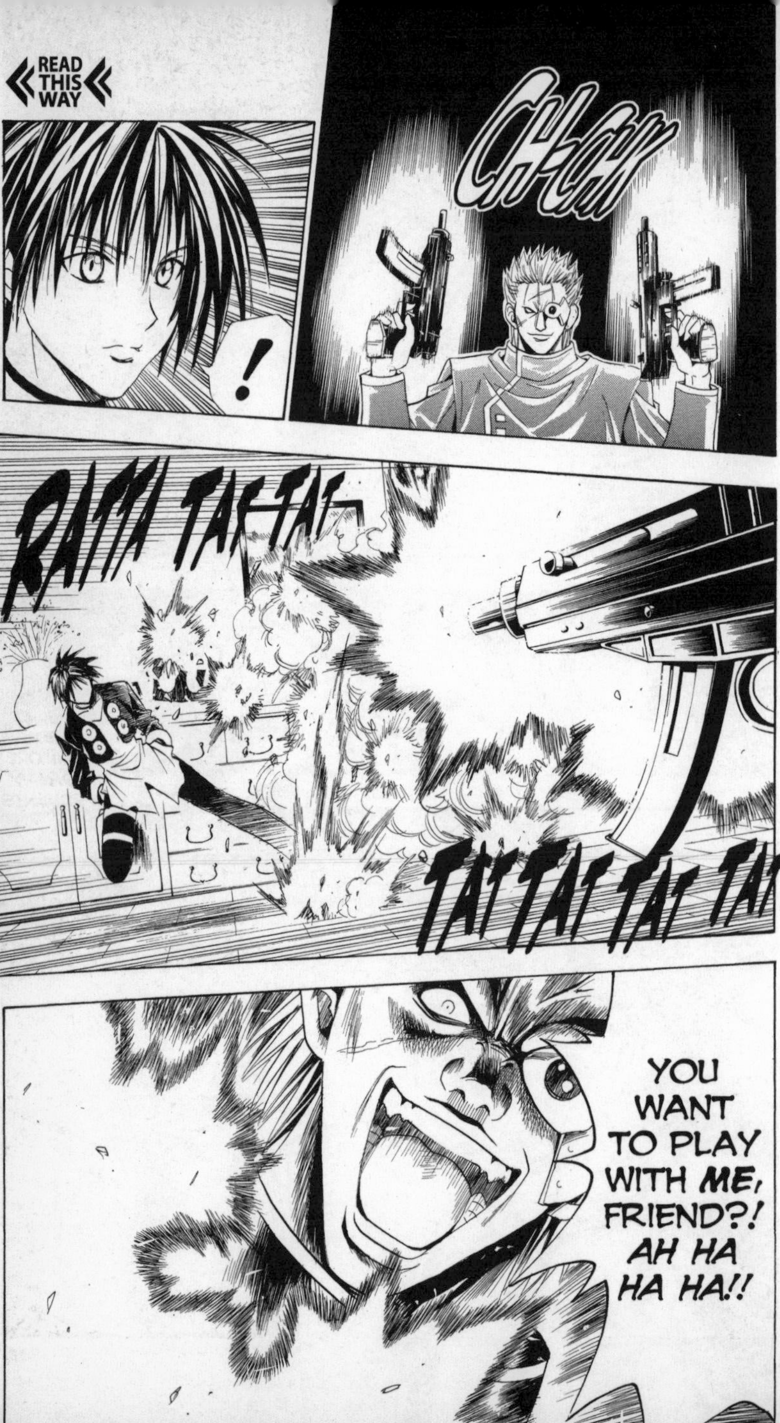
CHAK
!
RATTA TAT-TAT
TAT TAT TAT TAT
YOU WANT TO PLAY WITH ME, FRIEND?! AH HA HA HA!!

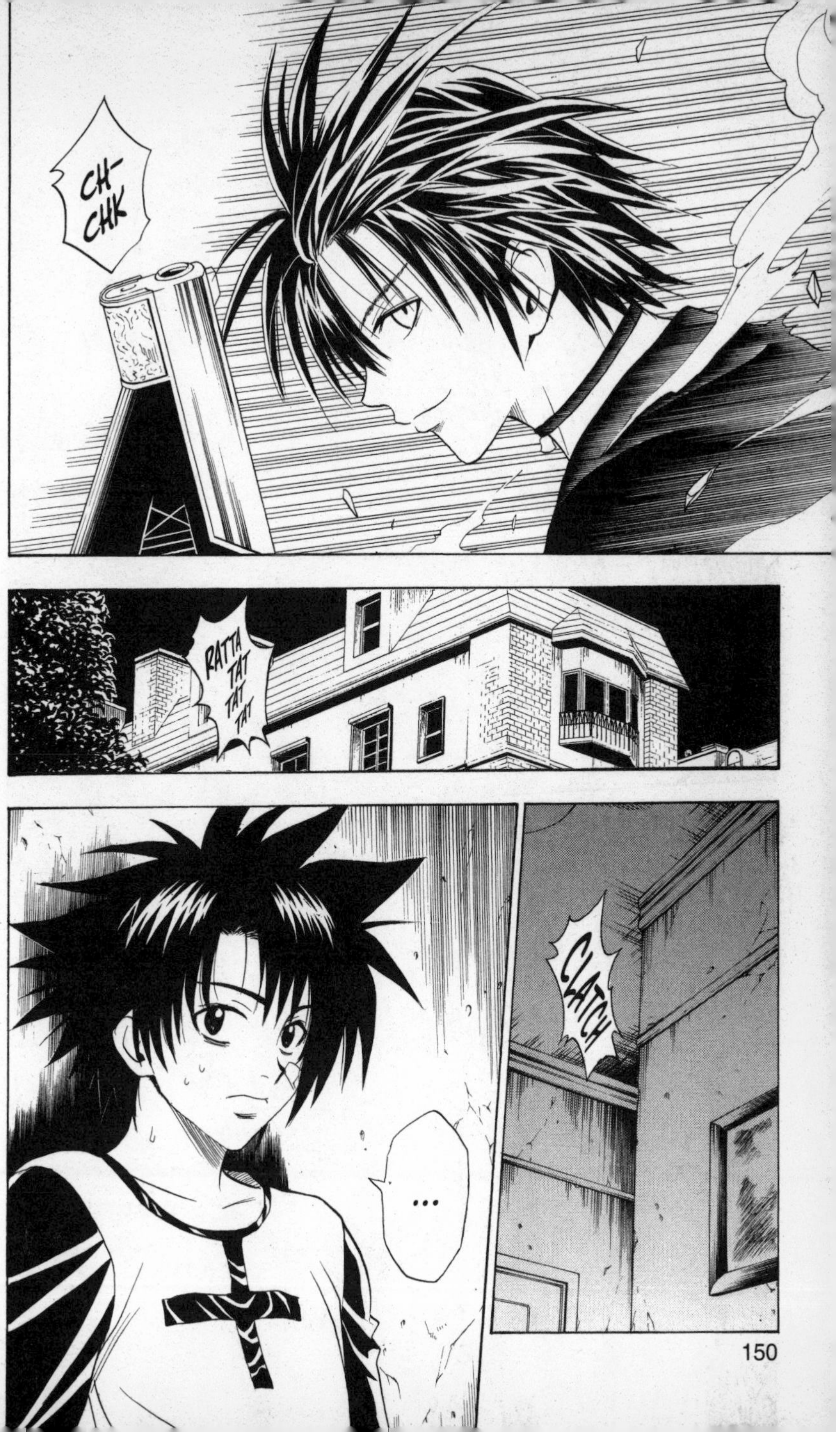
CH-CHK
RATTA TAT TAT TAT
CLATCH
...

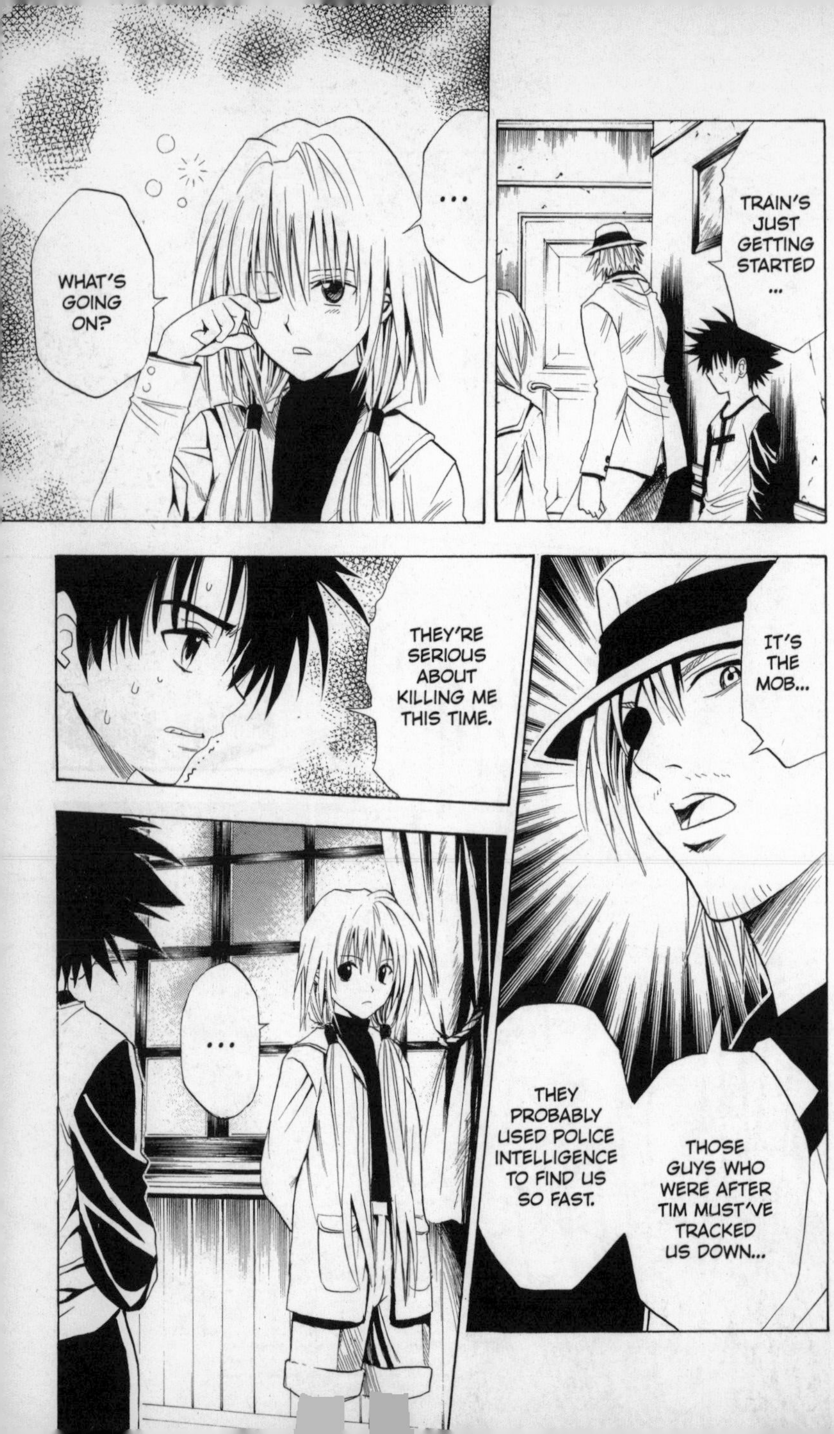
TRAIN'S JUST GETTING STARTED ...
...
WHAT'S GOING ON?
IT'S THE MOB...
THOSE GUYS WHO WERE AFTER TIM MUST'VE TRACKED US DOWN...
THEY PROBABLY USED POLICE INTELLIGENCE TO FIND US SO FAST.
THEY'RE SERIOUS ABOUT KILLING ME THIS TIME.
...

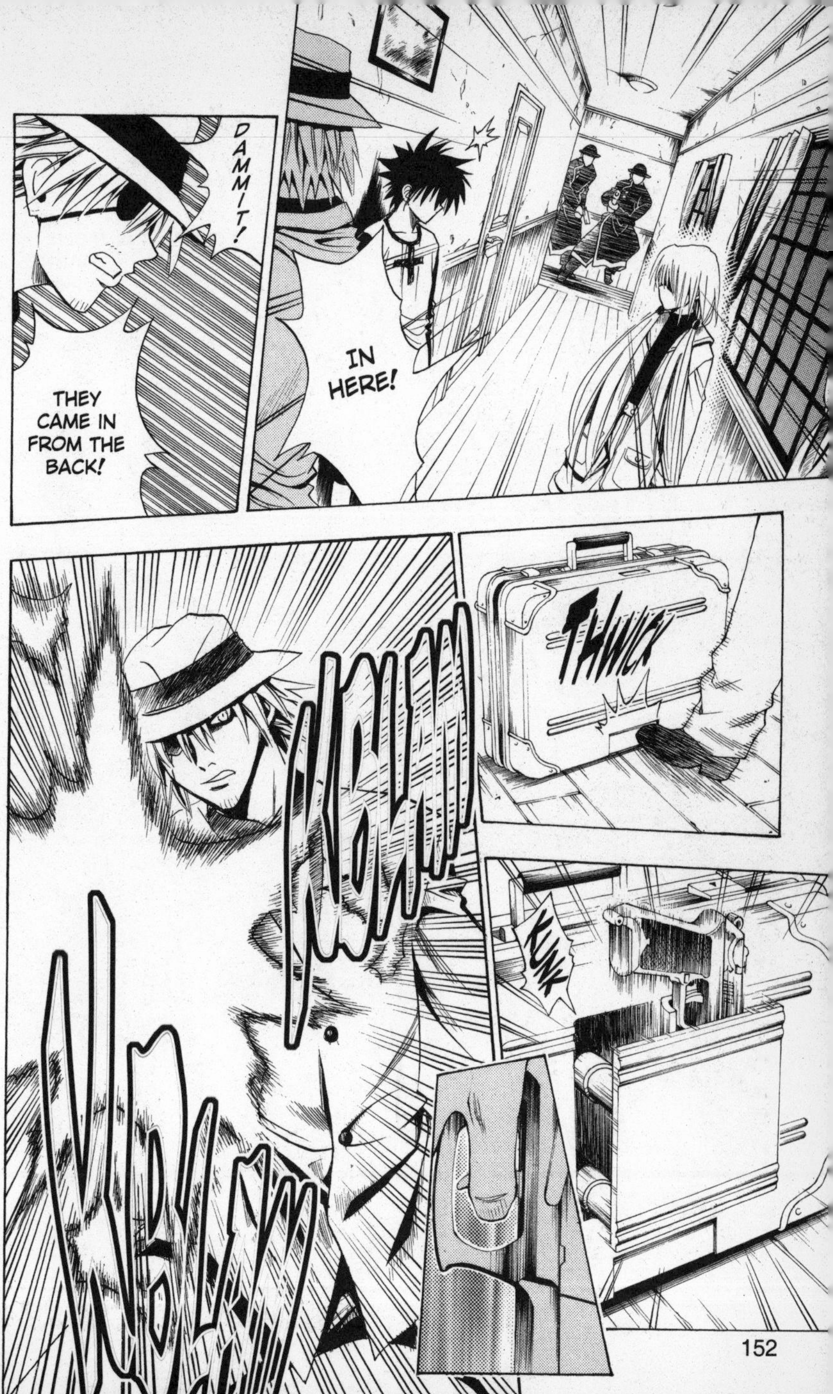
IN HERE!
DAMMIT!
THEY CAME IN FROM THE BACK!
THWICK
KLUNK
KBLAM!
WBLAM

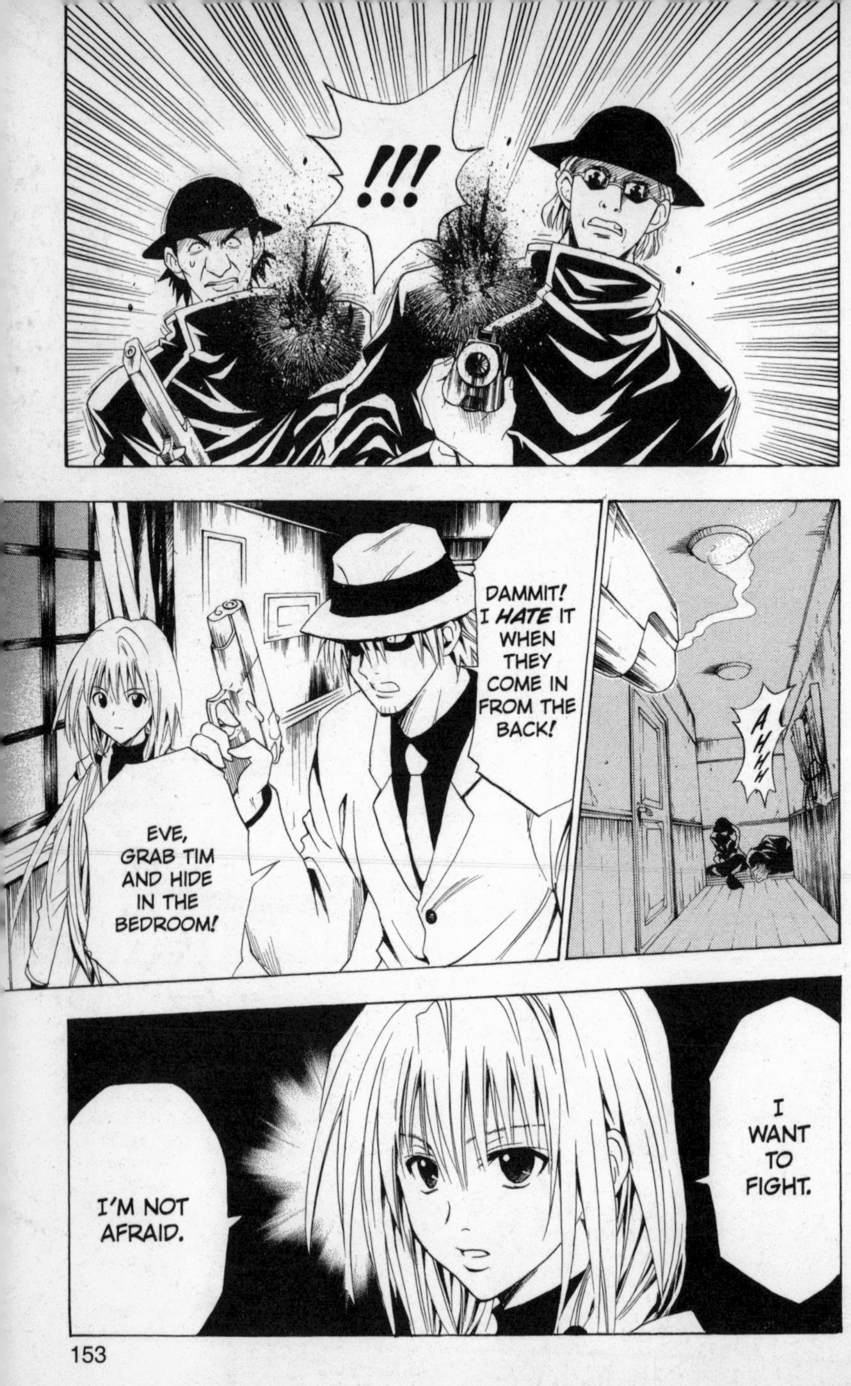
!!!
AHHH
DAMMIT! I HATE IT WHEN THEY COME IN FROM THE BACK!
EVE, GRAB TIM AND HIDE IN THE BEDROOM!
I WANT TO FIGHT.
I'M NOT AFRAID.

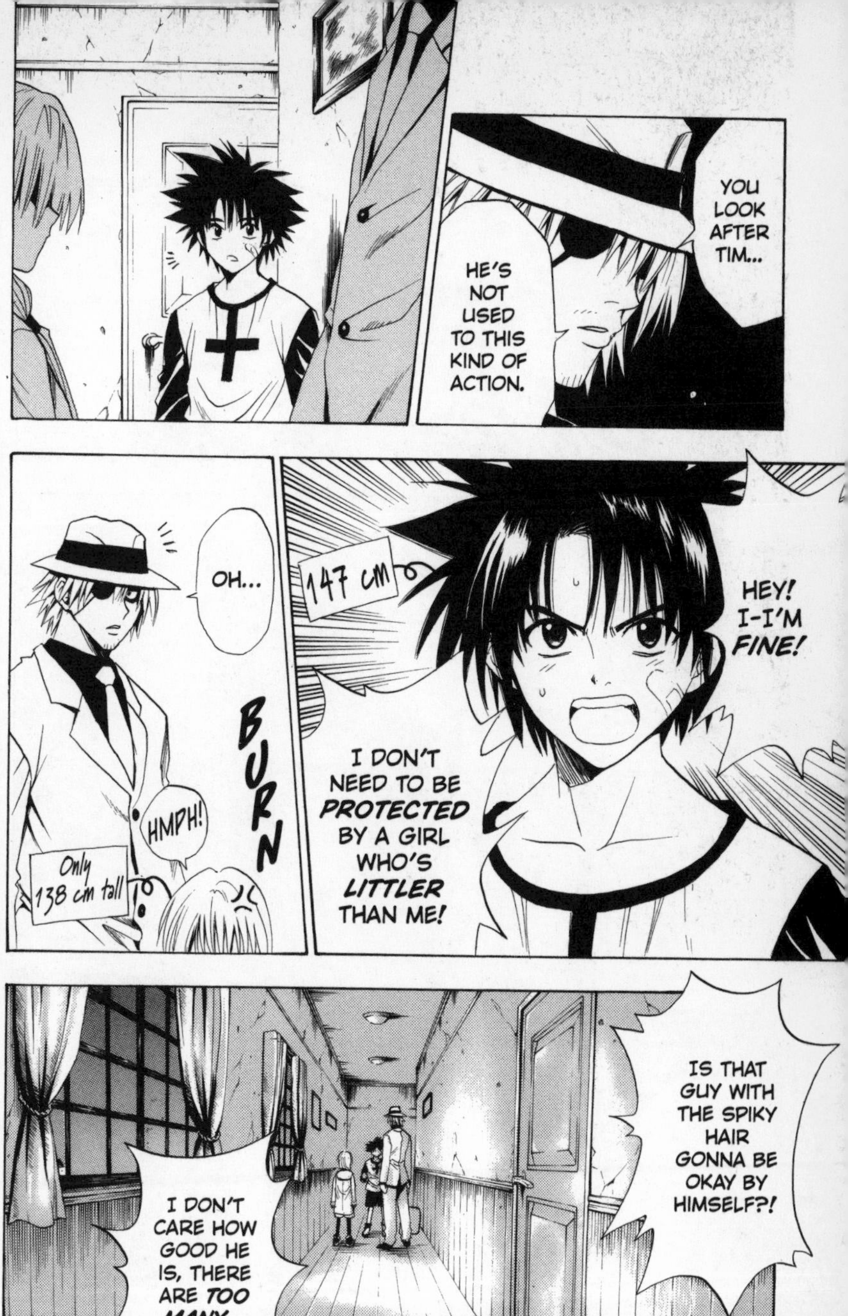
YOU LOOK AFTER TIM...
HE'S NOT USED TO THIS KIND OF ACTION.
HEY! I-I'M *FINE!*
147 cm
I DON'T NEED TO BE *PROTECTED* BY A GIRL WHO'S *LITTLER* THAN ME!
OH...
BURN
HMPH!
Only 138 cm tall
IS THAT GUY WITH THE SPIKY HAIR GONNA BE OKAY BY HIMSELF?!
I DON'T CARE HOW GOOD HE IS, THERE ARE *TOO MANY*...

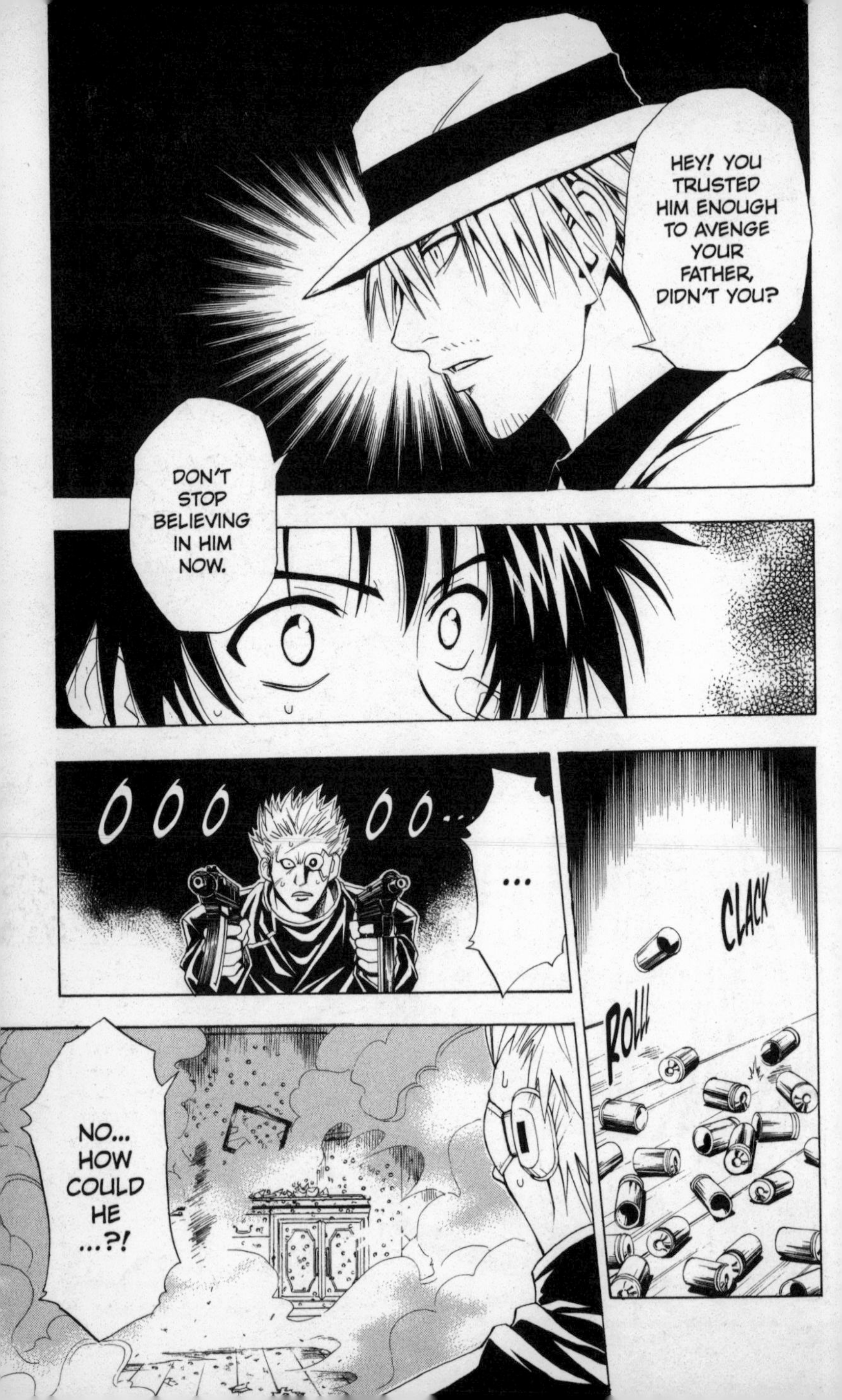
HEY! YOU TRUSTED HIM ENOUGH TO AVENGE YOUR FATHER, DIDN'T YOU?
DON'T STOP BELIEVING IN HIM NOW.
CLACK
ROLL
...
NO... HOW COULD HE ...?!

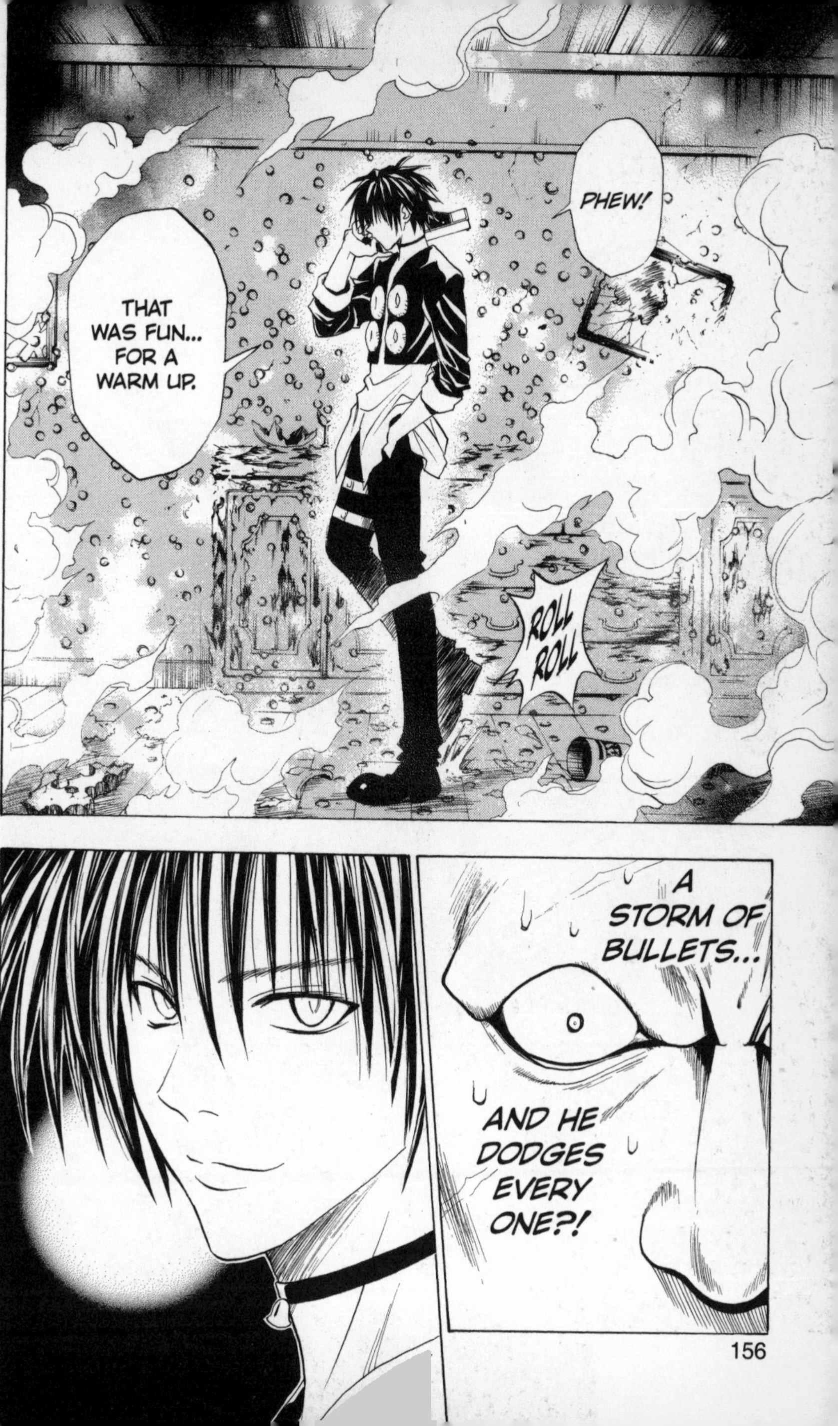
PHEW!
THAT WAS FUN... FOR A WARM UP.
ROLL ROLL
A STORM OF BULLETS...
AND HE DODGES EVERY ONE?!

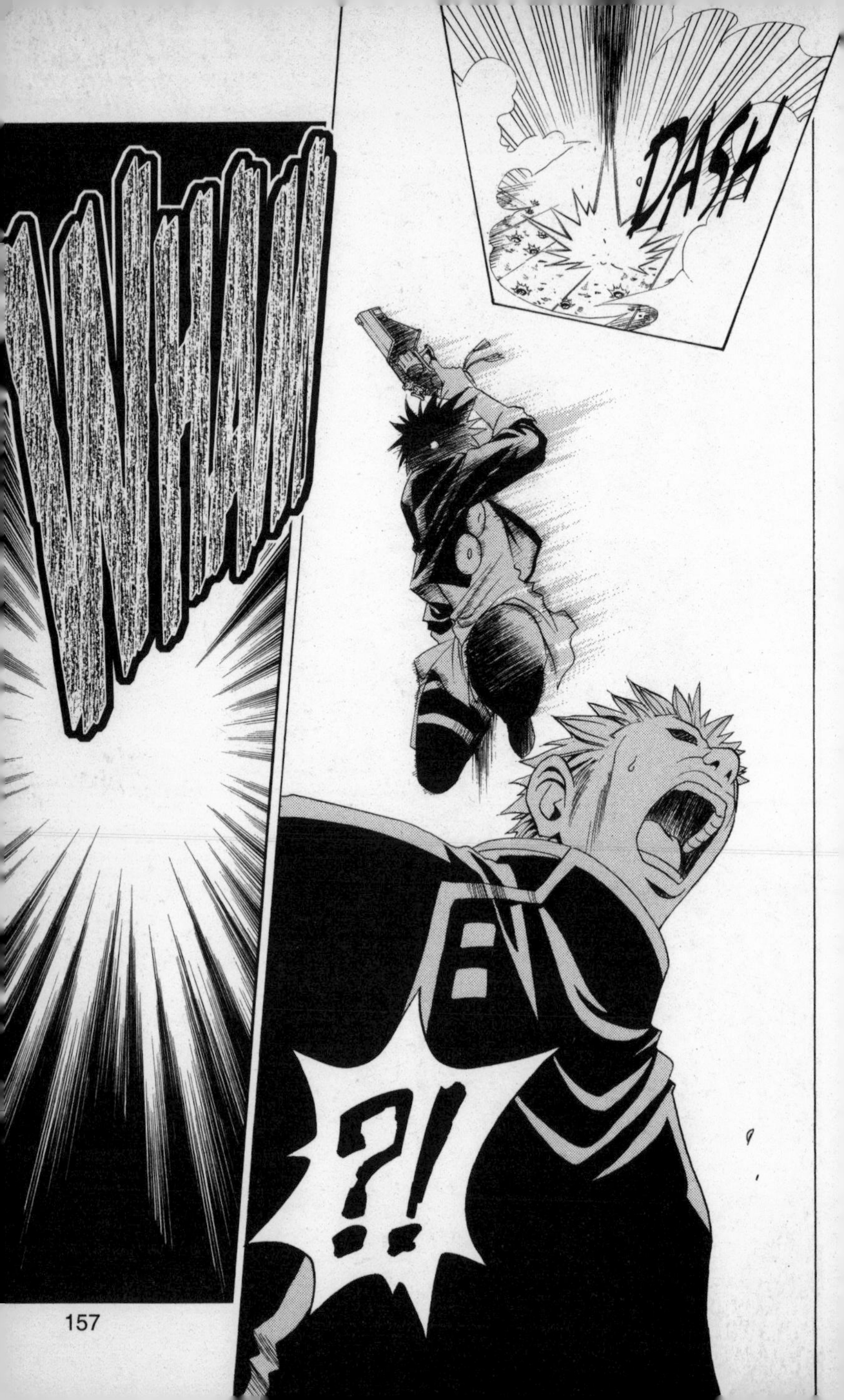
DASH
?!
WHAM!

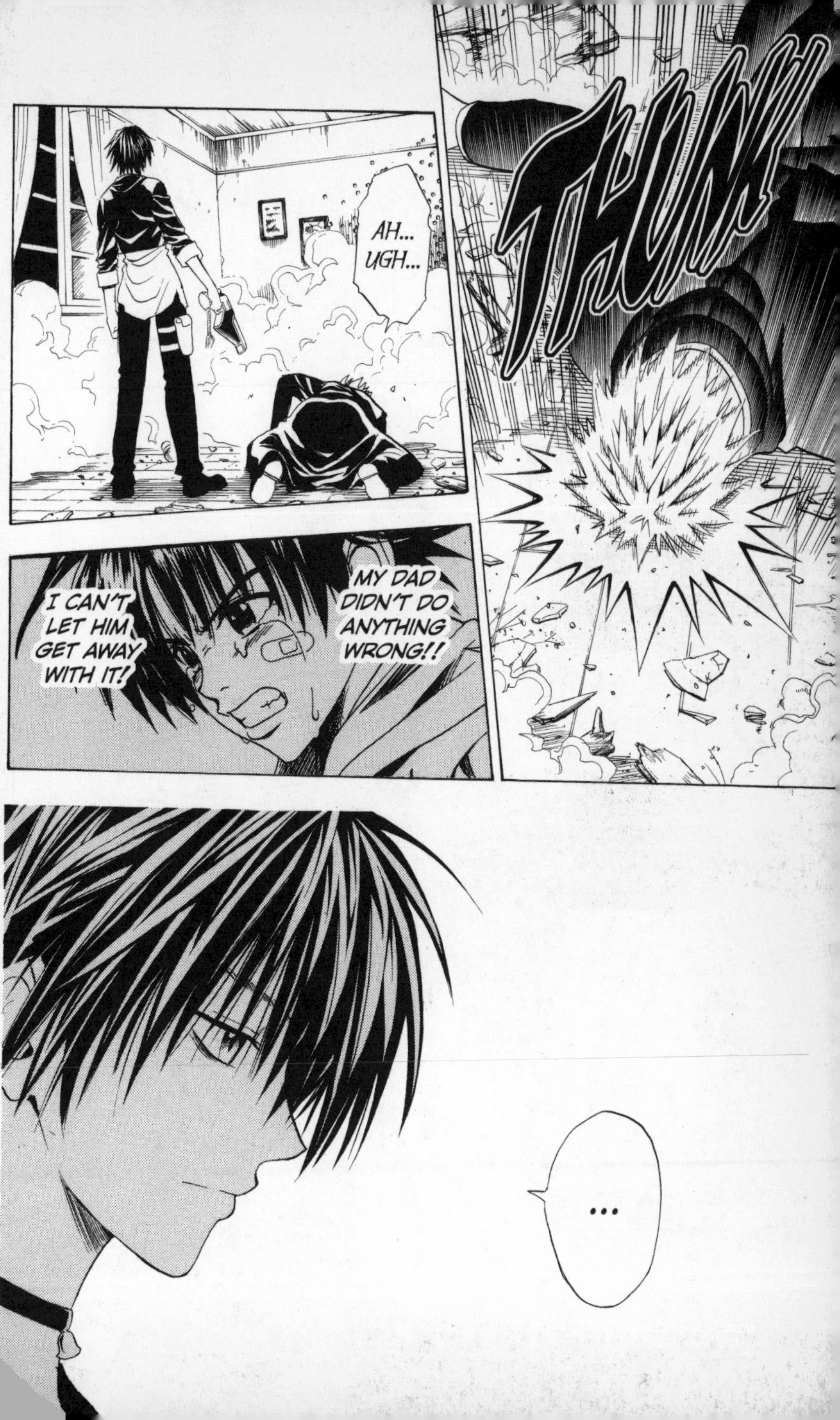
THOOM
AH... UGH...
MY DAD DIDN'T DO ANYTHING WRONG!!
I CAN'T LET HIM GET AWAY WITH IT!
...

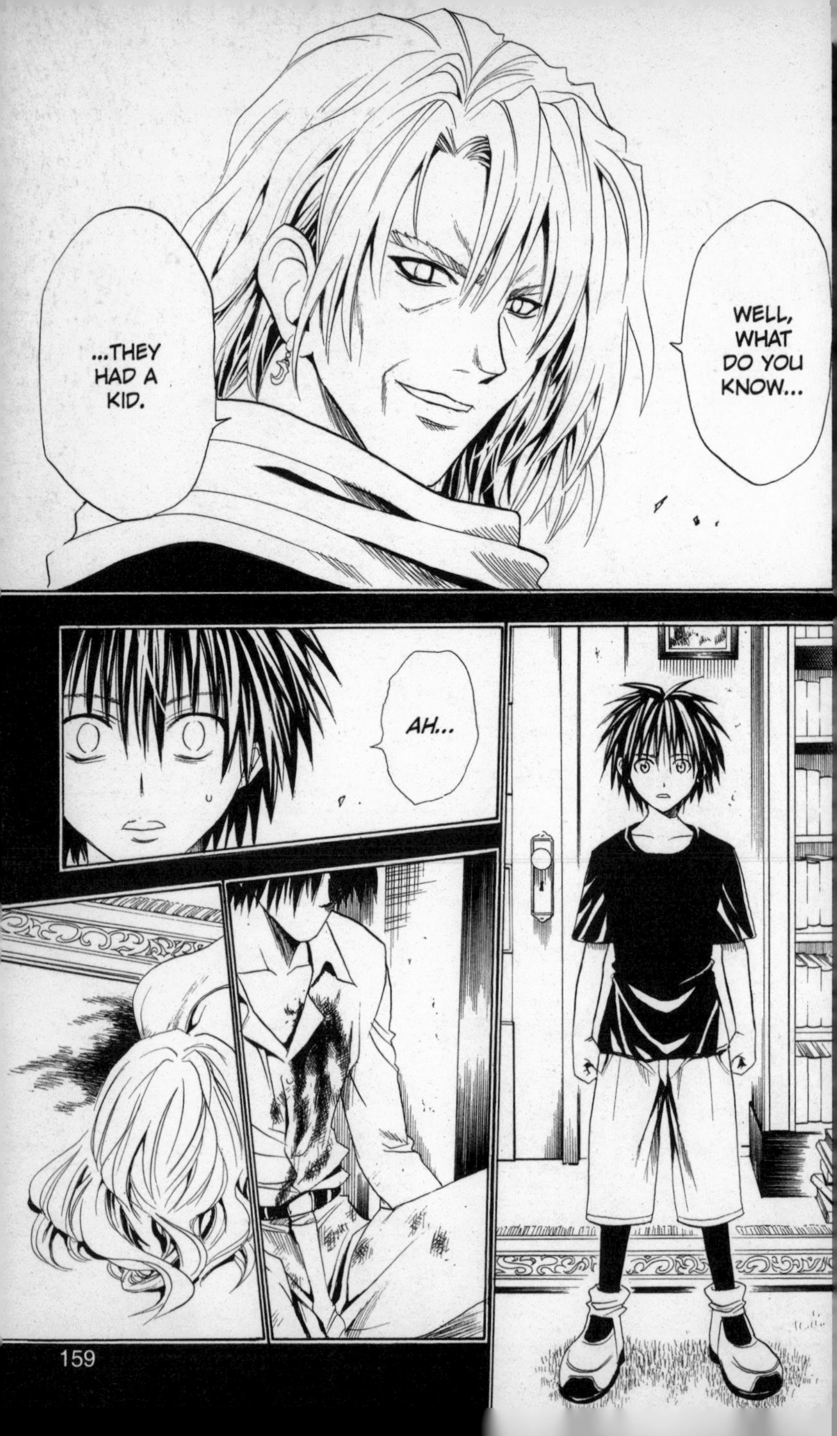
WELL, WHAT DO YOU KNOW...
...THEY HAD A KID.
AH...

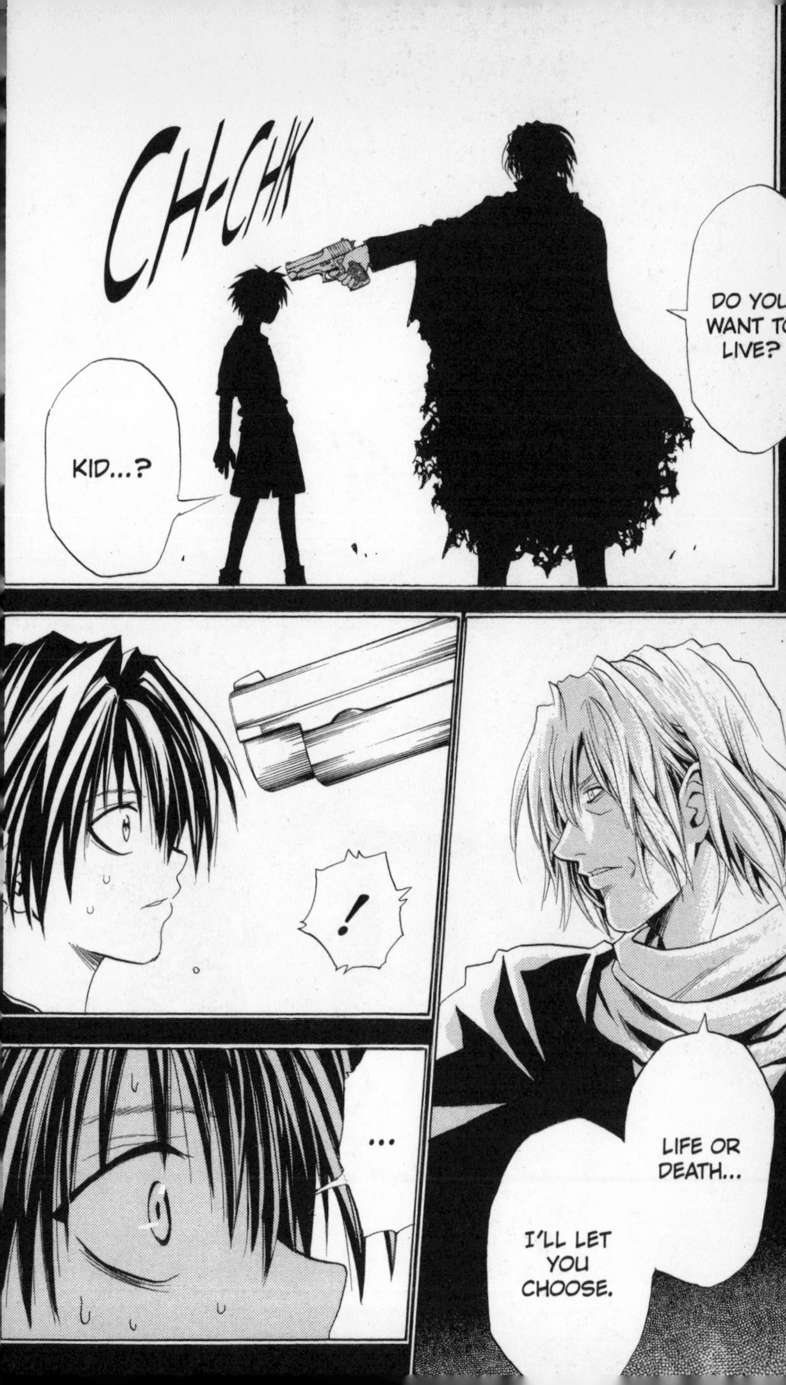
DO YOU WANT TO LIVE?
CH-CHK
KID...?
LIFE OR DEATH...
I'LL LET YOU CHOOSE.
!
...

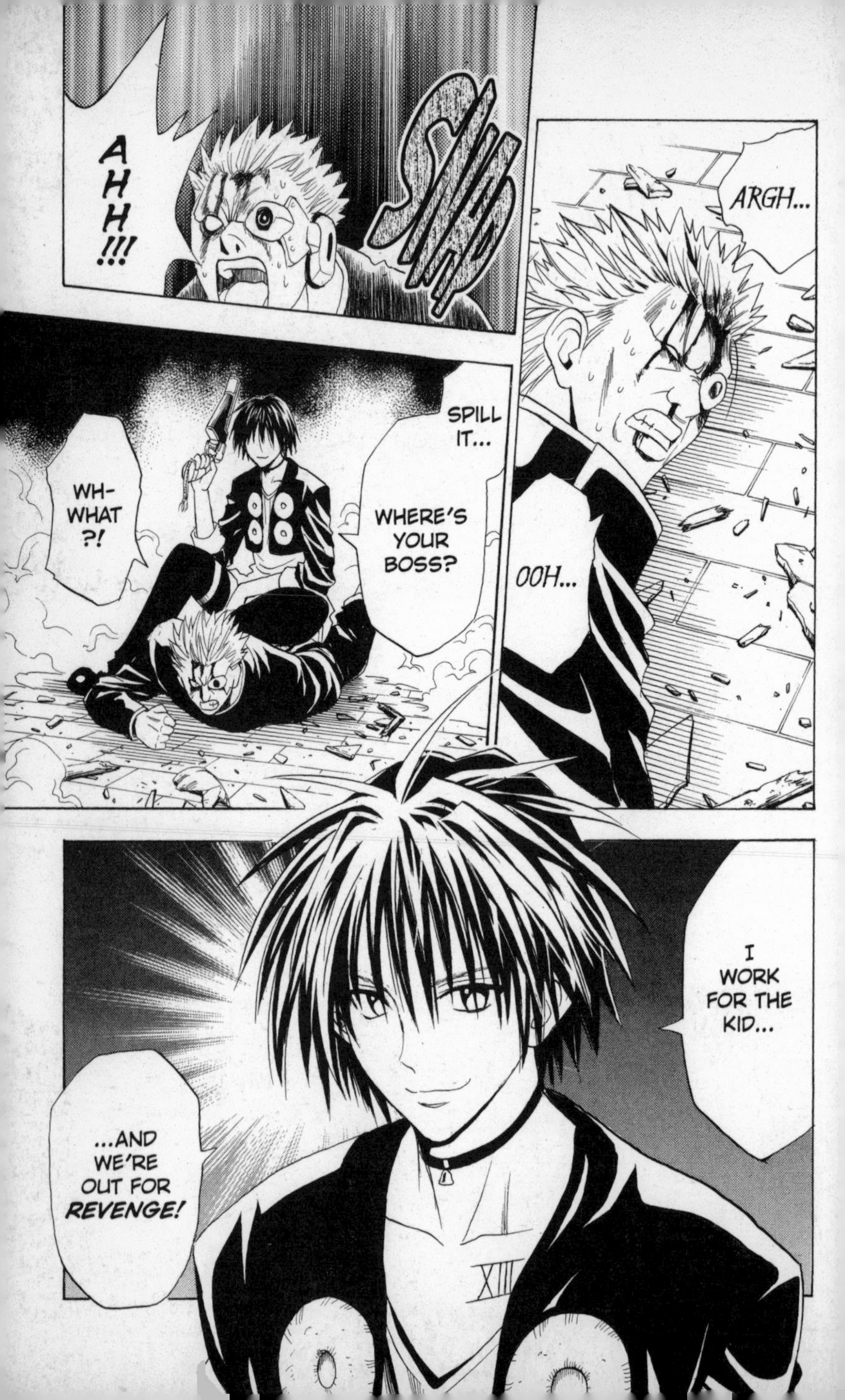
ARGH...
OOH...
AHH!!!
SHP
SPILL IT...
WHERE'S YOUR BOSS?
WH-WHAT?!
I WORK FOR THE KID...
...AND WE'RE OUT FOR REVENGE!

Train, Age 10

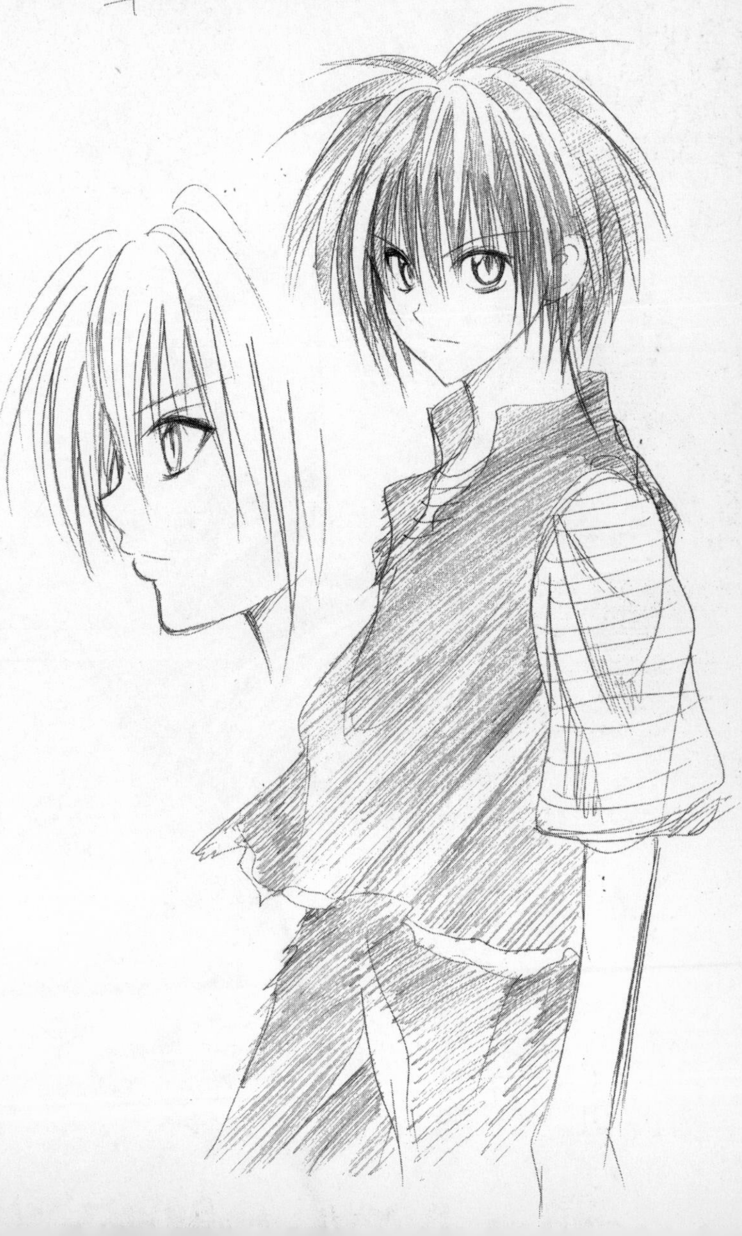

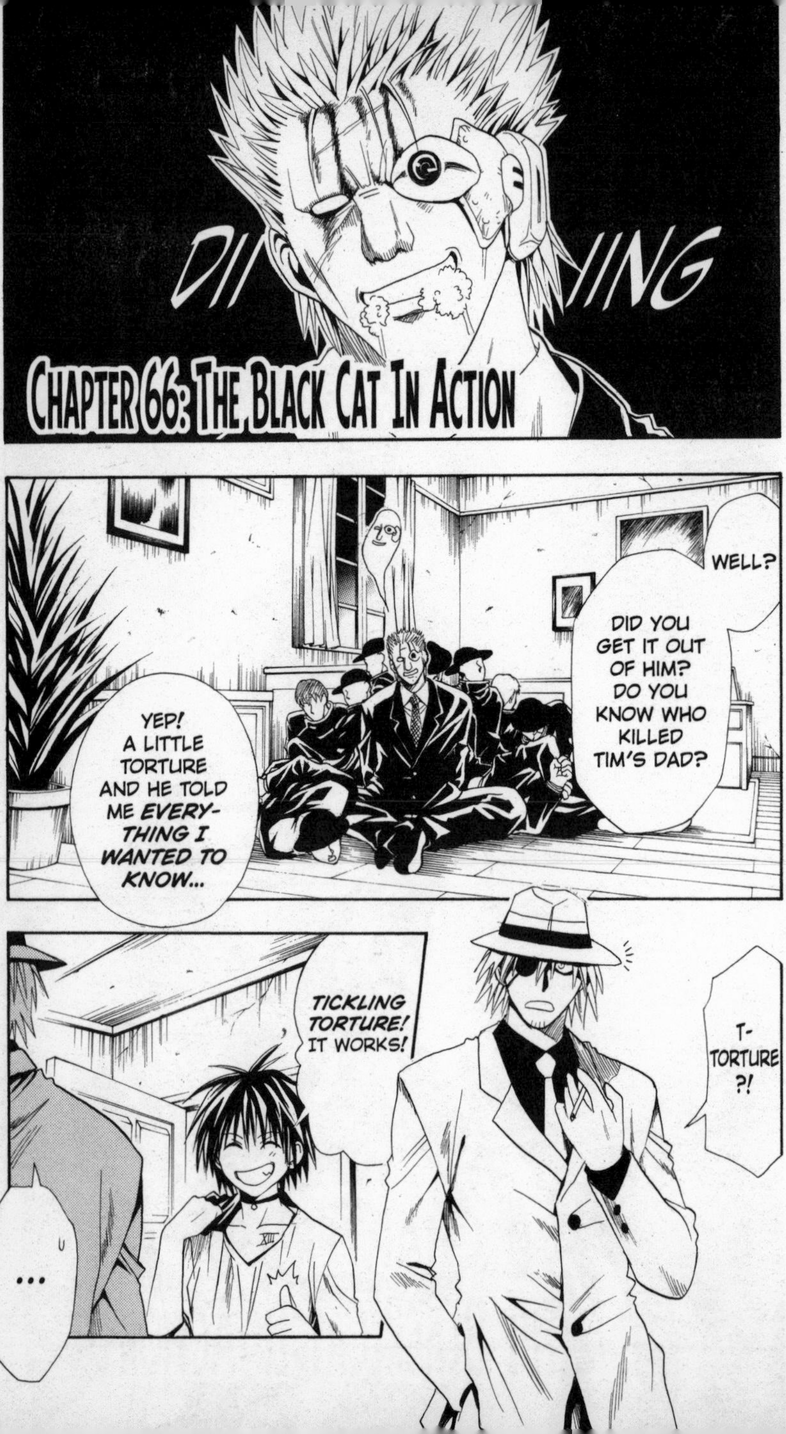
DIIIYING
Chapter 66: The Black Cat In Action
WELL?
DID YOU GET IT OUT OF HIM? DO YOU KNOW WHO KILLED TIM'S DAD?
YEP! A LITTLE TORTURE AND HE TOLD ME EVERY-THING I WANTED TO KNOW...
T-TORTURE?!
TICKLING TORTURE! IT WORKS!
...

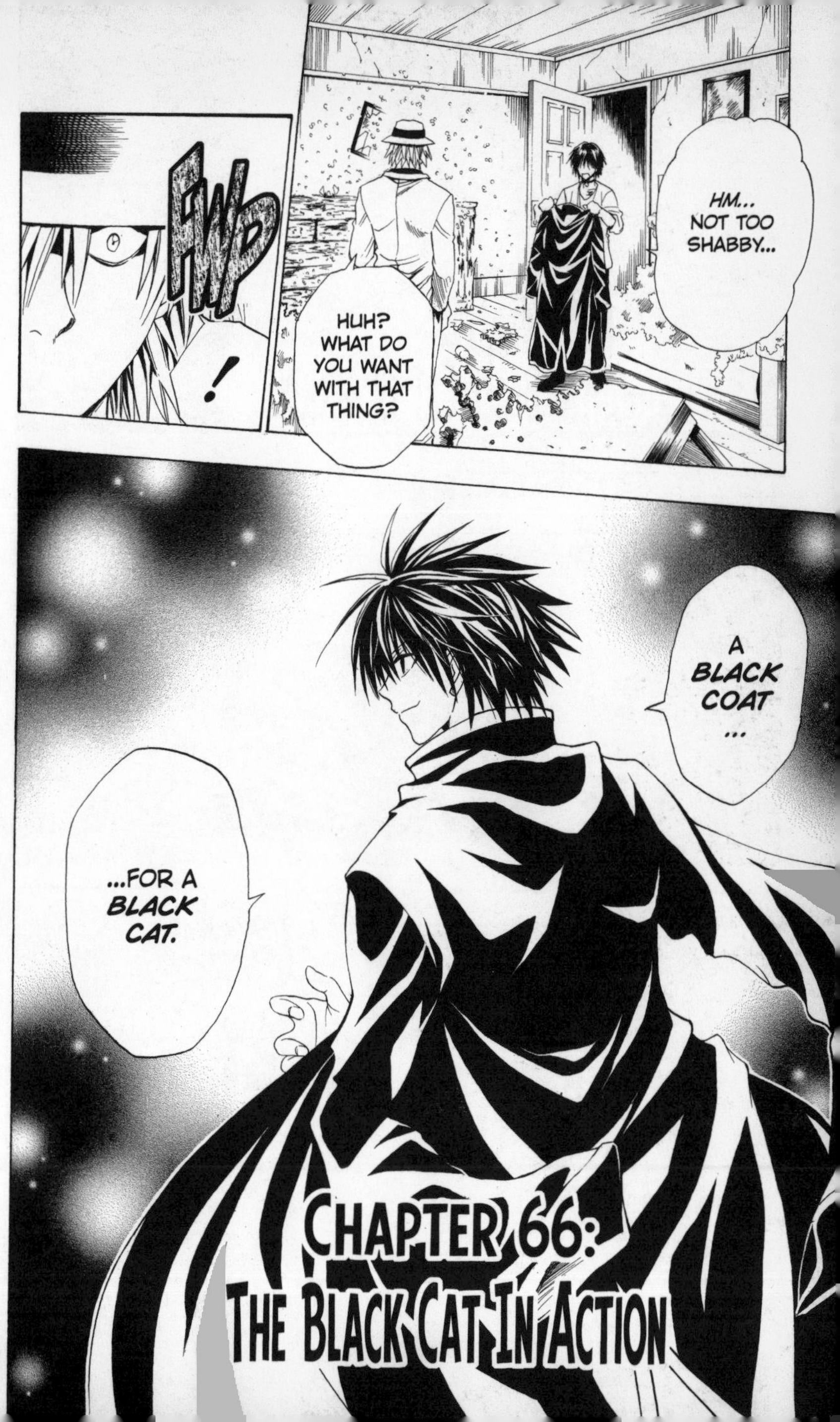
HM... NOT TOO SHABBY...
HUH? WHAT DO YOU WANT WITH THAT THING?
FWP
!
A BLACK COAT ...
...FOR A BLACK CAT.
CHAPTER 66:
THE BLACK CAT IN ACTION

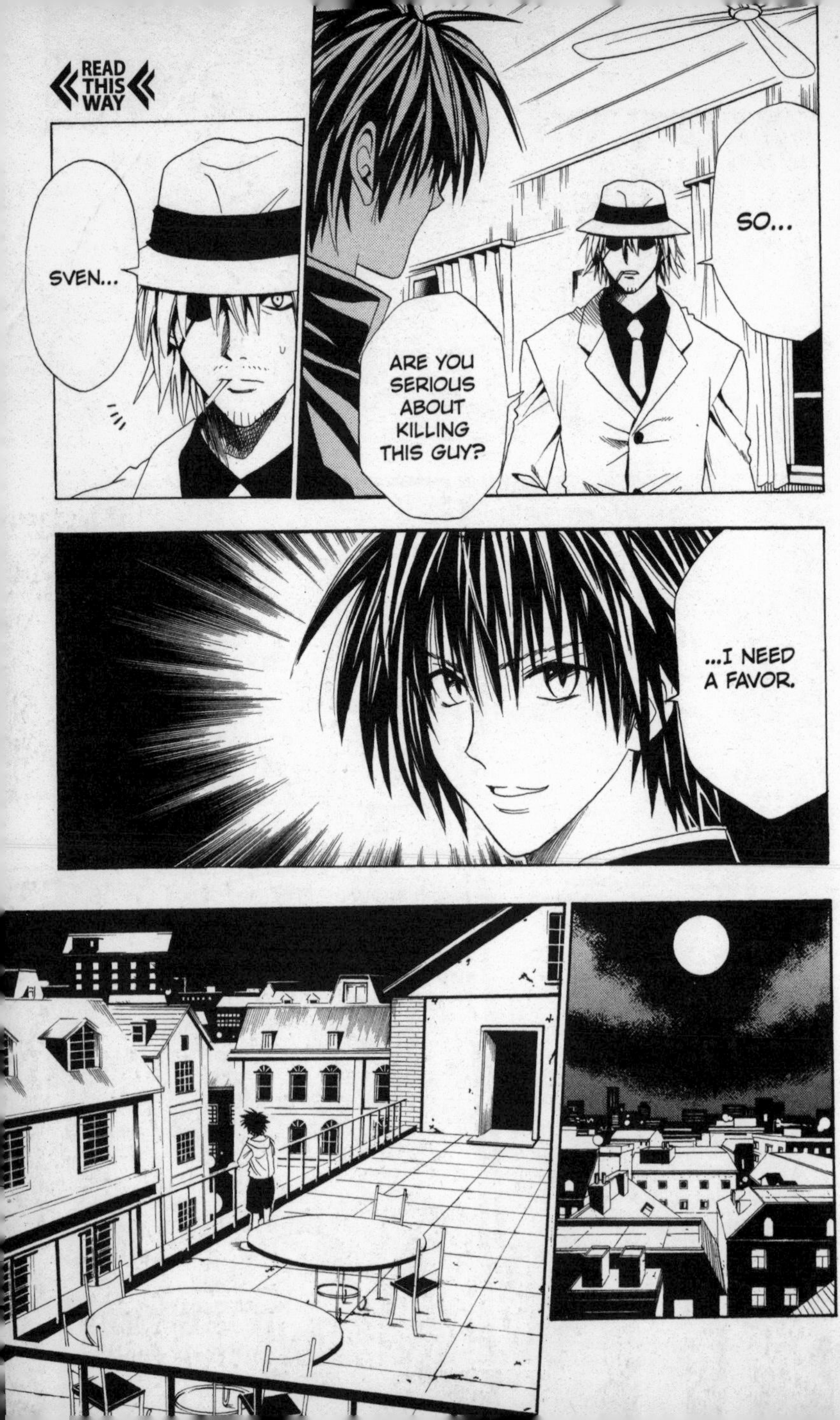
READ THIS WAY
SO...
ARE YOU SERIOUS ABOUT KILLING THIS GUY?
SVEN...
...I NEED A FAVOR.

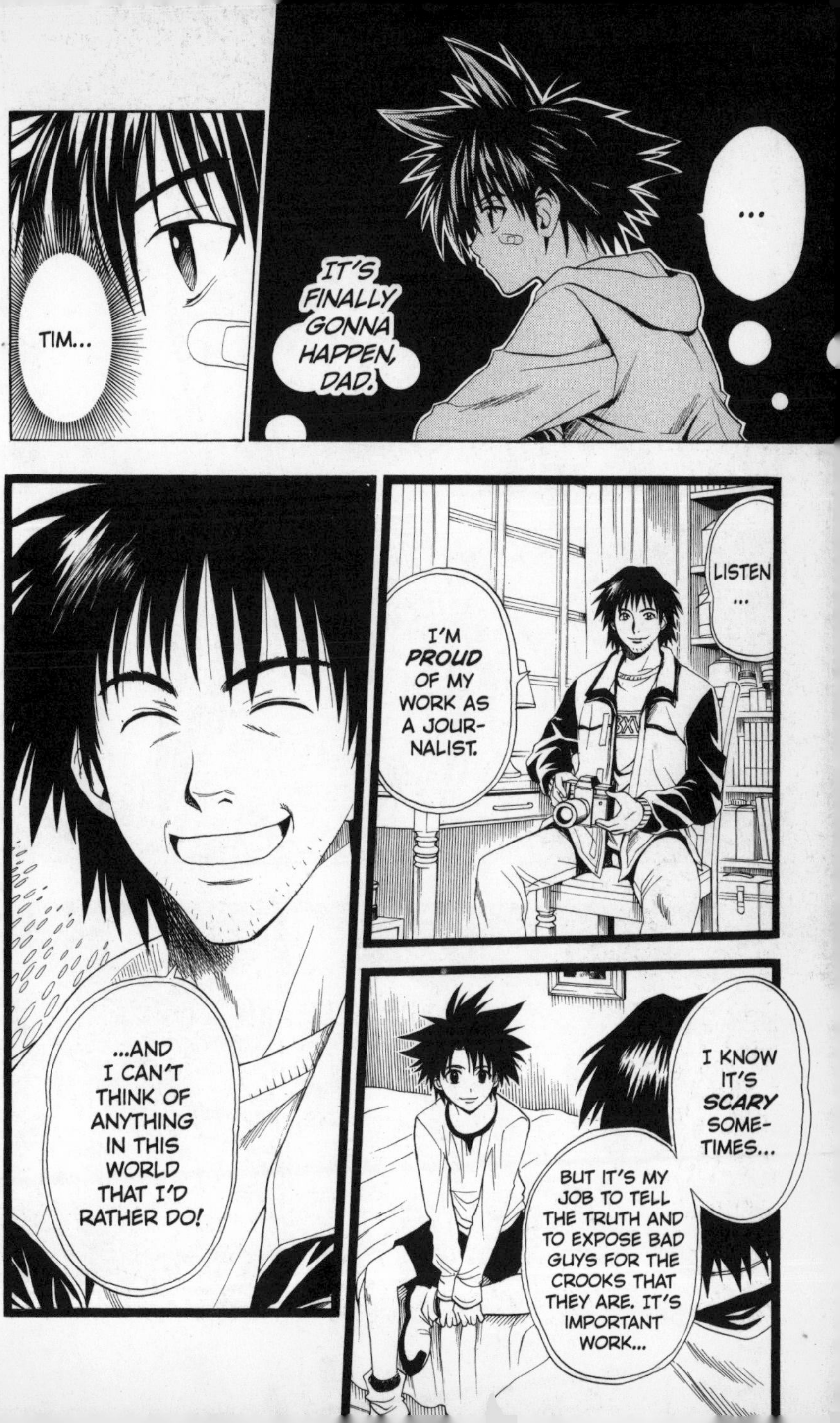
...
IT'S FINALLY GONNA HAPPEN, DAD.
TIM...
LISTEN...
I'M PROUD OF MY WORK AS A JOURNALIST.
I KNOW IT'S SCARY SOMETIMES...
BUT IT'S MY JOB TO TELL THE TRUTH AND TO EXPOSE BAD GUYS FOR THE CROOKS THAT THEY ARE. IT'S IMPORTANT WORK...
...AND I CAN'T THINK OF ANYTHING IN THIS WORLD THAT I'D RATHER DO!

READ THIS WAY

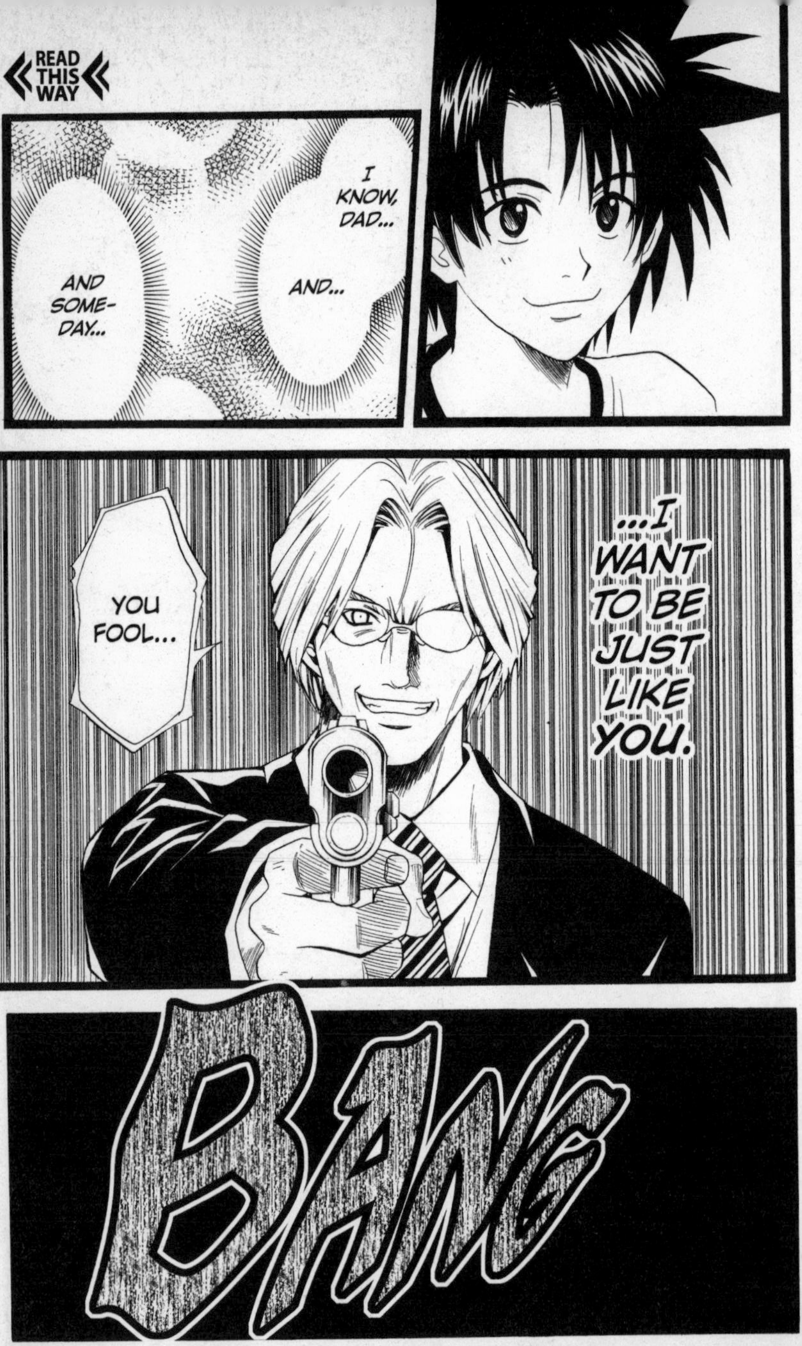
I KNOW, DAD...
AND...
AND SOME-DAY...
...I WANT TO BE JUST LIKE YOU.
YOU FOOL...
BANG

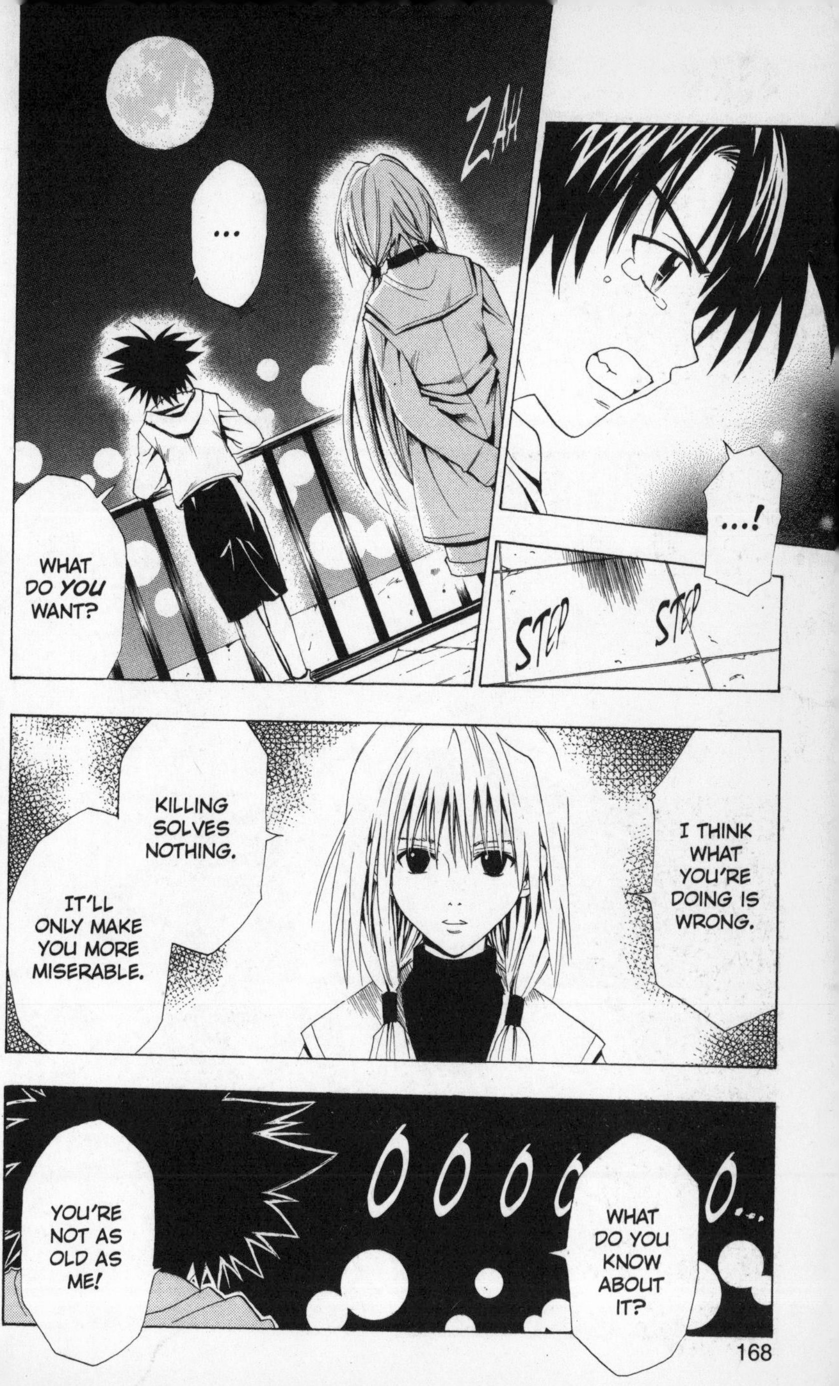
...!
STEP STEP
ZAH
...
WHAT DO *YOU* WANT?
I THINK WHAT YOU'RE DOING IS WRONG.
KILLING SOLVES NOTHING.
IT'LL ONLY MAKE YOU MORE MISERABLE.
WHAT DO YOU KNOW ABOUT IT?
OOOOOO...
YOU'RE NOT AS OLD AS ME!

READ THIS WAY

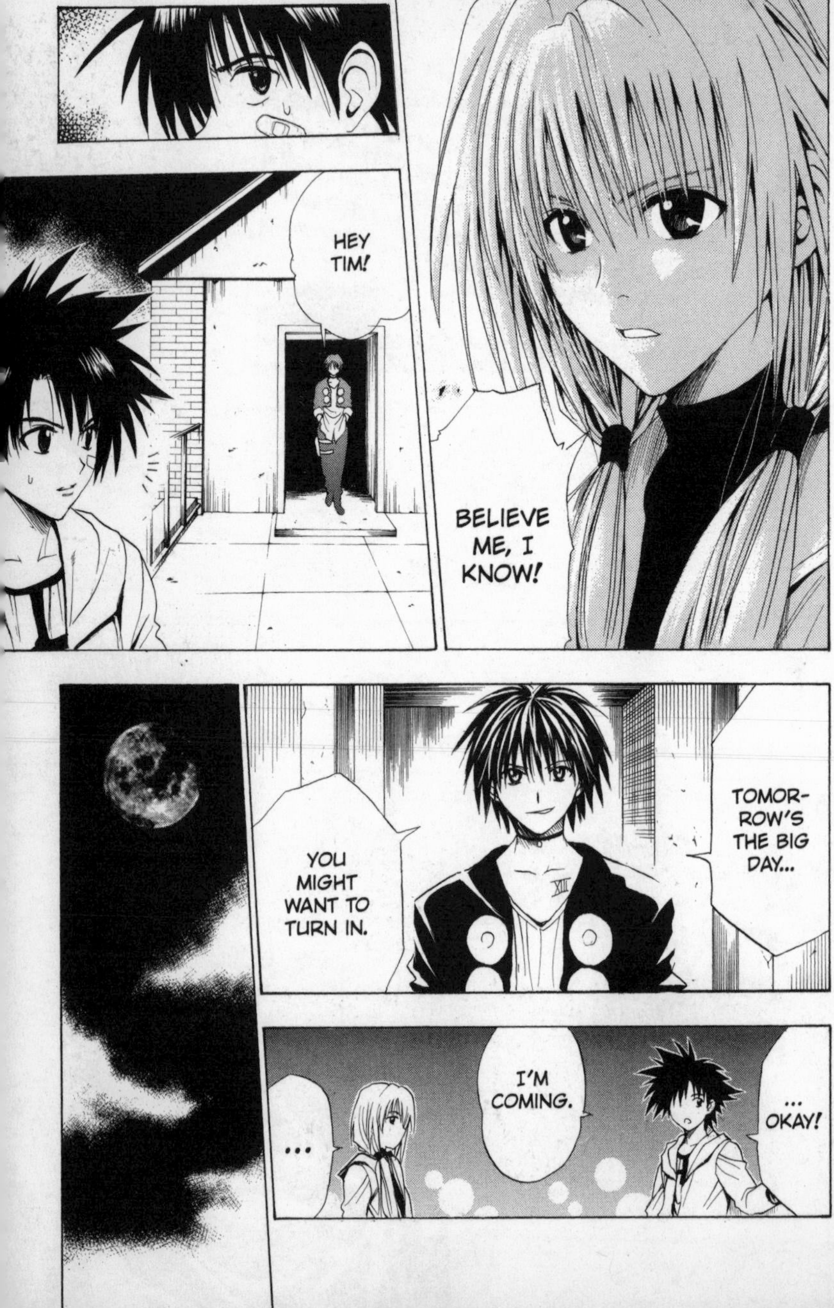
BELIEVE ME, I KNOW!
HEY TIM!
TOMOR-ROW'S THE BIG DAY...
YOU MIGHT WANT TO TURN IN.
...OKAY!
I'M COMING.
...

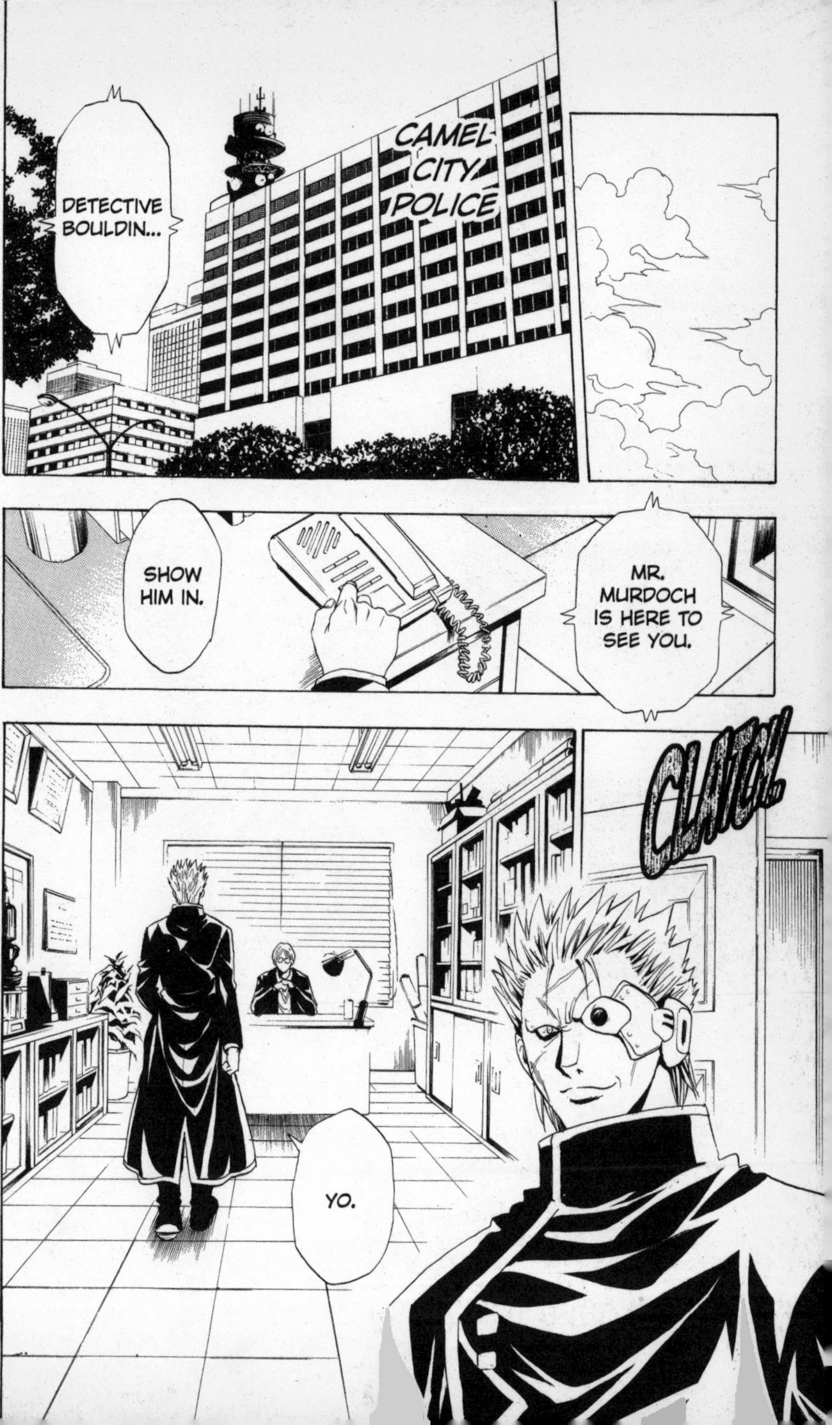
CAMEL CITY POLICE
DETECTIVE BOULDIN...
MR. MURDOCH IS HERE TO SEE YOU.
SHOW HIM IN.
CLATCH!
YO.

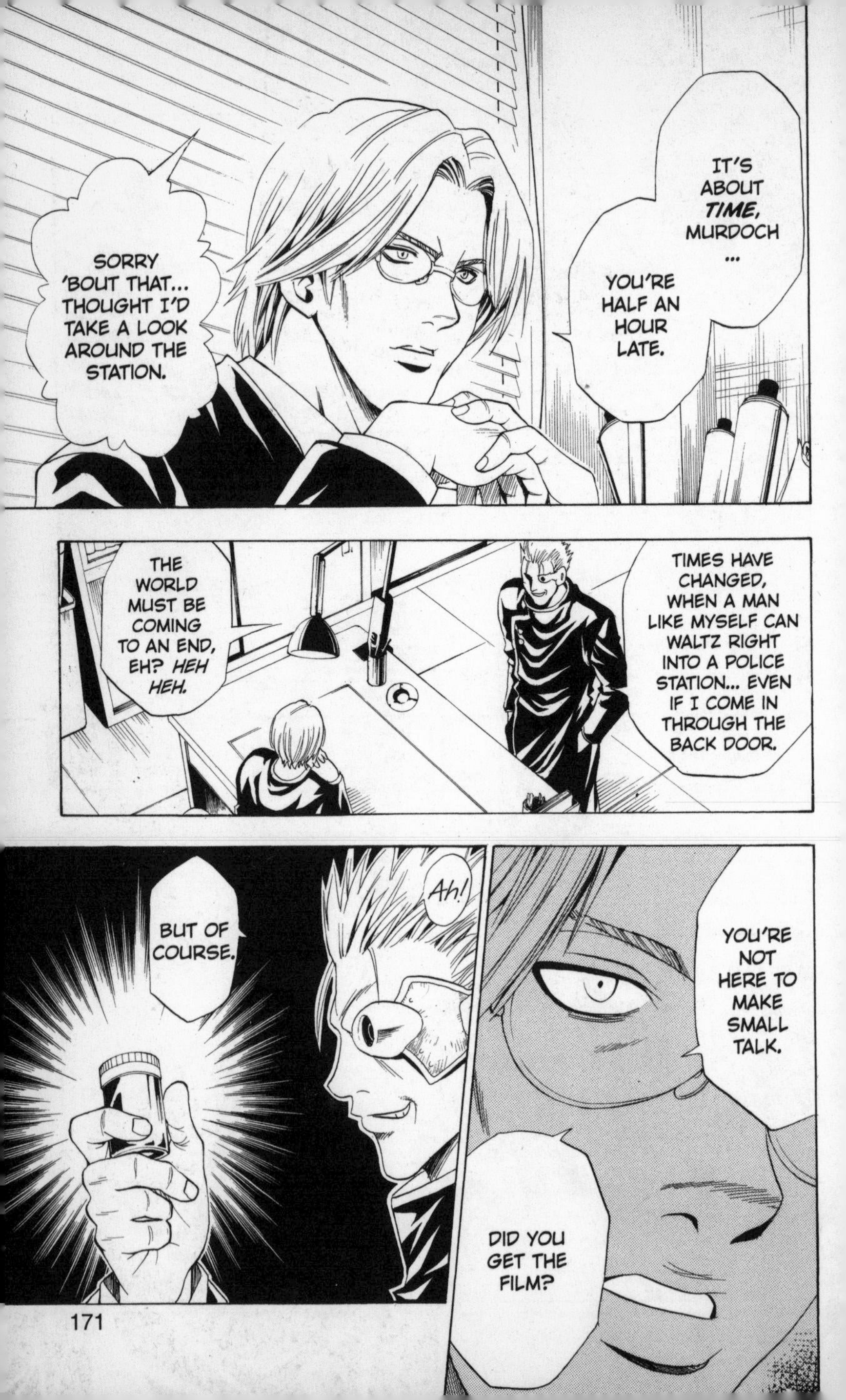
IT'S ABOUT *TIME,* MURDOCH ...
YOU'RE HALF AN HOUR LATE.
SORRY 'BOUT THAT... THOUGHT I'D TAKE A LOOK AROUND THE STATION.
TIMES HAVE CHANGED, WHEN A MAN LIKE MYSELF CAN WALTZ RIGHT INTO A POLICE STATION... EVEN IF I COME IN THROUGH THE BACK DOOR.
THE WORLD MUST BE COMING TO AN END, EH? *HEH HEH.*
YOU'RE NOT HERE TO MAKE SMALL TALK.
DID YOU GET THE FILM?
Ah!
BUT OF COURSE.

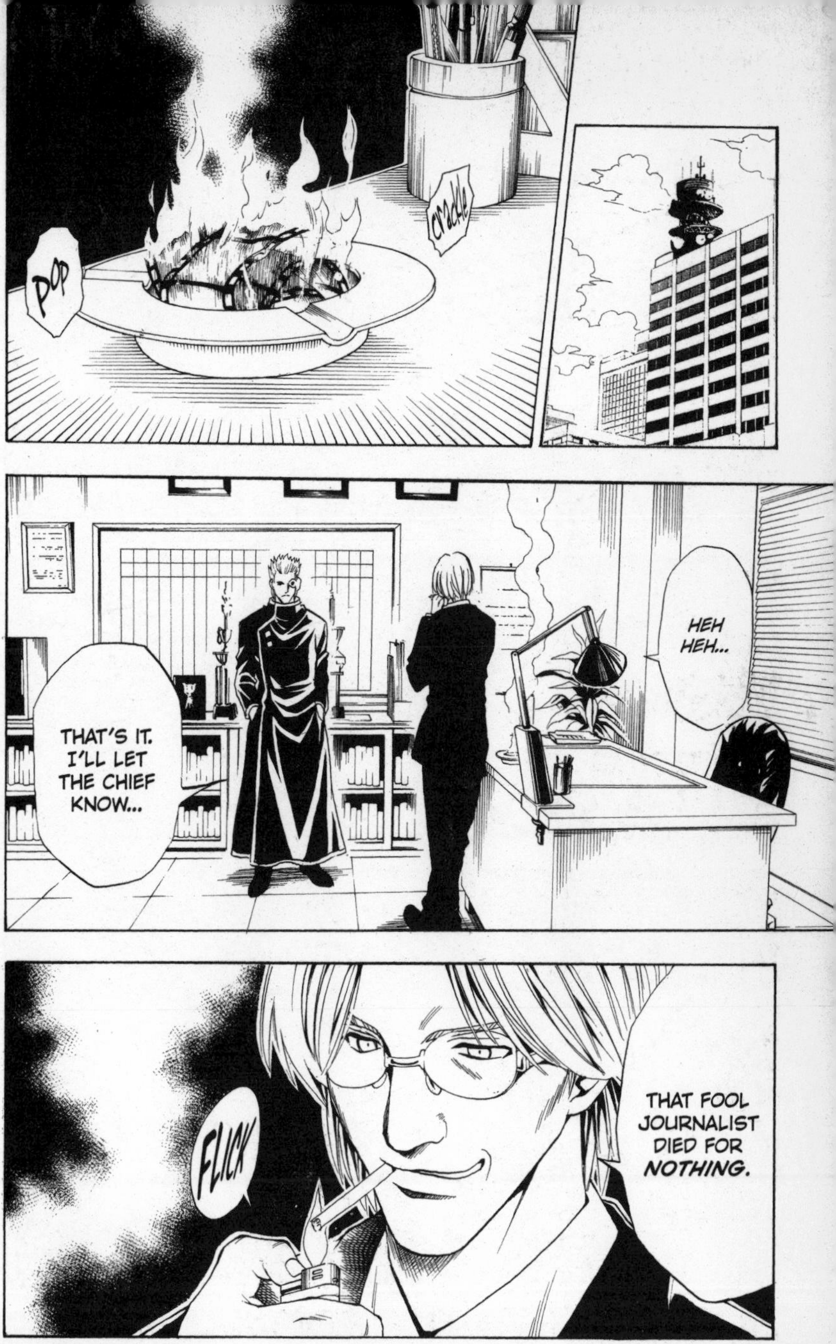
crackle
POP
HEH HEH...
THAT'S IT. I'LL LET THE CHIEF KNOW...
THAT FOOL JOURNALIST DIED FOR *NOTHING.*
FLICK

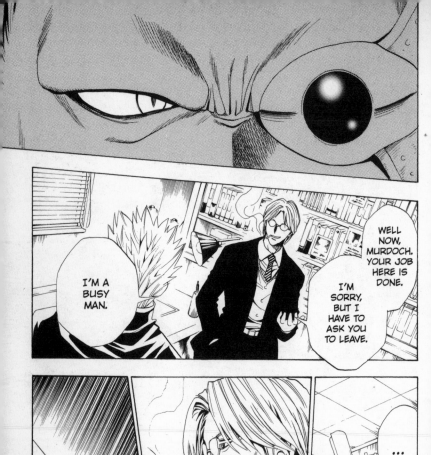

I'M A BUSY MAN.

I'M SORRY, BUT I HAVE TO ASK YOU TO LEAVE.

WELL NOW, MURDOCH. YOUR JOB HERE IS DONE.

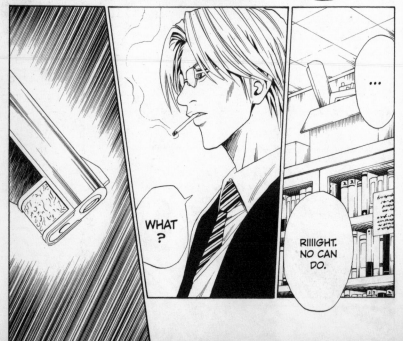

...

WHAT?

RIIIIGHT. NO CAN DO.

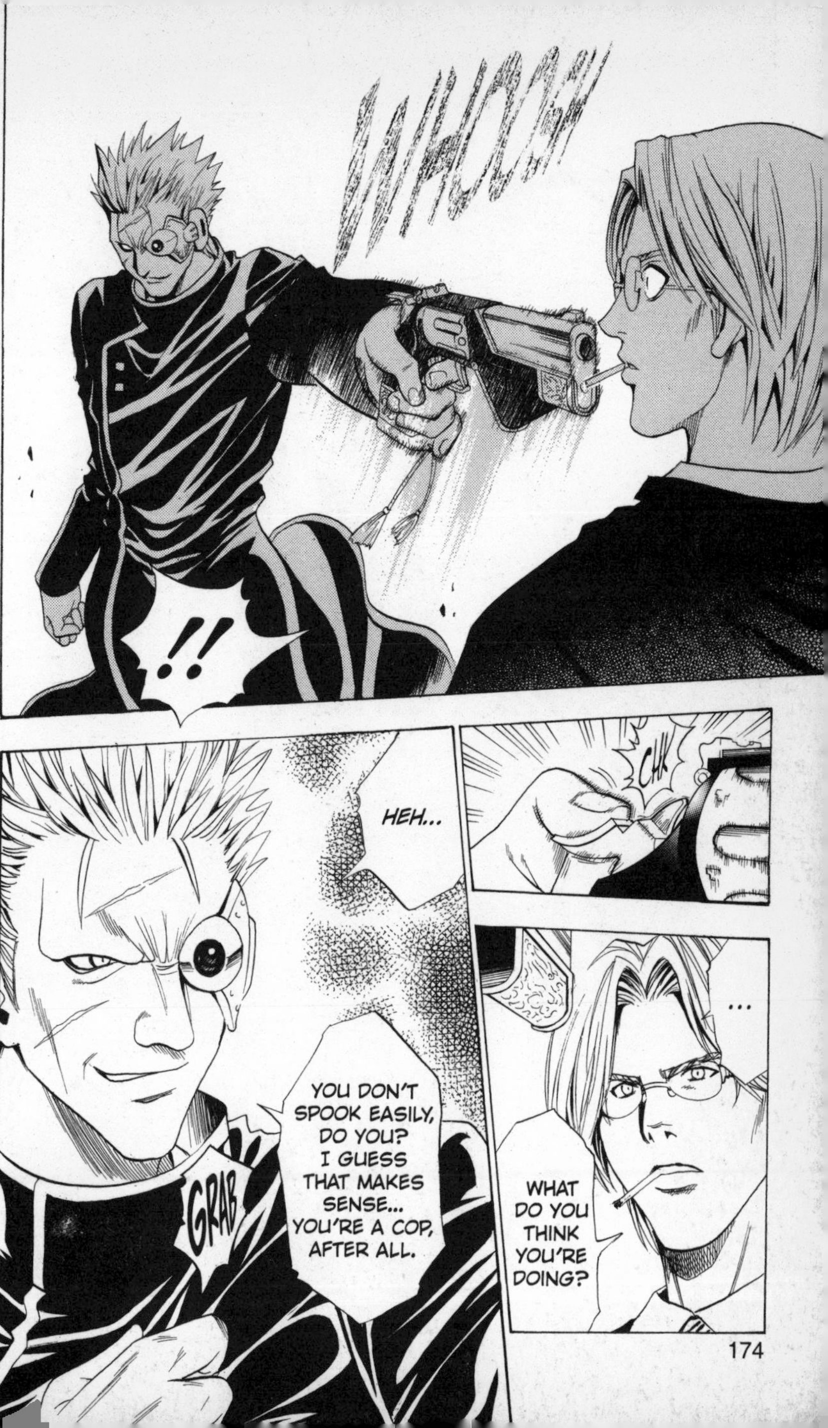
WHOOSH
!!
CHK
...
WHAT DO YOU THINK YOU'RE DOING?
HEH...
YOU DON'T SPOOK EASILY, DO YOU? I GUESS THAT MAKES SENSE... YOU'RE A COP, AFTER ALL.
GRAB

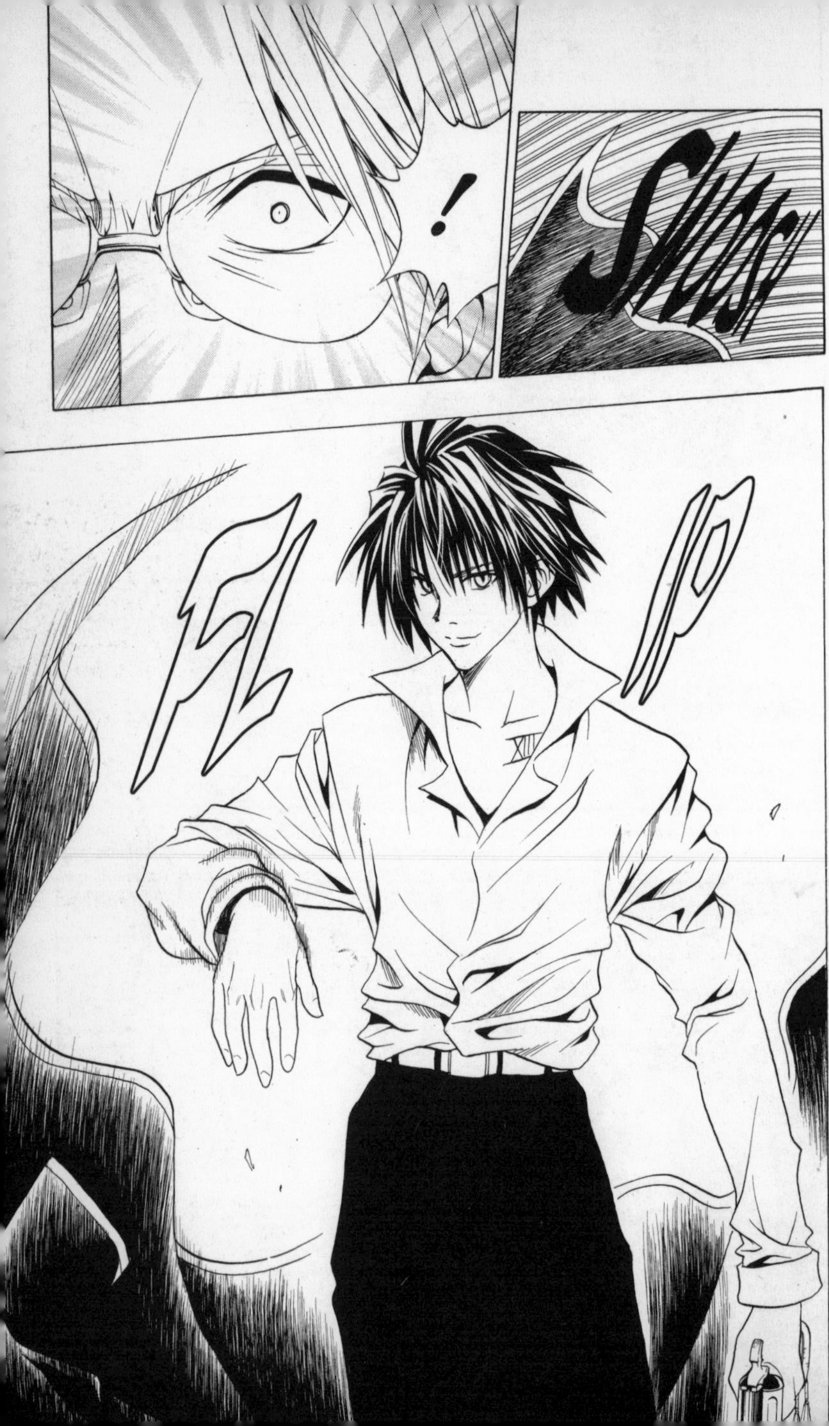
!
FLIP

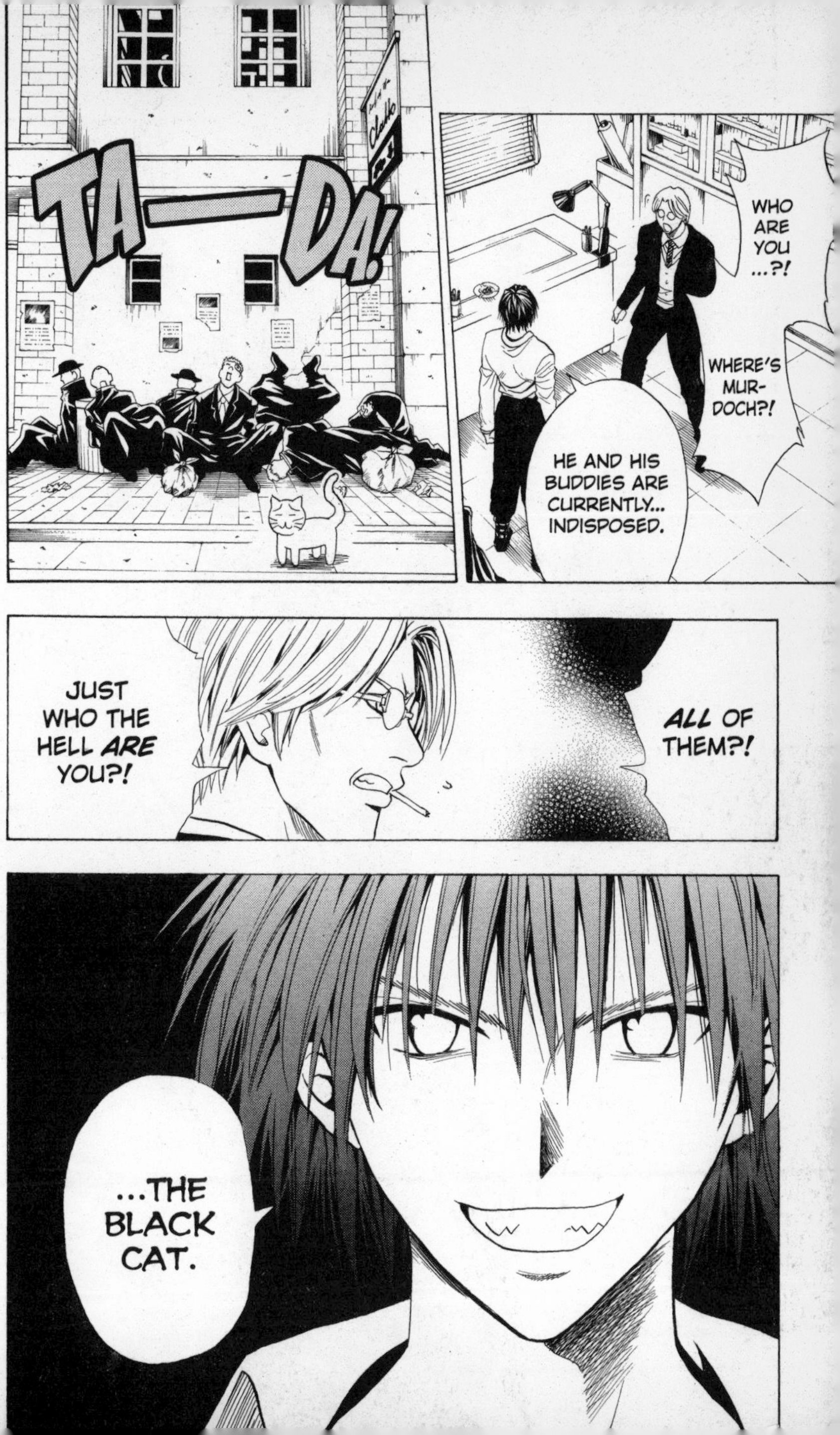
WHO ARE YOU ...?!
WHERE'S MUR-DOCH?!
HE AND HIS BUDDIES ARE CURRENTLY... INDISPOSED.
TA—DA!
ALL OF THEM?!
JUST WHO THE HELL ARE YOU?!
...THE BLACK CAT.

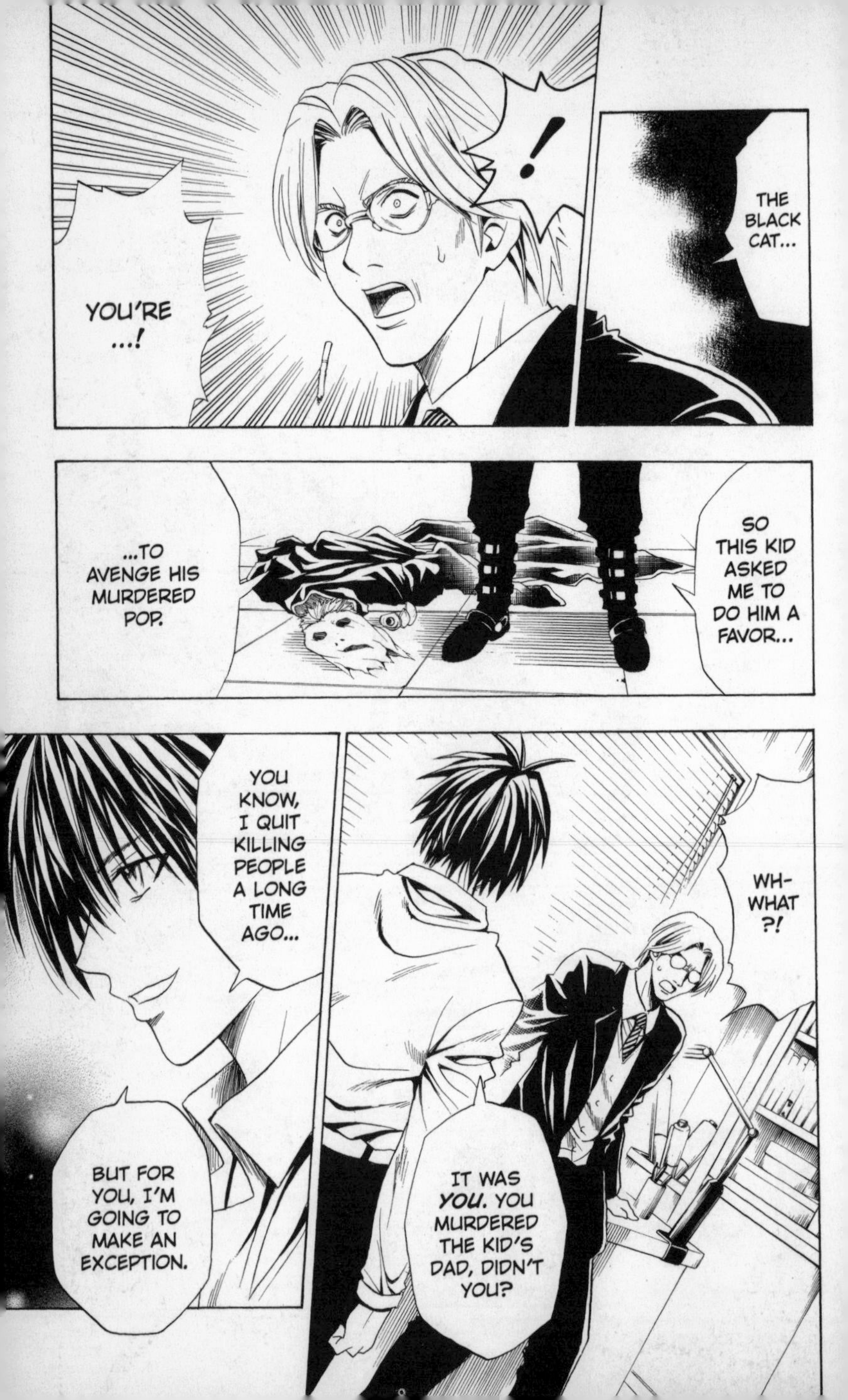
THE BLACK CAT...
!
YOU'RE ...!
SO THIS KID ASKED ME TO DO HIM A FAVOR...
...TO AVENGE HIS MURDERED POP.
WH-WHAT?!
IT WAS *YOU*. YOU MURDERED THE KID'S DAD, DIDN'T YOU?
YOU KNOW, I QUIT KILLING PEOPLE A LONG TIME AGO...
BUT FOR YOU, I'M GOING TO MAKE AN EXCEPTION.

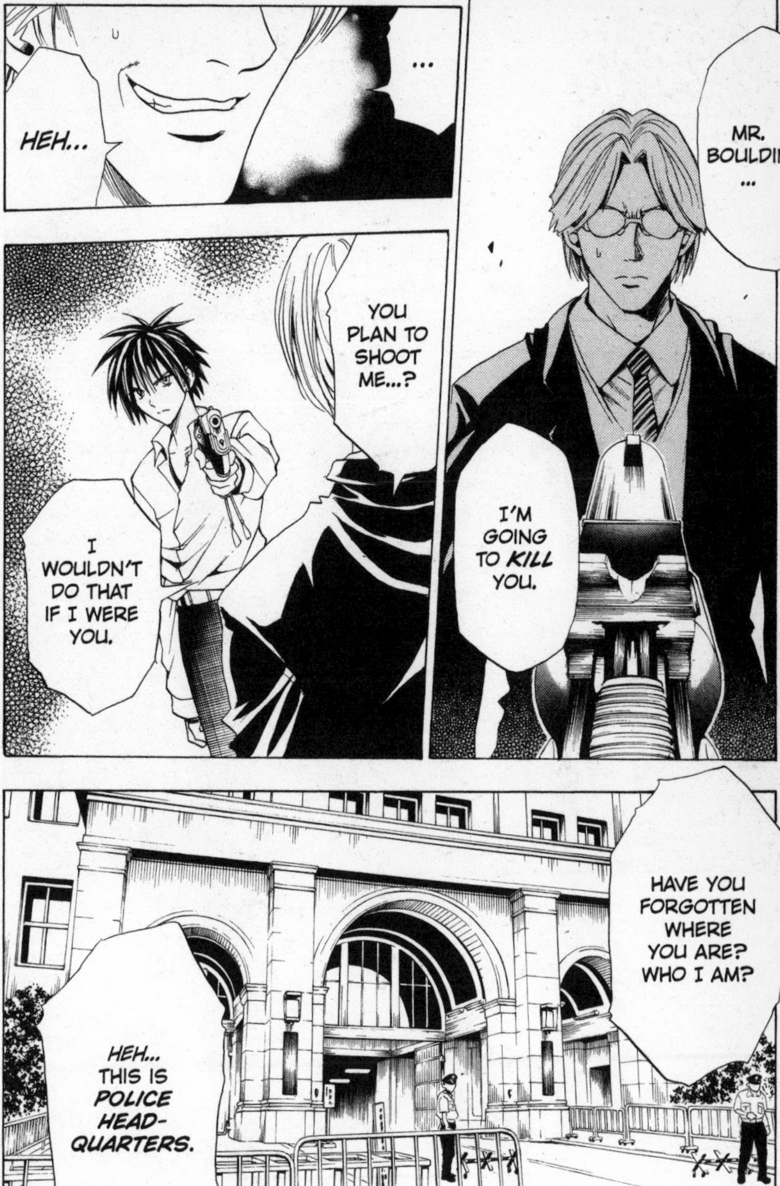
MR. BOULDIN ...
I'M GOING TO KILL YOU.
...
HEH...
YOU PLAN TO SHOOT ME...?
I WOULDN'T DO THAT IF I WERE YOU.
HAVE YOU FORGOTTEN WHERE YOU ARE? WHO I AM?
HEH... THIS IS POLICE HEAD-QUARTERS.

READ THIS WAY

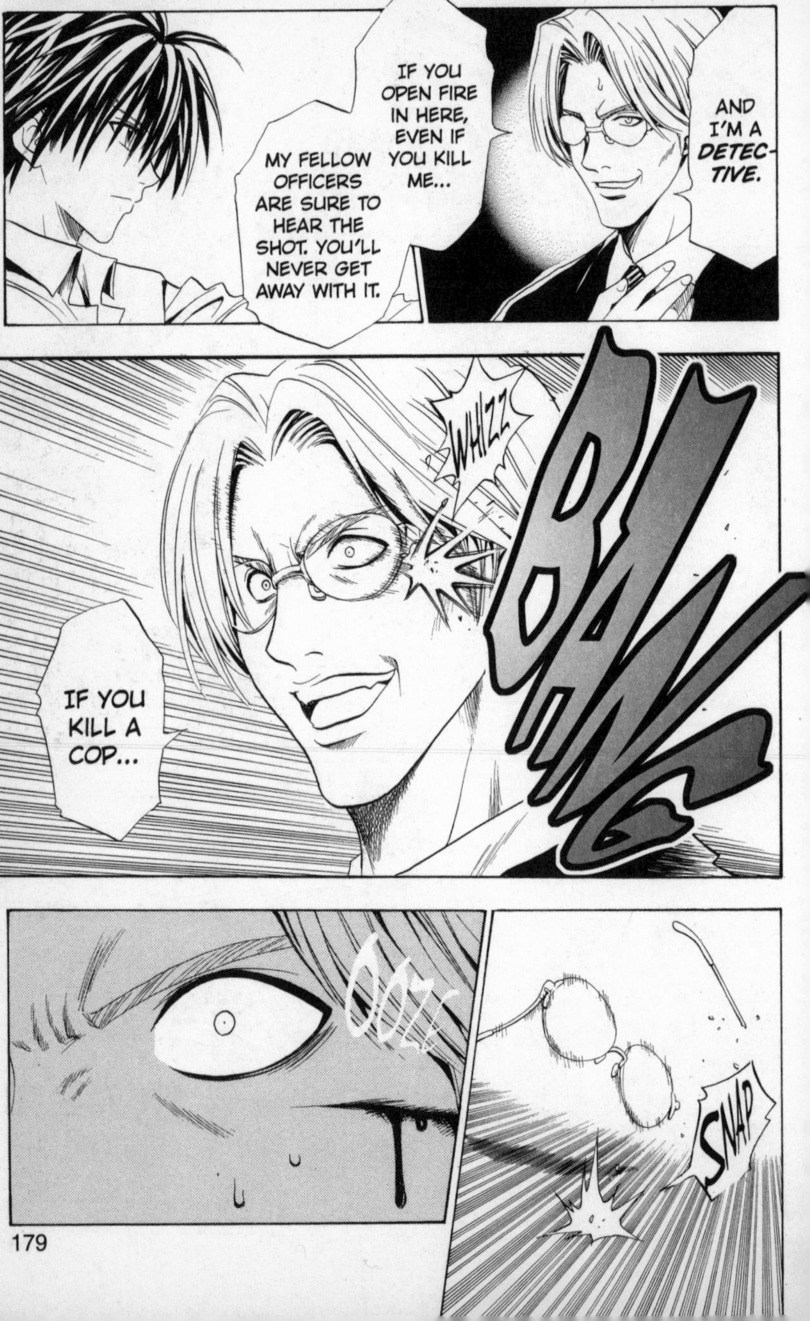
AND I'M A DETECTIVE.
IF YOU OPEN FIRE IN HERE, EVEN IF YOU KILL ME...
MY FELLOW OFFICERS ARE SURE TO HEAR THE SHOT. YOU'LL NEVER GET AWAY WITH IT.
BANG
WHIZZ
IF YOU KILL A COP...
SNAP
OOZE

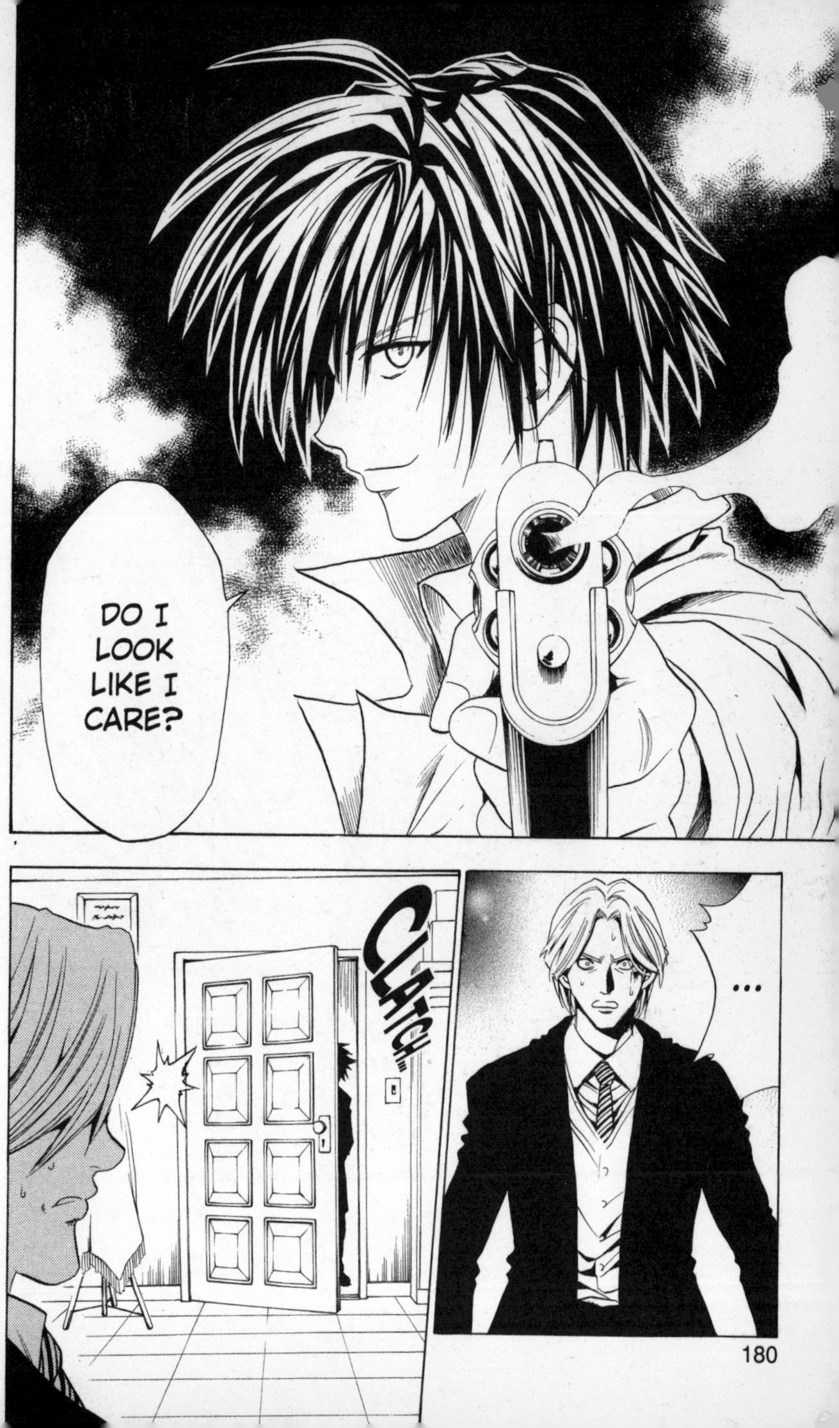
DO I LOOK LIKE I CARE?
...
CLATCH...

READ THIS WAY

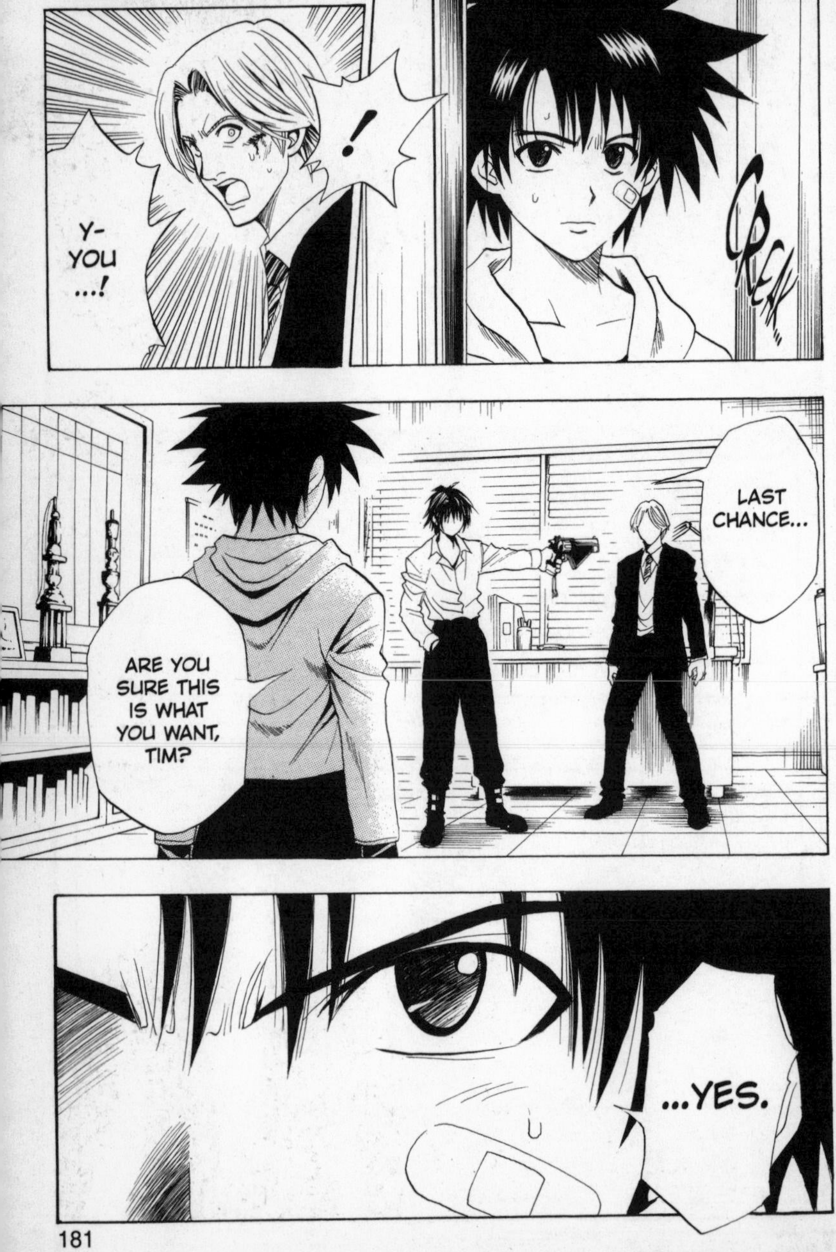
CREAK...
!
Y-YOU...!
LAST CHANCE...
ARE YOU SURE THIS IS WHAT YOU WANT, TIM?
...YES.

BLACK CAT

profile

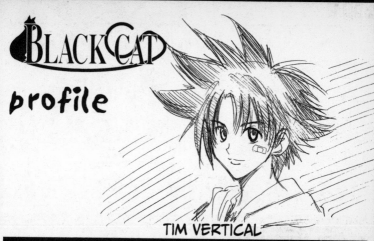

TIM VERTICAL

DATA	
BIRTHDATE:	MARCH 26
AGE:	13 YEARS OLD
BLOOD TYPE:	AB
HEIGHT:	147 CM
WEIGHT:	44 KG
INTERESTS:	VIDEO GAMES, MODEL BUILDING
FAVORITE FOODS:	HAMBURGERS, DAD'S SPECIAL PASTA
FAMILY BACK-GROUND:	LIVED WITH HIS FATHER. (HIS MOTHER DIVORCED HIS FATHER NINE YEARS EARLIER.)

READ THIS WAY

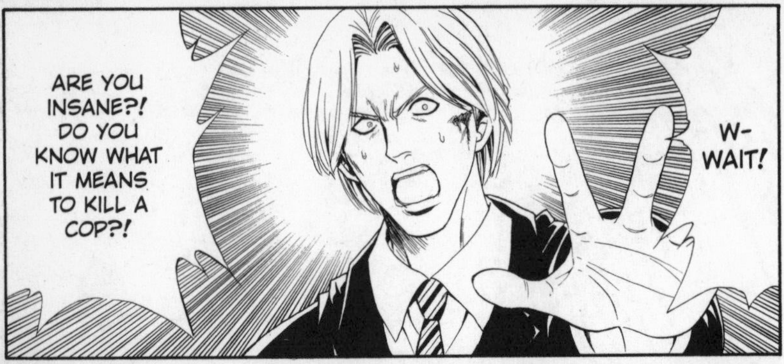
W-
WAIT!
ARE YOU INSANE?! DO YOU KNOW WHAT IT MEANS TO KILL A COP?!

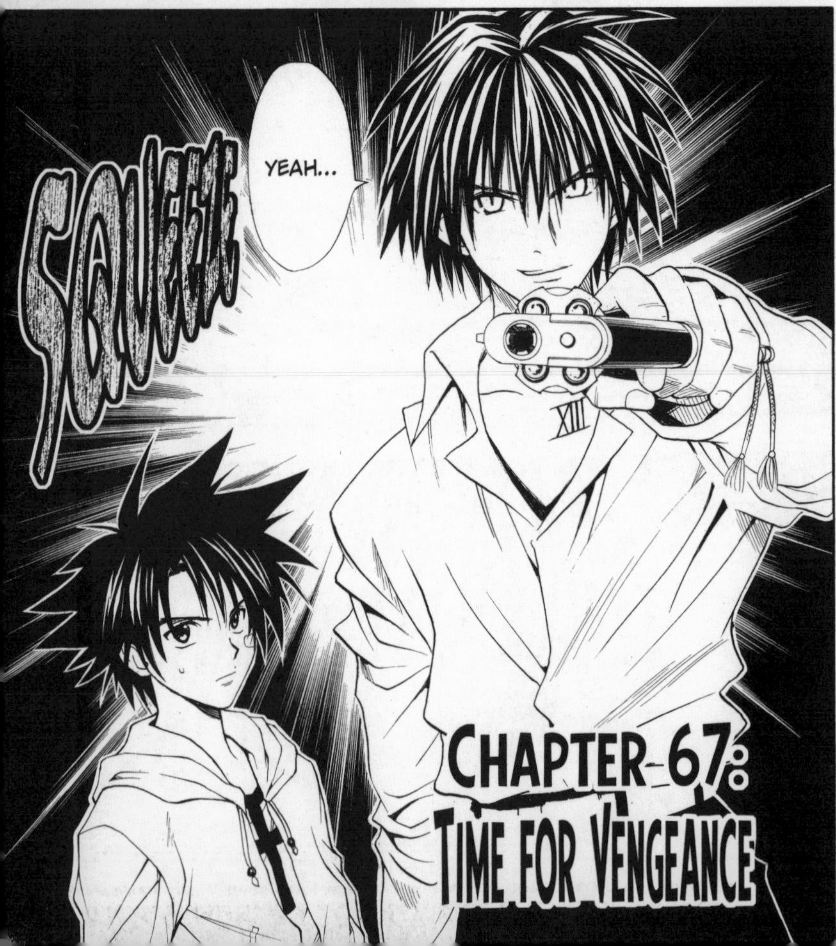
YEAH...
SQUEEZE
CHAPTER 67: TIME FOR VENGEANCE

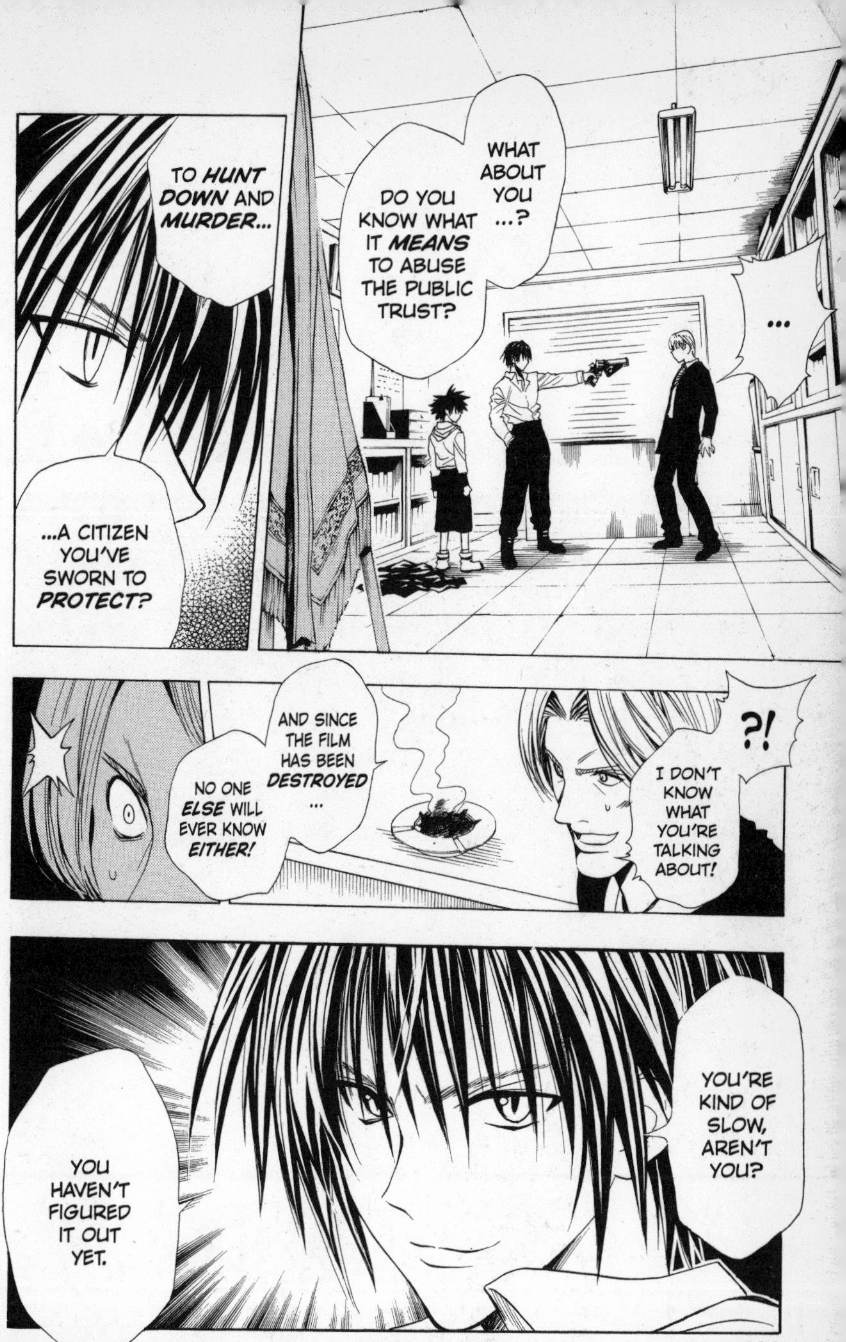
WHAT ABOUT YOU ...?
DO YOU KNOW WHAT IT MEANS TO ABUSE THE PUBLIC TRUST?
...
TO HUNT DOWN AND MURDER...
...A CITIZEN YOU'VE SWORN TO PROTECT?
?!
I DON'T KNOW WHAT YOU'RE TALKING ABOUT!
AND SINCE THE FILM HAS BEEN DESTROYED ...
NO ONE ELSE WILL EVER KNOW EITHER!
YOU'RE KIND OF SLOW, AREN'T YOU?
YOU HAVEN'T FIGURED IT OUT YET.

READ THIS WAY

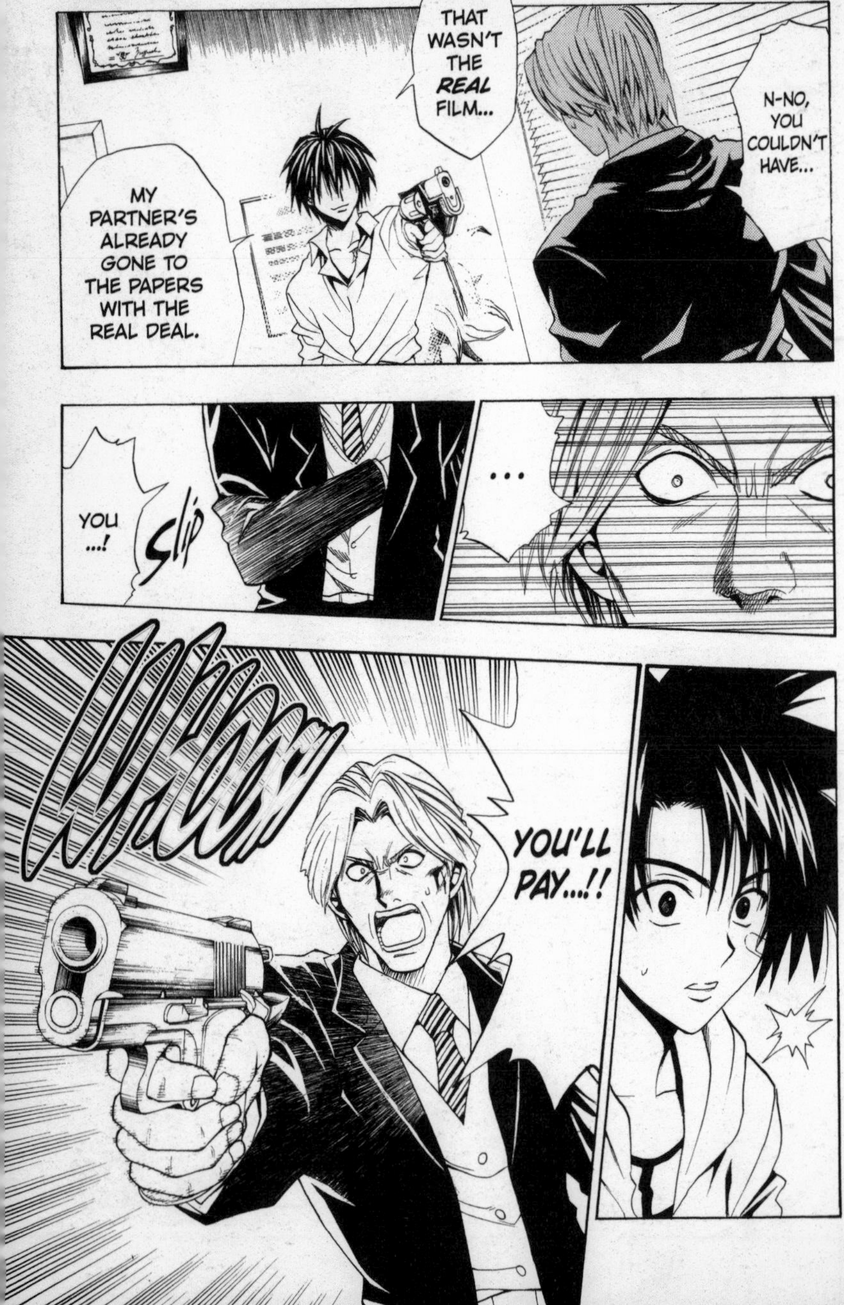
THAT WASN'T THE *REAL* FILM...
N-NO, YOU COULDN'T HAVE...
MY PARTNER'S ALREADY GONE TO THE PAPERS WITH THE REAL DEAL.
...
YOU ...!
SLIP
YOU'LL PAY...!!

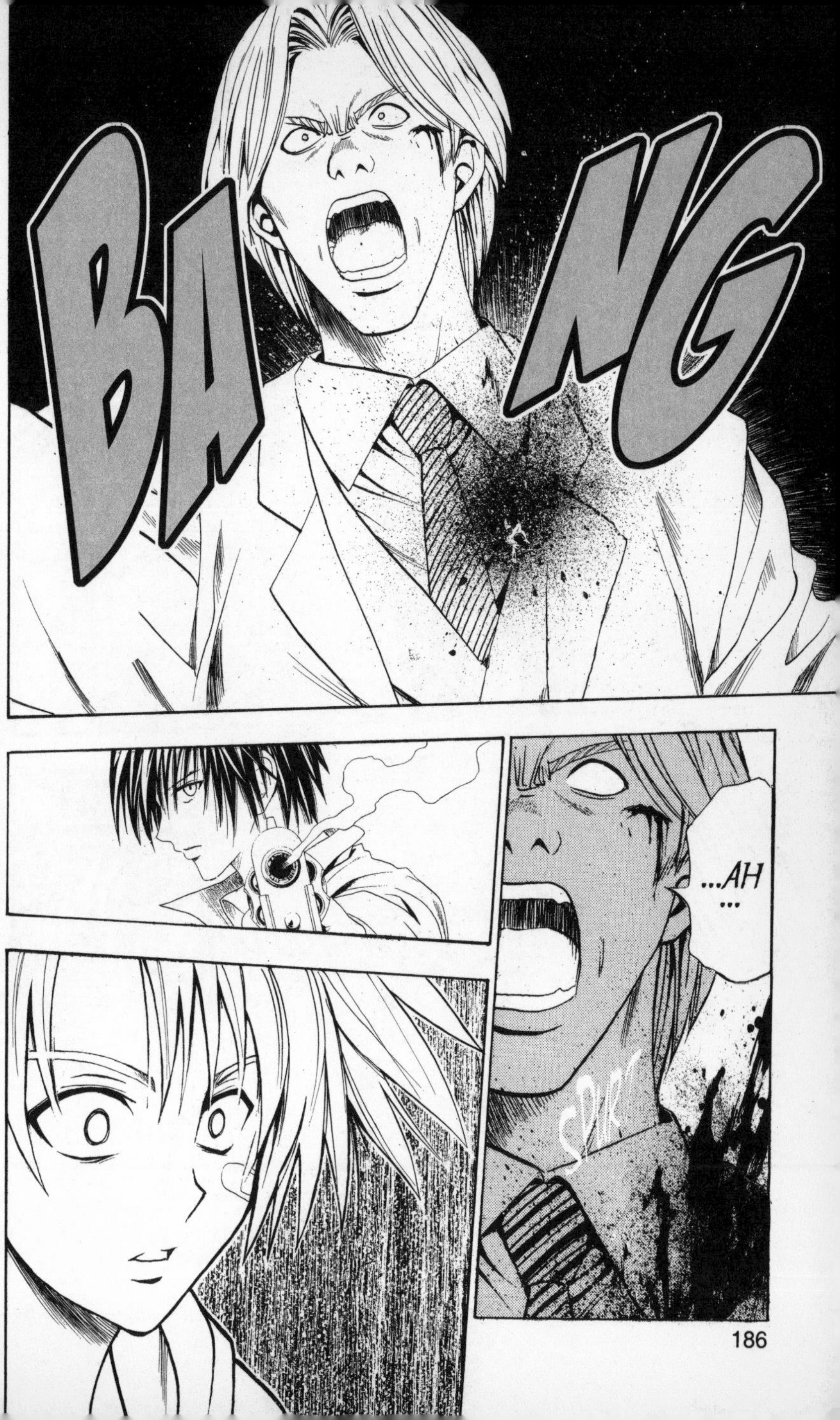
BANG
...AH ...
SPURT

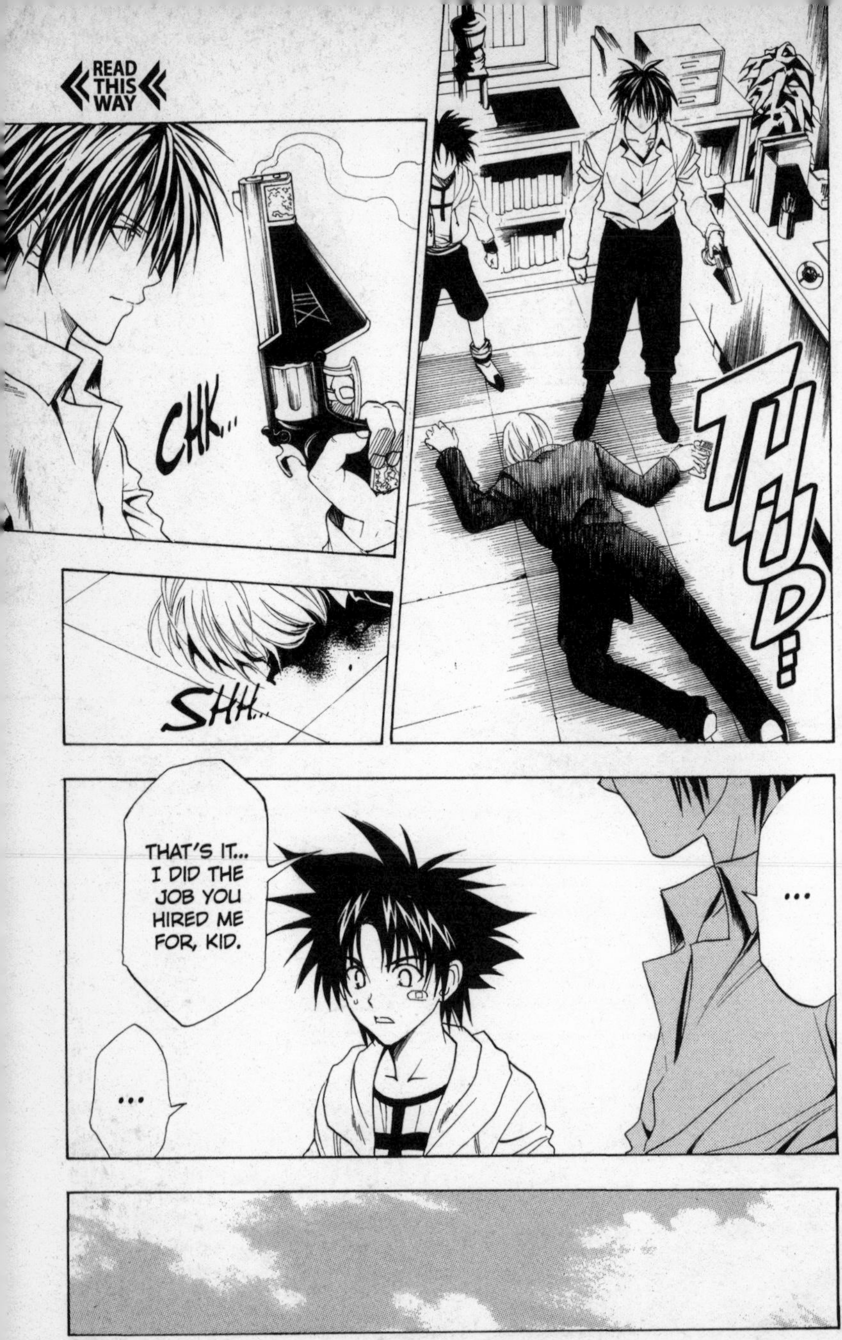
READ THIS WAY
THUD...
CHK...
SHH...
...
THAT'S IT... I DID THE JOB YOU HIRED ME FOR, KID.
...

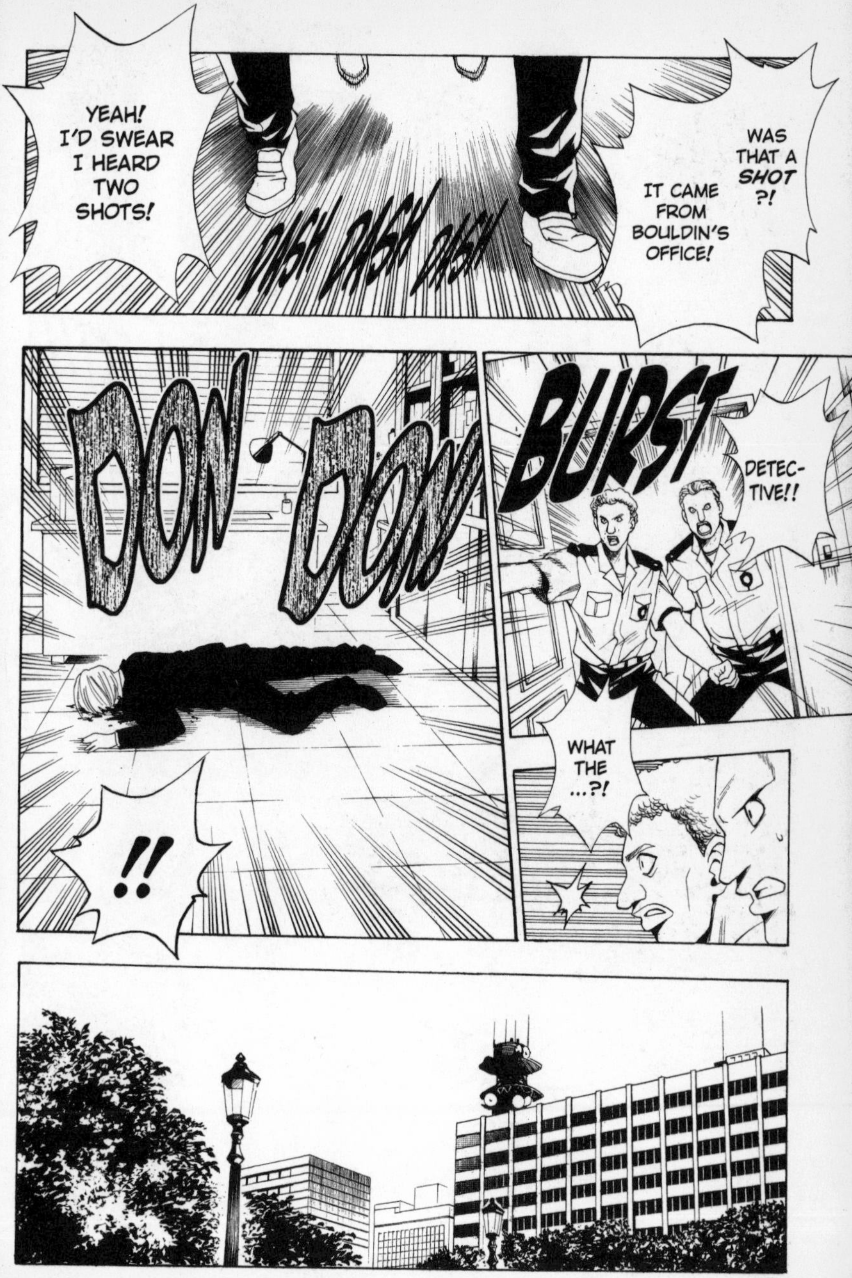
WAS THAT A SHOT ?!
IT CAME FROM BOULDIN'S OFFICE!
YEAH! I'D SWEAR I HEARD TWO SHOTS!
DASH DASH DASH
BURST
DETECTIVE!!
WHAT THE ...?!
DON DON
!!

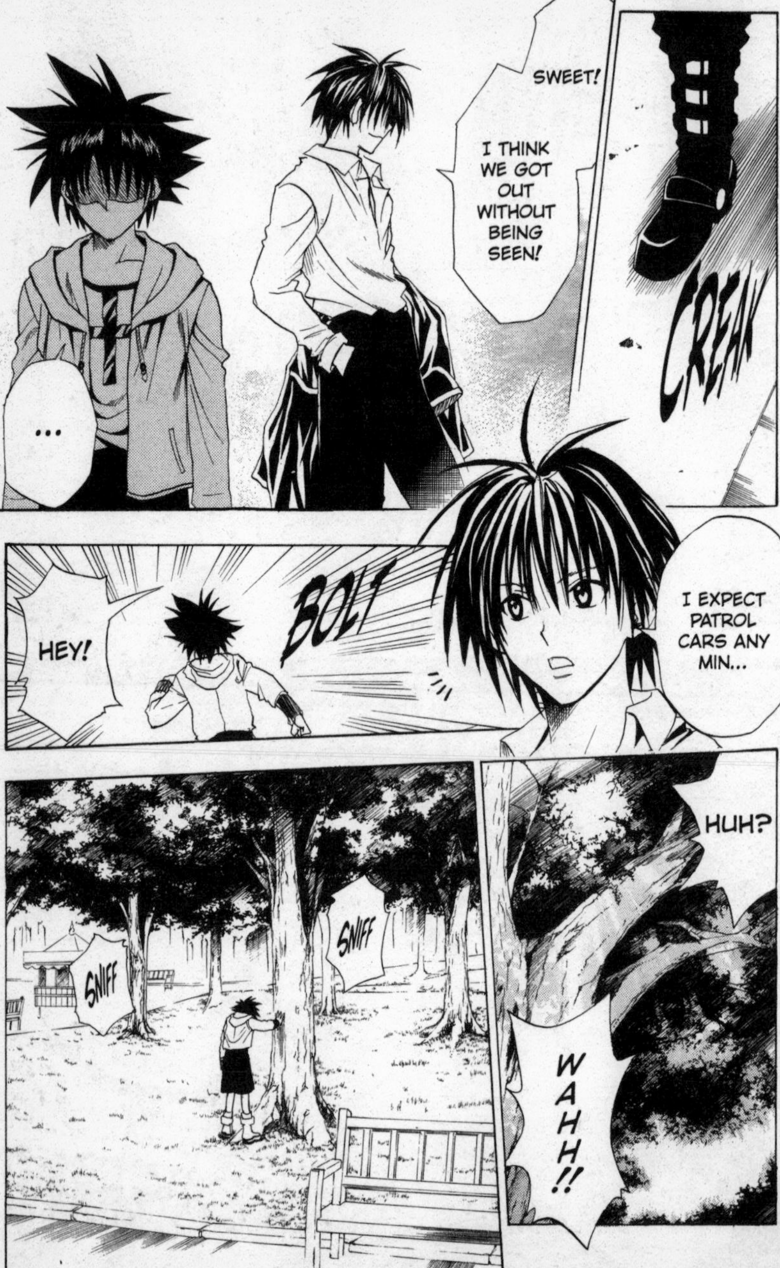
CREAK
SWEET!
I THINK WE GOT OUT WITHOUT BEING SEEN!
...
I EXPECT PATROL CARS ANY MIN...
BOLT
HEY!
HUH?
WAHH!!
SNIFF
SNIFF

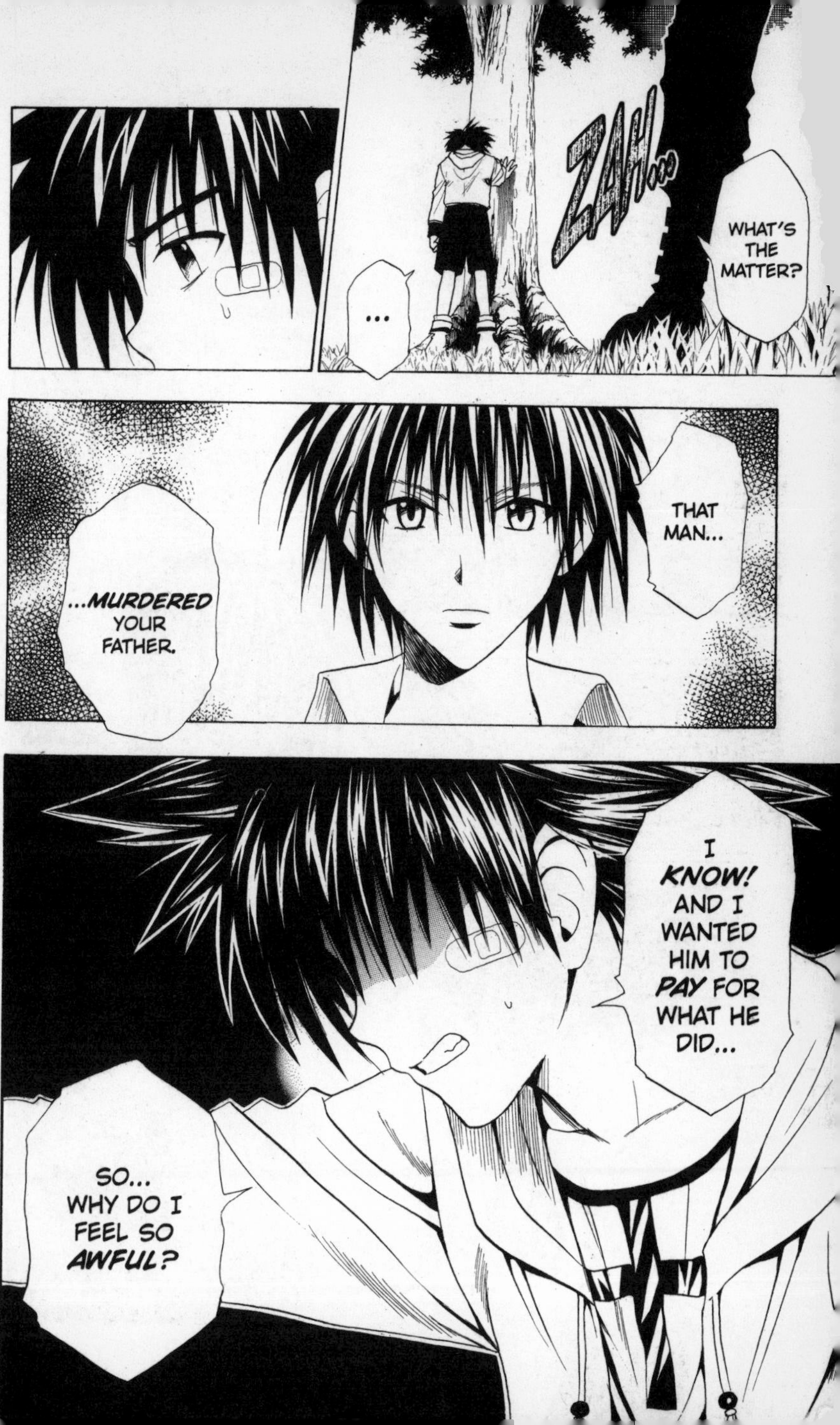
WHAT'S THE MATTER?
ZAH...
...
THAT MAN...
...MURDERED YOUR FATHER.
I KNOW! AND I WANTED HIM TO PAY FOR WHAT HE DID...
SO... WHY DO I FEEL SO AWFUL?

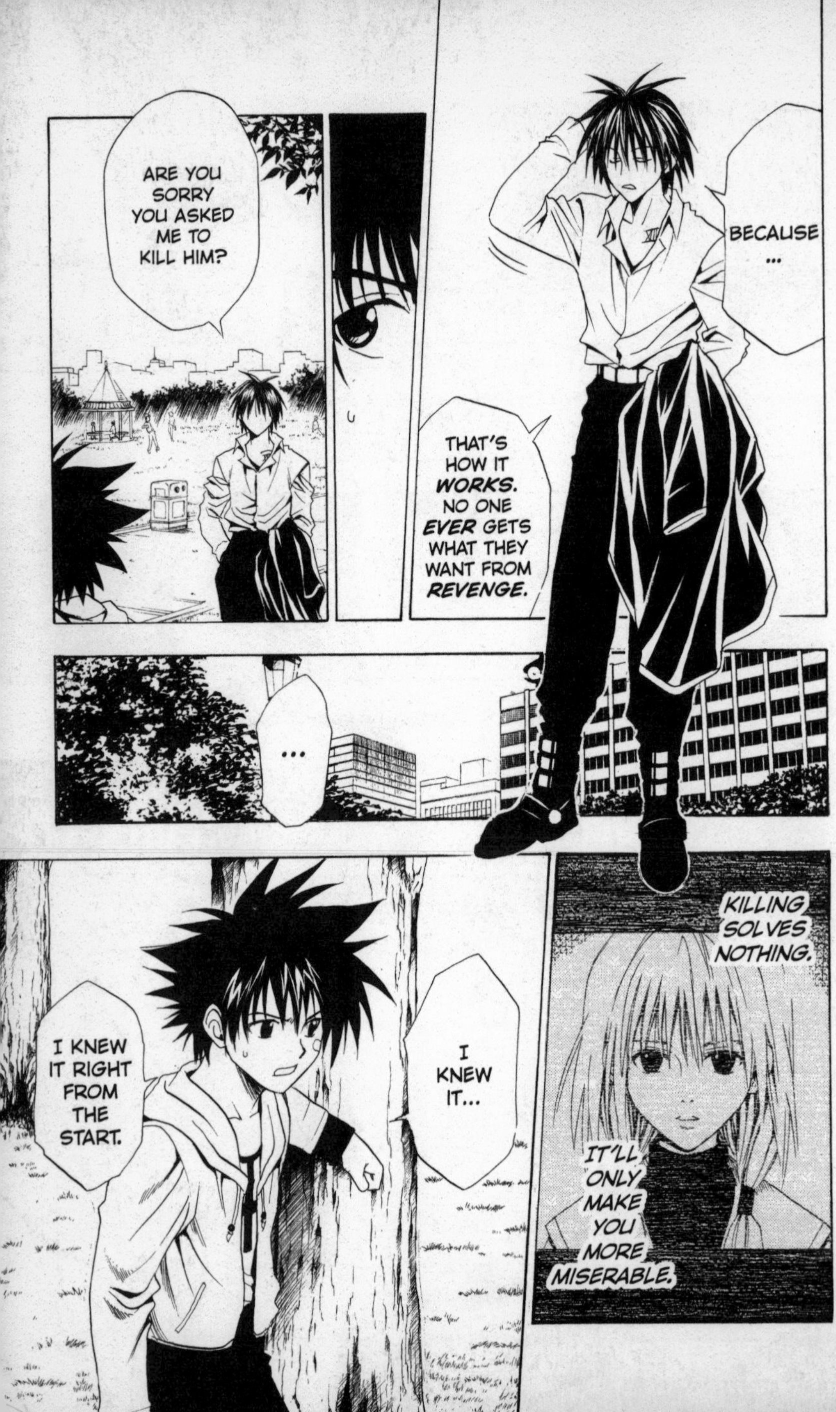
BECAUSE ...
THAT'S HOW IT WORKS. NO ONE EVER GETS WHAT THEY WANT FROM REVENGE.
ARE YOU SORRY YOU ASKED ME TO KILL HIM?
...
KILLING SOLVES NOTHING.
IT'LL ONLY MAKE YOU MORE MISERABLE.
I KNEW IT...
I KNEW IT RIGHT FROM THE START.

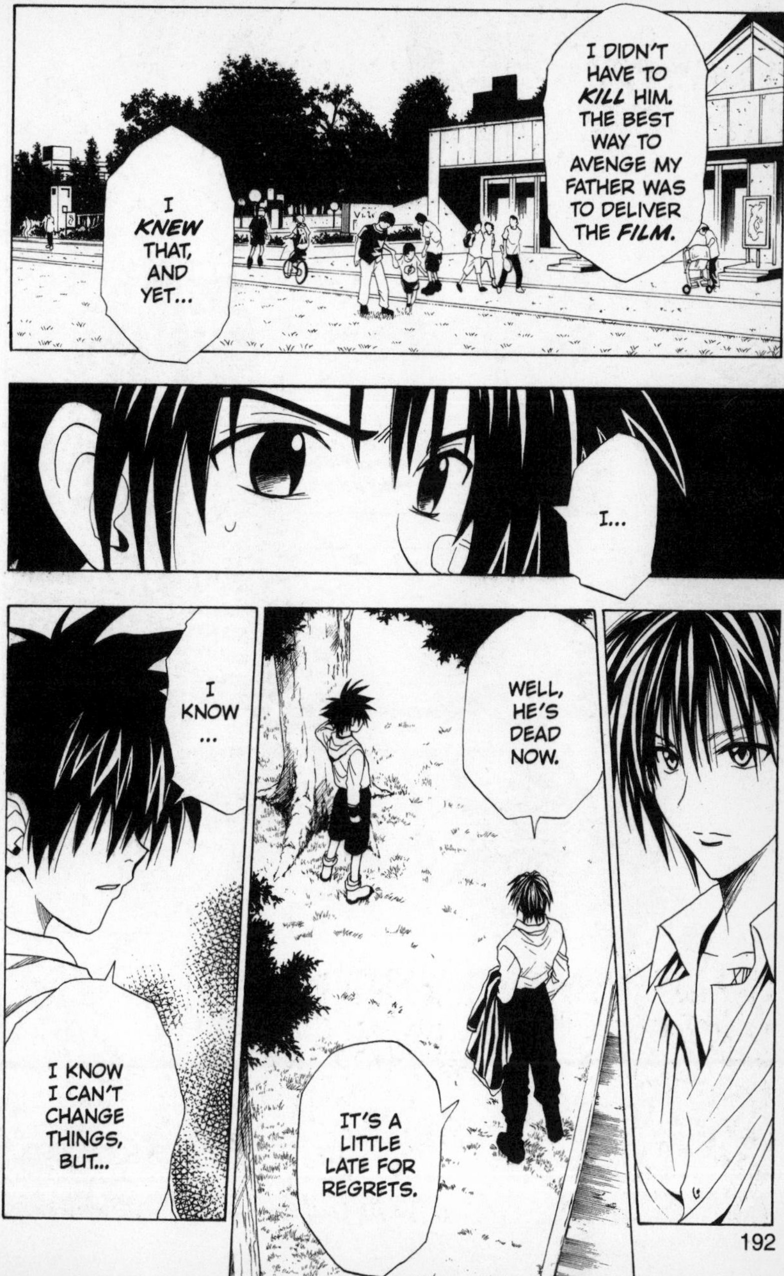
I DIDN'T HAVE TO KILL HIM. THE BEST WAY TO AVENGE MY FATHER WAS TO DELIVER THE FILM.
I KNEW THAT, AND YET...
I...
WELL, HE'S DEAD NOW.
IT'S A LITTLE LATE FOR REGRETS.
I KNOW...
I KNOW I CAN'T CHANGE THINGS, BUT...

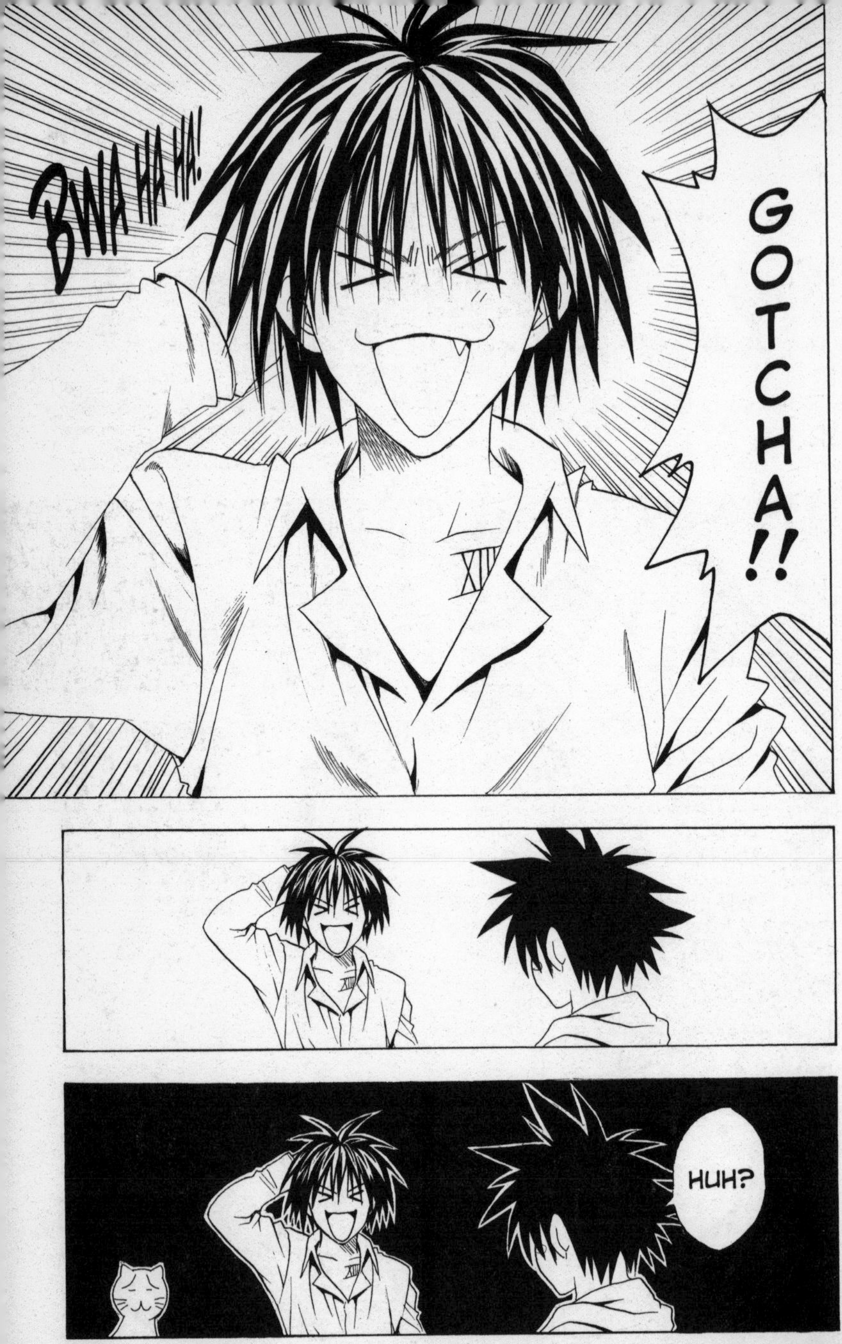
GOTCHA!!
BWA HA HA!
HUH?

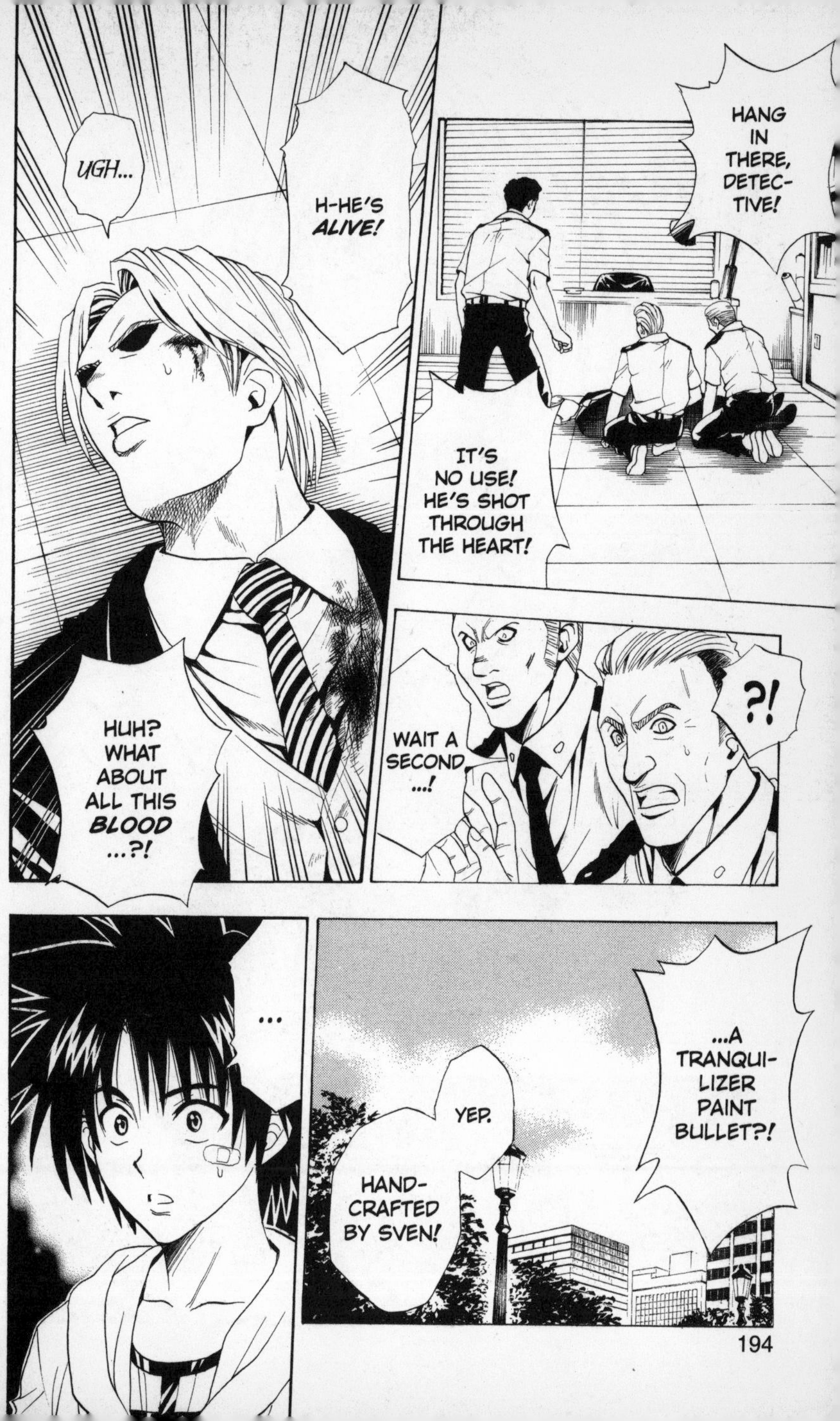
HANG IN THERE, DETECTIVE!
IT'S NO USE! HE'S SHOT THROUGH THE HEART!
?!
WAIT A SECOND ...!
UGH...
H-HE'S *ALIVE!*
HUH? WHAT ABOUT ALL THIS *BLOOD* ...?!
...A TRANQUILIZER PAINT BULLET?!
YEP.
HAND-CRAFTED BY SVEN!
...

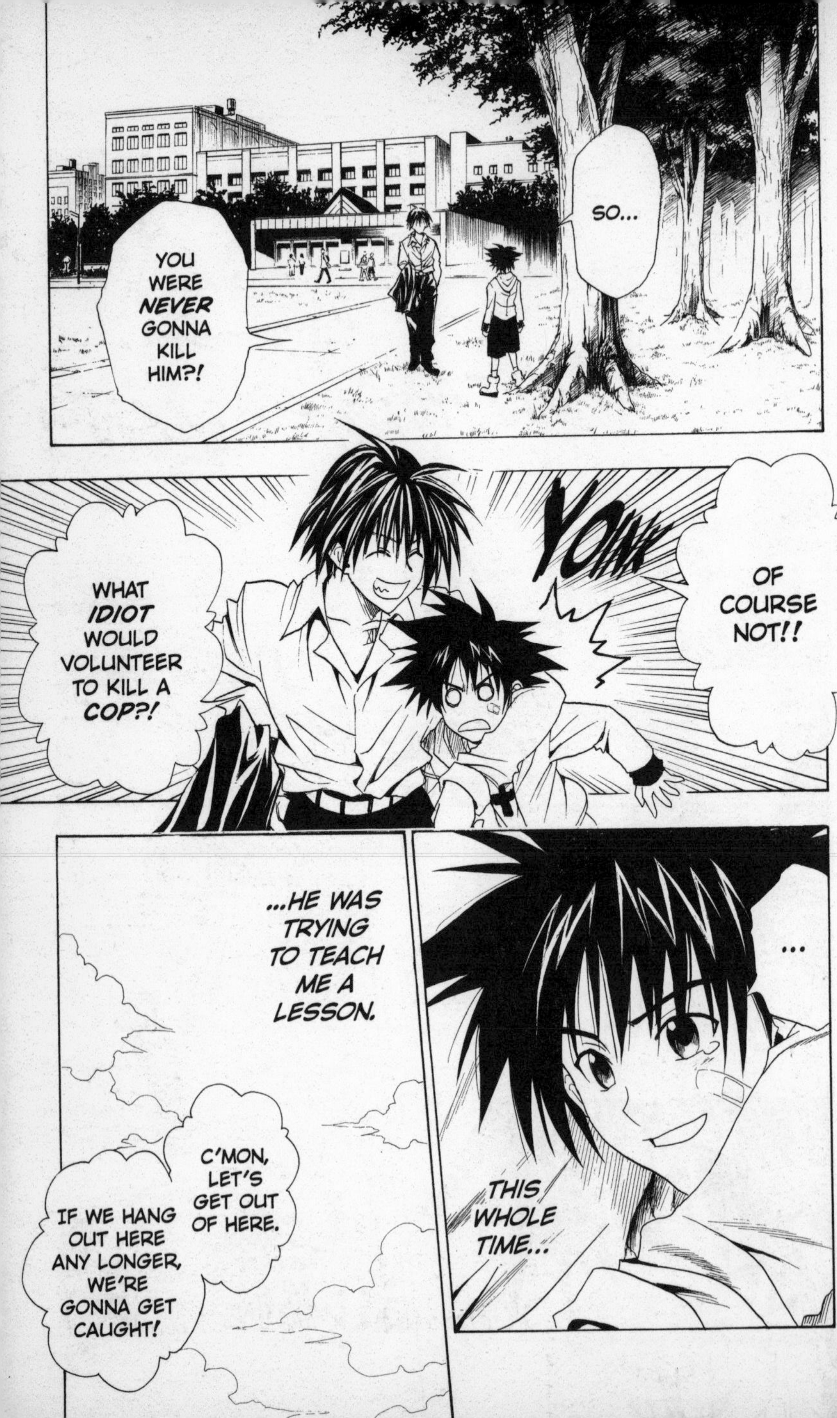
SO...
YOU WERE NEVER GONNA KILL HIM?!
OF COURSE NOT!!
YOINK
WHAT IDIOT WOULD VOLUNTEER TO KILL A COP?!
...
THIS WHOLE TIME...
...HE WAS TRYING TO TEACH ME A LESSON.
C'MON, LET'S GET OUT OF HERE.
IF WE HANG OUT HERE ANY LONGER, WE'RE GONNA GET CAUGHT!

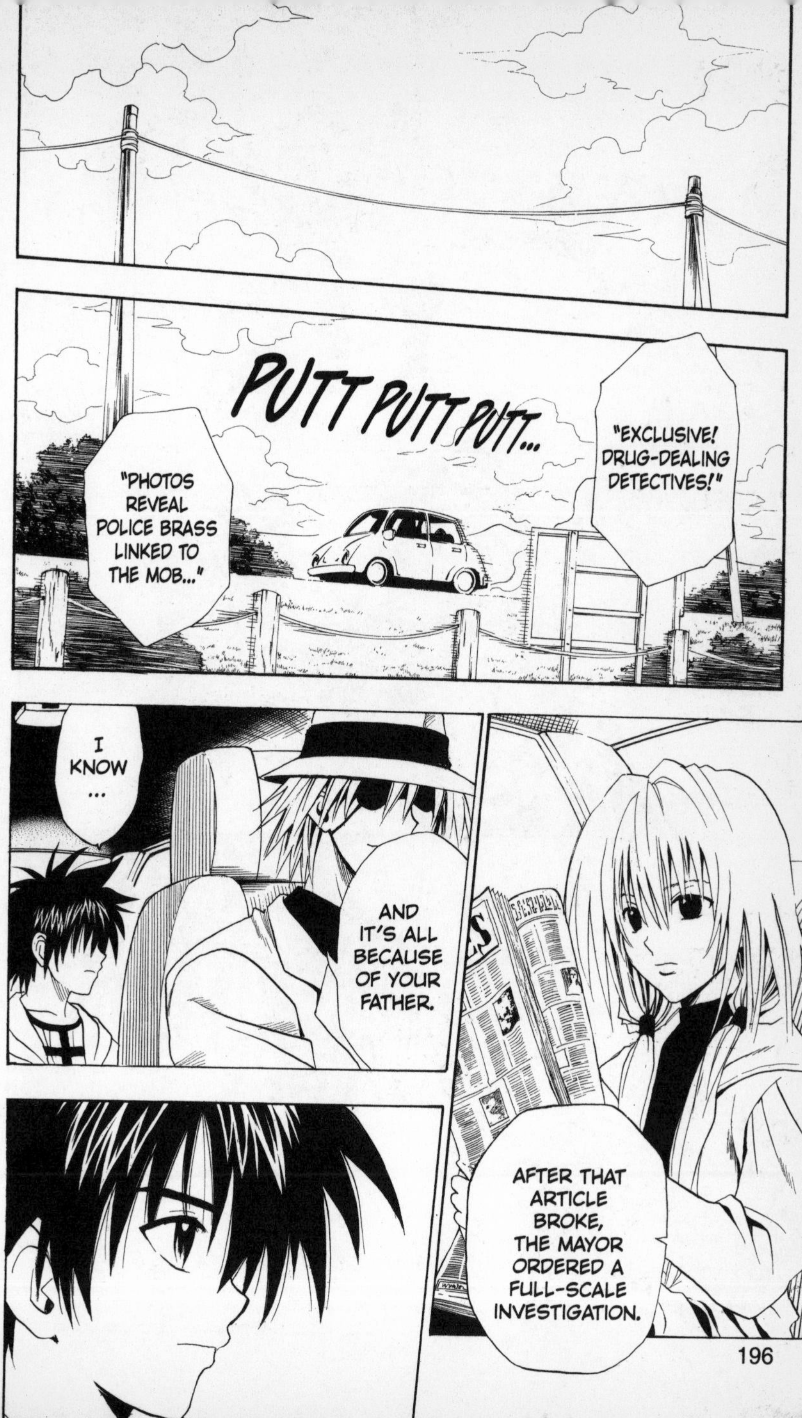
"EXCLUSIVE! DRUG-DEALING DETECTIVES!"
PUTT PUTT PUTT...
"PHOTOS REVEAL POLICE BRASS LINKED TO THE MOB..."
AFTER THAT ARTICLE BROKE, THE MAYOR ORDERED A FULL-SCALE INVESTIGATION.
AND IT'S ALL BECAUSE OF YOUR FATHER.
I KNOW ...

READ THIS WAY

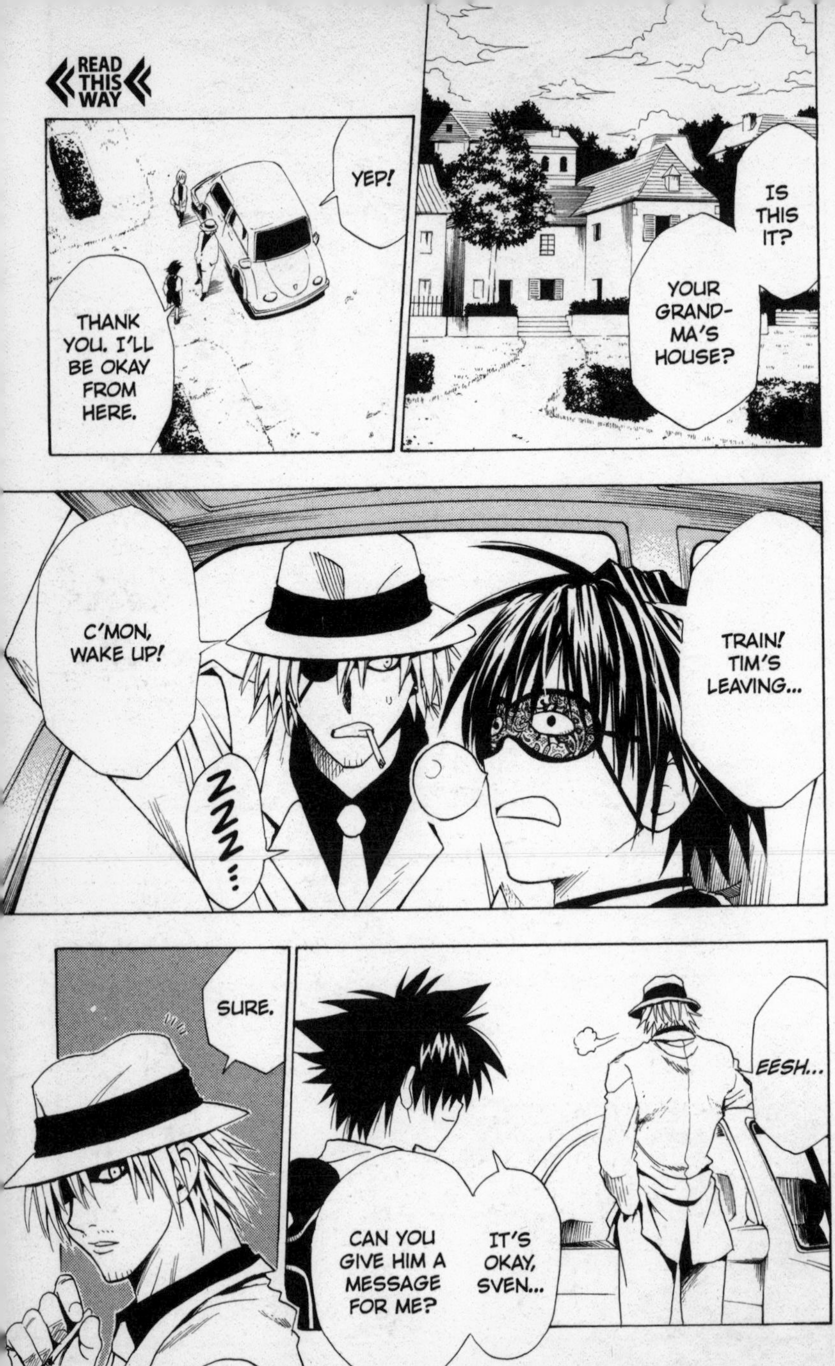
IS THIS IT?
YOUR GRAND-MA'S HOUSE?
YEP!
THANK YOU. I'LL BE OKAY FROM HERE.
TRAIN! TIM'S LEAVING...
C'MON, WAKE UP!
ZZZ...
EESH...
IT'S OKAY, SVEN...
CAN YOU GIVE HIM A MESSAGE FOR ME?
SURE.

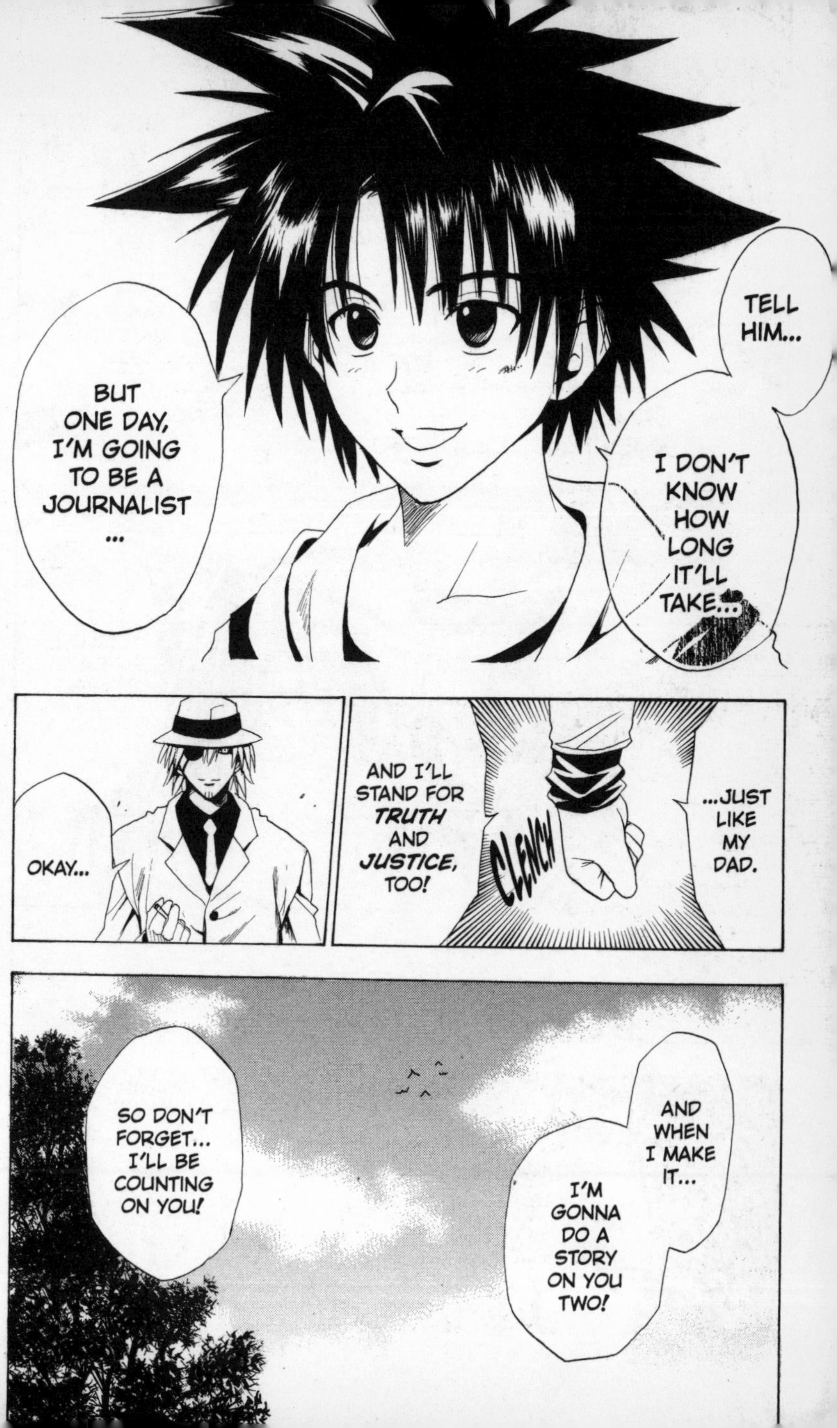
TELL HIM...
I DON'T KNOW HOW LONG IT'LL TAKE...
BUT ONE DAY, I'M GOING TO BE A JOURNALIST ...
...JUST LIKE MY DAD.
AND I'LL STAND FOR *TRUTH* AND *JUSTICE*, TOO!
CLENCH
OKAY...
AND WHEN I MAKE IT...
I'M GONNA DO A STORY ON YOU TWO!
SO DON'T FORGET... I'LL BE COUNTING ON YOU!

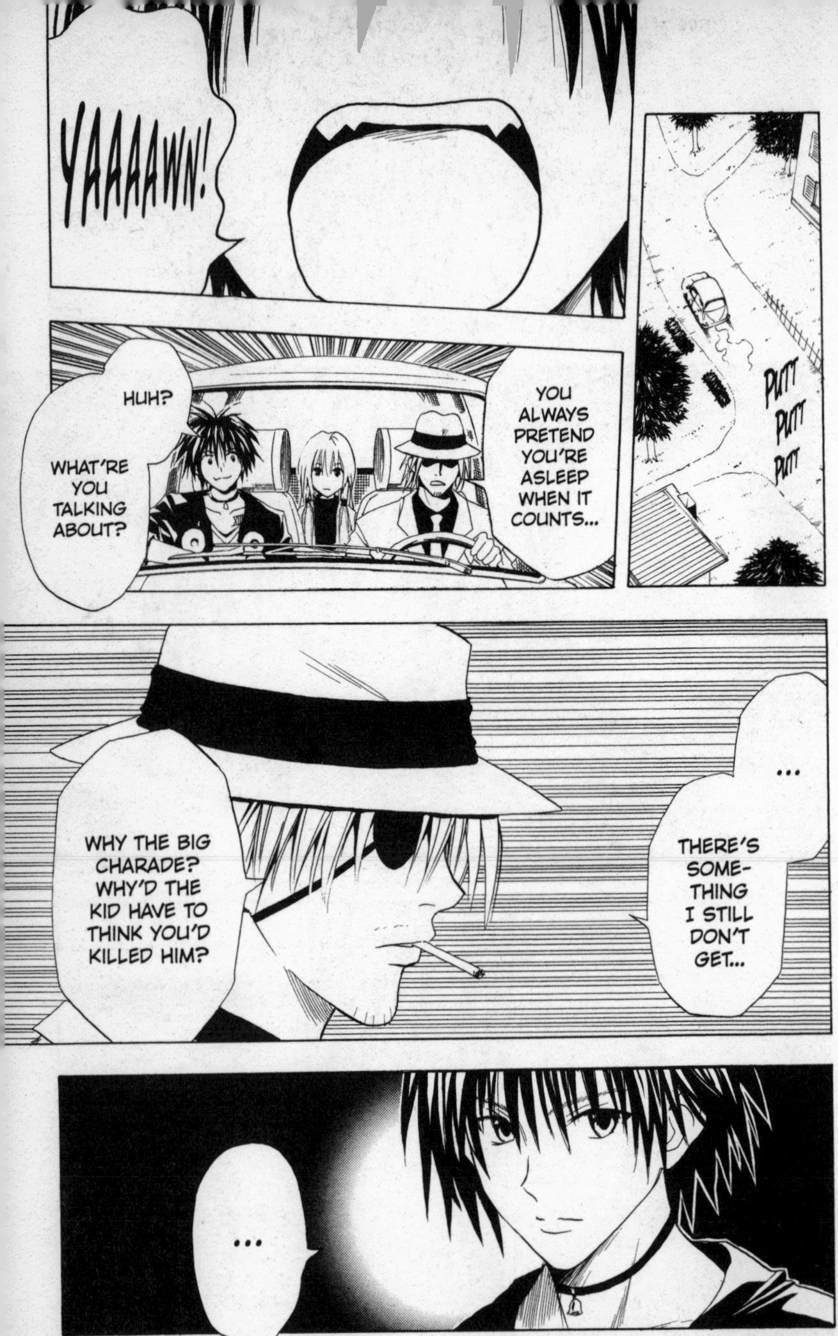
PUTT PUTT PUTT
YAAAAWN!
YOU ALWAYS PRETEND YOU'RE ASLEEP WHEN IT COUNTS...
HUH?
WHAT'RE YOU TALKING ABOUT?
...
THERE'S SOME-THING I STILL DON'T GET...
WHY THE BIG CHARADE? WHY'D THE KID HAVE TO THINK YOU'D KILLED HIM?
...

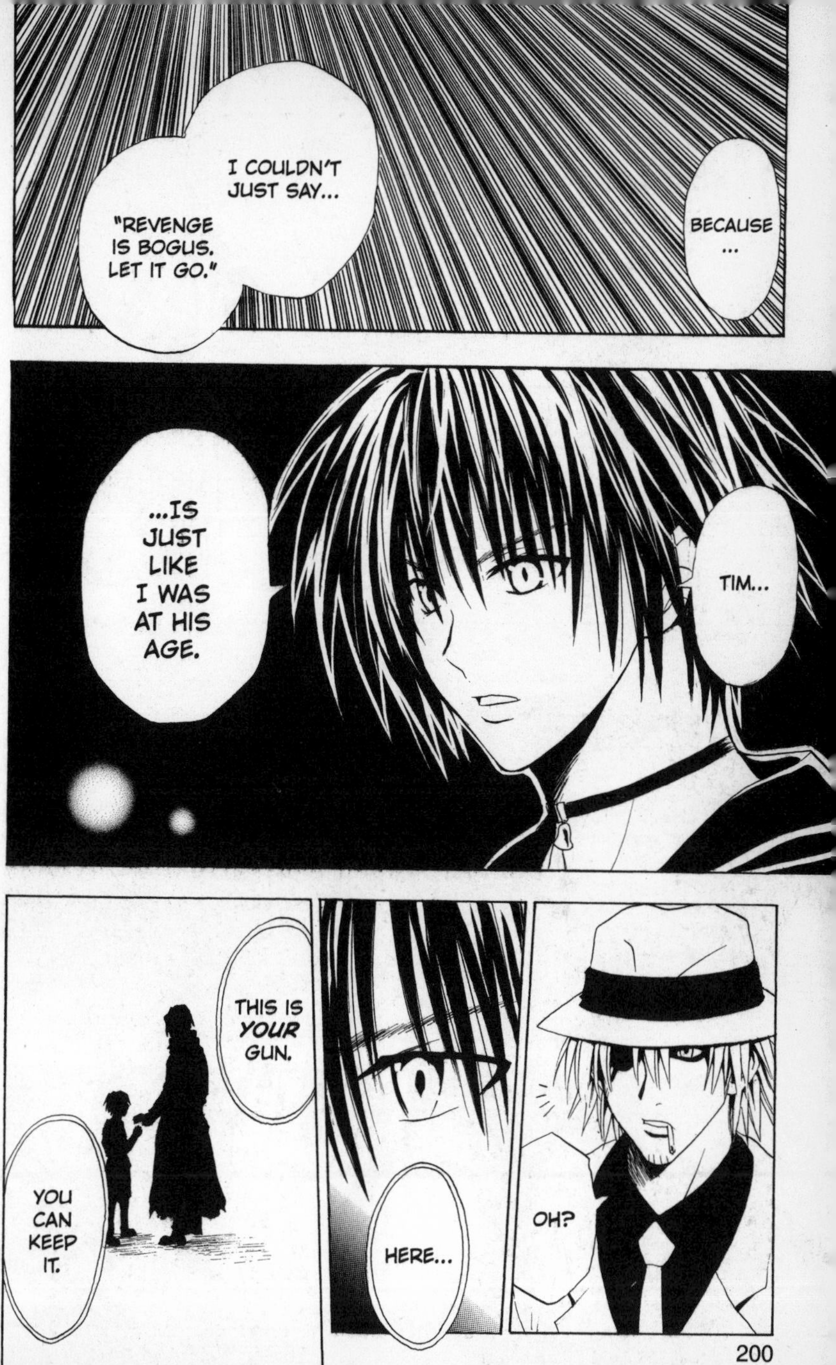
BECAUSE ...
I COULDN'T JUST SAY...
"REVENGE IS BOGUS. LET IT GO."
TIM...
...IS JUST LIKE I WAS AT HIS AGE.
OH?
HERE...
THIS IS *YOUR* GUN.
YOU CAN KEEP IT.

READ THIS WAY

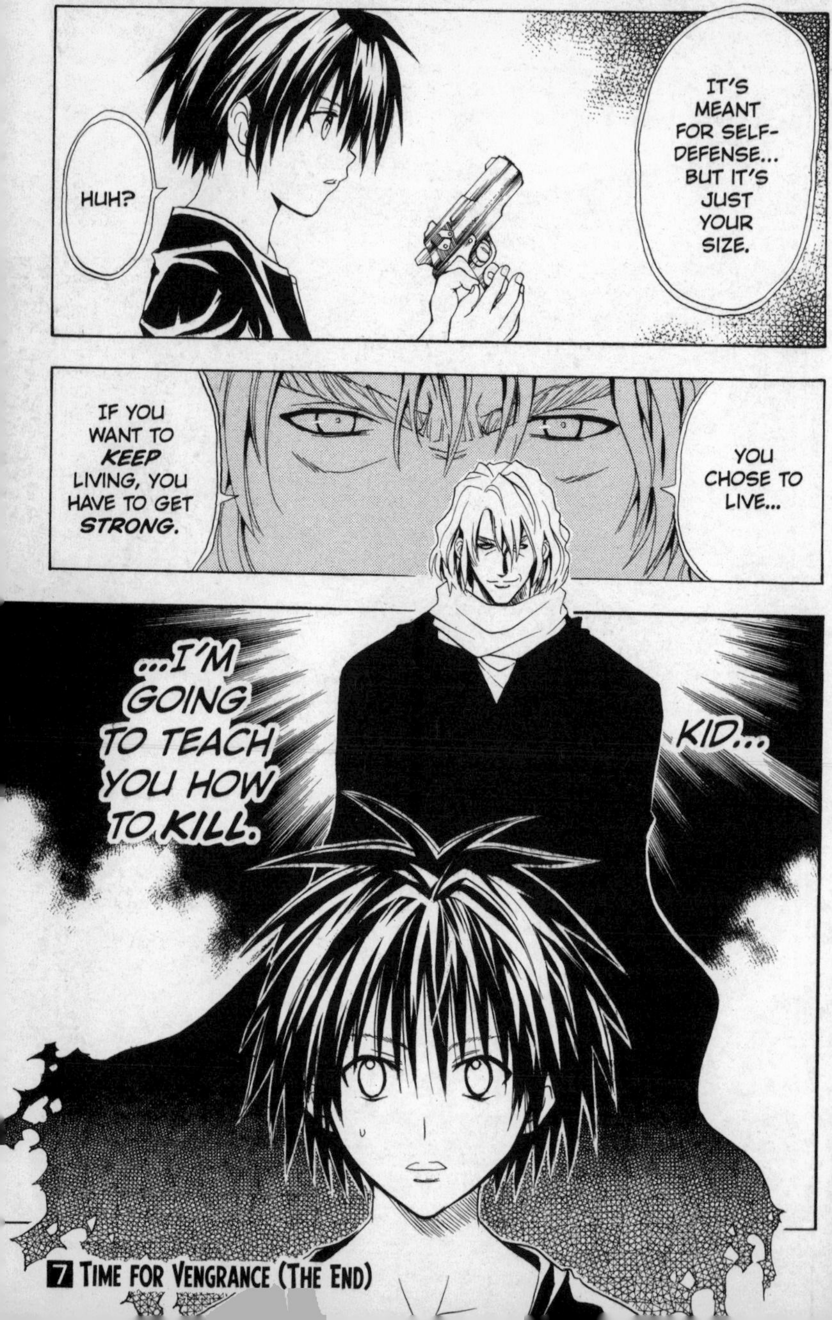

IT'S MEANT FOR SELF-DEFENSE... BUT IT'S JUST YOUR SIZE.
HUH?
YOU CHOSE TO LIVE...
IF YOU WANT TO KEEP LIVING, YOU HAVE TO GET STRONG.
KID...
...I'M GOING TO TEACH YOU HOW TO KILL.

7 TIME FOR VENGRANCE (THE END)

ブラック・キャット

BLACK CAT

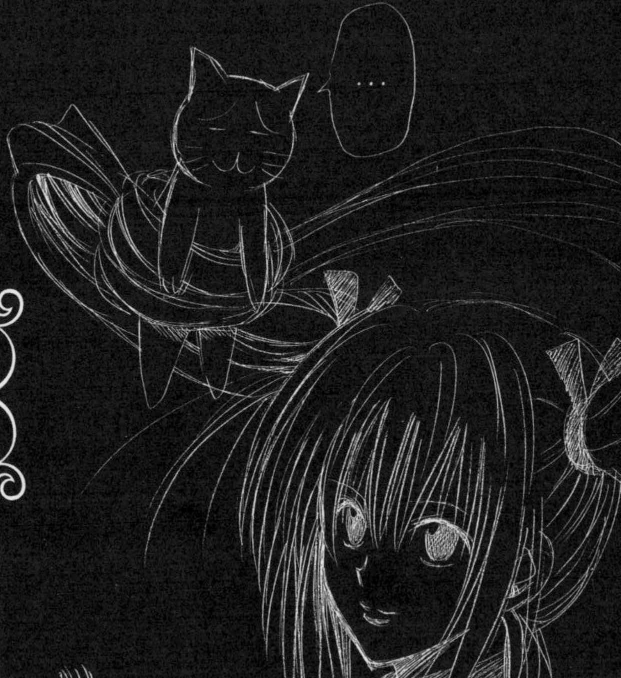
...

BONUS STORIES

WHAT HAPPENS TO FAN MAIL...

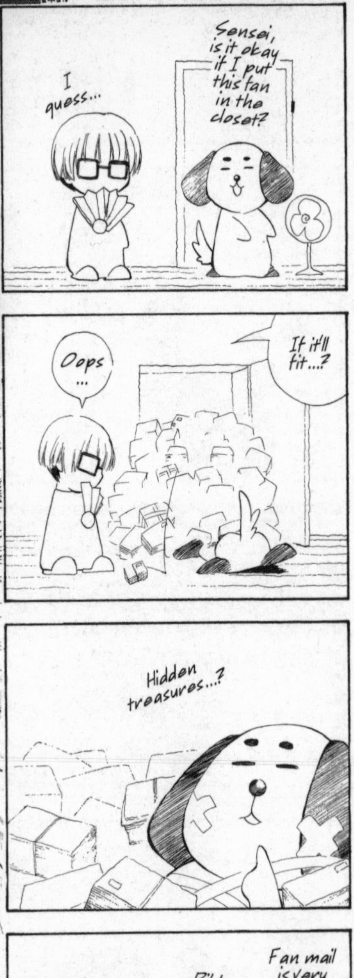
Sensei, is it okay if I put this fan in the closet?
I guess...
If it'll fit...?
Oops ...
Hidden treasures...?
Fan mail is very special, so it never gets thrown away.
Ribbons and paper.
Even boxes?
BONK

Running out of room.

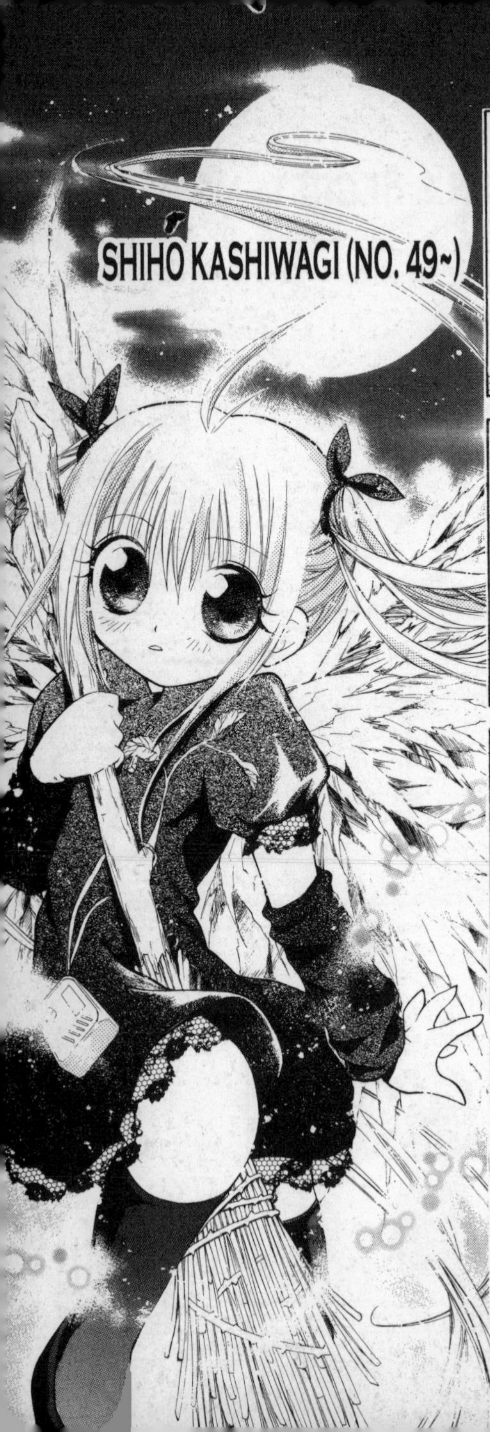
SHIHO KASHIWAGI (NO. 49~)

MURDOCH'S SECRET BY YOSHITAKA SAITO

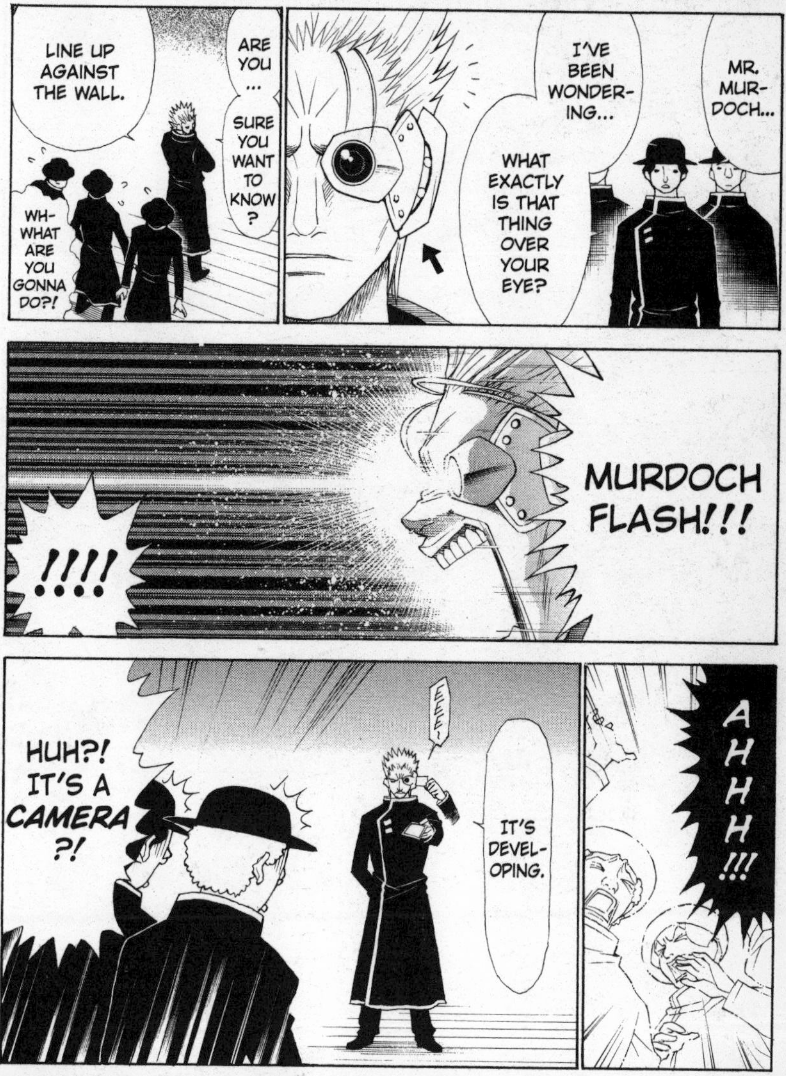
MR. MURDOCH...
I'VE BEEN WONDERING...
WHAT EXACTLY IS THAT THING OVER YOUR EYE?
ARE YOU ...
SURE YOU WANT TO KNOW?
LINE UP AGAINST THE WALL.
WH-WHAT ARE YOU GONNA DO?!
MURDOCH FLASH!!!
!!!!
AHHH!!!
IT'S DEVELOPING.
HUH?! IT'S A CAMERA?!

No Peaks, No Valleys, No Meaning By: Kentaro Honna

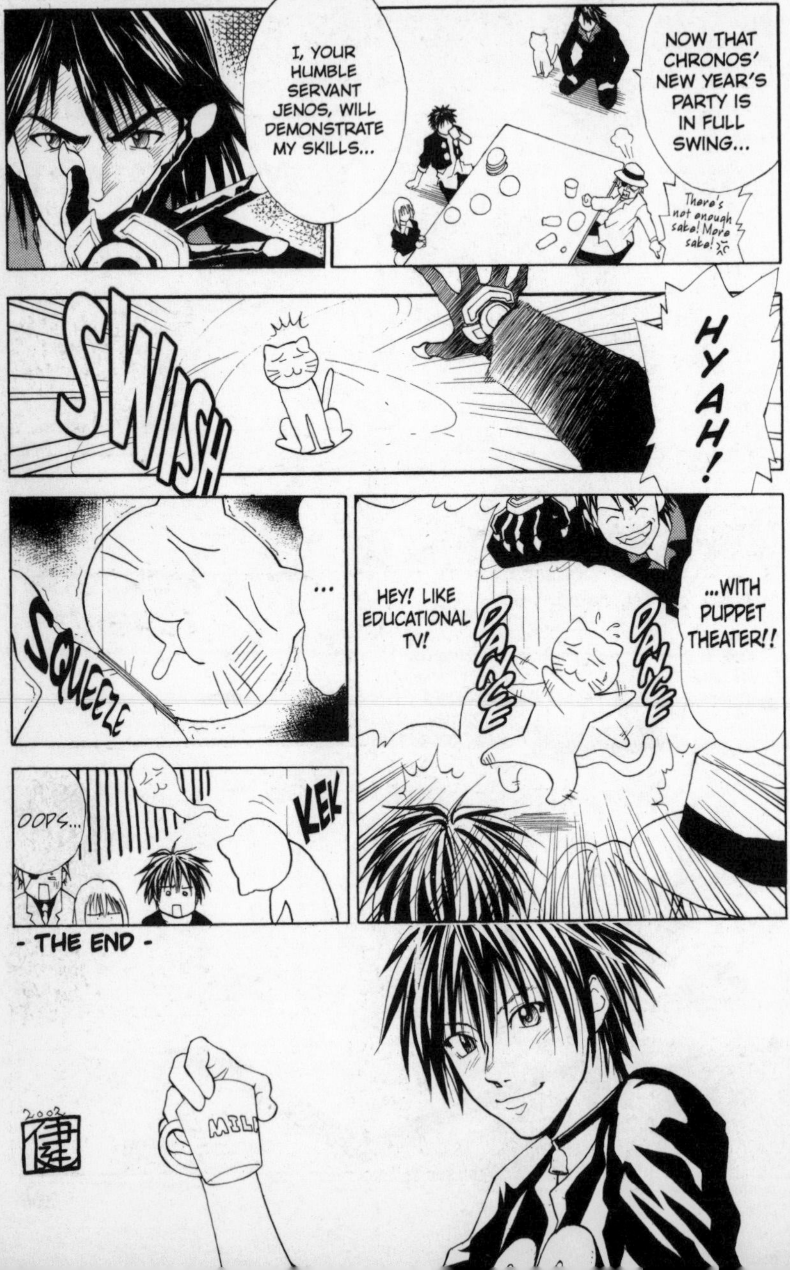
NOW THAT CHRONOS' NEW YEAR'S PARTY IS IN FULL SWING...
There's not enough sake! More sake!
I, YOUR HUMBLE SERVANT JENOS, WILL DEMONSTRATE MY SKILLS...
HYAH!
SWISH
...WITH PUPPET THEATER!!
DANCE
DANCE
HEY! LIKE EDUCATIONAL TV!
...
SQUEEZE
KEK
OOPS...
- THE END -

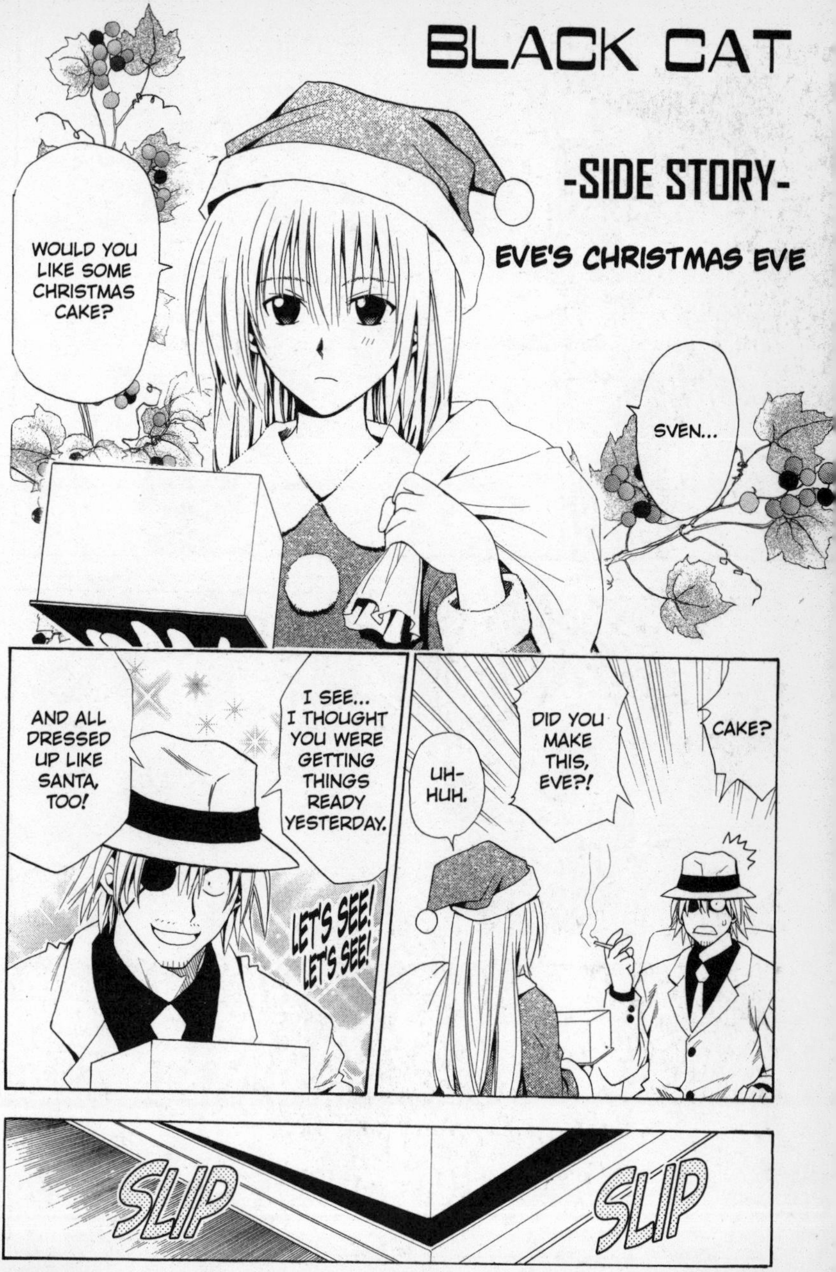
BLACK CAT
-SIDE STORY-
EVE'S CHRISTMAS EVE
SVEN...
WOULD YOU LIKE SOME CHRISTMAS CAKE?
CAKE?
DID YOU MAKE THIS, EVE?!
UH-HUH.
I SEE... I THOUGHT YOU WERE GETTING THINGS READY YESTERDAY.
AND ALL DRESSED UP LIKE SANTA, TOO!
LET'S SEE! LET'S SEE!
SLIP
SLIP

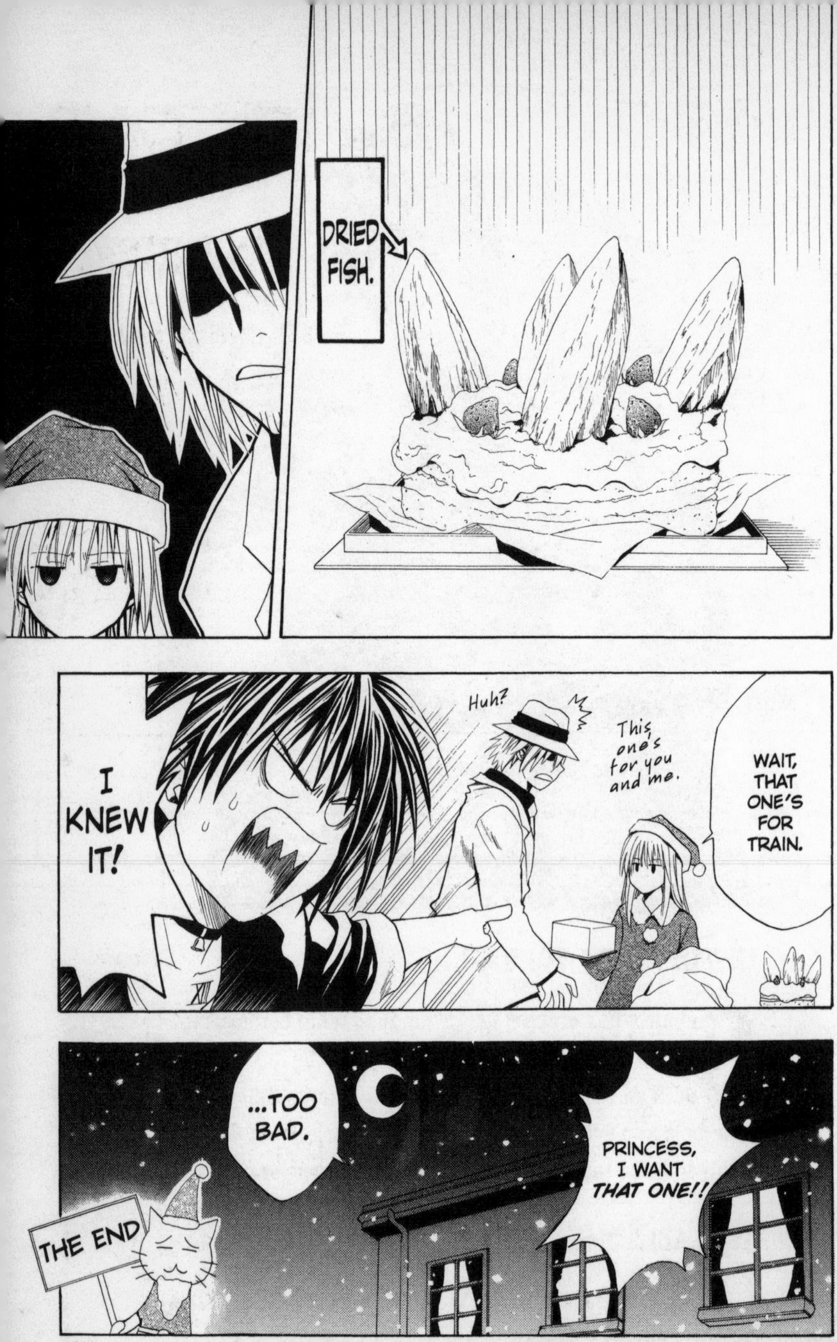
DRIED FISH.
WAIT, THAT ONE'S FOR TRAIN.
This one's for you and me.
Huh?
I KNEW IT!
PRINCESS, I WANT *THAT ONE!!*
...TOO BAD.
THE END

BLACK CAT-SIDE STORY- THE END

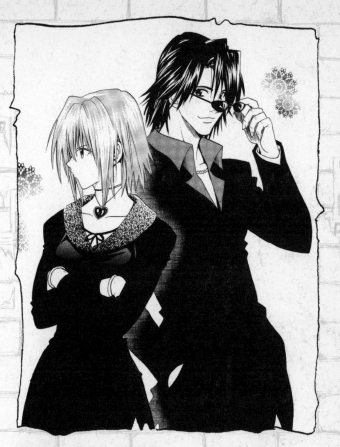

IN THE NEXT VOLUME...

Sephiria has ordered her commando team Cerberus to find Creed and destroy the Apostles of the Stars. To get data on their hideout, she decides to force Rinslet to be a mole and get inside. Rinslet tries to back out of the plan ...only to learn that she has no choice but to cooperate, or die.

AVAILABLE MAY 2007! ◁◁◁◁◁◁◁◁

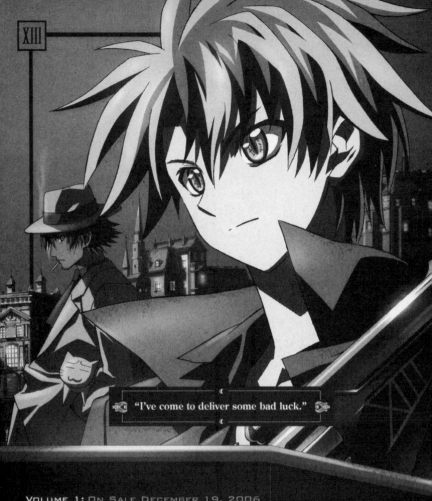

   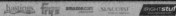

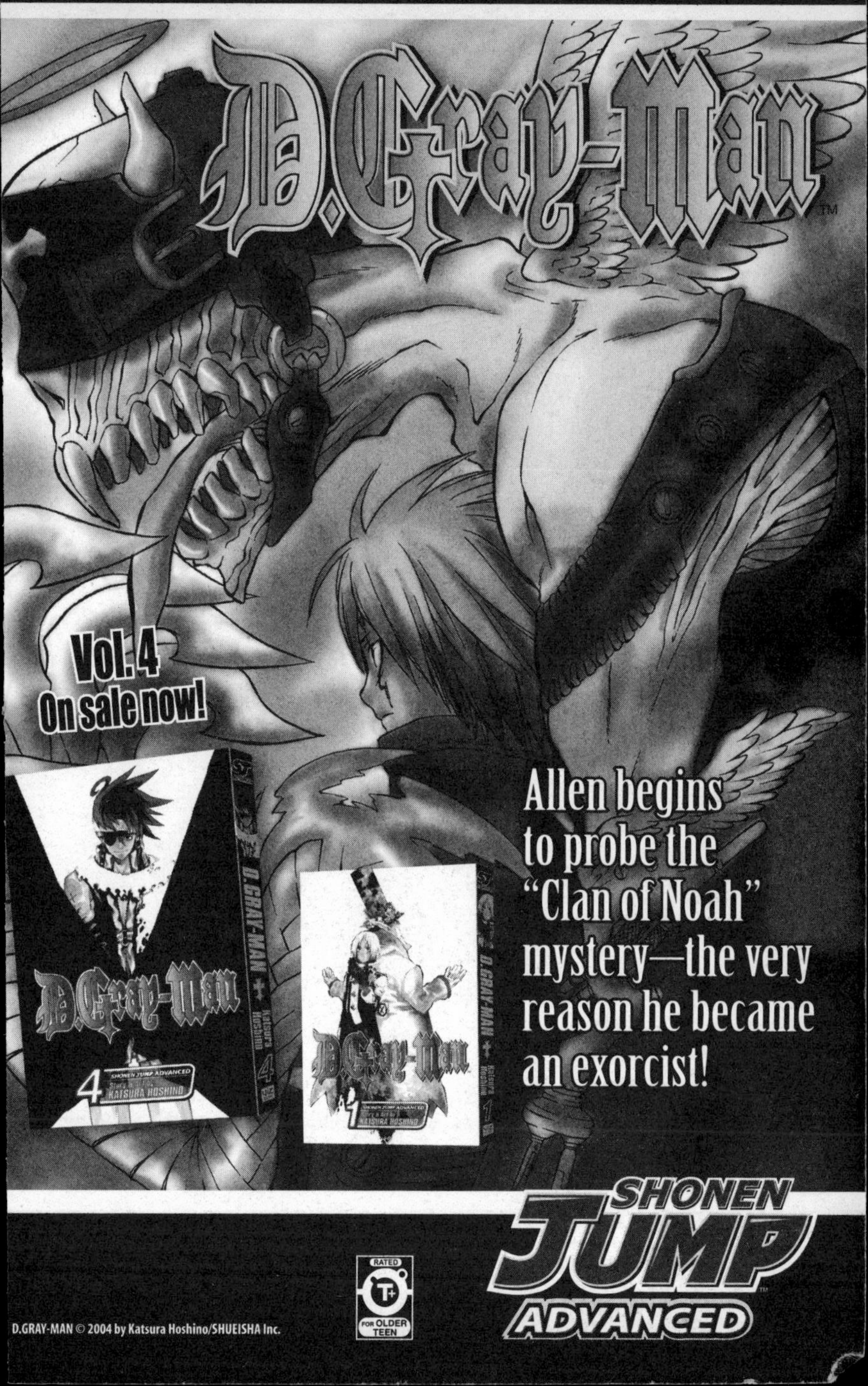

D.Gray-man™
Vol. 4
On sale now!
Allen begins to probe the "Clan of Noah" mystery—the very reason he became an exorcist!
D.GRAY-MAN
Katsura Hoshino
SHONEN JUMP ADVANCED
KATSURA HOSHINO
RATED T+ FOR OLDER TEEN
SHONEN JUMP ADVANCED
D.GRAY-MAN © 2004 by Katsura Hoshino/SHUEISHA Inc.

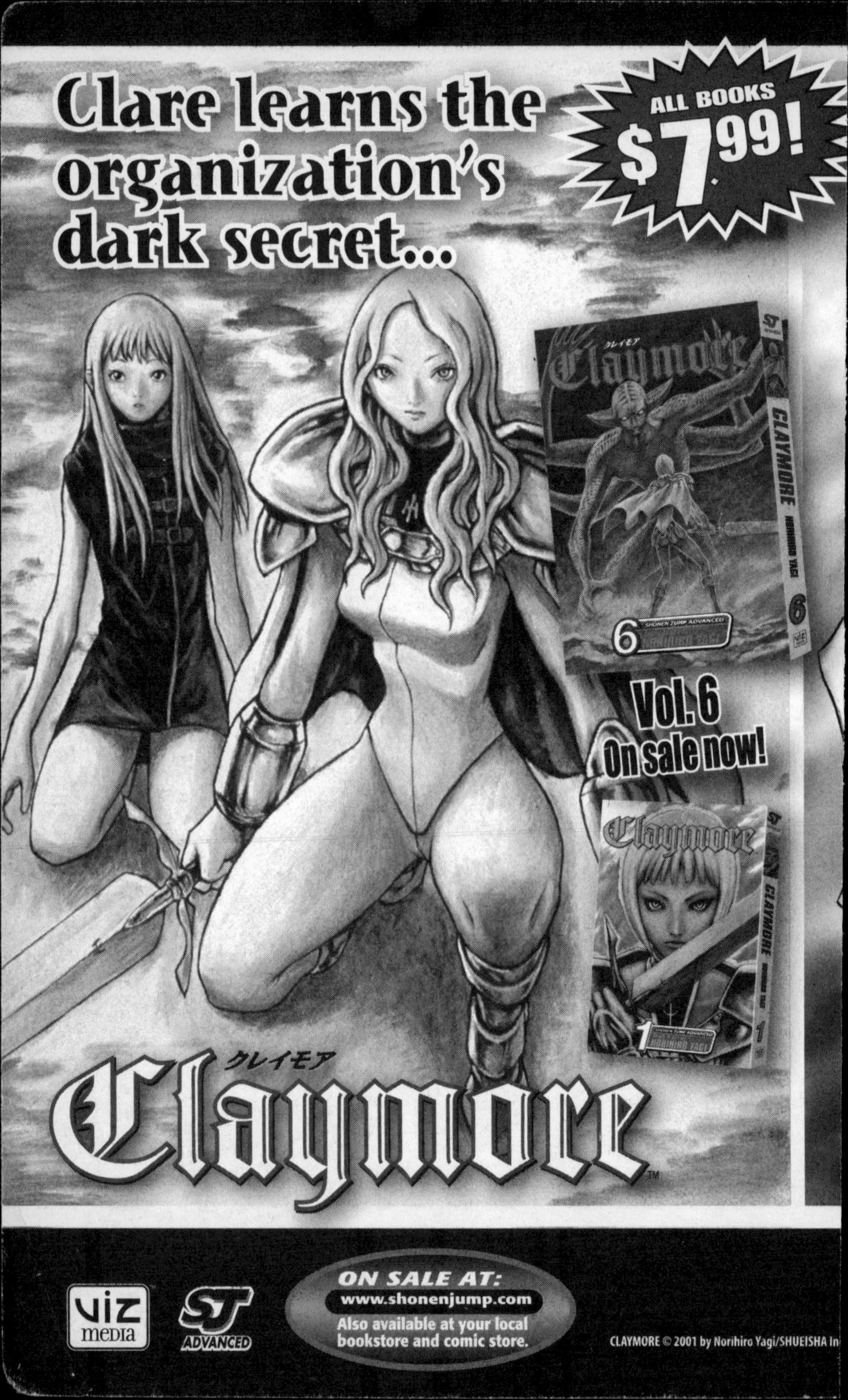

Clare learns the organization's dark secret...
ALL BOOKS $7.99!
Vol. 6
On sale now!
Claymore
クレイモア
ON SALE AT:
www.shonenjump.com
Also available at your local bookstore and comic store.
CLAYMORE © 2001 by Norihiro Yagi/SHUEISHA In

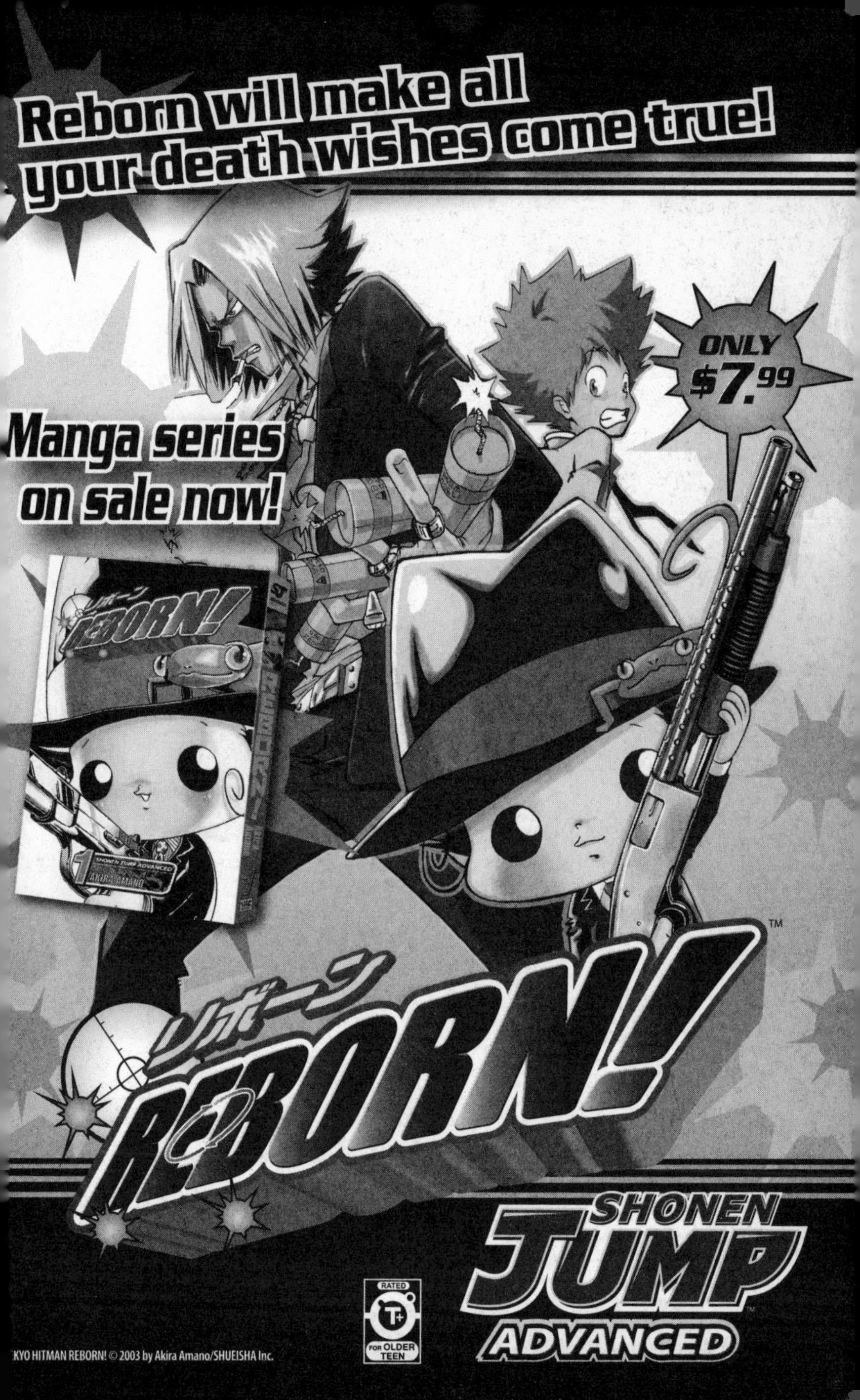
Reborn will make all your death wishes come true!
ONLY $7.99
Manga series on sale now!
REBORN!
SHONEN JUMP ADVANCED
AKIRA AMANO
REBORN!™
SHONEN JUMP ADVANCED
RATED T+ FOR OLDER TEEN

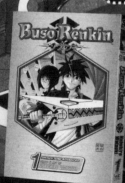
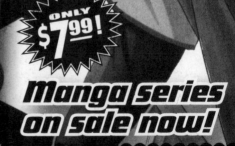

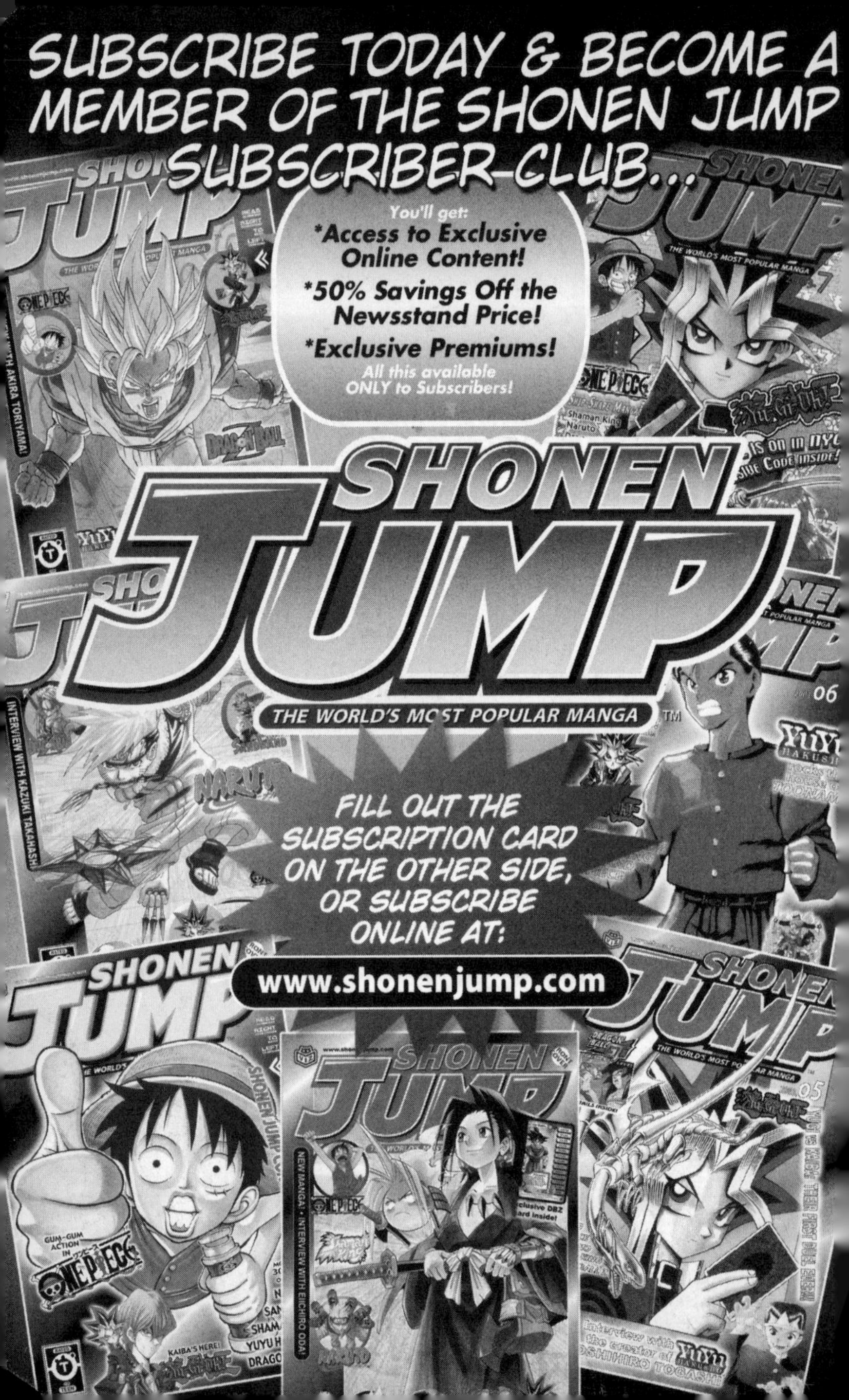

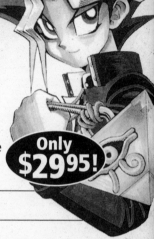